*Singapore → orange
beef

— Harmony

Case Studies
in Business Ethics

Case Studies in Business Ethics

fourth edition

Edited by

Thomas Donaldson
Georgetown University

Al Gini
Loyola University Chicago

PRENTICE HALL
Upper Saddle River, New Jersey 07458

Library of Congress Cataloging-in-Publication Data

Case studies in business ethics / edited by Thomas Donaldson, Al Gini.
  — 4th ed.
      p.   cm.
  Includes bibliographical references.
  ISBN 0–13–382433–0
  1. Business ethics—Case studies.   I. Donaldson, Thomas (date).
  II. Gini, Al (date).
  HF5387.C36 1996
  174'.4—dc20
                                  95–34941
                                    CIP

Acquisitions editor: Charlyce Jones-Owen
Editorial production/supervision
  and interior design: F. Hubert
Manufacturing buyer: Lynn Pearlman

© 1996, 1993, 1990, 1984 by Prentice-Hall, Inc.
Simon & Schuster / A Viacom Company
Upper Saddle River, New Jersey 07458

Printed in the United States of America

10 9 8

ISBN 0-13-382433-0

PRENTICE-HALL INTERNATIONAL (UK) LIMITED, *London*
PRENTICE-HALL OF AUSTRALIA PTY. LIMITED, *Sydney*
PRENTICE-HALL CANADA INC., *Toronto*
PRENTICE-HALL HISPANOAMERICANA, S.A., *Mexico*
PRENTICE HALL OF INDIA PRIVATE LIMITED, *New Delhi*
PRENTICE-HALL OF JAPAN, INC., *Tokyo*
SIMON & SCHUSTER PTE. LTD., *Singapore*
EDITORA PRENTICE-HALL DO BRASIL, LTDA., *Rio de Janeiro*

Contents

Preface   *xi*

Introduction to Ethical Reasoning   •   THOMAS DONALDSON
& PATRICIA WERHANE   *1*

The Case Method   •   THOMAS DONALDSON   *11*

ONE   •   Business or Ethics   *21*

CASE STUDY
Into the Mouth of Babes   •   JAMES TRAUB   *22*

CASE STUDY
Tylenol's Rebound   •   CARL CANNON   *29*

TWO   •   Communication in Business:
Truth Telling, Misinformation, and Lying   *33*

CASE STUDY
Toy Wars   •   MANUEL G. VELASQUEZ   *34*

CASE STUDY
Dow Corning Corporation: Marketing Breast Implant
Devices • N. CRAIG SMITH, ANDREW D. DYER, & TODD E. HIMSTEAD   *39*

CASE STUDY
Uptown, Dakota, and PowerMaster • N. CRAIG SMITH   *53*

CASE STUDY
Manville: The Ethics of Economic Efficiency? • AL GINI   *58*

CASE STUDY
When Did Johns-Manville Know? • JEFF COPLON   *67*

CASE STUDY
Italian Tax Mores • ARTHUR L. KELLY   *69*

THREE • Pollution and Environment   72

CASE STUDY
The AES Corporation • THE MANAGEMENT INSTITUTE
FOR ENVIRONMENT AND BUSINESS   *74*

CASE STUDY
The Chainsaws of Greed: The Case of Pacific
Lumber • LISA H. NEWTON   *86*

CASE STUDY
Exxon's Knee Deep in the Big Muddy • MICHAEL G. BOWEN
& F. CLARK POWER   *107*

FOUR • Employee–Employer Relations   *117*

CASE STUDY
AIDS in the Workplace: Options and Responsibilities • AL GINI
& MICHAEL DAVIS   *120*

CASE STUDY
The Case of the Willful Whistle-Blower • SALLY SEYMOUR   *130*

CASE STUDY
The DC–10's Defective Doors • BARBARA HIMES, TOM L. BEAUCHAMP,
& CATHLEEN KAVENY   *135*

CASE STUDY
The Hazards of the Enterprise • JOHN HASNAS   *141*

COURT DECISION
Weber v. Kaiser Aluminum and United Steelworkers • U. S.
SUPREME COURT   *144*

CASE STUDY
The Aggressive Ad Agency: Selling Experience or Confidential
Information? • JOHN R. BOATRIGHT   *153*

CASE STUDY
Management Dilemma • FRED E. SCHUSTER   *155*

CASE STUDY
Vital Information at Complex • THOMAS DONALDSON   *157*

FIVE • Diversity in the Workplace   *159*

ESSAY
Management Women and the New Facts of Life • FELICE N.
SCHWARTZ   *161*

ESSAY
Blowing the Whistle on the "Mommy Track" • BARBARA EHRENREICH
& DIERDRE ENGLISH   *172*

ESSAY
How to Get 'Em on Track • CAROL KLEIMAN   *176*

ESSAY

Woman's Work: Seeking Identity Through Occupation • AL GINI & TERRY SULLIVAN *178*

CASE STUDY

Sexual Discrimination at Eastern Airlines? • AL GINI *184*

CASE STUDY

The Oil Rig *189*

CASE STUDY

Foreign Assignment • THOMAS DUNFEE & DIANA ROBERTSON *190*

CASE STUDY

Gender Issues at *Your House* • JOHN HASNAS *192*

ESSAY

A Note on Sexual Harassment • ANDREW WICKS *198*

ESSAY

A Note of Sexual Harassment Policy • ANDREW WICKS *203*

SIX • Obligations to Stakeholders: Employees, Customers, Community, and Stockholders *205*

CASE STUDY

The Ford Pinto • W. MICHAEL HOFFMAN *207*

CASE STUDY

A. H. Robins: The Dalkon Shield • AL GINI & TERRY SULLIVAN *215*

CASE STUDY

Dorrence Corporation Trade-offs • HANS WOLF *224*

CASE STUDY

Sears Auto Shock • RONALD M. GREEN *230*

CASE STUDY

Commission on Sales at Brock Mason Brokerage • Tom L. Beauchamp *236*

CASE STUDY

Roger Hixon: Let the Buyer Beware • Clinton L. Oaks *239*

SEVEN • Multinationals *245*

CASE STUDY

Ethics and International Business Consulting:
The ERCI Episode • Peter Madsen *247*

CASE STUDY

Tropical Plywood Imports, Inc. • LaRue Tone Hosmer *258*

CASE STUDY

H. B. Fuller in Honduras: Street Children and Substance
Abuse • Norman Bowie & Stefanie Ann Lenway *267*

CASE STUDY

The Project at Moza Island • John Seeger & Balachandran
Manyadath *291*

CASE STUDY

Merck & Co., Inc. • The Business Enterprise Trust *299*

CASE STUDY

Three Scenarios • Thomas W. Dunfee *309*

EIGHT • Success Stories: It Can Be Done! *310*

ESSAY

Nice Guys Finish First? • Paul Gray *311*

CASE STUDY
Ice Cream & Integrity • MARY SCOTT & HOWARD ROTHMAN   *315*

CASE STUDY
Roger Meade: Running on People Power • MICHAEL A. VERESPEJ   *325*

ESSAY
Kresa's Cleanup • DAN CORDTZ   *329*

ESSAY
The Smoke at General Electric • NANETTE BYRNES   *332*

Preface

Not long ago the term *business ethics* was reserved for simple cases of fraud or honor. Customers complained about business ethics when they were victimized by bait-and-switch advertising, and corporate presidents boasted of business ethics in Christmas speeches and annual reports. But more recently the term has acquired greater complexity and sophistication. It has come to refer not only to matters of fraud and public relations, but to a growing field of study that encompasses standards of professionalism, corporate decision-making structures, and the interface between ethical theory and economic practice. Even as more and more business schools are introducing courses in business ethics, scholars in the humanities and social sciences are expanding the boundaries of research into the field.

In its evolution toward greater sophistication, business ethics has shed its "antibusiness" reputation. Repeatedly pointing the finger of blame—at the latest corporate watergate, at the latest Firestone 5, or at Three Mile Island—has come to be recognized as having limited pedagogical value. Such knee-jerk indignation promotes ethical simple-mindedness and avoids many of the deeper problems that vex even the most conscientious of managers.

In the face of this rising tide of academic interest in business ethics, it was inevitable that teachers and scholars would seek out better and more challenging case studies. *Case Studies in Business Ethics* is an attempt to fill that need by collecting into a single package some of the better case studies available. This book contains cases that deal not only with ethical failures, but with ethical successes, and each case attempts to confront the reader with the same complex value trade-offs that characterize real-life business decision making. Its cases are also designed to complement the new, more philosophically oriented approach taken in contemporary business ethics courses. Most instructors will want to use the book in conjunction with other materials dealing with specific topics in ethics, business, and economics. For those who wish to learn more about teaching with the aid of cases, we have provided an introductory essay that explains the case method and shows its special application to ethics. Each case study is followed by a set of discussion questions highlighting issues in the case.

It would be hard to thank sufficiently all those who helped design, prepare, and critique this book. These people include Jeanne Huchthausen, Ray O'Connell, Manuel Velasquez, and Pat Werhane. Special thanks go to Jeffrey A. Barach of Tulane University and Michael S. Pritchard of Western Michigan University for their careful reading of the manuscript. Research assistant Marci Lehe provided invaluable editorial advice and production editors Pattie Amoroso, Jan Stephan, Bridget Mooney, and Frank Hubert saved us from numerous embarrassments while doing a thoroughly professional job. Special thanks also have to be extended to Mark D. Schneider, assistant managing editor, *Business Ethics Quarterly,* Cynthia Rudolph, Sally Kowalkowski, and Tom McInerney for diligence in preparing the final manuscript; Caroline Carney, Ted Bolen, Diane Schaible, and Helen Brennan for their advice and support; and the Oak Park Public Library for its up-to-date holdings and professional courtesy.

THOMAS DONALDSON
AL GINI

Case Studies
in Business Ethics

Introduction to Ethical Reasoning*

Thomas Donaldson • Patricia H. Werhane

What is the basis for making ethical decisions? Should Joan challenge Fred the next time he cracks a chauvinist joke? Should John refrain from lying on his job application despite his temptation to do so? What, if anything, should make Hillary decide that eating meat is corrupting, whereas vegetarianism is uplifting? It is obvious that the kind of evidence required for an ethical decision is different from that needed to make a nonethical one; but what is the nature of the difference? These questions give rise to a search for a *method* of ethical justification and decision making, a method that will specify the conditions that any good ethical decision should meet.

To see how such questions arise concretely, consider the following case.[1]

Some years ago, a large German chemical firm, BASF, decided to follow the lead of many other European firms and build a factory in the United States. BASF needed land, lots of it (1,800 acres), an inexpensive labor pool, almost 5 million gallons of fresh water every day, a surrounding area free of import taxes, and a nearby railroad and ocean port. Obviously, only a handful of locations could meet all these requirements. The spot the company finally picked seemed perfect, an area near the coast of South Carolina called Beaufort County. It purchased 1,800 acres.

South Carolina and Beaufort County were pleased with BASF's decision. The surrounding area, from which the company would pick its workers, was economically depressed and per capita income stood well below the national average. Jobs of any kind were desperately needed. Even the Governor of South Carolina and his staff were eager for BASF to build in South Carolina, and although BASF had not yet finalized its exact production plans, the State Pollution Central Authority saw no problems with meeting the State pollution laws. BASF itself said that although it would dump chemical byproducts into the local Colleton River, it planned not to lower the river's quality.

But trouble started immediately. To see why, one needs to know that Beaufort County is the home of the internationally famous resort area called "Hilton Head." Hilton Head attracts thousands of vacationers every year—most of them with plenty of money—and its developers worried that the scenic splendor of the area might be marred by the air and water pollution. Especially concerned about water pollution, resort developers charged that the proposed chemical plant would pollute the Colleton River. They argued that BASF plants in Germany had polluted the Rhine and, in Belgium, the Schelde River. Further, they noted that on BASF's list of proposed expenditures, pollution control was allocated only one million dollars.

The citizens of Beaufort County, in contrast to the Hilton Head Developers, welcomed BASF. They presented the company with a petition bearing over 7,000 signatures endorsing the new plant. As one local businessman commented, "I would say 80 percent of the people in Beaufort County are in favor of BASF. Those who aren't rich." (William D. McDonald, "Youth Corps Looking for Jobs," *The State*, February 23, 1970.)

The manager of BASF's U.S. operations was clearly confronted by an economic and moral dilemma. He knew that preventing massive pollution was virtually impossible and, in any case, outrageously expensive. The eagerness of South Carolina officials for new industry suggested that pollution standards

*This article is a revised version of one appearing in Thomas Donaldson and Patricia H. Werhane, eds., *Ethical Issues in Business*, 4th ed. (Englewood Cliffs, N.J.: Prentice Hall, 1993) pp. 5–17.

might be "relaxed" for BASF. If it decided to go ahead and build, was the company to push for the minimum pollution control it could get away with under the law? Such a policy might maximize corporate profits and the financial interests of the shareholders, while at the same time it would lower the aesthetic quality of the environment. It might make jobs available to Beaufort County while ignoring the resort industry and the enjoyment of vacationers. Moreover, the long-term effects of dumping chemicals were hard to predict, but past experience did not give the manager a feeling of optimism. Pollution seemed to be not only a business issue, but a *moral* one. But how should the manager sort out, and eventually decide upon, such a moral issue?

To solve his moral problem, BASF's manager might try a variety of strategies. He might, for example, begin by assuming that he has three basic options: (1) Build with minimal pollution control; (2) build with maximal pollution control; or (3) do not build.

Then, he might reason

> The consequences of option 1 will be significant but tolerable water pollution, hostility from the Hilton Head Developers, high short-term corporate profits, and satisfied shareholders.
>
> The consequences of option 2 will be unnoticeable pollution, no complaints from the Hilton Head Developers, high pollution-control costs, low profits, and unsatisfied stockholders.
>
> The consequences of 3 will be approval from the Hilton Head Developers, low short-term profits (while a search for a new location is underway), strong disapproval from the local townspeople.
>
> My job from a *moral* perspective is to weigh these consequences and consider which of the alternatives constitutes a maximization of good. Who will benefit from each decision? How many people will be adversely affected and in what ways?

Or the manager might reason

> Both BASF Corporation and I are confronted with a variety of *duties, rights,* and *obligations.* First there is the company's obligation to its stockholders, and my duty as manager is to protect the economic interests and rights of our stockholders. Next there are the rights of those Beaufort residents and visitors in the area to clean air and water. Finally there are the rights of other property owners in the area, including the Hilton Head Developers, not to be harmed unreasonably by other industries. There is an implied obligation to future generations to protect the river. And finally, there are broader considerations: Is this an act I would want others to do? What kind of moral example will I be setting?
>
> My job from a *moral* perspective is to balance and assess these duties, rights, and obligations, and determine which have priority.

Finally, the manager might reason

> I cannot confront a moral problem from either the abstract perspective of "consequences," or of "duties, rights, and obligations." Instead, I must use a concrete concept of *human nature* to guide my deliberations. Acts that aid persons to develop their potential human nature are morally good; ones that do the opposite are bad.
>
> I believe that the crucial potentialities of human nature include such things as health, knowledge, moral maturity, meaningful employment, political freedom, and self-respect.
>
> My job from a *moral* perspective is to assess the situation in terms of its harmony or disharmony with these basic concepts of human potential.

Notice how different each of these approaches is. The first focuses on the concept of *consequences;* the second on *duties, rights, and obligations;* and the third on *human nature.* Of course, the three methods may overlap; for example, applying the concept of "human nature" in the third approach may necessitate referring to concepts drawn from the first and second, such as "consequences" and "rights," and vice versa. Even so, the approaches reflect three classical types of ethical theory in the history of philosophy. Each has been championed by a well-known traditional philosopher, and most ethical theories can be categorized under one of the three headings. The first may be called *consequentialism,* the second, *deontology,* and the third, *human nature ethics.*

CONSEQUENTIALISM

As its name implies, a consequentialist theory of ethical reasoning concentrates on the consequences of human actions, and all actions are evaluated in terms of the extent to which they achieve desirable results. Such theories are also frequently labeled *teleological,* a term derived from the Greek word *telos,* which means "end" or "purpose." According to consequentialist theories, the concepts of right, wrong, and duty are subordinated to the concept of the end or purpose of an action.

There are at least two types of consequentialist theory. The first—advocated by only a few consequentialists—is a version of what philosophers call ethical egoism. It construes right action as action whose consequences, considered among all the alternatives, maximizes *my* good—that is, action that benefits *me* the most or harms *me* the least. The second type—advocated by most consequentialists—denies that right action concerns only *me.* Rather, right action must maximize *overall* good; that is, it must maximize good (or minimize bad) from the standpoint of the entire human community. The best-accepted label for this type of consequentialism is *utilitarianism.* This term was coined by the eighteenth-century philosopher Jeremy Bentham, although its best-known proponent was the nineteenth-century English philosopher John Stuart Mill. As Bentham formulated it, the principle of utility states that an action is right if it produces the greatest balance of pleasure or happiness and unhappiness in light of alternative actions. Mill supported a similar principle, using what he called the "proof" of the principle of utility—namely, the recognition that the only proof for something's being desirable is that someone actually desires it. Since everybody desires pleasure or happiness, it follows, according to Mill, that happiness is the most desirable thing. The purpose of moral action is to achieve greatest overall happiness, and actions are evaluated in terms of the extent to which they contribute to this end. The most desirable state of affairs, the greatest good and the goal of morality, said Mill, is the "greatest happiness for the greatest number."

While later utilitarians accept the general framework of Mill's argument, not all utilitarians are hedonists. That is, not all utilitarians equate "the good" with pleasure or happiness. Some utilitarians have argued that in maximizing the "good," one must be concerned not only with maximizing pleasure, but with maximizing other things, such as knowledge, moral maturity, and friendship. Although it could be claimed that such goods also bring pleasure and happiness to their possessor, it is arguable whether their goodness is ultimately *reducible* to whatever pleasure they bring. These philosophers are sometimes called pluralistic utilitarians. Still other philosophers have adapted utilitarianism to modern methods of economic theory by championing what is known as preference utilitarianism. Instead of referring to the maximization of specific goods, such as pleasure or knowledge, preference utilitarians understand the ultimate foundation of goodness to be the set of preferences people actually possess. One person prefers oysters to strawberries; another prefers rock music to Mozart. Each person has a set of preferences, and so long as the set is internally consistent, it makes no sense to label one set morally superior to another. Preference utilitarianism thus interprets right action as that which is optimal among alternatives in terms of everyone's preferences. Disputes, however, rage among preference utilitarians and their critics over how to specify the meaning of *optimal.*

Bentham and Mill thought that utilitarianism was a revolutionary theory, both because it accurately reflected human motivation and because it had clear application to the political and social problems of their day. If one could measure the benefit or harm of any action, rule, or law, they believed, one could sort out good and bad social and political legislation as well as good and bad individual actions.

But how, specifically, does one apply the traditional principle of utility? To begin with, one's race, religion, intelligence, or condition of birth is acknowledged to be irrelevant in calculating one's ultimate worth. Each person counts for "one," and no more than "one." Second, in evaluating happiness, one must take into account not only present generations, but ones in the future. In calculating the effects of pollution, for instance, one must measure the possible effects pollution might have on health, genetics, and the supply of natural resources for future generations. Third, pleasure or happiness is measured *en toto* so that the thesis does not reduce to the idea that "one ought to do what makes the most persons happy." Utilitarianism does not reduce to a dictatorship of majority interests. One person's considerable unhappiness might outweigh the minor pleasures of many other persons added together. Utilitarians also consider the long-term consequences for single individuals. For instance, it might be pleasurable to drink a full bottle of wine every evening, but the long-term drawbacks of such a habit might well outweigh its temporary pleasures.

Finally, according to many utilitarians (such as Mill), some pleasures are *qualitatively* better than others. Intellectual pleasure, for example, is said to be higher than physical pleasure. "Better to be Socrates unsatisfied," writes Mill, "than a pig satisfied." The reasons that drove Mill to formulate this qualitative distinction among pleasures are worth noting. Since Mill believed that the optimal situation was one of "greatest happiness for the greatest number," then what was he to say about a world of people living at the zenith of merely *physical* happiness? If science could invent a wonder drug, like the "soma" in Aldous Huxley's *Brave New World,* which provided a permanent state of drugged happiness (without even a hangover), would the consequence be a perfect world? Mill believed not, and to remedy this difficulty in his theory, he introduced *qualitative levels* of happiness. For example, he said that the happiness of understanding Plato is "higher" than that of drinking three martinis. But how was Mill to say *which* pleasures were higher? Here he retreated to an ingenious proposal: When deciding which of two pleasures is higher, one should poll the group of persons who are experienced—that is, who know *both* pleasures. Their decision will indicate which is the higher pleasure. Ah, but might the majority decision not be wrong? Here Mill provides no clear answer.

Modern-day utilitarians divide themselves roughly into two groups: *act utilitarians* and *rule utilitarians*. An *act* utilitarian believes that the principle of utility should be applied to individual acts. Thus one measures the consequences of each *individual action* according to whether it maximizes good. For example, suppose a certain community were offered the opportunity to receive a great deal of wealth in the form of a gift. The only stipulation was that the community force some of its citizens with ugly, deteriorated homes to repair and beautify them. Next, suppose the community held an election to decide whether to accept the gift. An act utilitarian would analyze the problem of whether to vote for or against the proposal from the standpoint of the *individual voter*. Would an individual's vote to accept the gift be more likely to maximize the community's overall good than would a vote to the contrary?

A *rule* utilitarian, on the other hand, believes that instead of considering the results of specific actions, one must weigh the consequences of adopting a *general rule* exemplified by that action. According to the rule utilitarian, one should act according to a general rule which, if adopted, would maximize good. For example, in the hypothetical case of the community deciding whether to accept a gift, a rule utilitarian might adopt the rule "Never vote in a way that lowers the self-respect of a given class of citizens." She might accept this rule because of the general unhappiness that would ensue if society systematically treated some persons as second-class citizens. Here the focus is on the general rule and not on the individual act.

Critics raise objections to utilitarianism. Perhaps the most serious objection is that it is unable to account for justice. Because the utilitarian concentrates on the consequences of an action for a majority, the employment of the principle of utility can be argued to allow injustice for a small minority. For example, if overall goodness were maximized in the long run by making slaves of 2 percent of the population, utilitarianism seemingly is forced to condone slavery. But clearly this is unjust. Utilitarianism's obvious response is that such slavery will not, as a matter of empirical fact, maximize goodness. Rule utilitarians, as we have seen, can argue that society should embrace the rule "Never enslave others," because following such a principle will, in the long run, maximize goodness. Even so, the battle continues between utilitarians and their critics. Can utilitarianism account for the widely held moral conviction that injustice to a minority is wrong *regardless* of the consequences? The answer is hotly contested.

Another criticism concerns the determination of the good to be maximized. Any consequentialist has the problem of identifying and ranking whatever is to be maximized. For a utilitarian such as Mill, as we have seen, the problem involves distinguishing between higher and lower pleasures. But for pluralistic utilitarians, a similar problem exists: What is the basis for selecting, for example, friendship and happiness as goods to be maximized and not, say, aesthetic sensitivity? And even granted that this problem can be solved, there is the future problem of arbitrating trade-offs between goods such as happiness and friendship when they *conflict*. When one is forced to choose between enhancing happiness and enhancing friendship, which gets priority? And under what conditions?

An interesting fact about consequentialist reasoning is that most of us employ it to some degree in ordinary decisions. We weigh the consequences of alternatives in choosing colleges, in deciding on a career, in hiring and promoting others, and in many other judgments. We frequently weigh good consequences over bad ones and predict the long- and short-term effects of our choices. We often even cite consequentialist-style principles—for example, "No one should choose a college where he or she will be unhappy," or, "No one should pollute the environment when his or her action harms others."

However, for a variety of reasons including the objections to utilitarianism mentioned earlier, some philosophers refuse to acknowledge consequentialism as an adequate theory of ethics. They argue that the proper focus for ethical judgments should not be consequences, but moral *precepts*—that is, the rules, norms, and principles we use to guide our actions. Such philosophers are known as deontologists, and the next section will examine their views.

DEONTOLOGY

The term *deontological* comes from the Greek word for "duty," and what is crucial according to the deontologist are the rules and principles that guide actions. We shall discuss here two approaches to deontological ethical reasoning that have profoundly influenced ethics. The first is that of the eighteenth-century philosopher Immanuel Kant and his followers. This approach focuses on duty and universal rules to determine right actions. The second—actually a subspecies of deontological reasoning—is known as the "social contract" approach. It focuses not on individual decision making, but on the general social principles that rational persons in certain ideal situations would agree upon and adopt.

Kantian Deontology

Kant believed that ethical reasoning should concern activities that are rationally motivated and should utilize precepts that apply universally to all human actions. To this end, he opens his treatise on ethics by declaring

> It is impossible to conceive anything at all in the world, . . . which can be taken as good without qualification except a *good* will.[2]

This statement sums up much of what Kant wants to say about ethics and is worth unraveling. What Kant means is that the only thing that can be good or worthwhile without any provisos or stipulations is an action of the will freely motivated for the right reasons. Other goods such as wealth, beauty, and intelligence are certainly valuable, but they are not good *without qualification* because they have the potential to create both good and bad effects. Wealth, beauty, and intelligence can be bad when they are used for purely selfish ends. Even human happiness—which Mill held as the highest good—can, according to Kant, create complacency, disinterest, and excessive self-assurance under certain conditions.

According to Kant, reason is the faculty that can aid in the discovery of correct moral principles; thus it is *reason,* not *inclination,* that should guide the will. When reason guides the will, Kant calls the resulting actions ones done from "duty." Kant's use of the term *duty* turns out to be less formidable than it first appears. Kant is simply saying that a purely good and free act of the will is one done not merely because you have an *inclination* to do it, but because you have the right reasons for doing it. For example, suppose you discover a wallet belonging to a stranger. Kant would say that despite one's inclination to keep the money (which the stranger may not even need), one should return it. This is an act you know is right despite your inclinations. Kant also believes you should return the wallet even when you believe the *consequences* of not returning it are better. Here his views are at sharp odds with consequentialism. Suppose that the stranger is known for her stinginess, and you plan to donate the money to a children's hospital. No matter. For Kant, you must return the wallet. Thus the moral worth lies in the act itself and not in either your happiness or the consequences brought about by the act. Acts are good because they are done for the sake of what is right and not because of the consequences they might produce.

But how do I know what my duty is? While it may be clear that one should return a wallet, there are other circumstances in which one's duty is less evident. Suppose you are in a six-person lifeboat at sea with five others and a seventh person swims up? What is one's duty here? And how does one even know that what one *thinks* is right *is* right? To settle such problems, Kant claims that duty is more than doing merely what you "feel" is right. Duty is acting with *respect for other rational beings*. It almost goes without saying, then, that "acting from duty" is not to be interpreted as action done in obedience to local, state, or national laws, since these can be good or bad. Instead, "duty" is linked to the idea of universal principles that should govern all our actions.

But is there any principle that can govern *all* human beings? Kant believes the answer is yes, and he calls the highest such principle the "categorical imperative." He formulates the categorical imperative in three ways (although we shall only consider two formulations here). The first formulation, roughly translated, is

> One ought only to act such that the principle of one's act could become a universal law of human action in a world in which one would hope to live.

For example, one would want to live in a world where people followed the principle "Return property that belongs to others." Therefore, one should return the stranger's wallet. We do not, however, want to live in a world where everyone lies. Therefore, one should not adopt the principle "Lie whenever it seems helpful."

The second formulation of the categorical imperative is

> One ought to treat others as having intrinsic value in themselves, and *not* merely as means to achieve one's ends.

In other words, one should respect every person as a rational and free being. Hitler treated one group of persons as nonpersons in order to achieve his own ends, and thus he acted contrary to the categorical imperative. Another instance of treating persons as means would occur if a teacher looked up the grade records of new students to determine how to assign grades in her own class. She would be treating students as if they had no control over their destinies. Such actions are immoral according to Kant because they fail to respect the inherent dignity of rational beings.

Ethical reasoning for Kant implies adopting principles of action and evaluating one's actions in terms of those principles. Even Kant grants that the evaluation is sometimes difficult. For example, there is the problem of striking the proper level of generality in choosing a principle. A principle that read, "If one is named John Doe and attends Big State University and has two sisters, then he should borrow fifty dollars without intending to repay it," is far too specific. On the other hand, the principle "You should always pay your debts" might be too general, since it would require that a starving man repay the only money he possesses to buy a loaf of bread. Because of the problem of striking the proper degree of generality, many modern deontologists have reformulated Kant's basic question to read, "Could I wish that everyone in the world would follow this principle *under relevantly similar conditions?*"

As with utilitarianism, critics challenge deontological reasoning. Some assert that fanatics such as Hitler could at least *believe* that the rule "Persecute Jews whenever possible" is one that the world should live by. Similarly, a thief might universalize the principle "Steal whenever you have a good opportunity." Moreover, a strict interpretation of deontological ethical reasoning is said to allow no exceptions to a universal principle. Such strict adherence to universal principles might encourage moral rigidity and might fail to reflect the diversity of responses required by complex moral situations. Finally, critics argue that, in a given case, two principles may conflict without there being a clear way to decide which principle or rule should take precedence. Jean-Paul Sartre tells of his dilemma during World War II when he was forced to choose between staying to comfort his ill and aging mother and fighting for the freedom of France. Two principles seemed valid: "Give aid to your father and mother," and "Contribute to the cause of freedom." But with conflicting principles, how is one to choose? Nevertheless, deontological ethical reasoning represents a well-respected and fundamentally distinctive mode of ethical reasoning, one which, like consequentialism, appears in the deliberations of ordinary persons as well as philosophers. We have all heard actions condemned by the comment, "What would it be like if everyone did that?"

The Contractarian Alternative

Kant assumes that the categorial imperative is something all rational individuals can discover and agree upon. A different version of deontology is offered by many philosophers who focus less on the actions of individuals and more on the principles that govern society at large. These include two philosophers whose writings appear in our book: the seventeenth-century political philosopher John Locke and the twentieth-century American philosopher John Rawls. They and others try to establish universal principles of a just society through what might be called "social contract thought experiments." They ask us to imagine what it would be like to live in a situation where there are no laws, no social conventions, and no political state. In this so-called state of nature, we imagine that rational persons gather to formulate principles or rules to govern political and social communities. Such rules would resemble principles derived through the categorical imperative in that they are presumably principles to which every rational person would agree and which would hold universally.

Locke and Rawls differ in their approach to establishing rules or principles of justice, and the difference illustrates two distinct forms of contractarian reasoning. Locke argues from a "natural rights" position, while Rawls argues from a "reasonable person" position. Locke claims that every person is born with, and possesses, certain basic rights that are "natural." These rights are inherent to a person's nature, and they are possessed by everyone equally. Like other inherent traits, they cannot be taken away. They are, in the words of the Declaration of Independence, "inalienable." When rational persons meet to formulate principles to govern the formation of social and political communities, they construct a social contract that is the basis for an agreement between themselves and their government and whose rules protect natural rights. Rights, then, become deontological precepts by which one forms and evaluates rules, constitutions, government, and socioeconomic systems. While many philosophers disagree with Locke's view that each of us has inherent or *natural* rights, many do utilize a theory of human rights as the basis for justifying and evaluating political institutions.

Rawls adopts a different perspective. He does not begin from a natural rights position. Instead, he asks which principles of justice rational persons would formulate if they were behind a "veil of ignorance"—that is, if each person knew nothing about who he or she was. That is, one would not know whether one were old or young, male or female, rich or poor, highly motivated or lazy, or anything about one's personal status in society. Unable to predict which principles, if picked, will favor them personally, Rawls argues, persons will be forced to choose principles that are fair to all.

Rawls and Locke are not in perfect agreement about which principles would be adopted in such hypothetical situations, and more will be said about their views later in this book. For now it is important to remember that the social contract approach maintains a deontological character. It is used to formulate principles of justice that apply universally. Some philosophers note, however, that from an original position in a "state of nature" or behind a "veil of ignorance," rational persons *could* adopt consequentialist principles as rules for a just society. Thus, while the social contract approach is deontological in style, the principles it generates are not necessarily ones that are incompatible with consequentialism.

In the moral evaluations of business, all deontologists—contractarians included—would ask questions such as the following:

1. Are the rules fair to everyone?
2. Do the rules hold universally even with the passage of time?
3. Is every person treated with equal respect?

What may be missing from a deontological approach to ethical reasoning is a satisfactory means of coping with valid exceptions to general rules. Under what circumstances, if any, are exceptions allowed? Deontologists believe that they can answer this question, but their solutions vary. Suffice it to say that deontologists, just as utilitarians, have not convinced everyone.

HUMAN NATURE ETHICS

According to some contemporary philosophers, the preceding two modes of ethical reasoning exhaust all possible modes. That is to say, all theories can be classified as either teleological or deontological. Whether this is true cannot be settled here, but it will be helpful to introduce briefly what some philosophers consider to be a third category, namely the *human nature* approach.

A *human nature* approach assumes that all humans have inherent capacities that constitute the ultimate basis for all ethical claims. Actions are evaluated in terms of whether they promote or hinder, coincide with or conflict with these capacities. One of the most famous proponents of this theory was the Greek philosopher Aristotle. In Aristotle's opinion, human beings have inherent *potentialities,* and thus human development turns out to be the struggle for self-actualization, or in other words, the perfection of inherent human nature. Consider the acorn. It has the natural potential to become a sturdy oak tree. Its natural drive is not to become an elm or a cedar or even a stunted oak, but to become the most robust oak tree possible. Diseased or stunted oak trees are simply deficient; they are instances of things in nature whose potential has not been fully developed. Similarly, according to Aristotle, persons are born with inherent potentialities. Persons, like acorns, naturally are oriented to actualize their potentialities, and for them this means more than merely developing their physical potential. It also means developing their mental, moral, and social potential. Thus, human beings in this view are seen as basically good; evil is understood as a deficiency that occurs when one is unable to fulfill one's natural capacities.

It is important to understand that the concept of human nature need not be an individualistic one. According to Aristotle, persons are "social" by nature and cannot be understood apart from the larger community in which they participate. "Man," Aristotle wrote, is a "social animal." For Aristotle, then, fulfilling one's natural constitution implies developing wisdom, generosity, and self-restraint, all of which help to make one a good member of the community.

The criterion for judging the goodness of any action is whether or not the action is compatible with one's inherent human capacities. Actions that enhance human capacities are good; those that deter them are bad unless they are the best among generally negative alternatives. For example, eating nothing but starches is unhealthy, but it is clearly preferable to starving.

This theory puts great emphasis on the nature of persons, and obviously how one understands that "nature" will be the key to determining both what counts as a right action and how one defines the proper end of human action in general. Aristotle argued that intelligence and wisdom are uniquely human potentialities and consequently that intellectual virtue is the highest virtue. The life of contemplation, he believed, is the best sort of life, in part because it represents the highest fulfillment of human nature. Moral virtue, also crucial in Aristotle's theory, involves the rational control of one's desires. In action where a choice is possible, one exercises moral virtue by restraining harmful desires and cultivating beneficial ones. The development of virtue requires the cultivation of good habits, and this in turn leads Aristotle to emphasize the importance of good upbringing and education.

One problem said to affect human nature theories is that they have difficulty justifying the supposition that human beings *do* have specific inherent capacities and that these capacities are the same for all humans. Further, critics claim that it is difficult to warrant the assumption that humans are basically good. Perhaps the famous psychoanalyst Sigmund Freud is correct in his assertion that at bottom we are all naturally aggressive and selfish. Third, critics complain that it is difficult to employ this theory in ethical reasoning, since it appears to lack clear-cut rules and principles for use in moral decision making. Obviously, any well-argued human nature ethic will take pains to spell out the aspects of human nature which, when actualized, constitute the ultimate ground for moral judgments.

CONCLUSION

The three approaches to ethical reasoning we have discussed—consequentialism, deontology, and human nature ethics—all present theories of ethical reasoning distinguished in terms of their basic methodological elements. Each represents a type or model of moral reasoning that is applicable to practical decisions in concrete situations. Consider, for example, the case study with which we began our discussion, involving BASF and its proposed new plant. As it happened, BASF chose option 3 and decided to build elsewhere. In making his decision, did the BASF manager actually use any or all of the methods described earlier? Although we cannot know the answer to this question, it is clear, as we saw earlier, that each method was applicable to his problem. Indeed, the three methods of moral reasoning are sufficiently broad that each is applicable to the full range of problems confronting human moral experience. The question of which method, if any, is superior to the others must be left for another time. The intention of this essay is not to substitute for a thorough study of traditional ethical theories—something for which there is no substitute—but to introduce the reader to basic modes of ethical reasoning that will help to analyze the ethical problems in business that arise in the remainder of this book.

Notes

1. "BASF Corporation vs. The Hilton Head Island Developers," in *Business and Society,* Robert D. Hay, et al., eds. (Cincinnati: South-Western Publishing Co., 1984), pp. 100–12.

2. Immanuel Kant, *Groundwork of the Metaphysic of Morals,* trans. H. J. Paton (New York: Harper & Row, 1948, 1956), p. 61.

The Case Method*

THOMAS DONALDSON

Professor Gragg of the Harvard Business School, himself a master of the case method, once said the belief that knowledge can simply be "told" and passed on is "the great delusion of the ages."[1] Gragg's remark concurs with the view of Socrates, the Greek philosopher, whose well-known style of teaching was never a one-way street, with the instructor talking and the student listening, but rather a two-way exchange in which the student actively participated by questioning, searching, and answering. Thus the fundamental basis of the case method, the belief that knowledge cannot simply be "told," is in step with an age-old norm of good teaching. And it is a norm that for centuries has been recognized as valid by philosophers. One should not be surprised, then, to learn that the case method is gaining wide acceptance even outside schools of business. Philosophers, theologians, and social scientists are using it to confront issues of public policy, distributive justice, and ethics.

The purpose of this essay is to describe the case method, its strategies and aims, and to apply it to the teaching of ethics.

The Case Method: A Different Style of Learning

"You can lead a person to the university," someone once quipped, "but you can't make him think." What too often passes for learning is the repetition of facts by students during standardized exams. The case method, however, does not allow a student the luxury of memorizing a body of accepted wisdom. Rather, it forces the student to confront a set of facts that demands analysis; and these facts, the student soon discovers, are not understood by the application of memorized truths.

Thus, a philosophy of education undergirds the case method—namely, that people must be taught to think well in the presence of new situations and to arrive at reasoned courses of action. In this way the method emphasizes *judgment* as much as *understanding*. Moreover, it attempts to develop skills of judgment that can be applied to situations in the real world. Although it varies from practitioner to practitioner, the case method may be defined as a method of instruction that confronts students with descriptions of realistic human events, and then requires the students to analyze, evaluate, and make recommendations about those events.

What is known today as the case method began at Harvard University in 1908 with the opening of the new business school. The business school's first catalog stated that the "problem method" would be utilized "as far as practicable." After years of struggle and experimentation, the case method reached maturity at Harvard from 1919 to 1942 under the encouragement of the dean of the business school, Wallace Donham. It was during these years that the method became the trademark of the Harvard Business School, a position it retains to this day.

The Role of the Instructor

Just as there is no such thing as a "typical" case, there is no such thing as a "typical" case-method teaching style. Each instructor develops his or her own questions, responses, and style. Certain pedagogical virtues, however, are obvious, such as approachability, enthusiasm, and articulateness.[2]

The responsibilities of the instructor using a case-method approach have been summed up as follows:

1. Assign cases for discussion
2. Act as a responsible member of the group delegated to provoke argumentative thinking
3. Guide discussions through remarks and questions toward points of major importance
4. Take a final position on the viewpoints at the end of the discussion *if* the instructor chooses[3]

Sometimes an instructor has a remarkable teaching experience in which it is necessary only to ask an opening question—"Mr. Y., would you begin our discussion?"—and the class is off and running. More frequently, the instructor must help the discussion through contributions of his or her own. To accomplish this, the instructor may

1. Ask further questions
2. Restate and reconstruct what has been said
3. Voice his or her own opinions and draw upon his or her knowledge of fact[4]

To open a discussion, an instructor may ask such questions as

Do you see a problem in this case? If so, what is it?

Would someone volunteer to give us a brief sketch of the facts in the case?

(Or simply) What's happening in this case?

Once the discussion is underway, the instructor may invite a student to play the part of one of the managers who has a central role in the case. Thus, the instructor might ask, "What would you do if you were Mr. Jones?" Indeed, unless an instructor pushes a student to speak in terms of decisions, the advantage of the case method may be undercut as the discussion regresses into a fragmented series of general observations.

Discussion leaders frequently summarize or attempt to interpret a student's remark. Doing so has a double advantage: It helps to confirm what the student actually meant, and it helps to ensure that other students interpreted the remark correctly. In a surprisingly large number of cases, the student will want to qualify a remark once it has been interpreted by the instructor. This has the welcome consequence of encouraging the student to reflect upon both the nature of the view being expressed and the reasons for it.

Professor Andrews has summarized the role of the instructor as follows:

The instructor provides the impromptu services which any group discussion requires. He keeps the proceedings orderly. He should be able to ask questions which . . . advance . . . group thinking and at the same time reveal the relevance of talk that has gone before. . . . He needs the sense of timing which tells him that a discussion is not moving fast enough to make good use of available time or is racing away from the comprehension of half the class. . . . He exercises control over an essentially "undirected" activity, but at the same time he keeps out of the way. . . . Since unpredictable developments always distinguish real learning, he examines his class rather than his subject. His workshop is not the study but the classroom. . . . He must himself be a student.[5]

An instructor may block a direct question from a student. When a student asks a specific question about the material, the instructor may decide that to answer the question would stifle the thinking of other students. Hence the instructor may reply by saying "Well, what does the class think?" or "My opinion is X, but is that really the right opinion?" Here the attempt is to turn the question into a catalyst rather than a retardant of the ongoing discussion.

The following are sample questions asked by case-method instructors:

Where does this idea lead?

You said X. May I add Y?

Do others disagree?

Do you mean X?

Do you have more to say about Y?

Do you think that is true in all cases?

How does that apply to the situation in the case?

Is your point related to Ms. Y's?

What does that have to do with the bigger question?[6]

An instructor can do more than ask questions. He or she can identify unstated assumptions that one of the participants is making and hold them up to the class for inspection. Or if a discussion is really dragging, the instructor may frankly ask the class what's wrong and attempt to generate discussion about the *process* of the discussion itself. (Sometimes this will have surprising results.) Blackboards can be used to list options, relevant facts, pros and cons, and assumptions.

When a discussion is well under way, it is not unusual for an instructor to retire to an inconspicuous place and simply observe.

The Role of the Student

In the case method, the active cooperation of the student is essential. Previous schooling habituates a student to the role of receiver. In the case method, this previous schooling must be undone; the student must learn the habit of being active, of being a force in the teaching process. Hence the student must master a number of skills. First he or she must learn to synthesize material on his or her own. Although infrequently an instructor's summary of the main lines of the preceding discussion will help the student to integrate important aspects of the discussion, ordinarily the act of synthesis must be undertaken by the student. Equally important, the student must learn to separate irrelevant from relevant information. (Cases are frequently constructed intentionally to contain both kinds.) Finally, the student must invest sufficient time in preparing a case to make the discussion productive. With other methods, a failure to prepare is problematic; with the case method, it is disastrous.

Sometimes students benefit from discussing a case in a small, preclass group. In such a group they often discover crucial items around which ordinary group discussions will turn; moreover they gain experience in the presentation of ideas.

Discouragement is routine when students begin the case method. They jump to the conclusion that they are making no progress because they are accustomed to defining "progress" differently. After discussing the first case or two, they recognize that not all issues have been resolved, and may be left with a sense of incompleteness, like hearing a piece of music with no resolving chord. Gradually, however, they will experience a growing confidence in their ability to analyze complex case materials and, in turn, a growing conviction of the value of the case method. At this stage it is not uncommon for the original skepticism to turn to an uncritical endorsement of the method.

The Case Method Applied to Ethics

Any given method is related to the function and object of the method's activity. Thus, we should begin by noting—as Aristotle and others have before us—that the end or aim of ethical enquiry is different from that of empirical enquiry. Whereas the goal of empirical enquiry is factual or empirical knowledge, the goal of ethical enquiry is ethical insight. By "ethical insight" I mean insight about good and bad, right and wrong, and permissible and impermissible behavior. We want to be able to distinguish false or irrational convictions (e.g., that of first-century Romans that when a slave owner was killed by one of his slaves, *all* of his slaves should be executed) from correct ones (e.g., the more modern conviction that this Roman custom was unfair). Although ethics intersects frequently with matters of taste, and hence involves a certain amount of relativity, the very possibility of ethical insight recognizes a difference in the truth status of the belief that torturing children for sport is permissible, and the belief that it is not.

Ethical and empirical knowledge must be distinguished because although they both may be kinds of knowledge, they not only have different subjects but different epistemological foundations. The belief that salt is soluble in water is a piece of empirical knowledge because it is known through experience. It depicts a "fact," and if one were to doubt it, the proper response would be to take a pinch of salt and throw it into water. But the belief that patricide is wrong is an *ethical* belief, not an empirical one, and doubters may well not be persuaded by undertaking the "experiment" of killing their fathers. Indeed, it is difficult to see just what killing one's father could possibly "prove" about the rightness or wrongness of patricide.

The reasoning necessary to make sense of ethical issues has a different logic from that of empirical reasoning. Consider the traditional distinction offered by philosophers such as Aristotle and Aquinas between practical and theoretical reasoning. The end of theoretical reasoning is a general concept, while that of practical reasoning is an action. Thus, using theoretical reasoning I might conclude from the fact that all ravens I have seen are black to the general proposition that all ravens are black. Or I might reason from the premises that all healthy corporations have a strong corporate culture, and that the XYZ Corporation is a healthy corporation, to the deductive conclusion that the XYZ Corporation has a strong corporate culture. Both would be pieces of theoretical reasoning.

However, in practical reasoning, the tables are turned. I reason from the acknowledgment of a general value or desire to a practical action, and I do so typically through a process of means-ends reasoning. Thus, given that I hold the value of "honoring valid contracts," and that I believe that giving you a check in the amount of $10,000 is a means of "honoring a valid contract," my reasoning may lead me to write you a check in the amount of $10,000.

Notice that I have employed means-ends reasoning; that is, I reason that writing the check is a *means* of honoring the contract, but that my process of reasoning is not deductive in nature. The necessary conclusion that is characteristic of deductive reasoning is absent in practical reasoning. For although writing a check for $10,000 is one means of achieving my value, it may not be the only means. I might similarly honor the contract by giving you $10,000 in cash, or by arranging to release you from a prior debt. So whereas the conclusion that "XYZ Corporation has a strong corporate culture" is necessarily true if the premises, "All healthy corporations have a strong corporate culture" and "XYZ Corporation is a healthy corporation" are true, it does not follow necessarily that *if* I hold the value of honoring valid contracts and *if* I believe that writing you a check is a means of honoring a valid contract,

I *will* write you a check. It does not even necessarily follow that I *should* write you a check.

Practical reasoning occurs in a variety of contexts, not only those dealing with ethics. It occurs whenever one employs means-ends reasoning as a guide for action. Yet ethical reasoning, in contrast to nonethical reasoning, has another identifying feature: It necessarily involves evaluation of ends and principles as well as means. If I assume that I want to sell a given piece of property and reason about the best means of selling it, I am using a practical, though not necessarily ethical, mode of reasoning. Ethical reasoning also requires that I deliberate about the act of selling itself, and that I evaluate whether the end of selling the piece of property is morally justified. This feature adds to the complexity of business decisions enormously. For insofar as we can assume that the end or guiding principle of a corporation is the maximization of profit, our reasoning about corporate behavior is simplified. Moral analysis, however, requires that at least from time to time the corporate goal of profit maximization itself come under scrutiny.

Let us now apply our conclusions about ethical reasoning to the matter of teaching business ethics through cases.

The first thing to notice is that adapting the case method to ethics is relatively easy because this method emphasizes practical reasoning, which is a crucial component of ethical reasoning. Cases traditionally have been used to hone a student's judgment in concrete business situations. They emphasize means-ends reasoning and can be used to do the same when the ends are not only market share and profits, but fairness and corporate integrity. A major pedagogical difference between traditional business subjects and that of ethics, however, stems from ethics' concern with ends and principles. Because ethics requires investigation of values to be achieved as well as the means used to achieve them, cases must be adapted to evaluate broader issues. As we shall see, this implies a difference in the structure of cases and the style of pedagogy.

To begin with, teaching ethics requires a different selection of cases. Cases must be structured to raise issues about ends and principles, and this implies a backing away from the traditional insistence, associated with the Harvard case method, that every case must pose a decision-making problem confronted by an individual manager. A case dealing with the FDA's decision to ban the manufacture of Laetrile may not yield to the traditional format of "What should manager A do now?" Yet it may be a good case nonetheless if it confronts students with some of the difficult trade-offs between the liberties of individual actors in a market, and the (supposed) well-being of consumers.

Nor is the enormous detail championed by some case-method practitioners always necessary. Whereas practical reasoning always occurs in the context of a maze of facts, reasoning about ends sometimes thrives in rarefied atmospheres. Consider, for example, the following "case," which is only two sentences long:

> Two equally qualified candidates, one of whom is a black female and the other a white male, have applied for a job. Should the prospective employer hire the black female?

Admirably brief, these two sentences could serve as the focus of a highly profitable, hour-long discussion.

Cases alone are not sufficient when teaching business ethics and should be augmented by theoretical material. The examination of ends and principles is enhanced by reference to the inquiries of others. Whereas it may be possible to gain a reasonable sense of good marketing practice merely through an analysis of cases (although I have my doubts even here), it is nearly impossible to do so in the case of ethics. Again, unlike empirical disciplines, basic ethical knowledge owes little to experience per se. Like mathematics, ethics requires sustained reflection on specific concepts. Thus, just as teaching mathematics would be impossible through an approach involving nothing but cases, so too would ethics. One benefits greatly by examining the theoretical investigations of specialists in the field of ethics, and it follows that any casebook should be supplemented by theoretical materials.

Even as the structure of cases must be adapted to the teaching of ethics, so too must the instructor's teaching style. The "neutrality" of the instructor is a well-respected fixture of the case method in its ordinary setting. Should instructors be similarly neutral when teaching ethics? Although the answer is somewhat a matter of opinion, there seems little reason for sacrificing openness in ethical contexts. We are reminded of the long-standing Socratic irony: Socrates believed that virtue could not be taught, yet he spent his life teaching virtue. The solution to the seeming paradox, of course, is that Socrates believed that one teaches ethics in a quite different manner than one teaches other disciplines. One does not convey facts to the student; instead one plays the role of midwife, attempting to engage the student in a process of reflection that will yield ethical understanding. The truths of ethics cannot be drummed into one's head; rather they must instead be discovered and respected by oneself. Otherwise, they cannot be "known" in a meaningful sense.

Because of this, the instructor must struggle to preserve his or her own openness in the face of the student's own investigations. But openness should not be confused with moral relativism. As the philosopher Ralph Barton Perry notes, it "is easy to raise doubts, to point out the ignorance and conflicting evidence that beset the mind on every side. It is well to do this and an honest and trained mind will do it . . . (but) if beliefs are demolished, they should be built again, or others built in their place."[7]

Openness does not imply that there are no givens in ethics. As in any practical sphere, some things can be assumed: We can assume that murder, torture, and the intentional harming of innocents is bad, and that fairness and happiness are good. Documents such as the United Nation's *Universal Declaration of Human Rights* are good examples of how much we have in common even with peoples of distant lands and different tastes. Signed by virtually every country in the world, the *Declaration* lays down a basic floor of values that deserve the name "universal": rights to freedom, adequate medical care, safe working conditions, participation in government, and the ownership of property. So too, an instructor teaching ethics can make certain basic assumptions about values without compromising his pedagogical openness.

In empirical science, success implies that we have discovered the structure of the subject—and finally of the world itself—by perception and experiment. In ethical theory, success implies that we in some sense create the structure of the world, and that we do so in the image of a design that is beautiful and not ugly. As the German philosopher Immanuel Kant once remarked, "Things in nature act according to laws; only people act in accordance with the *concept* of laws." In business, people should be guided by concepts not only related to profitability and efficiency, but of professional integrity, responsibility, and fairness. The latter concepts demand an attention to ends and principles that is uncharacteristic of traditional case-method technique. Thus case-method instructors must make a concession to the unique demands of the discipline of ethics.

Shortcomings of the Case Method

The case method is not foolproof. Like any other method, it is susceptible to the foibles and failings of those who use it and, badly handled, produces classroom disasters. At its worst, the method becomes a boring exposure to the prejudices of others.

Cases necessarily oversimplify business situations. Whereas cases can imitate reality by demanding decisions on the basis of incomplete facts (no real-world decision maker has *all* the facts), cases are at odds with reality in presenting a "static" rather than a dynamic decision-making context. A case presents a situation in which the action has already occurred, but everyday situations unfold gradually, and every hour brings fresh information to the decision maker. Hence the skills of knowing when to seek new information, and of knowing when the proper moment has arrived to make a decision, are not developed by the case method.

Essential to a good case discussion is adequate discussion time. A case done hurriedly is an unrewarding experience in which most of the analysis is either superficial or wrong. At first, students may find the discussion of many problems in a short time stimulating. But soon the frustration of approaching case after case without in-depth analysis will bring discouragement with the entire method.

Finally, although the case method is an excellent method for most students, one or two students may benefit little if at all. However, this is not a characteristic drawback of the case method per se, since every approach to teaching misses some students. Indeed, a special advantage of the case method is that it can bring to life a joy in learning for students who have been turned off by traditional methods.

Structuring the Learning Experience

The following are suggestions for designing a case discussion process.

Lecturing in Conjunction with Cases. Depending on the style and preference of a given instructor, a lecture may precede or follow a case discussion. Most instructors in business ethics courses use cases only as one part of their course, with lectures and discussions of theoretical material constituting the remaining parts.

Time. A case may occupy a full class period or, in the instance of exceedingly long and complicated cases, two or more periods. Two or three short cases can sometimes be discussed in an hour. Even the shortest of cases (perhaps a paragraph or two in length) will usually require twenty minutes of discussion time.

Call Lists. Some instructors work entirely with volunteers, but others call on specific students, especially in the beginning, to get things moving. Calling on students increases pressure on them to be prepared, although some instructors and students find such pressure uncomfortable and distracting. Of those who do call on students, many use "call lists" containing the names of participants and their frequency of participation. Near the end of a discussion, an instructor may stop recognizing volunteers and move to call on those who haven't yet participated.

Assigning Additional Work. The usual assignment for students is to read and study the case carefully. With complicated cases, instructors sometimes ask for a brief written analysis to be submitted on the day of the discussion.

Role Playing. Role playing is a device sometimes used to simulate a living situation. Choosing an opportune moment, the instructor invites a student (or students) to assume the role of a participant in the case. In a case dealing with government regulation, for example, one student may remark that the corporation's best option is to stall the regulatory agency. The teacher, knowing that other students do not agree with this strategy, may ask, "Does anyone want to play the role of the regulator?" When someone accepts the invitation and responds directly to the student who advocates stalling, the former student has a chance to respond directly to the regulator. Such exchanges can enliven a discussion and reveal difficulties that otherwise might be glossed over.

Concluding Evaluation. At the end of a discussion, some instructors will ask for a vote among various options that have been explored in the discussion. This is not to affirm that correct answers are simple products of democratic vote, but to indicate how others have interpreted the points made in the discussion.

Grading. The method of grading, of course, is the prerogative of the instructor. Most instructors, however, try to form a general impression of a student's performance and then record it either after each class discussion or at one or two points during the semester.

Students may also be given exams that ask them to analyze cases in a written essay. In ethics courses where theoretical material is being covered in addition to cases, it is common to ask students to analyze a case by using concepts drawn from the theoretical readings.

• • •

The case method, though not foolproof, offers clear rewards. Socrates' insight that moral truth cannot simply "be told" is reflected in the case method's emphasis on analysis, discussion, and decision making. Like any method, it is subject to the failings of its practitioners. Like any method, it must be carefully adapted to the special territory it covers. But handled properly it can spark the search for skills and values of utmost human import. It can, perhaps more effectively than any other method, demonstrate the need for intellectual solutions to practical problems.

Notes

1. Charles I. Gragg, "Because Wisdom Can't Be Told," in *The Case Method at the Harvard Business School,* ed. Malcolm P. McNair (New York: McGraw-Hill, Inc., 1954), p. 10.
2. Kenneth R. Andrews, "The Role of the Instructor in the Case Method," in *The Case Method at the Harvard Business School,* ed. Malcolm P. McNair (New York: McGraw-Hill, Inc., 1954), p. 99.
3. Gragg, "Wisdom Can't Be Told," p. 12.
4. Andrews, "Role of the Instructor," p. 105.
5. Ibid., 98–99.
6. Ibid., 105–6.
7. Ralph Barton Perry, *The Citizen Decides: A Guide to Responsible Thinking in Time of Crisis* (Bloomington: Indiana University Press, 1951), Chapter VII.

Suggested Supplementary Readings

ANDREWS, KENNETH R., ed. *The Case Method of Teaching Human Relations and Administration.* Cambridge, Mass.: Harvard University Press, 1953.

ANDREWS, KENNETH R. "The Role of the Instructor in the Case Method," in *The Case Method at the Harvard Business School,* ed. Malcolm P. McNair. New York: McGraw-Hill, Inc., 1954, pp. 98–109.

CANTOR, NATHANIAL B. "Learning Which Makes a Difference," in *To Study Administration by Cases,* ed. Andrew Towl. Cambridge, Mass.: Harvard University Press, 1969, pp. 153–58.

COPELAND, MELVIN P. "The Genius of the Case Method in Business Instruction," in *The Case Method at the Harvard Business School,* ed. Malcolm P. McNair. New York: McGraw-Hill, Inc., 1954, pp. 25–33.

GLOVER, JOHN D., and RALPH M. HOWER. "Some Comments on Teaching by the Case Method," in *The Case of Teaching Human Relations and Administration,* ed. Kenneth R. Andrews, Cambridge, Mass.: Harvard University Press, 1953, pp. 13–24.

MCNAIR, MALCOLM P., ed. *The Case Method at the Harvard Business School.* New York: McGraw-Hill, Inc., 1954.

STENZEL, ANNE, and HELEN FEENEY. *Learning by the Case Method.* New York: The Seabury Press, Inc., 1970.

• ONE •

Business or Ethics

Relatively few issues in life are ever clear cut, especially when they involve a complex series of facts and decisions. However, there are times when the issues, though complex, are clear and demand our attention. Such is the case with two classic examples of what's right and wrong in business ethics: the Beech-Nut apple juice incident and the Tylenol tampering episode.

The Beech-Nut incident asks the question, Why would one of America's most venerable food companies knowingly produce apple juice that completely omitted apples from its recipe and contained nothing but sugar water and vitamin C? After all, Beech-Nut is not a "mom and pop" outfit, but a firm that annually earned 17 to 20 percent of the United States' then $760 million annual baby food market. This was a firm that was managed at the top by two pillars of the community. So how did it happen that Beech-Nut broke its sacred trust with the public—"Safe Food for Healthy Kids"?

The Tylenol tampering episode and the position that top management at Johnson and Johnson took begs the question, In doing the right thing, can a corporation and business also do well? Is the lesson of this case that honesty works and that the truth can be effective both ethically and economically? Or is the real lesson a cynical self-serving one vis-à-vis Mark Twain—"When in doubt tell the truth. It will disarm your friends and befuddle your enemies."

Given the two preceding essays, "Introduction to Ethical Reasoning" and "The Case Method," readers are invited to examine what happened at Beech-Nut and Tylenol and ask themselves the following questions:

1. What is at stake? (or) What is the problem?
2. What are the non-normative or factual issues involved?
3. What are the normative or ethical issues involved?
4. What alternatives are available?
5. What decision would you make?[1]

Notes

1. A. R. Gini, "The Case Method: A Perspective," *Journal of Business Ethics,* 4 (1985), 351–52. (D. Reidel Publishing Company.)

• *Case Study* •

Into the Mouth of Babes*

JAMES TRAUB

It is well within the reach of most white-collar criminals to assume an air of irreproachable virtue, especially when they're about to be sentenced. But there was something unusually compelling about the hearing of Niels L. Hoyvald and John F. Lavery as they stood before Judge Thomas C. Platt of the United States District Court in Brooklyn last month—especially in light of what they were being sentenced for. As president and vice president of the Beech-Nut Nutrition Corporation, Hoyvald and Lavery had sold millions of bottles of "apple juice" that they knew to contain little or no apple juice at all—only sugars, water, flavoring and coloring. The consumers of this bogus product were babies.

One prosecutor of the case, Thomas H. Roche, had summed up Beech-Nut's behavior as "a classic picture of corporate greed and irresponsibility." The company itself had pleaded guilty the previous fall to 215 counts of violating Federal food and drug laws, and had agreed to pay a $2 million fine, by far the largest ever imposed in the 50-year history of the Food, Drug and Cosmetic Act. Beech-Nut had confessed in a press release that it had broken a "sacred trust."

Yet there was Niels Hoyvald, 54 years old, tall, silver-haired, immaculately dressed, standing before Judge Platt with head bowed, as his attorney, Brendan V. Sullivan, Jr., described him as "a person we would be proud to have in our family." When it was Hoyvald's turn to address the judge, he spoke firmly, but then his voice cracked as he spoke of his wife and mother: "I can hardly bear to look at them or speak to them," he said. "I ask for them and myself, please don't send me to jail."

Judge Platt was clearly troubled. He spoke in a semiaudible mutter that had the crowd in the courtroom craning forward. Though it was "unusual for a corporate executive to do time for consumer fraud," he said, he had "no alternative" but to sentence Hoyvald to a prison term of a year and a day, plus fines totaling $100,000. He then meted out the same punishment to the 56-year old Lavery, who declined to speak on his own behalf. He received his sentence with no show of emotion.

The combination of babies, apple juice and a well-known name like Beech-Nut makes for a potent symbol. In fact, apple juice is not especially nutritious (bottlers often fortify it with extra Vitamin C), but babies love it and find it easy to digest. Parents are pleased to buy a product that says "no sugar added"—as Beech-Nut advertised—and seem to regard it as almost as pure and natural as mother's milk. That, of course, was the sacred trust Beech-Nut broke, and is now struggling to repair. The company's share of the $760 million United States baby-food market has dropped from a high of 20 percent in 1986, when Beech-Nut and the two executives were indicted, to 17 percent this year. Its losses in the fruit-juice market have been even more dramatic. Richard C. Theuer,

*From *The New York Times Magazine,* July 24, 1988. Copyright © 1988 by The New York Times Company. Reprinted by permission.

the company's president since 1986, still gets a stream of letters from outraged parents "who don't realize that it was a long time ago." Some of them, he says are "almost obscene."

If parents are outraged by Beech-Nut's actions, many people are also baffled. Even after the trial and verdict, the question of motive lingers: why would two men with impeccable records carry out so cynical and reckless a fraud? Except for Theuer, no current Beech-Nut employee who was involved in the events of the trial agreed to be interviewed for this article, nor did Hoyvald or Lavery. But a vivid picture of the economic and psychological concerns that impelled the company along its ruinous course emerges from court documents and a wide range of interviews. The Beech-Nut baby food scandal is a case study in the warping effects of blind corporate loyalty.

For three-quarters of the century after its founding in 1891 as a meat-packing company, Beech-Nut expanded steadily into a large, diversified food concern, eventually including Life Savers, Table Talk pies, Tetley tea, Martinson's coffee, chewing gum and, of course, baby food. The company had an image straight from Norman Rockwell—pure, simple, healthful. In 1969, Beech-Nut was taken over by the Squibb Corporation. Only four years later, a remnant of the old company was spun off and taken private by a group led by a lawyer, Frank C. Nicholas. The company that emerged from the Squibb umbrella sold only baby food, and, as in earlier years, regularly divided with Heinz the third or so of the market not controlled by Gerber. It was a completely new world for Beech-Nut's newly independent owners, and an extremely precarious one. Beech-Nut was in a continuous financial bind.

After an expensive and unsuccessful effort in the mid-1970's to market Beech-Nut as the "natural" baby food, the imperative to reduce costs became overwhelming. In 1977, when a Bronx-based supplier, who would later take the name Universal Juice, offered Beech-Nut a less-expensive apple-juice concentrate, the company abandoned its longtime supplier for the new source. The savings would never amount to much more than $250,000 a year, out of a $50 million-plus manufacturing budget, but Beech-Nut was under the gun.

At the time, the decision may have seemed insignificant. Ira Knickerbocker, head of agricultural purchasing at the main Beech-Nut plant in Canajoharie, N.Y., who has since retired, says that in 1977 the new concentrate was only slightly less expensive than the competition's. "There was never a question about the quality or anything else," he insists. Yet no other baby-food company, and no large apple-juice manufacturer, ever bought significant quantities of concentrate from Universal. In early 1981, Heinz would return the product to Universal after samples had failed to pass conventional laboratory tests and the supplier refused to let company officials visit the plant.

Another Federal prosecutor, John R. Fleder, contends that the low price of the Universal concentrate, which eventually reached 25 percent below the market, "should have been enough in itself to tip off anybody" that the concentrate was diluted or adulterated. Jack B. Hartog, a supplier who had sold Beech-Nut much of its apple concentrate until 1977, agrees with Fleder: "There was no question about it in the trade."

John Lavery, Beech-Nut's vice president of operations and manager of the plant in Canajoharie, did not question the authenticity of the concentrate. After spending his entire career at Beech-Nut, Lavery had risen to a position in which he managed almost 1,000 employees. In the small hamlets around Canajoharie, a company town in rural Montgomery County, northwest of Albany, Lavery was known as a figure of propriety and rectitude. "He was as straight and narrow as anything you could come up with," says Ed Gros, an engineer who worked with Lavery at Beech-Nut. Lavery was a fixture in the Methodist church, on the school board and in community organizations.

In 1978, after initial testing indicated the presence of impurities in the new concentrate, Lavery agreed to send two employees to inspect the "blending facility" that Universal's owner, Zeev Kaplansky, claimed to operate in New Jersey. The two reported that all they could find was a warehouse containing a few 55-gallon drums. The bizarre field trip aroused further suspicions among executives at the Canajoharie plant, but only one, Jerome J. LiCari, head of research and development, chose to act on them.

LiCari sent samples of the concentrate to an outside laboratory. The tests, he reported to Lavery, indicated that the juice was adulterated, probably with corn syrup. Rather than return the concentrate, or demand proof of its authenticity, as Heinz would do three years later, Lavery sent down the order that Kaplansky sign a "hold-harmless agreement," indemnifying Beech-Nut against damages arising from consumer and other complaints. (Ironically, in May 1987 Beech-Nut settled a class-action suit against it totaling $7.5 million.)

LiCari, however, was scarcely satisfied by Lavery's legalistic approach. Like Lavery, LiCari was also every bit the local boy. Born and raised in neighboring Herkimer County, he had worked in the Beech-Nut plant during summers home from college, and, after 14 years with Beech-Nut, he had achieved his greatest ambitions. Yet it was LiCari who accepted the solitary role of institutional conscience. In April 1979, and again in July, he sent samples of the concentrate to a second laboratory, in California. The April test again found signs of adulteration, but the July test did not. LiCari concluded that Kaplansky had switched from corn syrup to beet sugar, an adulterant that current technology could not detect. Once again he approached Lavery, suggesting that Beech-Nut require Kaplansky to repurchase the concentrate. This time, Lavery instructed that the concentrate be blended into mixed juices, where adulteration is far harder to detect. Lavery's attorney, Steven Kimelman, says that his client does not recall his rationale for the decision, but argues that on this matter, as on others, he acted in concert with other executives, including LiCari.

Lavery and LiCari were locked in a hopeless conflict of roles, values, and personality. Steven Kimelman characterizes Lavery as "more like a general. He's the kind of guy who gives orders, and he has no trouble making up his mind; LiCari was too much of a scientist type to him, and not practical enough." LiCari had become consumed by the issues of the concentrate. By spring of 1981 he was working almost full time on tests to determine its purity. Finally, on Aug. 5, LiCari circulated a memo to executives, including Lavery. "A tremendous amount of circumstantial evidence," he wrote, makes for "a grave case against the current supplier" of apple concentrate. No matter what the cost, LiCari concluded, a new supplier should be found.

Several days later, LiCari was summoned to Lavery's office, where, as he told the jury, "I was threatened that I wasn't a team player, I wasn't working for the company, threatened to be fired." The choice could not have been more stark: capitulate, or leave.

Many of those who know Lavery find this picture of him simply unbelievable. The Canajoharie view is that Lavery was victimized. Ed Gros, Lavery's former colleague, speculates that LiCari "had a personal vendetta" against Lavery. Ira Knickerbocker blames the Government. Yet even Lavery's friends admit to a kind of moral bafflement. "I've lost a lot of sleep over this," says a former company vice president, Bill Johnsey.

Steven Kimelman denies that Lavery threatened LiCari, but concedes that his client made a "mistake in judgment." The mistake was in not kicking the matter up to Hoyvald when he received the Aug. 5 memo. Kimelman insists that Lavery "thought that LiCari tended to overreact," and in any case felt that there was no other concentrate whose purity he could entirely trust. In fact, LiCari's tests showed no signs of adulteration in several other, more expensive, concentrates. A harsher view is that Lavery acted quite consciously. "He just didn't care," says Thomas Roche, one of the prosecutors. "He showed an extraordinary amount of arrogance. I think his sole objective was to show Beech-Nut and Nestlé's (since 1979, the corporate parent) that he could do well."

Or perhaps Lavery had simply blinded himself to the consequences of his acts. The apple juice had become merely a commodity and the babies merely customers. One exchange between another prosecutor, Kenneth L. Jost, and an executive at the Canajoharie plant, Robert J. Belvin, seemed to sum up Lavery's state of mind:

> "Mr. Belvin, what did you do when you found that Beech-Nut had been using a product in what is called apple juice that was not in fact apple juice?"
>
> "I—I became very upset."
>
> "Why were you very upset?"
>
> "Because we feed babies . . ."
>
> "Did you ever hear Mr. Lavery express a sentiment similar to that you have just described to the jury?"
>
> "No."

By 1979, Beech-Nut's financial condition had become so parlous that Frank Nicholas admitted failure and sold the company to Nestlé S.A., the Swiss food giant. Nestlé arrived with $60 million in working capital and a commitment to restore a hallowed brand name to health. The view in the food industry was that Beech-Nut had been rescued from the brink. Yet evidence presented at the trial gives the exact opposite impression—of a Procrustean bed being prepared for nervous managers. Hoyvald, who chose to testify on his own behalf, admitted that in 1981, his first year as chief executive, he had grandiosely promised Nestlé that Beech-Nut would earn $700,000 the following year, though there would be a negative cash flow of $1.7 million. Hoyvald had arrived at Nestlé only a year before, but he was a seasoned executive in the food business. The answer nevertheless shot back from Switzerland: the cash flow for Beech-Nut, as for all other Nestlé subsidiaries, would have to be zero or better. "The pressure," as he conceded, "was on."

Hoyvald testified that he knew nothing about adulterated concentrate until the summer of 1982. In January 1981, however, LiCari had sent to both Lavery and Hoyvald a copy of an article in a trade magazine discussing signs of adulteration in apple juice, and had written and attached a memo noting, among other things, that "Beech-Nut has been concerned over the authenticity of fruit juice products." LiCari also told the jury that in August of that same year, several weeks after his disastrous confrontation with Lavery, he went to Beech-Nut's corporate headquarters in Fort Washington, Pa., to appeal to Hoyvald—an uncharacteristic suspension of his faith in the chain of command. Hoyvald had been appointed president only four months earlier, and LiCari testified that he liked and trusted his new boss, whom he felt had a mandate from Nestlé to restore Beech-Nut's prestige. The meeting in Fort Washington persuaded LiCari that he had finally found an ally. Hoyvald, LiCari testified, "appeared shocked and surprised" at LiCari's report, and left him feeling "that something was going to be done and they would stop using it."

Then, month after month, nothing happened. Finally, at a late-fall company retreat at a ski resort in Vermont, LiCari raised the issue with Hoyvald one last time. Hoyvald told him, he testified, that he was unwilling to fire Lavery. (In his own testimony, Hoyvald denied that either meeting had taken place.)

LiCari was now convinced that the company was bent on lawbreaking, as he later testified, and rather than acquiesce, he quit, in January 1982. His allies concerned with quality control remained behind, but evidently none was stubborn or reckless enough to press his point.

Hoyvald, like Lavery, was a man with an exemplary background, though one that was a good deal more varied and sophisticated than his subordinate's. Born and raised in a provincial town in Denmark, he had relocated to the United States and received his Master of Business Administration degree from the University of Wisconsin in 1960. An ambitious man, Hoyvald had hopscotched across five companies before joining Beech-Nut as head of marketing in 1980, with the promise that he would be promoted to president within a year. Throughout his career, Hoyvald's watchword had been "aggressively marketing top quality products," as he wrote in a three-page "Career Path" addendum to a 1979 resumé. He had turned around the faltering Plumrose Inc., a large food company, by emphasizing quality, and he viewed the job at Beech-Nut as a chance to do just that.

In June 1982, Hoyvald's principles were abruptly tested when the quality of his own product was decisively challenged. A trade association, the Processed Apples Institute, had initiated an investigation into longstanding charges of adulteration throughout the apple-concentrate business. By April 1982, an investigator working for the institute, a former New York City narcotics detective named Andrew Rosenzweig (who is now chief investigator for the Manhattan District Attorney's office), was prowling around the Woodside, Queens, warehouse of a company called Food Complex, which was Universal's manufacturing arm. By diligent questioning, and searching by flashlight through a dumpster in the middle of many nights, Rosenzweig discovered that Food Complex omitted apples from its recipe altogether, and that its biggest customer was Beech-Nut. On June 25, Rosenzweig tracked a tanker truck full of sugar water out of the Food Complex loading dock and up the New York State Thruway to Canajoharie, where he planned to confront management with his findings. He was hoping to persuade the company to join a civil suit being prepared against Universal and Food Complex; but, expecting the worst, he secretly tape-recorded the ensuing conversation.

At the trial, the tape proved to be a damning piece of evidence. In the course of the discussion, Lavery and two other executives, instead of disputing Rosenzweig's claim that Beech-Nut was making juice from suspect concentrate, unleashed a cascade of tortuous rationalizations. When Rosenzweig explained that the trade association had made new strides in lab testing, Lavery, obviously panicking, suddenly announced: "At this point, we've made our last order from" Universal. But despite considerable pressure, Lavery refused to give Rosenzweig samples of the concentrate, and declined to join the suit. The one anxiety he expressed was the possibility of bad publicity.

On June 28, Paul E. Hillabush, the head of quality assurance at Canajoharie, called Hoyvald to tell him of Rosenzweig's visit. Hillabush testified that he suggested Beech-Nut recall the product. But Beech-Nut would not only have had to switch to a new and more expensive concentrate, it would have had to admit publicly that the product it had been selling since 1978 was bogus. The cover-up, which Lavery had begun three years earlier with the order to blend the concentrate in mixed juices, was attaining an irresistible momentum.

Hoyvald made the fateful decision to reject Hillabush's advice, and to devote the next eight weeks to moving the tainted products as fast as possible. It would be aggressive marketing, though not of a quality product.

The Apple Institute's suit, as it turned out, was only the first wave to hit the beach. Federal and state authorities had been investigating suppliers of adulterated concentrate since the spring, and the trail led them, too, to Canajoharie. On July 29, an inspector from the United States Food and Drug Administration arrived at the plant, announced that samples taken from supermarket shelves had proved to be adulterated, and took away cases of apple juice ready to be shipped. On Aug. 11, Paul Hillabush received a call from an old friend, Maurice Guerrette, an assistant director with the New York State Department of Agriculture and Markets, who reported much the same conclusion. Guerrette recalls receiving one of the great shocks of his life when Hillabush tried to laugh the whole thing off. It was only then that he realized—as would each investigator in his turn—that Beech-Nut was not the victim of a crime, but its conscious perpetrator.

Guerrette's phone call persuaded Lavery and others—incorrectly, as it turned out—that a seizure action was imminent. After consulting with Hoyvald, executives in Canajoharie decided to move the entire inventory of tainted juice out of the state's jurisdiction. And so, on the night of Aug. 12, nine tractor-trailers from Beech-Nut's trucking company were loaded with 26,000 cases of juice and taken in a ghostly caravan to a warehouse in Secaucus, N.J. One of America's most venerable food companies was fleeing the law like a bootlegger.

By the late summer of 1982, Beech-Nut was racing to unload its stock before regulators initiated a seizure action. On Sept. 1, Hoyvald managed to unload thousands of cases of juice from the Secaucus warehouse to Puerto Rico, despite the fact that the Puerto Rican distributor was already overstocked. Two weeks later, Hoyvald overruled his own lawyers and colleagues, who again suggested a recall, and ordered a feverish "foreign promotion"; under certain circumstances, American law does not prohibit the selling abroad of products banned at home. Within days, 23,000 cases were trucked at great expense from the company's San Jose, Calif., plant to Galveston, Tex., where they were offloaded for the Dominican Republic, where they were sold at a 50 percent discount.

While Beech-Nut's sales staff shipped the evidence out to sea, its lawyers were holding the Federal and state agencies at bay. On Sept. 24, lawyers scheduled a meeting with F.D.A. officials that was designed to placate their adversaries. It worked. Three more weeks passed before the F.D.A. Administrator, Taylor M. Quinn, threatened to seize the juice, and thus finally wrung from the company a pledge to begin a nationwide recall. New York State authorities, less patient, threatened a seizure before Beech-Nut hurriedly agreed to a state recall. But the delay allowed Niels Hoyvald to virtually complete his master plan.

By the middle of November Hoyvald could boast, in a report to his superior at Nestlé: "The recall has now been completed, and due to our many delays, we were only faced with having to destroy approximately 20,000 cases. We received adverse publicity in only one magazine." As it turned out, of course, Hoyvald's self-congratulation was premature.

Further Federal and state investigations exposed details of the cover-up, as well as the fact that Beech-Nut had continued to sell the juice in its mixed-juice product for six months after the recall. New York State sued Beech-Nut for selling an adulterated and misbranded product, and imposed a $250,000 fine, by far the largest such penalty ever assessed in the state for consumer violations. In November 1986, the United States Attorney obtained indictments of Hoyvald, Lavery, Beech-Nut, Zeev Kaplansky and Kaplansky's colleague Raymond H. Wells, the owner of Food Complex. Beech-Nut eventually settled by agreeing to pay a $2 million fine. Kaplansky and Wells, who had earlier settled the apple-institute with a financial agreement and by ceasing production of their concentrate, also pleaded guilty, and await sentencing. The F.D.A. referred the case to the Justice Department for criminal prosecution.

The case against Hoyvald and Lavery seemed overwhelming—so overwhelming that Lavery's first attorney suggested he plead guilty. Why did Lavery and Hoyvald insist on standing trial? Because both men, by most reports are still convinced that they committed nothing graver than a mistake in judgment.

Hoyvald and Lavery seem to think of themselves as corporate patriots. Asked by one of the prosecutors why the entire inventory of concentrate was not destroyed once it came under suspicion, Hoyvald shot back testily: "And I could have called up Switzerland and told them I had just closed the company down. Because that is what would have been the result of it."

The questions of what Nestlé would have said, or did say, was not resolved by the trial. Jerome LiCari testified that in 1980 and 1981 he had expressed his concerns to six different Nestlé officials, including Richard Theuer, who was then a vice president of Nestlé and would become Beech-Nut's president in 1986. In an extraordinary effort to clear its reputation, Nestlé brought all six officials to court, mostly from Switzerland, and each one either contradicted LiCari's account or stated he had no memory of the alleged conversation. Nestlé is acutely sensitive to its public image, which was tarnished in the 1970's and early 80's when it aggressively promoted infant formula in third-world countries despite public health concerns, sparking international controversy and boycott campaigns.

Nestlé has defended its subsidiary's acts as vigorously as it defended its own in the past. The company has spent what sources close to the case estimate as several million dollars in defending the two executives, and has agreed to keep both men on the payroll—at annual salaries of $120,000 and $70,000—until their current appeals are exhausted.

In a memo sent to Canajoharie employees after the verdict, James M. Biggar, president of Nestlé's American operations, claimed that LiCari had confused "what he wished he had said" with "what he actually said or did," and faulted management only for failing to keep an "open door."

Richard Theuer, the man Nestlé chose to replace Hoyvald, promises to keep that door open. He hopes to convince the public that at "the new Beech-Nut" decisions will be taken, as he says, "on behalf of the babies."

• *Case Study* •

Tylenol's Rebound*

CARL CANNON

It's "easier to turn water into wine than to bring back Tylenol. It is dead."

That obituary by the head of a large advertising agency came at the height of the Tylenol crisis, which began a year ago this coming Friday. In the bitter wake of seven deaths in the Chicago area from cyanide-laced Extra-Strength Tylenol capsules, millions of bottles were yanked off the shelves by panicky retailers, unsure of their own liability, and by a confounded manufacturer, Johnson & Johnson. A product that had become almost a household word virtually disappeared in the first weeks after the tragedy.

From 35.4% of the over-the-counter analgesic market before the killings, Tylenol sank to a shaky 18.3% at the end of last year, when the red-and-white capsules began to reappear on the shelves. Johnson & Johnson, an international health-products giant based in New Brunswick, N.J., saw its stock price plunge.

"Textbook" Recovery Plan

But that ad executive has since profusely apologized. Today, through a recovery plan that some say will be studied in textbooks on marketing, advertising and public relations, the product that only 12 months ago was "buried" by doomsayers has more than a 28.6% share of the $1.2-billion non-prescription pain reliever market, or more than 80% of its total before the crisis.

Johnson & Johnson's management, its agency, Compton Advertising, the unique confidence the public had in the product itself and even the news media share credit for the resurgence of Tylenol. It came against difficult odds, against a backdrop of national fear and a host of copycat crimes that not only threatened Tylenol but for a time cast a pall over the entire non-prescription analgesic industry as well. It was expensive—Johnson & Johnson's massive product recall, media messages and tests of the capsules cost it in the tens of millions of dollars. And it has permanently affected the way non-prescription drugs are packaged as makers of everything from aspirin to eye drops followed Johnson & Johnson's lead in tamper-proofing.

Within the first few hours after the poisonings were traced to Tylenol capsules, Johnson & Johnson set up a task force of its top executives to first assess the damage to the company and then determine how to overcome it.

Over the next two weeks, during which this task force and a Compton Advertising team struggled to come up with a plan for recovery, outside marketing experts were advising that the only course was to change the name and come out with a "new" product. But there was legitimate concern that if such a tactic as merely reissuing Tylenol under a different name were tried, the press would quickly learn of it and the situation for the company would be worse.

There was no feeling within the company or within the agency that the name Tylenol should be dropped, according to Richard Earle, Compton's senior vice president and creative director, and Thomas Lom, senior vice president and managing supervisor for the advertising agency, both of whom worked on the recovery plan.

Tylenol was introduced in the late 1950's to the medical profession and built its reputation in those first years on being medically endorsed as a substitute for aspirin. The company contends its research shows that 70% of the users of the product first tried it on the recommendation of a physician. "With that kind of a profile as a foundation, advertising for the product began in 1976," Earle said. "We did some research and found that it was pretty well known among consumers then as a substitute for aspirin. Over the years our commercials used ordinary people with hidden cameras and showed the relief of actual headaches. The whole emphasis of our campaigns was how well the product worked."

Advertising Criticized

It was a type of advertising that had been criticized by other Madison Avenue agencies as both boring and insulting to viewers. Critics say consumers were not naive enough to believe that people featured in the commercials were unaware they were on camera. But sales results had proved these critics wrong. Viewers obviously not only believed the advertising, but had faith in the product as well. This was later to stand the company in good stead in the midst of the crisis when competing products saw an opportunity to increase their market share at Tylenol's expense.

The first major decision by Johnson & Johnson, even before the crisis task force was set up, according to a company spokesman who took part, was to pull two lots of Tylenol capsules off the shelves in Chicago. The second was to halt all advertising. In the next few days capsules were taken off shelves across the country.

Johnson & Johnson's next step was to launch consumer research, to judge how the public perceived the company. "Then it was deemed necessary to make sure consumers got rid of Tylenol capsules," a Johnson & Johnson spokesman said. To accomplish this, Compton ran newspaper ads 10 days after the tragedy offering to swap Tylenol tablets for Tylenol capsules. "The press had informed the public so well that the whole country realized the danger was not in tablets, so the response was good" Lom said.

At the same time, decisions were being made to investigate tamper-resistant packaging, to develop marketing strategies to rebuild the brand—coupons for consumers and discounts for retailers—and to figure out the type of advertising to employ once the crisis was over.

During this period the company also obtained a letter from the Food and Drug Administration stating that the agency was satisfied that there had been no criminal tampering with the product at the plant in which it was manufactured. "We were encountering people in our research who still expressed some lingering doubt, who thought perhaps the damage had been done on our premises," a company spokesman said. Johnson & Johnson widely exhibited the FDA letter to the press to try to erase the doubts.

Then the counterattack—a low-key one—began. "We wrote some ad copy which was essentially a corporate statement," Earle said. "We felt the public should be told that Tylenol would be back. We wrote a commercial early but it was held up and not aired for about four weeks."

The reluctance was born of uncertainty, according to the Compton team. "The company had worries of stirring everything up. So we did some research. Starting a week after the tragedy, we began to conduct man-on-the-street interviews to get a good reading of the general mood of the country. Over the next four weeks, we interviewed more than 800 people in 12 or 15 cities and found little negative feeling against the company itself. Many said they would buy Tylenol again if it were packaged in tamper-proof containers.

"But Mr. Burke (James E. Burke, chairman and chief executive of Johnson & Johnson) wanted to go slowly. He decided not to rush in. There were some concern over the timing. It was very close to Halloween and we were afraid it might spark a 'copycat' crime," Earle said.

Aired "Roadblock" Ad

It was finally concluded that, since the Tylenol killings had been so extensively covered in the press and since Compton's research showed that the public wanted to hear from the company, the commercial should be run. "Our statement was rewritten many times," Lom said.

The first Tylenol commercial after the killings was what ad agencies and networks call a "roadblock": A viewer would see the same commercial no matter which of the three television networks was being watched at, say, 9 p.m. The ad featured Dr. Thomas N. Gates, medical director of McNeil Consumer Products, the Johnson & Johnson subsidiary that produces the analgesic. Gates, obviously used as a symbol of reliability, urged trust in the product and promised tamper-resistant containers.

"We thought about that spot hard and long," acknowledged a Johnson & Johnson spokesman. "There was some risk that it would be interpreted as being too commercial. After all, there were no capsules on the shelves for people to even buy. But, fortunately, it did what the country was expecting from the company and told them Tylenol would be back and it would be safe."

Long thought was given, too, to the press conference by Burke in which he announced—five weeks after McNeil Consumers Products withdrew 22 million bottles from the market—that Tylenol would start to reappear on store shelves in triple-sealed, tamper-resistant packages.

"We had more than 200 inquiries from the media and there simply was no other way" to answer them all, a company spokesman said. Burke appeared in New York and was linked by television to 29 other cities across the country. He said it was a "moral imperative" not to be destroyed by a "terrorist" act. And Johnson & Johnson emerged with the perception of being a responsible company and a champion of consumers.

Granted Access to Media

Both Earle and Lom acknowledge that "a lot that might have been handled by advertising at this time was handled in a public relations sense." They mean that over these weeks Johnson & Johnson executives made themselves extremely available to the press. Burke and aides accepted virtually any and all appearances on talk shows, for instance, in an attempt to get across the company's viewpoint.

Still, according to one of those involved, the Johnson & Johnson task force agonized over a request for an appearance on "60 Minutes" because of the combative and sometimes abrasive style of questioning often used on the show. Among the seven key members of the Burke task force, two voted against the appearance. "We discussed it at length, and decided we had nothing to hide and the rest of the press had done a very complete job, and we thought '60 Minutes' would, too."

Burke not only appeared, but CBS reporter Mike Wallace and a camera crew were also allowed to attend and film a strategy session of the task force. In the telecast, as it had publicly and editorially most other places, the company won empathy from its plight.

It was a plight that would have sunk a smaller and less diverse company than Johnson & Johnson. If Tylenol had been its lone product, the story probably would have been different. As it was, Johnson & Johnson took a $100-million pretax write-off on the Tylenol losses for 1982. Tylenol contributed an estimated 7% of Johnson & Johnson's worldwide sales of $5.4 billion and between 15% and 20% of its profits of $467.6 million in 1981.

Still, despite Tylenol's vulnerability, competitors made surprisingly small headway in grabbing off chunks of its market share. For one thing, some of their products, too, were adulterated in a wave of copycat incidents at the height of the scare. Consumers were frightened by then of most analgesic capsules.

There was apparently an amazing level of brand loyalty. Anacin, the next-biggest seller, picked up only an estimated 1% to give it a 13.5% market share, and Datril's share remained at less than 1%.

A Johnson & Johnson official said the company is currently in litigation with some of its insurance firms over whether or not the company was covered for such product-tampering resulting in deaths.

Finally, the company was confident enough to return to pretty much the same type of advertising it had done before the crisis—non-actors with headaches. On Jan. 3, a San Diego woman appeared in an ad, expressing her trust in the brand. An announcer pointed out the new tamper-resistant packaging, but the crisis was never mentioned.

"We reviewed our advertising campaign just the other day," a company spokeswoman said last week. "We decided to go with the same thing with about the same level of spending."

TWO

Communication in Business
Truth-Telling, Misinformation, and Lying

Unlike the ancient cynic Diogenes, who is said to have searched the streets of Athens for an honest man, modern cynics have special fears about the world of business. Business, they say, is a medium in which honesty cannot flourish; the two repel each other like oil and water. The cases in this section deal with hard choices in business that are made more complicated by the fact that they revolve around questions of communication and honesty. Does business have a special set of rules covering the issue of truth-telling? Are these rules more lenient than those that exist in the non-business world?

The issue of truth-telling in business is far broader than that of whether to lie to the boss about one's expense account. It reaches into questions of misleading advertising, reporting procedures for complex government regulations, issues of public health and product safety, and bargaining styles during negotiation sessions. It is probably fair to say that no aspect of business life is completely free of the issue of truth-telling. In turn, every business manager should strive to develop and correct his or her own view of acceptable business communication.

Although even the most callous tend to grant that business requires a minimal level of honesty, disputes arise about the extent to which business requires adherence to strict principles of truth-telling. At one end of the spectrum of views, we find the claim that business is analogous to the game of poker and that, just as bluffing is acceptable in poker, so a certain amount of deception is acceptable in business.[1] When the automobile company Avis claimed, "You have a friend at Avis," no one seriously believed it; rather, it is acceptable puffery. Similarly, when a man in his fifties suspects that he may be discriminated against because of his age when applying for a job, then his lying about how old he is, is acceptable bluffing.

At the opposite end of the spectrum are views like that of the philosopher Immanuel Kant which condemn any lie, however small. Kant is quick to distinguish a lie from what he calls a false statement, thus distinguishing between a genuine lie and merely a false statement in a game (where doing so is part of the game), or a false statement when being tortured by a malicious enemy. Thus a few false statements are not lies. But with these exceptions, Kant insists that falsehoods are never justified.[2] Even when someone is planning to make bad use of requested information, and even when the consequences seem to justify it, Kant argues that one must refrain from lying. One *can* remain silent, of course, but one must never lie. Kant views his analysis as extending throughout the entire range of human activities, including both the world of personal affairs and business.

The cases in this section deal with honesty and truth-telling in a variety of contexts. "Toy Wars" shows a manager's personal struggle to act morally when choosing to advertize children's toys by glamorizing violence. The cases "Dow-Corning Corporation: Marketing Breast Implant Devices" and "Uptown, Dakota, and PowerMaster" raise two larger questions regarding the relationship between ethics and marketing: (1) What are or what should be the rules in any advertizing or marketing campaign for any product? (2) Does the notion of *caveat emptor* (let the buyer beware) sum up the sole moral constraint in any marketing activity? Both cases also question whether corporations should market a desire for dubious goods to traditionally disadvantaged/vulnerable groups. By extension this case also asks if there should be limits placed on the promotional activity involved in the marketing of certain kinds of products and services, e.g., alcoholic beverages, cigarettes, medical services, legal services. The two cases on Manville's high product liability losses and subsequent bankruptcy proceedings examine the question: What did Manville really know, and when did they know it? "Italian Tax Mores" considers the issue of truth-telling in the context of Italian culture, a culture that at least appears to condone financial dishonesty.

Notes

1. See Albert Carr, "Is Business Bluffing Ethical?", *Harvard Business Review* (January–February, 1968).

2. Immanuel Kant, "Ethical Duties Towards Others: Truthfulness," rpt. *Ethical Issues in Business,* ed. Thomas Donaldson and Patricia Werhane (Englewood Cliffs, N.J.: Prentice Hall, Inc., 1983).

• *Case Study* •

Toy Wars*

Manuel G. Velasquez

Early in 1986, Tom Daner, president of the advertising company of Daner Associates, was contacted by the sales manager of Crako Industries, Mike Teal.[1] Crako Industries is a family-owned company that manufactures children's toys and had long been a favorite and important client of Daner Associates. The sales manager of Crako Industries explained that the company had just developed a new toy helicopter. The toy was modeled on the military helicopters that had been used in Vietnam and that had appeared in the "Rambo" movies. Mike Teal explained that the toy was developed in response to the craze for military toys that had been sweeping the nation in the wake of the Rambo movies. The family-owned toy company had initially resisted moving into military toys, since members of the family objected to the violence associated with such toys. But as segments of the toy market were increasingly taken over by military toys, the family came to feel that entry into the military toy market was crucial for their business. Consequently, they approved development of a line of military toys, hoping that they were not entering the market too late. Mike Teal now wanted Daner Associates to develop a television advertising campaign for the toy.

The toy helicopter Crako designers had developed was about one and one-half feet long, battery-operated, and made of plastic and steel. Mounted to the sides were detachable replicas of machine guns and a detachable stretcher modeled on the stretchers used to lift wounded soldiers from a battlefield. Mike Teal of Crako explained that they were trying to develop a toy that had to be perceived as "more macho" than the top-selling "G. I. Joe" line of toys. If the company was to compete successfully in today's toy market, according to the sales manager, it would have to adopt an advertising approach that was even "meaner and tougher" than what other companies were doing. Consequently, he continued, the advertising clips developed by Daner Associates would have to be "mean and macho." Television advertisements for the toy, he suggested, might show the helicopter swooping over buildings and blowing them up. The more violence and mayhem the ads suggested, the better. Crako Industries was relying heavily on sales from the new toy, and some Crako managers felt that the company's future might depend on the success of this toy.

Tom Daner was unwilling to have his company develop television advertisements that would increase what he already felt was too much violence in television aimed at children. In particular, he recalled a television ad for a tricycle with a replica machine gun mounted on the handlebars. The commercial showed the tricycle being pedaled through the woods by a small boy as he chased several other boys fleeing before him over a dirt path. At one point the camera closed in over the shoulder of the boy, focused through the gun sight, and showed the gun sight apparently trying to aim at the backs of the boys as they fled before the tricycle's machine gun. Ads of that sort had disturbed Tom Daner and had led him to think that advertisers should find other ways of promoting these toys. He suggested, therefore, that instead of promoting the Crako helicopter through violence, it should be presented in some other manner. When Teal asked what he had in mind, Tom was forced to reply that he didn't know. But at any rate, Tom pointed out, the three television networks would not accept a violent commercial aimed at children. All three networks adhered to an advertising code that prohibited violent, intense, or unrealistic advertisements aimed at children.

This seemed no real obstacle to Teal, however. Although the networks might turn down children's ads when they were too violent, local television stations were not as squeamish. Local television stations around the country regularly accepted ads aimed at children that the networks had rejected as too violent. The local stations inserted the ads as spots on their non-network programming, thereby circumventing the Advertising Codes of the three national networks. Daner Associates would simply have to place the ads they developed for the Crako helicopter through local television stations around the country. Mike Teal was firm: if Daner Associates would not or could not develop a "mean and tough" ad campaign, the toy company would move their account to an advertiser who would. Reluctantly, Tom Daner agreed to develop the advertising campaign. Crako Industries accounted for $1 million of Daner's total revenues.

Like Crako Industries, Daner Associates is also a family-owned business. Started by his father almost fifty years ago, the advertising firm that Tom Daner now ran had grown dramatically under his leadership. In 1975 the business had grossed $3 million; ten years later it had revenues of $25 million and provided a full line of advertising services. The company was divided into three departments (Creative, Media, and Account Executive), each of which had about 12 employees. Tom Daner credited much of the company's success to the many new people he had hired, especially a group with M.B.A.s who had developed new marketing strategies based on more thorough market and consumer analyses. Most decisions, however, were made by a five-person executive committee consisting of Tom Daner, the Senior Account Manager, and the three-department heads. As owner-president, Tom's views tended to color most decisions, producing what one of the members called a "benevolent dictatorship." Tom himself was an enthusiastic, congenial, intelligent, and widely read person. During college he had considered becoming a missionary priest but had changed his mind and was now married and the father of three daughters. His personal heros included Thomas Merton, Albert Schweitzer, and Tom Dooley.

When Tom Daner presented the Crako deal to his Executive Committee, he found they did not share his misgivings. The other Committee members felt that Daner Associates should give Crako exactly the kind of ad Crako wanted: one with a heavy content of violence. Moreover, the writers and artists in the Creative Department were enthused with the prospect of letting their imaginations loose on the project, several feeling that they could easily produce an attention-grabbing ad by "out-violencing" current television programming. The Creative Department, in fact, quickly produced a copy-script that called for videos showing the helicopter "flying out of the sky with machine guns blazing" at a jungle village below. This kind of ad, they felt, was exactly what they were being asked to produce by their client, Crako Industries.

But after viewing the copy, Tom Daner refused to use it. They should produce an ad, he insisted, that would meet their client's needs but that would also meet the guidelines of the national networks. The ad should not glorify violence and war but should somehow support cooperation and family values. Disappointed and somewhat frustrated, the Creative Department went back to work. A few days later they presented a second proposal: an ad that would show the toy helicopter flying through the family room of a home as a little boy plays with it; then the scene shifts to show the boy on a rock rising from the floor of the family room; the helicopter swoops down and picks up the boy as though rescuing him from the rock where he had been stranded. Although the Creative Department was mildly pleased with their attempt, they felt it was too "tame." Tom liked it, however, and a version of the ad was filmed.

A few weeks later Tom Daner met with Mike Teal and his team and showed them the film. The viewing was not a success. Teal turned down the ad. Referring to the network regulations, which other toy advertisements were breaking as frequently as motorists broke the 55 mile per hour speed law, he said, "That commercial is going only 55 miles an hour when I want one that goes 75." If the next version was not "tougher and meaner," Crako Industries would be forced to look elsewhere.

Disappointed, Tom Daner returned to the people in his Creative Department and told them to go ahead with designing the kind of ad they had originally wanted: "I don't have any idea what else to do." In a short time the Creative Department had an ad proposal on his desk that called for scenes showing the helicopter blowing up villages. Shortly afterwards a small set was constructed depicting a jungle village sitting next to a bridge stretching over a river. The ad was filmed using the jungle set as a background.

When Tom saw the result he was not happy. He decided to meet with his Creative Department and air his feelings. "The issue here," he said, "is basically the issue of violence. Do we really want to present toys as instruments for beating up people? This ad is going to promote aggression and violence. It will glorify dominance and do it with kids who are terrifically impressionable. Do we really want to do this?" The members of the Creative Department, however, responded that they were merely giving their client what the client wanted. That client, moreover, was an important account. The client wanted an aggressive "macho" ad, and that was what they were providing. The ad might violate the regulations of the television networks, but there were ways to get around the networks. Moreover, they said, every other advertising firm in the business was breaking the limits against violence set by the networks. Tom made one last try: why not market the toy as an adventure and fantasy toy? Film the ad again, he suggested, using the same jungle backdrop. But instead of showing the helicopter shooting at a burning village, show it flying in to rescue people from the burning village. Create an ad that shows excitement, adventure, and fantasy, but no aggression. "I was trying," he said later, "to figure out a new way of approaching this kind of advertising. We have to follow the market or we can go out of business trying to moralize to the market. But why not try a new approach? Why not promote toys as instruments that expand the child's imagination in a way that is positive and that promotes cooperative values instead of violence and aggression?"

A new film version of the ad was made, now showing the helicopter flying over the jungle set. Quick shots and heightened background music give the impression of excitement and danger. The helicopter flies dramatically through the jungle and over a river and bridge to rescue a boy from a flaming village. As lights flash and shoot haphazardly through the scene the helicopter rises and escapes into the sky. The final ad was clearly exciting and intense. And it promoted saving of life instead of violence against life.

It was clear when the final version was shot, however, that it would not clear the network censors. Network guidelines require that sets in children's ads must depict things that are within the reach of most children so that they do not create unrealistic expectations. Clearly the elaborate jungle set (which cost $25,000 to construct) was not within the reach of most children, and consequently most children would not be able to recreate the scene of the ad by buying the toy. Moreover, network regulations stipulate that in children's ads scenes must be filmed with normal lighting that does not create undue intensity. Again clearly the helicopter ad, which created excitement by using quick changes of light and fast cuts, did not fall within these guidelines.

After reviewing the film Tom Daner reflected on some last-minute instructions Crako's sales manager had given him when he had been shown the first version of the ad: The television ad should show things being blown up by the guns of the little helicopter and perhaps even some blood on the fuselage of the toy; the ad had to be violent. Now Tom had to make a decision. Should he risk the account by submitting only the rescue mission ad? Or should he let Teal also see the ad that showed the helicopter shooting up the village, knowing that he would probably prefer that version if he saw it? And was the rescue mission ad really that much different from the ad that showed the shooting of the village? Did it matter that the rescue mission ad still violated some of the network regulations? What if he offered Teal only the rescue mission ad and Teal accepted the "rescue approach" but demanded he make it more violent; should he give in? And should Tom risk launching an ad campaign that was based on this new untested approach? What if the ad failed to sell the Crako toy? Was it right to experiment with a client's product, especially a product that was so important to the future of the client's business? Tom was unsure what he should do. He wanted to show Teal only the rescue mission commercial, but he felt he first had to resolve these questions in his own mind.

Note

1. Although the events described in this case are real, all names of the individuals and the companies involved are fictitious; in addition, several details have been altered to disguise the identity of participants.

Questions for discussion

1. Should Tom Daner simply have refused to take the job?
2. Did he have other options?
3. What would you have done?

• *Case Study* •

Dow Corning Corporation: Marketing Breast Implant Devices*

N. Craig Smith • Andrew D. Dyer • Todd E. Himstead

In December, 1991, a federal court jury in California awarded a $7.3 million payment against Dow Corning to Mariann Hopkins, a silicone gel breast implant wearer who claimed injury to her autoimmune system.[1] The recipient was just one of thousands of women who had undergone breast implant surgery over the past twenty-five years. Throughout the 1980's there had been considerable questioning of the safety of these implants. The federal court judgment was seen as a landmark victory by the plaintiff's lawyers. Dow Corning and other breast implant manufacturers now were facing the possibility of substantial litigation from women claiming to be harmed by silicone gel implants. With perhaps as many as two million breast implant operations completed, the potential existed for thousands of lawsuits to be filed against the manufacturers.[2]

As it entered 1992, Dow Corning's exposure to product safety issues with silicone gel implants became more apparent. On January 6, 1992, the Food and Drug Administration (FDA) requested that breast implant producers and medical practitioners halt the sale and use of silicone gel breast implants, pending further review of the safety and effectiveness of the devices.[3] As a precautionary measure, Dow Corning retained former attorney general Griffin Bell on January 19, 1992, to conduct a complete investigation of the company's development, production and marketing of silicone gel breast implants. On February 3, 1992, Dow Corning took a pretax charge of $25 million to earnings in 1991 to cover costs associated with frozen inventories, dedicated equipment and other related costs.[4]

On February 10, 1992, Dow Corning's board elected Keith R. McKennon chairman and CEO. McKennon was a career Dow Chemical employee. His previous role was president of Dow Chemical USA. Having managed two previous product crises for Dow Chemical (including Dow's Agent Orange pesticide crisis) now he was charged with the decisions of what to do with the silicone gel implant product line and how to manage the legal, regulatory and public relations challenges facing Dow Corning. Since breast implants represented less than 1% of total 1991 revenues,[5] McKennon might have been tempted to question whether Dow Corning even should continue with the implant products, despite the benefits to women resulting from their use in reconstructive and cosmetic surgery.

*Andrew D. Dyer and Todd E. Himstead of Georgetown University School of Business prepared this case from public sources under the direction of Professor N. Craig Smith as the basis for class discussion rather than to illustrate either effective or ineffective handling of an administrative situation. Some material also was drawn from a report compiled by Georgetown MBA students Kirsten D. Marlatt, Daniel Rabbit and Michael Vechery. Copyright Andrew D. Dyer, Todd E. Himstead and N. Craig Smith, 1995 (forthcoming in *Business Case Journal*, the journal of the Society for Case Research).

DOW CORNING

Dow Corning Corporation was founded in 1943 with a mission to develop the potential of silicones. Silicones were new materials, unlike anything found in nature or previously manufactured. They were based on silicon, which was an element refined from quartz rock, a form of silica. The resulting chemical compounds were the basis for an infinite range of versatile, flexible materials that ranged from fluids thinner than water to rigid plastics, each with unique properties.

Dow Corning was established as a 50/50 joint venture by The Dow Chemical Company of Midland, Michigan and Corning Glass Works (now Corning Inc.) of Corning, New York. Corning provided the basic silicone technology while Dow Chemical supplied the chemical processing and manufacturing know-how. Both companies provided initial key employees and maintained their ownership of Dow Corning from the outset.

The Dow Corning venture became successful in developing, manufacturing and marketing silicone based products. It grew steadily from 1943 in revenues, profits and employees and by 1991 generated revenues of $1.85 billion and income of $152.9 million, with some 8,300 employees.[6] In 1991, it was ranked 241 in the Fortune 500.[7] In addition to developing silicone products, it had expanded development to related specialty chemical materials, polycrystalline silicon and specialty health care products. With some 5,000 products, Dow Corning served a wide range of industries including aerospace, automotive, petrochemicals, construction, electronics, medical products, pharmaceuticals, plastics and textiles. It had become a global enterprise with 33 major manufacturing locations worldwide, R&D facilities in the US, Japan, France, Germany, Belgium and the UK, and over 45,000 customers from countries including the US, Europe, Canada, Latin America, Japan, Australia, Taiwan, and Korea.

In the early 1990s, Dow Corning was seen as a model corporate citizen. It was a pioneer in corporate ethics, renowned for its Business Conduct Committee. The committee comprised six managers, who performed an ethics audit of every business every third year and reported results to the Audit & Social Responsibility Committee of the Dow Corning board. In October 1990, the committee audited Dow Corning's implant operation. It found no substantial ethical problems related to implants.

In 1991, Dow Corning was headed by John Ludington as chairman and Larry Reed as president and CEO. The organization was divided into two primary line organizations, Area Operations and Business Organization. Area Operations was responsible for sales and service of Dow Corning products around the world and were grouped into the US, Inter-America (Canada and Latin America), Europe and Asia. The Business Organization was responsible for the development and manufacturing of Dow Corning's products and was organized on a product line-of-business approach.

Dow Corning's product line in 1991 included gasket sealants and windshields for the aerospace industry; silicone rubbers for the automotive industry; adhesives and sealants for the building trade and for consumer home improvement; and fluids, emulsions and transdermal patches for the pharmaceutical industry; as well as a variety of medical products, such as tubing, adhesives and surgical implants.

Dow Corning Wright

In 1991, Dow Corning Wright Corporation, a wholly owned subsidiary, manufactured and sold silicone gel breast implants for Dow Corning. It also manufactured and marketed metal orthopedic implants for Dow Corning. Dow Corning Wright was headquartered in Arlington, Tennessee and was headed up by chairman Bob Rylee and president and CEO Dan M. Hayes, Jr. It reported to Dow Corning's Business Organization and was considered a stand-alone line of business. Dow Corning Wright was established in 1978 when Dow Corning acquired Wright Medical, a small manufacturer of orthopedic hips and knees. Dow Corning then transferred all of its medical devices manufacturing and sales to this new subsidiary, including the breast implants.[a] Dow Corning Wright 1991 revenues were approximately $80 million.[8]

Breast Implant Devices

Various options had been tried to achieve breast augmentation since the sixteenth century. Materials such as ivory, glass and paraffin had been used for contour enhancement (by applying these materials to the breast externally). The first augmentation mammaplasty was accomplished in the late nineteenth century. Following this operation, a variety of non-silicone materials were injected or implanted to cosmetically alter or reconstruct breasts. The most successful implant device, developed during the 1950s, was a product with an outer sack made of polyurethane foam or silicone, and filled with saline.

The next breakthrough came in 1962, when Dow Corning was approached by two plastic surgeons who wanted help in further developing breast implants for mastectomy and congenital deformity victims. The surgeons had designed an implant and had begun limited production, but looked to Dow Corning to apply its silicone gel and manufacturing expertise. In 1964, as a result of this request, Dow Corning developed a product based on an envelope of silicone elastomer (a rubber-like elastic substance) filled with silicone gel. The product was touted to be superior in terms of its look and feel for the recipients and was less likely to migrate over time through body and muscle tissue that surrounded the breast, compared with saline fluid-filled implants. Silicone gel breast implants became the market leader from that time on.

The advantage of silicone gel implants was that the silicone could hold its shape. This was particularly important for reconstructive patients, where there was little or no foundation to build on. Saline implants (made with salt water contained in a silicone envelope) were "waterlike" and were unable to hold any shape by themselves. As a result, they were much less effective in providing either an enhanced figure or a complete reconstruction.

From 1965, when Dow Corning launched the first silicone gel breast implants, demand for the product was consistently high. Other manufacturers entered the market and the company became one of seven manufacturers in the US producing the silicone gel product. Dow Corning introduced new models over time, with improvements in gel texture and envelope characteristics. The implants were available in a variety of sizes and contours. During the period

---

[a]As Dow Corning Wright is 100% owned by Dow Corning Inc., it is referred to as "Dow Corning" from here on, unless specific reference to Dow Corning Wright is required.

1965 to 1992, Dow Corning sold approximately 600,000 implants, 45% of them outside the US.[9] Dow Corning's market share of breast implants never exceeded 25% (once the industry had become established). In 1991, chairman Bob Rylee admitted that the breast implant line had sustained five consecutive years of financial losses, but the company continued selling them because millions of women were "counting on them."[10] Dow Corning also supplied silicone to the other implant manufacturers. During the 1980s, Dow Corning's focus on medical devices moved to knee implants and breast implants were not viewed as a strategic product. In 1991, Dow Corning's market share of breast implant sales was approximately 18%. It was the third largest supplier behind McGhan and Mentor.

Sales Agents

Dow Corning Wright's medical devices were sold by independent agents who had contracts to sell the products in specified geographic areas. They were paid a commission on sales and were reimbursed for expenses. In 1991, Dow Corning had some 70 medical device agents across the United States that were managed by a Dow Corning national sales manager, supported by two marketing staff. Some of the more senior agents also coordinated or supervised other agents regionally.

Some independent agents also sold non-Dow Corning products, though typically these products did not compete with Dow Corning's line. The agents relied on their strong relationship with the surgeons to make sales and maintained that relationship by providing quality products and good service. Of the 70 independent agents operating in 1991, two relied heavily on Dow Corning's breast implants, with some 50% of their sales derived from Dow Corning implants. For the remaining agents, their primary focus was hip and knee implants, with between 5% to 25% (an average of 10%) of their sales coming from breast implants.[11]

Geography was the major contributor to variations in volume, with certain regions having a higher demand for implants than others. The Pacific region was the site of the most (approximately 25%) breast augmentation procedures in the early 1990s, followed by the South Atlantic region with 21%, according to the American Society of Plastic and Reconstructive Surgeons (ASPRS). New England had the fewest procedures, with only 1.5%. California represented 19% of the total, Florida 12%, Texas 10% and New York 4%.[12]

MEDICAL DEVICES INDUSTRY

Breast implant products were considered part of the medical devices industry, an industry that was generally fragmented, with 97% of manufacturers employing 500 employees or less and 70% of manufacturers employing 50 employees or less.[13] Medical devices (also known as surgical appliances and supplies) included crutches, wheelchairs, orthopedic devices and materials, surgical implants, bandages, hearing aids and protective clothing. In 1991, the US manufactured and shipped some $10.7 billion worth of medical devices, growing 6.4% from 1990. The industry employed an estimated 89,500 people in 1991, up 3% from 1990, 58,300 of these employees were engaged as production workers. US exports of medical devices also grew in 1991 by 18% to $1.4

billion, the fourth consecutive year of double digit growth.[14] The principal export items included respiratory products, orthopedic equipment and supplies, as well as artificial joints and internal fixation devices. The principal manufacturers of breast implants in 1991 were: Baxter Healthcare Corporation (Deerfield, IL), Bioplasty Inc. (St. Paul, MN), Cox-Uphoff (Carpinteria, CA), Dow Corning Corporation (Midland, MI), McGhan Medical Inc. (Santa Barbara, CA), Mentor (Santa Barbara, CA), Porex Technologies (Fairburn, GA), Surgitek (Racine, WI).

Regulation

When Dow Corning first sold implants in 1965, the medical devices industry was not subject to specific government regulation. The Food and Drug Administration unit of the US Department of Health and Human Services was given the responsibility to regulate all medical devices and device establishments on May 28, 1976, following the Medical Device Amendments to the Federal Food, Drug and Cosmetic Act of 1938. Its goal was to ensure that the medical devices consumed by the public were safe and effective by regulating the industry, by analyzing product samples and by researching the risks and benefits of those products. The 1976 amendments directed the FDA to issue regulations to set up an approval process for new devices and classify existing ones into Class I, II or III, depending on the degree of testing necessary to provide reasonable assurance of the safety of the device.

At that time, the FDA classified breast implants as "Class II" devices, a rating that did not demand testing as a condition for remaining on the market. While an advisory panel was formed in 1977 to look at cosmetic implants, the lack of conclusive studies and the panel members' own positive experience with breast implants allowed the implants to be classified as 'safe' with no more research necessary. Some FDA scientists disputed this finding, based on feedback from doctors who claimed that the implants could break or leak. A new panel in 1982 voted that there was insufficient evidence to establish the product's safety and efficacy. It went on to recommend that silicone gel filled breast implants be placed at the top of the FDA's list for review. But the lack of consumer complaints lowered the priority on implants, as the FDA screened its huge backlog of other devices. John Vilforth, the FDA's medical devices division manager during the 1980's, commented during a later interview that few of the million or more women with implants had complained to the FDA and that the longer term effects allegedly occurring in 1991 had not been observed in the previous decade. The FDA took no action on implants between 1982 and 1988.

In January, 1989, the FDA reclassified breast implants as "Class III," and on April 10, 1991, required all manufacturers (including Dow Corning) to submit, within 90 days, implant safety and effectiveness data in pre-market approval applications (PMAAs) for the FDA's evaluation. According to its 10-K filing, on July 8, 1991, Dow Corning submitted 30,000 pages of documentation along with its PMAA, detailing silicone gel breast implant manufacturing processes, product design and labeling, and 30 years of safety studies. After previewing the PMAAs, on September 25, the FDA ordered manufacturers to provide more implant risk data to the physicians that inserted them, while the FDA continued its review. In November, 1991, the FDA's Advisory Panel, after hearing testimony, recommended keeping implants on the market, noting that the psychological benefits outweighed the health risks. It was up to FDA Commissioner David Kessler to make the final decision, however, and on January 6, 1992, Kessler requested that producers and physicians halt the sale and use of breast implants for 45 days. Dow Corning voluntarily suspended shipments on that day.

PLASTIC SURGERY

Background

The plastic surgery profession began to formalize in the 1930's, although it had been practiced for centuries. Plastic surgeons were qualified surgeons that specialized in surgery to either reconstruct a human deformity or to enhance or modify a human feature. In 1992, there were over 5,000 certified plastic surgeons in the US. In the early 1990's, these plastic surgeons performed over 1.5 million procedures a year, with average fees ranging from $100 to over $6,000 per procedure.[15]

Plastic surgeons typically specialized in certain procedures and/or parts of the anatomy. For example, they would specialize in procedures such as skin grafts or nose surgery (rhinoplasty) or could specialize in a certain body part such as the hands or face. Plastic surgeons performing breast implant surgery typically became specialized in that procedure, and would average one implant operation per week. For these plastic surgeons, breast implant procedures represented between 20–40% of their income.[16]

Types of Plastic Surgery

The two main categories of plastic surgery were general reconstructive and cosmetic:

General Reconstructive Plastic Surgery. Over one million reconstructive procedures were performed yearly by plastic surgeons in the early 1990's in the US. Reconstructive surgery was performed on abnormal structures of the body, caused by birth defects, developmental abnormalities, trauma or injury, infection, tumors or disease. It was generally performed to improve the patient's function, but may also have been done to approximate a normal appearance. Reconstructive surgery met the needs of two different categories of patients: those who had congenital deformities (known as birth defects) and those with developmental deformities (resulting from an accident, infection, disease or aging). In the early 1990's, tumor removal was the leading procedure, constituting almost half of all reconstructive plastic surgery. Breast reconstruction was one of the top ten procedures. In 1990, 30,000 women received breast implants for reconstruction. Approximately 20% of all implant operations between 1965 and 1991 were for reconstructive surgery after undergoing a mastectomy operation.[17] In 1992, according to ASPRS statistics, 1% of reconstructive patients were under 19, 11% were between 19 and 34, 54% were between 35 and 50, 29% were between 51 and 64, and 5% were over 64. The average surgeon's fees for a breast reconstruction procedure using implants was $2,340 in 1992.[18]

Cosmetic Plastic Surgery. Cosmetic surgery was performed to reshape normal structures of the body to improve the patient's appearance and self esteem. In 1990, 120,000 women received breast implants for cosmetic reasons. It was the leading cosmetic plastic surgery procedure. Other popular procedures included eyelid surgery, nose reshaping, liposuction, collagen injections, and facelifts. Approximately 80% of all breast implant operations between 1965 and 1991 were cosmetic augmentations.[19] In 1992, according to the ASPRS, 3% of the breast augmentation (cosmetic) patients were under the age of 19, 60% were between 19 and 34, 34% were between 35 and 50, 3% were between 51 and 64, while none were over 64.[20] ASPRS estimated that its members billed $330 million a year for breast implant procedures in the early 1990s.[21] In 1992, the average surgeon's fees for a breast augmentation procedure using implants was $2,754.[22]

Surgeon Selection of Medical Devices

In buying medical devices such as breast implants, plastic surgeons looked primarily at four criteria in making their selection:

- **Quality.** The quality of the products had to be uniform and consistent. The surgeon could only inspect the product at the time of the operation, when the product was removed from its packaging. A faulty product would cause the operation to be delayed or postponed while backup supplies were sought.
- **Service.** Product availability was mandatory at the time of surgery, and had to meet the schedule of the surgeon. Successful suppliers therefore had to ensure very high service levels and were subject to high inventory carrying costs as a result.
- **Price.** Price, while not the dominant factor in the purchase decision, needed to be consistent with alternatives and enable the procedure to be affordable for the patient.
- **Relationship.** The relationship between the sales agent and the surgeon was critical. The surgeon relied on and trusted the agent to provide the best and latest products together with quality service. Without such a relationship, it was unlikely that a medical device manufacturer could sell its products to a surgeon regardless of how well it scored in the other three criteria above.

Dow Corning felt that its strongest attributes were quality and relationships. Dow Corning generally had very strong credibility with the plastic surgeons, based on its leadership and innovation of new products. Dow Corning's scientists and physicians were highly regarded by the plastic surgeons and were constantly researching and publishing on key areas of interest. The independent agents were well connected to the plastic surgeons and provided an effective channel for Dow Corning's products.

Patient Selection of a Plastic Surgeon

Patients requiring or requesting plastic surgery were either referred by their physician to a plastic surgeon or selected their plastic surgeon directly. The latter was especially the case for cosmetic surgery, where the costs were not covered by health insurance. In selecting a plastic surgeon, patients used a number of steps to decide which surgeon would be best:

- Gathering names of plastic surgeons from friends, family doctor, nurses, hospitals, advertisements and directories (e.g., the Plastic Surgery Information Service, state and city directories of certified plastic surgeons).

- Checking the credentials of the surgeons such as their training, board certification (i.e., certified by the American Board of Plastic Surgery), hospital privileges (i.e., approved to perform the specific procedure at an accredited hospital), experience and membership of professional societies (e.g., ASPRS, which required certification by the American Board of Plastic Surgery together with a peer review, adherence to a strict code of ethics and continuing education to maintain membership).
- Consulting and interviewing the surgeon to compare personalities and obtaining opinions on the type of surgery and approach. Typically, the interview also included discussion of the surgeon's fees and an assessment of the way the surgeon answered questions and described the risks involved. Generally, patients would pay a fee for this consultation and thus would have narrowed down the list of potential surgeons to two or three by this stage.

According to a pamphlet prepared by the ASPRS and distributed in plastic surgeons' offices, a good plastic surgeon should exhibit some or all of the following qualities:[23]

- Has been recommended by a friend who has had a similar procedure
- Has been recommended by a family doctor or operating room nurse
- Is listed by the American Society of Plastic and Reconstructive Surgeons
- Is board-certified by the American Board of Plastic Surgery
- Has completed a residency in a specialty related to (your) procedure
- Has answered all (your) questions thoroughly
- Has asked about the patient's motivations and expectations of the surgery
- Has offered alternatives, where appropriate
- Has welcomed questions about professional qualifications, experience, cost and payment policies
- Has clarified the risks of surgery and the variations in outcome
- Has made sure that the final decision to undergo surgery is the patient's decision.

CONSUMER NEED FOR IMPLANTS

Reconstructive breast surgery patients had usually contracted a form of breast cancer, but also could be accident victims, or women with a congenital deformity. The most common reconstructive surgery took place after a patient had undergone a mastectomy (surgical removal of one or both breasts). Augmentation surgery patients desired an increase in breast size to enhance their appearance (known as augmentation mammaplasty).

Reconstructive Surgery

Without plastic surgery, reconstructive surgery consumers faced spending the rest of their lives with one or both breasts removed. The silicone gel breast implant operation provided them with a solution to regain their original physical appearance. Hence, the availability of breast implants was a major breakthrough for women suffering from breast cancer. In the early 1990's, about one woman in nine developed breast cancer in the US. It was the most commonly occurring cancer in women, accounting for more deaths than cancer of any other part of the body except the lungs. It was the leading cause of death among US women aged 40–55.[24]

Before implants were available, some women refused to undergo a mastectomy, opting for lumpectomy (surgical removal of the breast tumor) or radiation or no action at all. While a lumpectomy or radiation abated the cancer's growth, neither treatment necessarily eliminated the breast cancer and, if unsuccessful, the patient could face a painful and premature death. Women refusing mastectomies were either afraid of the operation or were concerned with the permanent disfiguration and their perceived inability to be accepted back into society.

But with breast implants available, women were more accepting of the mastectomy operation. During the February 1992 FDA Advisory Panel hearing into breast implant safety, breast implant recipient Elaine Sansom testified:

> My mother's fear of losing her breast kept her from an early diagnosis, which allowed her cancer to spread before her mastectomy. She lived horribly from that point on, going through the rounds of chemo [therapy] and radiation; having a tumor eat through her first vertebra, ending up in a halo vest with bolts in her head.
>
> Being diagnosed with breast cancer [myself] was devastating . . . The choice to have implants was life-saving for me. Because I'm a diabetic, I wasn't a candidate for other types of reconstruction.[b] If silicone gel breast implants had not been available at that time, my decision would have been a different one.[25]

In a letter to the *Washington Times* on January 31, 1992, another silicone breast implant recipient wrote:

> Since the FDA's moratorium on silicone breast implants has occurred, I would like you to hear the other side (the majority)—from satisfied recipients. I am one of nearly 2 million.
>
> These lifelike implants have helped the majority of women to recover faster physically and psychologically by restoring their femininity. I would rather die than be denied the option of having to go through life horribly disfigured. The alternative saline implants are a poor substitute, and they, too, are surrounded by silicone.
>
> Just give us the facts—we will decide, along with our doctors. Don't legislate my life anymore.[26]

Breast Augmentation Surgery

Breast augmentation surgery consumers were women who wished to enlarge their breasts for appearance reasons. The images portrayed by fashion models and 'sex symbols' had created certain perceptions regarding the size of women's breasts. As a result, clothing sizes and designs, as well as male expectations, centered around the 'appropriate' size for a woman's breasts. However, normal variations in humans resulted in a wide variation in breast sizes and some women developed smaller breasts than others. Breast augmentation surgery offered an approach for these women to artificially enlarge their breasts permanently to a size that they felt was perceived as being more suitable for their figure and lifestyle.

---

[b]A diabetic is an individual suffering from diabetes, a disease that causes an insulin deficiency and is characterized by an excess of sugar in the blood and urine, and by hunger, thirst and gradual loss of weight. Other types of breast reconstruction, such as saline implants, can impact the sugar level further, increasing the severeness of diabetes.

Given the breast implant controversy, many examples were reported of women who had undergone augmentation surgery and their reasons why. Carol Lachnit, journalist with the *Los Angeles Times,* wrote:

> Back in 1991, Patricia Fodor was a newlywed with 'a cute little figure' and the belief that silicone gel breast implants would enhance it. It was "a self esteem issue," she said. Because she worked in a doctor's office, Fodor even got a discount on the procedure.
> . . . Catherine, a 64-year-old Orange County woman . . . [received] her implants in 1987, when she was 58. "I was one of those women who didn't get everything some women have," she said. "I have poor hair, fine, thin hair. I can't do much about my hair, but for my bust, I thought this would be great. I was so thrilled." Catherine immersed herself in the world of ballroom dancing. She had gowns made to show off her new figure. She made friends and "everyone commented on how good I looked," she said.[27]

Other comments from breast augmentation surgery patients were included in an article in the *Washington Times,* January 29, 1992:

> "I just wanted to be average," sighs Janet, 34, of Alexandria, Virginia. Having her breasts enlarged from a "boyish" 32 A to a "beautiful" 36 C has improved Janet's self-image and outlook. She says she can shop in half the time, buy clingy clothing on sale and doesn't feel at all self-conscious. "You wouldn't look at me on the street and say, 'There goes a busty woman,'" says the 5-foot-4-inch, full-time mother. "I look just right."
> "Look, there's a pressure on women for physical beauty," says Janet, who does aerobics regularly. "Models can get three times their salary when they get implants, and if that doesn't tell you something about our society . . ." She calls it an "unfair, idealized image of beauty," but Janet subscribes to it.
> . . . And Jacki Buckler, 26, credits her new 36 C breasts—"very round, very full"— with giving her the confidence to go back to the University of Maryland to finish her degree in oceanography. "I'm pushing myself now," the part-time Giant cashier and waitress says . . . "I did this [the surgery] for myself, for no one else," Miss Buckler says. She paid for the $3,500 procedure in monthly $600 installments and says she hasn't regretted the expense or the pain of surgery for a minute.[28]

CONSUMER PROBLEMS WITH THE PRODUCT

By 1985, some 1.3 million implant operations had been completed.[29] Already, though, complaints were being received by the manufacturers and the FDA from customers citing painful hardening lumps and seepage of the silicone gel into the body after the implant bag had ruptured. Concerns began to arise about the potential of implants to rupture, the tightening of scar tissue that often formed around implants, causing the breast to harden, and the possible seepage of silicone, which was alleged to be responsible for generating a host of immune-system disorders that were painful, debilitating and untreatable. Over the next seven years, consumer activists in Washington, DC, began to challenge the product's safety, while plastic surgeons and some women's groups lobbied to defend implants.

A variety of documents began to be released by Dow Corning and other manufacturers revealing that medical studies performed as early as the 1970's had warned of possible problems with implants.[30] Consumer activists criticized the manufacturers for 'hiding' the information, the plastic surgeons for not questioning the safety of the implants, and the government for being negligent and not acting on the studies earlier. Leading the charge was Public Citizen's Health Research Group (Public Citizen), an organization founded by Ralph Nader and Dr. Sidney Wolfe to represent consumer interests in health related matters. Public Citizen became actively involved in the implant controversy in 1988 after it obtained internal Dow Corning and FDA documents that suggested silicone gel implants were not safe for human use. It continued to lobby Congress and the FDA and also provided information packets to consumers and acted as a clearinghouse for plaintiff attorneys.

With growing legal activity and media attention, implants eventually assumed a higher priority on the FDA's agenda. FDA action increased by the end of the 1980's, when the FDA forced several implant products off the market after it was discovered that the foam covering the silicone slowly disintegrated at body temperature. This disintegration allowed a chemical known as TDA to be released, which in very high doses developed cancer in rats. By 1991 and the FDA's request that manufacturers provide evidence of research on the safety of implants, Public Citizen had begun selling $750 kits of evidence to trial lawyers interested in filing suits on behalf of disgruntled customers. The Command Trust Network, a nationwide educational network of 8,000 "implant victims," raised $30,000 and gave interviews to hundreds of reporters.[31]

The ASPRS, meanwhile, dedicated $1.3 million to lobby for the continued use of implants. In October, 1991, it orchestrated a Washington "fly in," during which it paid for 400 women to travel to Capitol Hill and lobby congress to keep implants a viable choice for women. Simultaneously, it placed newspaper ads and organized a letter writing campaign of 20,000 letters to the FDA.[32] In November 1991, the FDA hearings were given the report by its Advisory Panel which concluded that the psychological importance of the implants outweighed the medical risks.

In December, 1991 the verdict in the case of *Mariann Hopkins vs. Dow Corning* was announced, awarding Ms. Hopkins $7.3 million in damages, based on claims of damage to her autoimmune system.[33] Following the court's decision, Mariann Hopkins' lawyer, Dan C. Bolton, wrote to FDA Commissioner Dr. David A. Kessler about concerns with silicone breast implants.

The verdict was followed by the FDA moratorium on the sale of all silicone gel breast implant devices until such time as the agency received evidence to allay fears of any links to disease. Canada followed the US by placing a similar ban, however the UK and France allowed implants to remain on the market. The moratorium, which prevented the sale of silicone gel implants unless their installation was clinically supervised (i.e., a study sponsored by the manufacturer and the FDA), sparked strong reaction from plastic surgeons and feminist groups. The plastic surgeons stood by the product and their surgical procedures while the feminist groups claimed that women were being deprived the right to make their own medical decisions.

A lawsuit filed after this moratorium by an augmentation surgery patient, was reported in the *San Diego Union-Tribune,* January 30, 1992:

> A woman who was given Dow Corning Corp.'s silicone gel breast implants to improve her figure has sued the company, claiming they made her ill and accusing the company of ignoring safety warnings about the devices, her attorney said.
>
> Stanley Rosenblatt said yesterday the Dade County woman, identified only as "Jane Doe," is in her 30's and received the breast implants in 1985 to enhance her figure.

She is seeking $100 million in damages. The lawsuit, filed in Dade County Circuit Court, claims the woman was in perfect health before the operation but has since suffered "recurrent flu, recurrent strep throat, infections, excessive hair loss, constant fatigue, excruciating joint pain, rashes across her face and a constant low-grade fever." The woman has been bedridden "for months at a time" because of systemic lupus erythematosus, a disorder of the immune system, the suit claims.

Dow Corning ignored warnings from its own employees about implant defects and concealed the information from doctors, patients and federal regulators, the lawsuit alleges. "Plaintiff is a victim of an incredible 'con' perpetrated upon the public at large and women in particular," the lawsuit said. It accused Dow Chemical of constructing a "vast experiment" on 2 million women that should have been performed on laboratory animals instead.

The surgeon is not being sued because Dow Corning convinced him the implants were safe, Rosenblatt said. The woman still has the implants but is deciding whether to have them removed, he said. The lawsuit alleges an internal company memo shows Dow Corning salespeople misled surgeons by washing "the often greasy gel implants before showing them to physicians, with full knowledge that the product was dangerous to women."[34]

Pamela Johnson filed a lawsuit against another implant manufacturer. The following extract from the *Houston Chronicle* explains her complaint:

Johnson's first set of breast implants, manufactured by MEC, [were] surgically implanted in 1976. O'Quinn [her attorney] said the company led Johnson's doctor to believe the implants had been tested and engineered so that the outer shell would contain the silicone gel, that the gel was cohesive and would not run if the shell ruptured, and that, if the gel did escape the shell, it would not harm human tissue. The doctor was told [that] the product would last a lifetime, O'Quinn said.

In 1989, Johnson's implants ruptured. Her doctor, believing the product's problems had been solved, then inserted a new set of silicone gel implants . . . The second set was removed that same year, and another implant done, with a product made by a different manufacturer. Those implants were removed [in early 1992].[35]

But despite these suits, Dow Corning defended its product. Bob Rylee, Dow Corning Wright's chairman, stated that implants represented less than 1% of Dow Corning's $1.8 billion in revenues and the true risk with implants was less than 1%.[36]

Ongoing Investigations

The FDA Advisory Panel was scheduled to reconvene on February 18, 1992 to reconsider implant PMAA's. In addition to the FDA studies, another probe into Dow Corning's breast implants was launched on January 30, 1992, by the Los Angeles County district attorney's office, under its Corporate Criminal Liability Act.[37] The investigation was to determine whether Dow Corning sold the breast implants without fully disclosing health risk information required by law. District attorney Ira Reiner had requested that Dow Corning provide substantial information about the product, including laboratory data, internal memoranda and copies of informational and promotional material about the implants. LA County's Corporate Criminal Liability Act makes it a felony for corporate managers to fail to provide regulatory agencies with written notification of a "serious concealed danger" associated with a product and penalties included up to three years imprisonment and fines up to $1 million.

At the same time, Dow Corning had hired Griffin Bell, a former US attorney general and a circuit court judge, to investigate the company's development and marketing of the implants. He planned to select independent scientific and medical experts to assist his investigation, with free access to all of Dow Corning's records, resources and employees. Bell's final recommendations would be made available to the FDA and the public. Dow also announced on January 29, 1992, that it would make public internal memoranda and other information by the week of February 10.

Lawyers and Public Citizen criticized the delays in having the documents released, claiming that the documents had been locked up for years and that, if the FDA had been given earlier access to the information, breast implants would have been off the market a long time ago.[38] Dow Corning disputed this view, stating that the FDA had possession of the relevant documents for many years. Dow Corning also claimed to have performed some 900 studies into the safety of the implants, none of which concluded that implants would cause harm to the recipient.[39] Plaintiff lawyers, keen to obtain any new information surrounding implants, estimated that there were as many as 1,000 suits filed or about to be filed alleging that the implants had caused cancer, immune system disorders or connective tissue disease.[40]

NEW APPROACH REQUIRED

The seriousness of the implant issue had now escalated. On February 10, 1992, the same day Keith McKennon was appointed to chairman and CEO of Dow Corning, the company yielded to public pressure and disclosed 100 potentially embarrassing company documents that came to light in the Hopkins trial and more recently had been leaked to the press.[41] McKennon had been asked by the board to personally assemble Dow Corning's strategy and action plan to resolve conclusively the implant situation.

With many stakeholders to satisfy and ethical issues to deal with, the problem was going to be complex to solve. His first step was to understand what caused the implant controversy in the first place and to decide whether Dow Corning should continue to market this sensitive product. McKennon also had to assess the validity of the customer complaints, estimate the financial and legal exposure from future customer litigation, respond to the FDA's moratorium announcement and determine the potential damage to Dow Corning's brand name and reputation.

Endnotes

1. Marcotty, Josephine, "Implant Lawsuits: Floods of Litigation Possible Because of Health Problems with Silicone Gel," *Star Tribune,* January 30, 1992, p. D1.

2. Appleson, Gail, "Court Orders Kept Breast Implant Data Secret for Years," *Reuters,* AM cycle, January 30, 1992.

3. Ressberger, Boyce, "Silicone Gel Data Faked, Firm Says," *Houston Chronicle,* November 3, 1992, p. A7.

4. Dow Corning Corporation, Form 10-K, December 31, 1991.

5. Marcotty, op. cit., p. D1.

6. Dow Corning Corporation, Form 10-K, December 31, 1991.

7. *Fortune,* April 20, 1992.

8. *Ward Business Directory of U.S. Private and Public Companies,* 1992.

9. McMurray, Scott and Thomas M. Burton, "Dow Corning Plans to Quit Implant Line," *Wall Street Journal,* March 19, 1992, p. A3.

10. Burton, Thomas M., Bruce Ingersoll, and Joan E. Rigdon, "Dow Corning Makes Changes in Top Posts," *Wall Street Journal,* February 11, 1992, p. A3.

11. Gary E. Anderson, Executive Vice President, Dow Corning Corporation, interview, January 7, 1994.

12. American Society of Plastic Reconstructive Surgeons (ASPRS), *1992 Statistics,* Arlington Heights, IL, 1992.

13. According to the U.S. Food and Drug Administration.

14. U.S. Department of Commerce, *U.S. Industrial Outlook 1993* (Lanham, MD: Bernan Press).

15. ASPRS, op. cit.

16. Pisik, Betsy, "Dangerous Curves; For Many Women, Rewards of Breast Implants Worth Risks," *Washington Times,* January 29, 1992, p. E1.

17. Lachit, Carroll, "Controversy That Won't Go Away," *Los Angeles Times,* October 7, 1993, p. E1.

18. ASPRS, op. cit.

19. Lachit, op. cit.

20. Ibid.

21. Ibid.

22. ASPRS, op. cit.

23. ASPRS, "How To Choose a Qualified Plastic Surgeon," (Arlington Heights, IL: ASPRS, 1992).

24. U.S. Department of Commerce, *Statistical Abstract of the United States.* Bureau of the Census, Washington, D.C., 113th edition, 1993.

25. Samson, Elaine, National Organization for Women with Implants, FDA Panel Hearing, February 1992.

26. *Washington Times,* "FDA Chief David Kessler Joins the Hysteria Over Silicone," January 31, 1992, p. F2.

27. Lachit, op. cit.

28. Pisik, op. cit.

29. Drew, Christopher and Michael Tackett, "Access Equals Clout: The Blitzing of FDA," *Chicago Tribune,* December 8, 1992, p. C1.

30. Byrne, John A., "The Best Laid Ethics Programs," *BusinessWeek,* March 9, 1992, p. 69.

31. Ingersoll, Bruce, "Industry Mounts Big Lobbying Drive Supporting Implants," *Wall Street Journal,* February 14, 1992, p. A5.

32. Drew, op. cit.

33. Cooper, Clair, "Thousands Await Decision as Implant Suit Hits Appeals Court," *Sacramento Bee,* June 19, 1993, p. A6.

34. United Press International, "Dow Sued Over Breast Implants," *San Diego Union-Tribune,* January 30, 1992, p. A9.

35. Piller, Ruth, "Trial Starts in Lawsuit Against Maker of Silicone Gel Implants," *Houston Chronicle,* December 11, 1992, p. A33.

36. Marcotty, op. cit.

37. Steinbrook, Robert and Henry Weinstein, "County Will Investigate Maker of Breast Implants," *Los Angeles Times,* January 31, 1992, p. B1.

38. Appleson, op. cit.

39. Anderson, op. cit.

40. Appleson, op. cit.

41. Burton et al., op. cit.

Questions for discussion

1. What should McKennon do with Dow-Corning's implant business?
2. Who are the stakeholders? How can Dow-Corning reconcile their different interests?
3. How could Dow-Corning have avoided the present crisis?

• *Case Study* •

Uptown, Dakota, and PowerMaster*

N. Craig Smith

Uptown

In December 1989, the R. J. Reynolds Tobacco Co. (RJR) announced plans to introduce Uptown, a menthol cigarette designed to appeal strongly to black smokers. Cigarette sales had declined 6% in 1989 alone and tobacco companies were aggressively seeking new customers. While 29% of the adult U.S. population smoked at that time, the figure was 34% for blacks. Market research showed 69% of black smokers preferred menthol as against 27% for all smokers. RJR's Salem already was the top-selling menthol cigarette with a 6.8% market share (a 1% share was around $250 million in sales), but research suggested many blacks would favor the lighter menthol planned for Uptown. The company's marketing plan for the Philadelphia test market included advertising suggesting glamour, high fashion and nightlife, with the slogan "Uptown. The place. The taste." It would run in black newspapers and in black-oriented magazines such as *Jet* and *Ebony*. Research on the Uptown name suggested it was "classy sounding" and, accordingly, the product packaging was black and gold, in contrast to the usual green for menthol cigarettes. Moreover, the cigarettes were to be packed with the filters down, a response to a research finding showing that many blacks opened cigarette packs from the bottom. In short, RJR had studied carefully the market and customer needs and responded with a sharply focused marketing program targeting black smokers.

For a number of years, public health officials had attacked cigarette advertising directed at specific groups, especially minorities. Statistics showed that during the 1980s the gap between the number of black and white smokers was widening, as whites were more likely to quit. However, the attack on RJR's marketing plans for Uptown by the black Health and Human Services Secretary, Louis W. Sullivan, was unprecedented. In a January 18, 1990, speech to medical students at the University of Pennsylvania (in the city where RJR planned to test market Uptown) he said: "This brand is cynically and deliber-

*Professor N. Craig Smith of Georgetown University Business School prepared this case from public sources as the basis for class discussion rather than to illustrate either effective or ineffective handling of an administrative situation. Copyright © 1995 N. Craig Smith. Reprinted with permission.

ately targeted toward black Americans. At a time when our people desperately need the message of health promotion, Uptown's message is more disease, more suffering and more death for a group already bearing more than its share of smoking-related illness and mortality. At a time when we must cultivate greater personal responsibility among our citizens, Uptown's slick and sinister advertising proposes instead a greater degree of personal irresponsibility." In a letter to RJR's CEO, Sullivan wrote, "I strongly urge you to cancel your plans to market a brand of cigarettes that is specifically targeted to black smokers."

Sullivan's speech received extensive media coverage. Among those commenting on his remarks, Reed Tuckson, the D.C. health commissioner, noted: "The prevalence of smoking is by far the single most important issue that accounts for the poor quality of health for people of color in this country. The predatory behavior and the degree of intensity to which these companies market their products of death and disease for the sake of profit is just immoral." An RJR spokeswoman initially commented: "We believe that black smokers have the right to buy products that fit their preference. The introduction of a new brand will not affect the decision to smoke." However, on January 19, RJR announced that it had cancelled plans for Uptown. Peter Hoult, executive vice president for marketing commented: "We regret that a small coalition of anti-smoking zealots apparently believes that black smokers are somehow different from others who choose to smoke. This represents a loss of choice for black smokers and a further erosion of the free enterprise system."

RJR's conflict with Sullivan did not end with Uptown. Confidential RJR documents leaked to the Advocacy Institute were released to the press to coincide with a Senate hearing on cigarette advertising targeting specific groups. This time, the marketing plans were for a new brand that targeted women.

Dakota

RJR had planned to test market Dakota in April, 1990. It was positioned against Philip Morris Co.'s Marlboro, the leading cigarette brand with a 26% overall market share and the leading brand among women. Marlboro was the most popular entry-level brand for teenage women and was smoked by almost half of young female smokers aged 18 to 24. RJR saw an opportunity in addressing a weakness in Marlboro's appeal to women: the difficulty for a woman to completely identify with the "Marlboro man" image. Women were "one of the few bright spots" in the shrinking cigarette market, with a rate of smoking declining, but not as fast as for males. Moreover, while there were still more adult male smokers (32%) than females (27%), among teens, girls smoked at higher rates than boys. Philip Morris had pioneered female cigarettes in the late 1960s with Virginia Slims, the dominant brand with a 3% share. While around a dozen other brands only held in total a 3% market share, there had been much activity in the late 1980s; for example, BAT Industries' Capri, a much thinner cigarette, had gained a 0.5% market share in 16 months, prompting Philip Morris to launch Superslims and other innovations. As a marketing VP for Liggett commented, "if the female segment keeps growing, more companies will come into it." RJR was no exception.

Dakota was not positioned as a conventional female cigarette with a "soft, feminine sell." Its image was rugged. The target customer was a white, 18–24 year-old, "virile" female, with only a high school degree and for whom work was a job, not a career. Her free time was spent with her boyfriend, doing whatever he was doing, including tractor pulls and hot rod shows. Proposed promotions included "hunk-oriented" premiums, such as calendars, that would tie in with Dakota-sponsored male strip shows. The Dakota cigarette would be similar in taste and number of puffs to a Marlboro. Again, RJR had developed a marketing program clearly aimed at a well-defined target market.

Women's groups already had been strongly critical of the increased efforts by tobacco companies to target women. Twisting the Virginia Slims ad slogan, they were telling women smokers: "You've come the *wrong* way, baby." The Women's Tennis Association had been pressured to end its ties with Philip Morris, the sponsor of the Virginia Slims tennis tour. The marketing VP of Philip Morris commented that it was "reprehensible at best and sexist at worst to assume that adult women are not capable of making their own decisions about whether or not to smoke." Another industry spokesperson noted that it's "prudent marketing to go after your market." The demise of Uptown prompted increased attention to the targeting of women and the suggestion that they too could "resist exploitation by the tobacco industry." Having noted that slim cigarettes appealed to women with a "freedom from fat" message, one commentator suggested Sullivan should "blast cigarette companies for targeting women." With the announcement of RJR's plans for Dakota, Sullivan was able to oblige. He was also critical of the Virginia Slims tennis tour for fostering "a misleading impression that smoking is compatible with good health."

Primed by the Uptown story, commentators offered more insightful analysis on the controversy over target marketing, going beyond charges of "exploitation" and "manipulation." Consumer vulnerability was suggested in explanation: "Dakota is an unscrupulous attempt to exploit a vulnerable group" (Kornheiser 1990); "the company is under heavy fire for a plan to market the new brand to one of the industry's most vulnerable segments: young, poorly-educated, blue-collar women" (Freedman and McCarthy 1990). Target marketing was acknowledged as a standard marketing tool and a tactic of choice among tobacco companies because in a declining market the best opportunities were with specific groups: the poor, the young, blacks and Hispanics. These perceived vulnerable groups were left because "The well-to-do and well-educated . . . have quit smoking. Those who remain are the disadvantaged. It's logical to target them, except you are sending a message society can't accept." Targeting had become hazardous for tobacco companies because "targeting specific consumer groups suggests they're creating victims" (Freedman and McCarthy 1990).

However, the hazards of targeting were not restricted to tobacco. The alcohol industry soon realized that it too faced the prospect of similar pressures and going "down Tobacco Road" (Abramson 1991). With driving after drinking the leading cause of death among teenagers, the industry had already faced criticism over targeting youth from groups and public health officials, such as Surgeon General Koop.

PowerMaster

Like the tobacco industry, alcohol producers, also faced with declining consumption, were increasingly targeting their marketing programs, especially at heavy users. These targets included "the most vulnerable elements of society," according to Michael Jacobson of the Center for Science in the Public Interest

(CSPI), a consumer advocacy group coordinating a coalition of 22 public interest groups critical of the emphasis on black and Hispanic consumers in advertisements for malt liquor. A CSPI video, "Marketing Booze to Blacks," suggested alcohol was connected to many social problems, from spousal and child abuse to homicide. The Beer Institute charged the Center with elitism: "The elitists at CSPI believe that only middle- to upper-class white males have the capacity to view ads without endangering themselves" (Folt 1991). In San Francisco, the city's health commissioner commented: "It is the height of irresponsibility for the beer industry to target poor ethnic communities with these genocidal beer promotions." Community leaders charged that heavy promotion of "high octane" malt liquor in black and Latino neighborhoods resulted in social problems similar to those created by crack cocaine. The following year, another new product introduction was to go the way of Uptown and Dakota.

In 1990, G. Heileman Brewing Co., the fifth largest brewer in the U.S., had seen its volumes decline for the seventh year in a row. Market share was also down. It was in bankruptcy proceedings and desperately in need of successful new product introductions. It had developed 40% of the 87 new beer products introduced in the 1980s. While beer consumption was on the decline (along with most other alcoholic beverages), the $500m malt liquor market was growing. It experienced a 7% volume increase to 79.7 m. 2.5-gallon cases in 1990, about 3% of the total beer market. Some malts had even seen annual increases of 25–30%. Malt liquor, brewed from a base that contains a higher degree of fermentable sugars than regular beer, has a higher alcohol content, is paler in color and has a more aromatic and malty taste. It was disproportionately consumed in low income neighborhoods, where its appeal was attributed to its "quicker high." Heileman dominated the malt liquor market with a volume market share of around one-third. In July, 1991, it planned to introduce PowerMaster, which at 5.9% alcohol was 31% stronger than Heileman's Colt 45, the market leader, and had 65% more alcohol than regular beer. Heileman had spent more than $2m on research and marketing for the brand.

The announcement of PowerMaster had anti-alcohol groups and black leaders up in arms. CSPI and other groups asked the brewer to stop distribution of the product because "higher octane alcoholic beverages have no place on the market, especially in communities where residents already suffer disproportionately from alcohol and other drug problems." Boycotts were planned. Surgeon General Antonia Novello described the promotion of PowerMaster as "socially irresponsible." PowerMaster's target marketing to minorities also was criticized by Congressional representatives. On June 20, 1991, the Bureau of Alcohol, Tobacco and Firearms (BATF) announced that its approval of the PowerMaster label was a mistake and required Heileman to drop the word *power* because it was a veiled reference to alcohol strength. (The Federal Alcohol Administration Act banned the mention of alcohol content on beer labels to discourage competition on that basis.) On July 3, Heileman announced that it would discontinue PowerMaster following BATF's withdrawal of approval for its label, because "the brand name was the product," commented the Heileman director of marketing. BATF gave the brewer four months to sell existing stocks.

Anti-alcohol groups criticized the agency because it made its move only after public outrage over PowerMaster's potency and the targeting of low-income blacks, who suffer disproportionately from alcohol-related diseases (CSPI found that black men had a 40% higher death rate from cirrhosis of the liver than whites). Industry commentators, anticipating further action by BATF against power claims widely used by malt liquor brands, suggested this would "strip away the whole basis for business" in the category. Also under scrutiny was advertising that associated malt liquors with aphrodisiacs, drug use, and street gangs. The director of the National Coalition to Prevent Impaired Driving commented: "Alcohol producers will think twice before targeting vulnerable, inner-city groups again." While a *New York Times* editorial had lambasted Heileman for "deliberately zeroing in on a section of society that already has problems enough," the President of the Beer Institute accused critics of PowerMaster of "patronizing" blacks and Hispanics. The trade journal *Beverage World* in its obituary to PowerMaster said it became "a magnet of controversy from the moment it reared its alcohol-enhanced head. Federal officials, industry leaders, black activists, and media types weighed in with protests that PowerMaster . . . was an example of bad product, bad marketing, and, essentially, a bad idea."

Later in 1991, BATF cracked down on other malt liquors, such as Black Sunday, Crazy Horse, and St. Ides, while cans of PowerMaster fast became collectors' items. Some observers noted the failure of some black organizations and media to criticize alcohol and tobacco and educate on health effects, suggesting they were "bought off" by these industries. *Fortune* described Power-Master as one of the biggest business goofs of 1991, noting that "targeting black consumers with anything less wholesome than farina has become politically risky." A line extension of Colt 45, Colt 45 Premium, was introduced by Heileman in May 1992 and described by BATF as being identical in content to PowerMaster.

Sources

ABRAMSON, JILL (1991). "Selling Moderation; Alcohol Industry Is at Forefront of Efforts to Curb Drunkenness," *Wall Street Journal*, May 21, p. A1.

ALTERS, DIANE (1989). "As Youths Are Urged to Stay Sober, Beer-Ad Blitz Tries to Lure Them," *Boston Sunday Globe*, June 25, p. 1.

BUREAU OF NATIONAL AFFAIRS (1991). "Brewer Decides to Withdraw New High Alcohol Malt Liquor," *Antitrust and Trade Regulation Report*, Vol. 61, No. 1524 (July 11), p. 41.

CHICAGO TRIBUNE (1991). "U.S. Seeking to Dilute New Malt Liquor's Name," *Chicago Tribune*, June 21, p. 10.

COHEN, RICHARD (1990). "More Work for Dr. Sullivan," *Washington Post*, January 30, p. A19.

CORNWELL, RUPERT (1991). "Out of the West: Trouble Brews for a Powerful Beer," *The Independent*, July 3, p. 10.

FARNHAM, ALAN (1992). "Biggest Business Goofs of 1991," *Fortune*, January 13, p. 81.

FOLTZ, KIM (1991). "Alcohol Ads Aimed at Blacks Criticized," *New York Times*, January 16, p. D6.

FREEDMAN, ALIX M. (1991). "Potent New Heileman Malt Is Brewing Fierce Industry and Social Criticism," *Wall Street Journal*, June 17, p. B1.

FREEDMAN, ALIX M. (1991). "Malt Advertising That Touts Firepower Comes Under Attack by U.S. Officials," *Wall Street Journal*, July 1, p. B1.

FREEDMAN, ALIX M. (1991). "Heileman, Under Pressure, Scuttles PowerMaster Malt," *Wall Street Journal*, July 5, p. B1.

FREEDMAN, ALIX M. and MICHAEL J. MCCARTHY (1990). "New Smoke from RJR Under Fire," *Wall Street Journal*, February 20, p. B1.

GARDNER, MARILYN (1990). "Women and Cigarettes: Smoking out the Truth," *Christian Science Monitor*, January 30, p. 14.

GLADWELL, MALCOLM (1990). "HHS Chief Assails Tie Between Tobacco Firms, Sporting Events," *St. Petersburg Times,* February 24, p. 6A.

GLATER, JONATHAN (1992). "Federal Crackdown Alcohol, Regulators Target Ads Over Claims of Potency," *San Francisco Chronicle,* July 24, p. B1.

HARDIE, CHRIS (1994). "Heileman Shipments Cut in Half Since '83," *La Crosse Tribune,* January 13.

HILTS, PHILIP J. (1990). "Health Chief Assails a Tobacco Producer for Aiming at Blacks," *New York Times,* January 19, p. A1.

INMAN, DAVID (1990). "Blacks Strike Back at Ad Campaigns; Amidst Uproar, Will Marketing Change?" *Sunday Tennessean,* April 8, p. 1D.

JACKSON, DERRICK Z. (1991). "Miller's Mockery," *Boston Globe,* December 29, p. 63.

KORNHEISER, TONY (1990). "Cigarettes and Virile Chicks," *Washington Post,* February 23, p. B1.

LACEY, MARC (1992). "Marketing of Malt Liquor Fuels Debate," *Los Angeles Times,* December 15, p. A32.

LANG, PERRY (1990). "Hard Sell to Blacks of Potent Malt Brew Called 'Irresponsible'," *San Francisco Chronicle,* November 3, p. A2.

ROTHENBERG, RONDALL (1989). "Groups Plan to Protest Malt Liquor Campaigns," *New York Times,* August 23, p. D17.

SPECTER, MICHAEL (1990). "Sullivan Denounces Reynolds Tobacco; New Brand Said Aimed at Blacks," *Washington Post,* January 19, p. A1.

SPECTER, MICHAEL (1990). "Reynolds Cancels Plans to Market New Cigarette; Uptown Brand Attacked as Aimed at Blacks," *Washington Post,* January 20, p. A3.

WALDMAN, PETER (1989). "Tobacco Firms Try Soft, Feminine Sell; But in Targeting Women, They Spark Backlash," *Wall Street Journal,* December 19, p. B1.

Questions for discussion

1. How should tobacco products and alcoholic beverages be marketed and advertised, if at all?

2. Are there any special moral problems engendered by marketing such products to minority groups and women?

3. Are the moral issues surrounding alcohol and tobacco settled merely by the fact that they are legal?

• *Case Study* •

Manville: The Ethics of Economic Efficiency?*

AL GINI

On Friday, July 20, 1982, a short article appeared on page four of the *Wall Street Journal* announcing that yet another company, UNR Industries Inc. of Chicago, had filed for Chapter 11 of the Federal Bankruptcy Code of 1978. Given the present state of the economy the public notification of a bankruptcy proceeding is hardly a novel occurrence. However, the circumstances leading to the UNR petition were certainly far from usual.

At the time of filing UNR assets exceeded $200 million, with debts totaling only about $100 million. While sales had marginally declined, 4.2% in the second quarter of 1982, yearly sales figures were expected to remain relatively strong. UNR chairman, David S. Leavitt, said that the company was forced to file for bankruptcy because of the nearly 17,000 suits filed against it in regard to their asbestos pipe insulation product line. Although the company had stopped manufacturing asbestos insulation in 1970, the suits seek damages for alleged injuries and wrongful deaths supposedly attributable to exposure to the insulation. Mr. Leavitt claimed that the company simply could not survive the burden of the costs of all the present and possible future litigation.[1] While the general business community probably paid little or no attention to UNR's plight, their predicament did not go unnoticed by the Denver-based Manville Corporation, the nation's, if not the world's, single largest producer of asbestos and asbestos products.

On Thursday, August 26, 1982, the Manville Corporation (formerly Johns-Manville) and its principal American and Canadian affiliates filed for reorganization under Chapter 11 in the United States District Court for the Southern District of New York. Manville's unexpected bankruptcy petition stunned the financial community, surprised Congress, shocked their creditors, suppliers, and customers, outraged those who had filed damage suits against them, and raised a complex tangle of legal, political, and ethical issues that will have far-reaching implications for millions of Americans. The drama of the Manville announcement stems from the fact that this is the same Manville Corporation that last year earned $60.3 million on sales exceeding $2 billion with an unencumbered net worth of $1.1 billion. This is the same Manville that ranks 181 on the Fortune 500 list of American corporations. And this is the same Manville that has been traditionally included in the 30 companies used to calculate the prestigious Dow Jones industrial average, the most watched indicator of prices on the New York Stock Exchange. While there are many factors in the equation that resulted in Manville's final decision, like UNR's unprecedented decision less than a month earlier, Manville Chairman John A. McKinney angrily announced that this company could no longer sustain or survive the blitz of "toxic torts" that it was now facing.

Many of Manville's critics have claimed that Manville, and by implication UNR, is acting in an immoral and illegal manner. They are held to be immoral insofar as their critics feel that they are using the "bankruptcy boom" as a means of avoiding just compensation for those who have truly been injured or killed due to excessive or abusive exposure to asbestos. Manville is accused of acting illegally in that the spirit and purpose of the 1978 Bankruptcy Act is being violated because no company has ever filed for Chapter 11 given the size of their assets, their net worth, and their yearly sales figures. Other observers suggest that this is much too simplistic a response to the situation and that whatever the final merits of Manville's petition the factors involved in their decision warrant a careful and detailed analysis.

• • •

Asbestos is a naturally occurring mineral found in various concentrations across the earth's surface. Asbestos is the best known member of a family of fibrous silicate minerals, which share the common attribute of being able to be separated into relatively soft, silky strands. Because of its high tensile strength, superior flexibility, and durability and because of its resistance to fire, heat, and corrosion, asbestos finds broad use in many essential applications. In all, asbestos is a component in more than 3,000 industrial and consumer products. It is an essential ingredient in plastics, textiles, roofing tiles, brake linings, insulation and fire wall materials, cement water and sewerage pipes, and vinyl floor coverings. Because it is plentiful in nature and relatively inexpensive in cost, asbestos continues to be widely used. According to the Bureau of Mines, 349,000 metric tons of asbestos was used to make various products in this country in 1981.

Industry spokesmen are quick to point out that its unique combination of properties makes asbestos superior to any other natural or man-made fiber. After more than a decade of intense well-financed research for an asbestos substitute, none has been found that works as well or makes as much economic sense. Robert Clifton, asbestos commodities specialist for the National Bureau of Mines, stated that while there are substitutes for practically every application in which asbestos is used, they are either inferior, more costly, or contain serious health hazards.[2]

Like many of the naturally occurring materials, asbestos may also pose a health hazard unless properly handled. Today there is little doubt that excessive exposure to airborne asbestos fiber can cause disease, principally of the respiratory tract. Some forms of asbestos consist of fibers so small that 1,600 particles can occupy the space of a single human hair. Because of their minute size and needle-like shape asbestos fibers can be inhaled into the lungs; and because they are relatively indestructible they may be substantially resistant to the body's normal defense mechanisms.[3]

The insidious aspect of asbestos-related illness is that they have an incubation period of 10 to 40 years. Diseases of this type are usually referred to as "delayed emergence diseases." Asbestos has been primarily associated with three forms of respiratory illness: asbestosis, mesothelioma, lung cancer. Asbestosis is a chronic and sometimes fatal lung disease characterized by extensive scarring of the lung tissue and progressive shortness of breath much like emphysema. This disease has a latency period of 10 to 20 years. Mesothelioma is a fatal if rare cancer of the chest or abdomen lining. Its average latency is 25 to 40 years. Asbestos-related lung cancer is a highly virulent and always fatal form of the disease which has a latency period of 20 to 40 years. Moreover, modern research has also suggested a link between asbestos fibers and cancer of the gastrointestinal tract, larynx, and kidney.

In a recent statement in *Newsweek* magazine Dr. William Blot of the National Cancer Institute claims that excessive exposure to asbestos fibers "appears to be the greatest single source of occupational cancer."[4] Medical specialists estimate that over the past 40 years 9 to 20 million Americans have been exposed to large amounts of asbestos in the workplace and that *at least* 5,000 cancer related deaths directly linked to asbestos will occur annually until the end of the century. According to Manville, the major occupational groups that may have been exposed to excessive amounts of asbestos in the past are divided into three categories: (1) Workers in mines, mills, and factories where raw asbestos was used; (2) Insulation workers who worked with non-bonded or non-encapsulated asbestos-containing products; (3) Workers exposed to asbestos while in government controlled naval shipyards.[5]

For all intents and purposes the origins of Manville's present predicament begins with this country's preparation for World War II. Because of its fire resistant qualities, asbestos was extensively used in government owned or controlled shipyards in the production of 6,000 new warships and freighters and the refitting of 65,000 other vessels. Over 4 million workers were directly exposed to clouds of asbestos dust in their race to build and repair America's naval arsenal.[6] While it is the case that after the war asbestos came to be looked upon as the "miracle mineral" and was extensively used throughout the construction industry, the shipyard workers remain the largest single group exposed to the possible effects of asbestos poisoning. It is from this group that Manville is experiencing the largest number of lawsuits and claims.

By the summer of 1982 Manville was being sued at the rate of 500 new cases a month. Having already settled 3,500 suits at a cost of over $50 million[7] and with 16,500 suits still pending, Manville commissioned a study by Epidemiology Resources, Inc., a small, Boston based, health data research company, to determine how many new lawsuits would probably be filed against them. The report was filed on August 4, 1982, and it forecast by the year 2009 Manville could conservatively expect another 32,000 suits. Together these pending and probable suits could cost the company anywhere between $2 to $5 billion, budgeting $40,000 per settlement based on the assumption of a modest rate of inflation and an average win/loss ratio.

While many critics contend that Manville's figures are an excessive extrapolation, a number of independent authorities maintain that Manville's figures are not only conservative but very low estimates indeed. Dr. Irving J. Selikoff, chief of Environmental Health at Mt. Sinai Hospital in New York and a leading authority on asbestos-related disease, claims that Manville is vastly underestimating their future rate of litigation and probable liabilities. According to Dr. Selikoff's figures, from 1940 to 1980 about 27 million workers were exposed to asbestos. He claims that while only a fraction of those exposed developed cancer, the number of cancer deaths among asbestos workers exceeds the average in the population by 8,000 to 10,000 a year. This means, said Dr. Selikoff, that the total liabilities to Manville and other asbestos companies could reach $40 to $80 billion.[8]

Based on the "Epidemiology Resources Report" and after an intensive review by a "blue-ribbon committee," Manville's board of directors announced their decision to file for reorganization under Chapter 11 of the Bankruptcy Act. In filing for reorganization Manville has won at least a temporary respite from its legal woes. Although the company will continue operating during the reorganization, all suits now pending are frozen and no new suits can be filed. While the company develops a plan to handle its liabilities, it is up to the bankruptcy courts to deal with all present claims as well as establishing guidelines for the handling of any future claims.

In a full-page interview that appeared as an ad in 21 major newspapers one day after the bankruptcy filing, Manville Chairman John A. McKinney contended that while the decision to apply for Chapter 11 was a dramatic one, he stressed that the company was not in a desperate manner. "This is not a financial failure," McKinney emphasized.

Nothing is wrong with our business. Filing under Chapter 11 does not mean that the company is going out of business and that its assets will be liquidated. Lawsuits are the problem. We will continue to manufacture and ship high quality products and provide the same services, as always.[9]

McKinney went on to say that he was personally angered by and opposed to the decision to file for bankruptcy, but he agreed with the board of directors that there was no other logical recourse legally left to the company.

Mr. G. Earl Parker, Manville Senior Vice-President, in testimony before a "House Subcommittee on Labor Standards" on September 9, 1982, itemized the four chief reasons that forced Manville to the bankruptcy courts:

1. to avoid the largest tort litigation ever witnessed;
2. federal standards in regard to accounting principles and requirements;
3. legal disputes with insurance companies;
4. the federal government's unwillingness to establish a compensation fund for asbestos victims.[10]

The first two points are interconnected. With Manville being faced with the possibility of a minimum of $2 billion in litigation costs and liabilities, the company found itself, at least on paper, in a difficult financial position. As John McKinney pointed out, the company's net worth is only $1.1 billion. Therefore, if Manville did not file for bankruptcy

> we would have to strangle the company slowly, by deferring maintenance and postponing capital expenditures. We would also have to cannibalize our good businesses to just keep going. . . . We would have to mortgage our plants and properties and new credit would be most difficult and expensive to obtain.[11]

Because Manville is a publicly-held company it is required to comply with certain accounting requirements. Federal law states that a company is supposed to estimate the costs of all current and probable litigation whenever possible and create a reserve fund for the liability in an amount equal to the estimated costs. Given the volume of present and projected litigation facing Manville, it is clearly impossible for them to establish such a fund even on a liquidation basis. "Without court protection," McKinney insisted, "the lawsuits, one way or another, would cripple us."[12]

Perhaps the last appreciated factor in the equation that led Manville to Chapter 11 is the long disputes it has been having with its major insurance carriers. According to Manville spokesman John Lonnquist, "Except for one company, all are essentially withholding payments."[13] The insurance industry has been split into two warring camps by the flood of asbestos-related lawsuits that led Manville to declare bankruptcy. Some insurance experts suggest that it is the insurance industry's war, more than any other factor, that has prompted the bankruptcy filing. At the heart of the insurance battle is the question of whether an insurer's liability begins when the workers were exposed to asbestos or when the asbestos-related disease manifests itself, typically many years after exposure. As one might expect, insurance firms who covered the asbestos manufactures in the early years favor the manifestation theory. And the insurers who have written coverage for the asbestos industry more recently are fighting for the exposure theory. Manville's problem is that as long as the insurance companies are fighting among themselves about whose policies cover what, Manville must use its corporate assets to pay both the fees and damages involved in all suits. For its part, Manville is presently suing all its insurers (27 companies); they are asking that all outstanding claims be paid as well as $5 billion in punitive damages.[14]

No matter what the other reasons that have led Manville to apply for Chapter 11, in so doing it clearly hopes to encourage the support and active participation of the federal government in establishing a compensation program for all asbestos victims. Up until now the government has steadfastly denied responsibility and refused to participate in any further compensation fund beyond the presently mandated compensation programs.[15] John McKinney vigorously rejects the allegation that Manville is simply seeking a federal "bailout" vis-à-vis Chrysler or the railroads. Manville maintains that the government should pay a large portion of the asbestos claims for three reasons:

1. The government was the chief contractor for the shipyards and the major employer of the asbestos-exposed workers.
2. The government established the specifications for all aspects of the sale and use of asbestos in wartime shipbuilding.
3. Since the war the government has been responsible for the establishment and policing of all safety standards regarding asbestos.[16]

Manville insists that it has always conformed to government standards and that it always tried to establish company regulations that reflected the latest word in scientific achievement. Tragically for many workers, however, it has taken decades for the medical/scientific community, industry, and the government to obtain the broad knowledge we have today. The public literature has reported since the 1930s that factory workers exposed to 100 percent raw asbestos fiber experienced an increased risk of contracting a pulmonary fibrosis that has come to be called asbestosis. But there was no reason to believe that any worker faced a health risk from using finished asbestos products, and there was no reason to believe that workers faced any health risks other than asbestosis.[17] In 1964 Dr. Irving Selikoff of Mt. Sinai School of Medicine in New York reported the results of a study of insulation workers and changed everyone's understanding of the extent of potential health problems from excessive exposure to asbestos. Dr. Selikoff's findings showed that exposure to asbestos from products such as asbestos insulation, even though below the accepted standard, heightened the risk of disease among insulation workers. In addition, he showed that there was a markedly increased risk of lung cancer in asbestos insulation workers who smoked cigarettes. Studies since then have supported Dr. Selikoff's findings.[18]

Given this information and the new standards that have evolved, Manville is convinced that asbestos can and is being used safely. Today's disease problems, Manville contends, are a legacy of the past when the state of medical knowledge concerning asbestos was inadequate. Therefore, while Manville recognizes that it has participated in the mistakes of the past, the company feels that the government has been a full partner in these errors. As a partner Manville is willing to share costs with the government in the establishment of a statutory compensation program to aid all those who have contracted an asbestos disease. According to John McKinney, without such a program there will be no help for present and future victims of asbestos, and there will be no way to save the Manville Corporation from going defunct!

After all is said and done, the central issue in this case for most people is not that Manville is filing for Chapter 11 to avoid immediate and future liability, but that Manville is alive, doing well, highly solvent, and not even close to closing up shop and yet it is filing for bankruptcy! Manville claims that just because their actions are unprecedented (save for UNR) and highly unorthodox, it does not follow that they are acting in an immoral or illegal fashion. Manville officials insist that filing for bankruptcy was unavoidable and in the best interest of its stockholders, employees, and creditors. Moreover, they feel that in the long run their decision will better benefit the victims of asbestos-related diseases. Earl Parker testified that only by filing now could Manville ensure that the asbestos disease claimants will receive the money owed them in the coming decades.[19] Manville Chairman John McKinney insists that Chapter 11 is the only orderly way possible for the company to treat everyone fairly. He emphasized that Manville's failure is really our court and legislative systems' failure to provide a reasonable way to compensate victims of an unexpected occupational health catastrophe. McKinney is firmly convinced that Manville's problems are America's problems and the government should and must help![20]

In all candor it must be remembered that Manville's actions are not without danger. To the extent that Manville is using Chapter 11 as a shelter against the rush of asbestos litigation, the company is nevertheless taking a risky gamble. Manville must now operate under the eye of a federal bankruptcy judge, and, said Lawrence King, Professor of Law at New York University, "once you file, there is always a risk of liquidation." "It is not yet clear," said King, "that the bankruptcy proceeding will succeed in mooting the claims against Manville."[21] No one really knows how Manville's decision to apply for Chapter 11 will ultimately affect the status of the litigation and claims now in the courts. The only thing that is clear is that each decision in the Manville controversy will be breaking new legal ground each step of the way, whether it be in regard to Manville itself, the asbestos industry in general, government regulations and responsibilities, and/or the future status of public health and environmental policy.

AN UPDATE
Reorganization Gives Manville New Life Amid Asbestos Suits
Christopher Elias, *Insight*, August 1, 1988

Perhaps as soon as late August, Denver's Manville Corp. will emerge from bankruptcy proceedings that have lasted six years and cost the company $100 million in fees for lawyers and other professionals. When the last appeal has been made and the last legal argument has ended, the bankruptcy of Manville, once New York-based Johns-Manville Corp., undoubtedly will go down as one of the most complicated and successful ever. Instead of a corpse, Manville will be a going business, deeply in debt to be sure, but alive and earning money.

Its 550-page reorganization plan filed under Chapter 11 of the Federal Bankruptcy Code is already being counted among the most imaginative, since it reconciles the interests of an extraordinary number of disparate creditors with claims far greater than the total assets of company. Instead of wiping out shareholders, which could easily have occurred, the plan lets them hang on, though they must accept a dilution of the value of their holdings by as much as 98 percent, while relinquishing governance of the company to two trusts and ultimate control to a group of banks supplying new working capital of more than $200 million. . . .

In outline, the reorganization plan requires Manville to fund enormous known and unknown potential liabilities, resulting largely from asbestosis, a disease often contracted by people working with and around asbestos products sold by Manville for decades. . . .

Under its reorganization plan Manville has accepted an obligation of at least $2.5 billion and agrees to pay out as much as 20 percent of its earnings for as long as they "are needed to provide compensation for personal injury and property damage caused by asbestos." The plan also provides money for commercial creditors, including 12 banks, and Manville suppliers.

The plan enables the company to remain viable by setting up two independent trusts to administer and pay claims, freeing the company to tend to its diversified businesses. The separation, a pragmatic one agreed to by a variety of claimants, is essential if Manville is to fund claims initiated years, even decades from now. To shield the company from lawsuits bypassing the two trusts, Burton R. Lifland, chief judge of the U.S. Bankruptcy Court in New York, issued an injunction prohibiting further suits after the reorganization is consummated.

The injunction was a departure from Bankruptcy Code and is considered unique by lawyers, since the effect is to extend some of the protection of bankruptcy to a company no longer in bankruptcy. The order might be challenged one day, since doubt exists that future claims against Manville can be discharged before the fact by a Bankruptcy Court.

"It was the most imaginative bankruptcy proceeding yet," said attorney Roy Babitt, a retired New York bankruptcy judge and former associate of Lifland. "It shows that the bankruptcy system is working."

At Manville's headquarters, Chief Executive Officer W. Thomas Stephens, credited as one of the chief architects of the reorganization along with New York lawyer Leon Silverman, is jubilant. Legal opposition to the reorganization is winding down. Two groups of claimants may yet appeal to the Supreme Court, imposing new delays. But, as early as Aug. 25, six years from the day Manville declared its bankruptcy, Stephens might be able to start running the company without Lifland's approval of management decisions. . . .

. . . the plan separates Manville's operating companies from direct involvement in claim procedures. It establishes two trusts, one to pay asbestos-related personal injury claims, the other to pay claims related to property damage. The personal injury trust is being funded with an estimated $2.5 billion over the next 20 to 25 years. Insurance companies will contribute $615 million to the funding and the firm will contribute $150 million in cash as well as a $50 million interest-bearing note. It will also contribute the proceeds from the sale of $1.65 billion in bonds payable over 25 years and "an interest" in a second, $150 million bond. The company will double the 24 million shares outstanding and contribute half the total to the trust, which one day could own as much as 80 percent of Manville's outstanding shares. For as long as needed, the personal injury trust will also receive as much as 20 percent of Manville's net earnings. . . .

"We are going to come out of this smokin', there's no doubt about it," says the Arkansas-born Stephens, an engineer by training, a logger in his youth, and former president of Manville's Forest Products Group. . . .

Last year, Stephens' first complete year as chief executive officer, Manville's earnings rose 102 percent, to $164.1 million, as sales rose only from $1.9 billion to $2 billion. Most of these earnings, however—$91.5 million—was devoted to advance funding of the personal injury trust that will be born when the 130-year-old company emerges from bankruptcy. That charge reduced 1987 net earnings to about $72.6 million from $81.2 million in 1986. . . .[22]

Notes

1. *Wall Street Journal,* July 20, 1982, p. 4.

2. *New York Times,* September 2, 1982, Sec. D, p. 2.

3. *Compensating Workers for Asbestos-Related Disease,* Asbestos Compensation Coalition, 1981, p. 1.

4. *Newsweek,* September 6, 1982, pp. 54, 55.

5. *Asbestos, Health and Johns-Manville,* Johns-Manville Corporate Relations Department, September 1981, p. 5.

6. "Kirkland & Ellis Report: The Government's Legal Responsibilities," Manville Corporate Relations Department, September 8, 1982.

7. *Time,* September 6, 1982, p. 17.

8. *New York Times,* August 31, 1982, Sec. A, p. 13.

9. *New York Times,* August 27, 1982, Sec. D, p. 3.

10. "The Testimony of G. Earl Parker, U.S. House of Representatives," Manville Corporate Relations Department, September 9, 1982.

11. *New York Times,* August 27, 1982, Sec. D, p. 3.

12. Ibid.

13. *Science News,* September 18, 1982, Vol. 122, p. 183.

14. *New York Times,* September 7, 1982, Sec. D, p. 2.

15. *Sci Now,* September 18, 1982, Vol. 122, p. 182; *New York Times,* September 10, 1982, Sec. D, p. 1.

16. "Kirkland & Ellis Report: The Government's Legal Responsibilities," Manville Corporate Relations Department, September 8, 1982.

17. "The Testimony of G. Earl Parker, The Senate Subcommittee on Courts," Manville Corporate Relations Department, November 19, 1982.

18. *Asbestos, Health and Johns-Manville,* Johns-Manville Corporate Relations Department, September 1981, p. 6.

19. *New York Times,* August 31, 1982, Sec. A, p. 13.

20. *Chemical and Engineering News,* September 6, 1982, p. 6.

21. *Newsweek,* September 6, 1982, p. 55.

22. In effect, what this means is that Manville will be the first company to be operated primarily for the purpose of generating money for people injured by one of its products. According to Manville's CEO, W. Thomas Stephens, "The whole Manville reorganization is driven by the rights of the future claimants and that's what's unique about it." Estimates of the number of asbestos claims that may ultimately be filed run to 50,000 or more. (*New York Times, National Edition,* July 30, 1988, pp. 17, 18).

Questions for discussion

See questions: "When Did Johns-Manville Know?"

• Case Study •
When Did Johns-Manville Know?*

JEFF COPLON

Even if the Manville Corp. is thrown out of bankruptcy court, Ted Kowalski and his fellow plaintiffs will be fighting uphill to collect on their damage suits. To date, New Jersey workers have been shunted to workers' compensation in cases of job-related illness or injury; no one has ever successfully sued an employer in civil court.

But in California, the state Supreme Court ruled in 1980 that the family of a dead J-M employee could sue the company for "fraud and conspiracy" in concealing the dangers of long-term exposure to asbestos.

By 1981, under the same principle, several judges throughout the country had ordered six-figure punitive awards to people outside the company who had taken sick after handling J-M products. In one case, a widow of a Cleveland insulation worker won $350,000 in punitive damages, in addition to $500,000 in compensatory damages.

For the victims in Manville, then, the legal issue is this: what did J-M know, and when did the company know it?

In its defense, J-M says it protected its own workers from asbestosis as best it could since the 1930s, that it followed the U.S. Public Health Service standard set in 1938, and that it was aware of no cancer threat until 1964.

But a growing body of evidence suggests otherwise—that J-M knew more than it admits, and that it deliberately suppressed medical information from its workers in Manville.

The first case of asbestosis was reported in 1907 in England, followed by conclusive medical research in 1930 and documentation of a link with lung cancer in 1934. In this country, the Journal of the American Medical Association reported on asbestosis in 1928—the same year Prudential Insurance suspended all policies on the lives of asbestos workers.

In the 1930s, J-M responded by taking annual chest X rays at the Manville plant and partially funding a study of asbestosis at Saranac Lake. But at the same time, recently disclosed correspondence between officers at J-M and other asbestos firms shows they sought to keep the bad news from spreading.

In December 1934, after reviewing galley proofs of the Saranac Lake study, J-M attorney Vandiver Brown requested revisions: "All we ask is that . . . none of the unfavorable [aspects] be unintentionally pictured in darker tones than the circumstances justify." The study was duly revised.

In 1942 an outside attorney named Charles Roemer met with Brown. After his cousin, a doctor at a Paterson asbestos plant, found "lung changes" among many workers, Roemer approached J-M "to see how they were handling the asbestos health problem."

The answer, included in a sworn affidavit taken from the 83-year-old Roemer last September, pulled no punches: "Vandiver Brown stated that Johns-

Manville's physical examination program had, indeed, also produced findings of X-ray evidence of asbestos disease among workers exposed to asbestos and that it was Johns-Manville's policy not to do anything, nor to tell the employees of the X-ray findings. Vandiver Brown went on to say that . . . if Johns-Manville's workers were told, they would stop working and file claims against Johns-Manville, and that it was Johns-Manville's policy to let them work until they quit work because of asbestosis or died as a result of asbestos-related diseases."

In 1952, Dr. Kenneth Smith, J-M's medical director, asked company executives to place a warning label on some asbestos products, which he felt could be dangerous to insulation workers. Their reply, he attested in a 1975 deposition, was that the corporation "is in business . . . to provide jobs for people and make money for stockholders, and they had to take into consideration the effects of everything they did and if the application of caution label would cut out sales, there would be serious financial implications." The warning labels were deferred until 1964.

In 1950 Dr. Nicholas Demy, a Somerset radiologist, found asbestos fibers imbedded within the lung cancer of a deceased J-M worker—demonstrating a link the industry would deny for 14 more years. Subsequently, J-M refused to supply Demy with occupational histories he needed to pursue the lead.

When it was clear the controversy over asbestos would not blow over, J-M was selective as to what research it backed. When Dr. Maxwell Borow, a surgeon at Somerset Medical Center, asked for $3500 in 1966 to mount an exhibit on the worst Manville cancer of all, the company declined: "They said they were not prepared to admit a causal relationship between asbestos and mesothelioma."

Even as the conflagration raged full blast, some say the company shrank from sounding an alarm. According to Wilber Ruff, a former J-M manager at its Pittsburg, California plant, company doctors were barred until 1971 from telling workers about their X-rays or referring them to outside specialists.

"The company did not want to talk about these things and get employees upset," Ruff testified before Congress, "until such time as we knew our ground."

Few people will question a doctor who tells them they're healthy. It's what they want to hear, after all, that all will be well in the morning. And in a company town like Manville, filled with immigrants who spoke little English, the doctor was a man of learning, a high authority. If he said the X-ray showed nothing, they must be fine. They weren't much for complaining.

"They're good people, strong people, with strong beliefs," said Ted Kowalski. "Someone took advantage of their goodness."

That remains true today. For all the hoopla and network specials about the lethal white fiber, there is no research to determine why certain workers are susceptible to asbestosis and related cancers, or how they might get sick under current workplace conditions.

"Neither the companies nor the insurance companies nor the government have shown the slightest interest in finding out how these diseases occur," said Dr. Irving Selikoff, the Mt. Sinai researcher whose 1964 paper was the first accepted by J-M. "One side says the other should pay for it. There's been no interest. So people will continue to die."

Questions for discussion

1. Is Manville telling the truth about its knowledge of the health factors involved in excessive exposure to asbestos? Is it true that officers of the company were unaware of the connection between asbestosis and certain other respiratory diseases, including cancer? Or is it true, as many of J-M's critics contend, that company officers conspired for more than 40 years to both deny and cover up any knowledge of the long-term ill effects of working with and around asbestos and asbestos products?

2. If it is true that Manville did conspire to cover up any knowledge of ill effects of asbestos, is the company justified in petitioning the government for its support in establishing a compensation program for asbestos victims?

3. In regard to general product liability, how far back can claims be made against a company? More importantly, is it just to sue a company when, at the time, it acted legally, cautiously, and in good faith?

4. Given that Manville was simply the producer/supplier of a product and not the contractor, designer, or an agent in charge, is the federal government justified in denying further responsibility?

5. A major by-product of Manville's actions may be the restructuring of the legal responsibilities of industrial insurance carriers. Specifically, how does an insurance company determine a valid claim, and when may a company decide to deny or withhold a claim?

6. Can the 1978 Federal Bankruptcy Act be used as a means of seeking relief from possible future claims and liabilities?

• *Case Study* •

Italian Tax Mores*

ARTHUR L. KELLY

The Italian federal corporate tax system has an official, legal tax structure and tax rates just as the U.S. system does. However, all similarity between the two systems ends there.

The Italian tax authorities assume that no Italian corporation would ever submit a tax return which shows its true profits but rather would submit a return which understates actual profits by anywhere between 30 percent and 70 percent; their assumption is essentially correct. Therefore, about six months after the annual deadline for filing corporate tax returns, the tax authorities issue to each corporation an "invitation to discuss" its tax return. The purpose of this notice is to arrange a personal meeting between them and representatives of the corporation. At this meeting, the Italian revenue service states the

*This case was prepared by Arthur L. Kelly based on an actual occurrence. Mr. Kelly is a member of the Board of Directors of several corporations in the United States and Europe and formerly President and Chief Operating Officer of LaSalle Steel Company. Copyrighted 1977. Reprinted by permission of the author. All rights reserved.

amount of corporate income tax which it believes is due. Its position is developed from both prior years' taxes actually paid and the current year's return; the amount which the tax authorities claim is due is generally several times that shown on the corporation's return for the current year. In short, the corporation's tax return and the revenue service's stated position are the opening offers for the several rounds of bargaining which will follow.

The Italian corporation is typically represented in such negotiations by its *commercialista*, a function which exists in Italian society for the primary purpose of negotiating corporate (and individual) tax payments with the Italian tax authorities; thus, the management of an Italian corporation seldom, if ever, has to meet directly with the Italian revenue service and probably has a minimum awareness of the details of the negotiation other than the final settlement.

Both the final settlement and the negotiations are extremely important to the corporation, the tax authorities, and the *commercialista*. Since the tax authorities assume that a corporation *always* earned more money this year than last year and *never* has a loss, the amount of the final settlement, i.e., corporate taxes which will actually be paid, becomes, for all practical purposes, the floor for the start of next year's negotiations. The final settlement also represents the amount of revenue the Italian government will collect in taxes to help finance the cost of running the country. However, since large amounts of money are involved and two individuals having vested personal interests are conducting the negotiations, the amount of *bustarella*—typically a substantial cash payment "requested" by the Italian revenue agent from the *commercialista*—usually determines whether the final settlement is closer to the corporation's original tax return or to the fiscal authority's original negotiating position.

Whatever *bustarella* is paid during the negotiation is usually included by the *commercialista* in his lump-sum fee "for services rendered" to his corporate client. If the final settlement is favorable to the corporation, and it is the *commercialista*'s job to see that it is, then the corporation is not likely to complain about the amount of its *commercialista*'s fee, nor will it ever know how much of that fee was represented by *bustarella* and how much remained for the *commercialista* as payment for his negotiating services. In any case, the tax authorities will recognize the full amount of the fee as a tax deductible expense on the corporation's tax return for the following year.

About ten years ago, a leading American bank opened a bank subsidiary in a major Italian city. At the end of its first year of operation, the bank was advised by its local lawyers and tax accountants, both from branches of U.S. companies, to file its tax return "Italian-style," i.e., to understate its actual profits by a significant amount. The American general manager of the bank, who was on his first overseas assignment, refused to do so both because he considered it dishonest and because it was inconsistent with the practices of his parent company in the United States.

About six months after filing its "American-style" tax return, the bank received an "invitation to discuss" notice from the Italian tax authorities. The bank's general manager consulted with his lawyers and tax accountants who suggested he hire a *commercialista*. He rejected this advice and instead wrote a letter to the Italian revenue service not only stating that his firm's corporate return was correct as filed but also requesting that they inform him of any specific items about which they had questions. His letter was never answered.

About sixty days after receiving the initial "invitation to discuss" notice, the bank received a formal tax assessment notice calling for a tax of approximately three times that shown on the bank's corporate tax return; the tax authorities simply assumed the bank's original return had been based on generally accepted Italian practices, and they reacted accordingly. The bank's general manager again consulted with his lawyers and tax accountants who again suggested he hire a *commercialista* who knew how to handle these matters. Upon learning that the *commercialista* would probably have to pay *bustarella* to his revenue service counterpart in order to reach a settlement, the general manager again chose to ignore his advisors. Instead, he responded by sending the Italian revenue service a check for the full amount of taxes due according to the bank's American-style tax return even though the due date for the payment was almost six months hence; he made no reference to the amount of corporate taxes shown on the formal tax assessment notice.

Ninety days after paying its taxes, the bank received a third notice from the fiscal authorities. This one contained the statement, "We have reviewed your corporate tax return for 19– and have determined that [the lira equivalent of] $6,000,000 of interest paid on deposits is not an allowable expense for federal tax purposes. Accordingly, the total tax due for 19– is lira 3." Since interest paid on deposits is any bank's largest single expense item, the new tax assessment was for an amount many times larger than that shown in the initial tax assessment notice and almost fifteen times larger than the taxes which the bank had actually paid.

The bank's general manager was understandably very upset. He immediately arranged an appointment to meet personally with the manager of the Italian revenue service's local office. Shortly after the start of their meeting, the conversation went something like this:

GENERAL MANAGER: "You can't really be serious about disallowing interest paid on deposits as a tax deductible expense."

ITALIAN REVENUE SERVICE: "Perhaps. However, we thought it would get your attention. Now that you're here, shall we begin our negotiations?"[1]

Note

1. For readers interested in what happened subsequently, the bank was forced to pay the taxes shown on the original tax assessment, and the American manager was recalled to the United States and replaced.

Questions for discussion

1. Would you, as the general manager of the Italian subsidiary of an American corporation, "when in Rome" do as other Italian corporations do or adhere strictly to U.S. tax reporting practices?

2. Would you, as chief executive officer of a publicly traded corporation (subject to Securities Exchange Commission rules, regulations, and scrutiny), advise the general manager of your Italian subsidiary to follow common Italian tax reporting practices or to adhere to U.S. standards?

• THREE •

Pollution and Environment

The Eskimo and some subcultures in India regard pollution as a philosophical concept. For such persons, to pollute is to injure the harmony that exists between people and nature. Hence, one should avoid polluting not only the physical environment but also one's social environment. In western Europe and the United States, we have tended to view pollution more narrowly. We have defined it largely in a physical manner, referring primarily to air pollution, water pollution, radiation pollution, waste-disposal pollution, and noise pollution. For our present purposes we shall define "pollution" as "the presence in the environment of a substance produced by human beings that renders the environment less fit for life." Notice that this definition is sufficiently broad to accommodate pollution inside the workplace as well as outside it.

Concern about pollution mushroomed during the 1960s with the appearance of such books as Rachel Carson's *Silent Spring*, a chilling forecast of the destruction that pesticides such as DDT could bring to bird and animal populations. During the 1960s, not only were DDT and other pesticides restricted by congressional legislation, but broad regulatory mechanisms were also established under such acts as the Clean Air Act and the Clean Water Act. Unfortunately, for Congress to put legal teeth into its legislation sufficient to force business into compliance, these acts were forced to wait until the early 1970s and the passage of the Clean Air Amendments Act and the Clean Water Amendments Act.

An economic concept crucial to an understanding of pollution issues is that of an *external cost*. Economists define external costs as *costs of production borne by someone other than the producer*. Under this definition, the production of steel would involve both external and internal costs. Producing steel requires iron ore, coal, and skilled labor. These are all internal costs, since they are borne directly by the producer. But steel production also typically involves the discharge of pollutants such as sulfur dioxide and sulfur trioxide into the atmosphere, and such pollutants are notorious for defacing and weakening steel and marble structures. And since the structures damaged are typically not owned by the steelmaking firms themselves, these costs must be counted as external ones. From an ethical point of view then, the push is to make external costs internal. In other words, the push is either to require the steel company to compensate those who are harmed by the pollution, or—as is usually done—to require the company to pay for pollution-control devices sufficient to deter pollution damage.

Becoming clearer about pollution issues requires a healthy sense of realism. The goal of *zero discharge*—in other words, no pollution at all—is probably a dream. Pollution experts note that the cost of eliminating pollutants from a given production process is inversely and exponentially related to the percentage of pollution remaining. That is, as a manufacturer spends money to control pollution, the first 50 percent of the pollution is relatively inexpensive to eliminate; but eliminating each remaining percentage point of pollution is dramatically more expensive. Indeed, for many production processes, eliminating 100 percent of the pollution is infinitely expensive, or, practically speaking, impossible.

The cases in this section focus on the question of the extent to which corporations must exercise internal moral responsibility in addition to simply following laws in regard to environmental use. The "AES Corporation" brings into focus some of the fundamental issues and questions that should be raised in the formalization of any environmentally sensitive production policy: the size of the project; short-term vs. long-term impact; alternatives and options; financial vs. social costs. The "Chainsaws of Greed" case deals with a number of fundamental issues confronting the environmentalist movement and the needs of an industry based on limited natural resources. It asks, How can we, as a society, balance our needs to do business with our ever-diminishing supply of national resources? Can we rely on business to protect the environment? Or is state regulation absolutely essential to carry out the goals of the conservationist movement? Finally, the Exxon case deals with the 1989 oil spill in Prince William Sound, Alaska. This case deals with an ecological disaster at many levels: Exxon's lack of contingency plans for the possibility of an accident; Exxon's lack of screening procedures for employees in critical positions; and Exxon's and the government's recalcitrance in regard to clean-up and restoration.

• *Case Study* •

The AES Corporation

THE MANAGEMENT INSTITUTE FOR ENVIRONMENT AND BUSINESS

A*

On an afternoon in mid-1987, Roger W. Sant was in a rush to get back to his office. As Chairman of the Board and CEO of the AES Corporation, and a board member of several environmental organizations, Sant felt the company ought to assume more accountability for its contribution to the build-up of greenhouse gases in the atmosphere. He had just spent another day as a member of a World Resources Institute global warming panel where he had become more convinced than ever that excessive carbon dioxide in the lower layer of the earth's atmosphere would be one of the main causes of global warming, should global warming occur.

As one of the nation's leading independent power producers, AES had a commitment to meeting the energy needs of its customers at the lowest possible cost, a strategy which Sant and his colleagues had developed and written about while with the Mellon Institute ten years previously. Although they had successfully operationalized their mission on "least cost," they felt a competing responsibility to minimize the company's impact on the environment. This accountability for social costs was integral to AES's value system, which put social responsibility as the first, and conditional order of business. Unfortunately, the least cost option for power generation in the U.S. does not have the lowest environmental impact. Coal-fired cogeneration plants are significant emitters of carbon dioxide, a gas which is not regulated by law, but which is the key greenhouse gas. As soon as he arrived at the office, Sant called Roger Naill, Vice President of Planning Services, and Sheryl Sturges, Director of Strategic Planning, to discuss the problem of how to offset these carbon dioxide emissions so that AES could bring its cost strategy in line with its value system.

The Company

The AES Corporation was co-founded in 1981 by Roger W. Sant and Dennis W. Bakke to capitalize on the market potential for cogeneration (the sequential generation of steam for industrial uses and electricity for sale to utilities). The company entered the business of developing, owning and operating independent (i.e., non-utility) cogeneration facilities in 1981, and in 1983 began the construction of its first plant. By 1987, AES had grown to 215 employees with annual revenues of over $40 million and two operating cogeneration facilities: AES Deepwater, a 140-megawatt petroleum coke-fired facility and AES Beaver Valley, a 120-megawatt coal-fired cogeneration facility.

AES's primary objective in 1987 was to meet the growing need for electricity by being a safe, reliable and efficient power supplier in the independent power market. AES used a six-part strategy to develop its core cogeneration business and maintained a critical corporate value system to achieve this objective. The six-part strategy was as follows:

- *Project Size:* AES typically focused on larger projects, generally greater than 100-megawatts in size and $100 million in construction costs. The customer base for the electricity produced from these projects was electric utilities.
- *Least Cost:* AES offered its customers the "least cost" supply of energy. In the company's judgment, coal generally provided the best alternative to meeting this criteria. Coal is expected to be abundant and available from U.S. reserves for over 200 years. Also, prices for coal are less likely to rise than those of other fuels due to threatened shortages or political disruptions, enabling the company to obtain long-term coal supply contracts at competitive rates.
- *Long-term Contracts:* AES entered into long-term power sales contracts with electric utilities (i.e., 30 years) at a set electric rate with escalators that match those of the projected fixed and variable costs of operating the plant.
- *Careful Site Selection:* The company attempted to find appropriate facility sites before extensive capital commitment by optimizing the following key variables: access to fuel and waste transportation, water availability, potential steam or thermal markets, and local government and community acceptance.
- *Stand-alone Financing:* Each project, to the maximum extent possible, was financed without recourse to the Company or to other projects.
- *Commitment to Operations:* Because of the Company's commitment to the electric utility customer, it emphasized excellence in operations and believed strongly that it should operate all projects which it developed or acquired.

Key to AES meeting their stated objective apart from the above six-part strategy was maintaining a strong corporate value system integral to all operating decisions. The four shared corporate values at AES included:

- *Integrity:* To act with integrity and honor its commitments.
- *Fairness:* To treat fairly its employees, customers, suppliers and the governments and communities in which it operates.
- *Fun:* To create and maintain an atmosphere where employees can advance in their skills while enjoying their time at work.
- *Social Responsibility:* To undertake projects that provide social benefits, such as lower costs to customers, a high degree of safety and reliability, increased employment, and a cleaner environment.

This value system was created by and represented the personal values of Roger Sant and Dennis Bakke. They were of such importance to the founding members of AES that the company would adhere to these values even at the cost of a lost profit opportunity.

The Thames Plant

During 1987, the company competed in and won the bidding competition to furnish Connecticut Power & Light 181-megawatts of base load power on an annual basis. Montville, Connecticut on the Thames River was chosen as the site for the new "Thames" coal-fired cogeneration plant—estimated to begin commercial operation in 1990.

The 181-megawatts to be furnished under the 25 year contract was enough power to provide electricity to over 100,000 homes. The Thames plant would also supply up to 100,000 pounds per hour of steam to Stone Container Corporation's Uncasville paper recycling plant under a 15 year contract.

The fuel source for the plant was planned to be West Virginia coal, supplied by CSX Transportation, Inc. under a 15 year contract. The coal would be burned in two state-of-the-art circulating fluidized bed boilers, which produce lower stack emissions than conventional boilers, and are significantly cleaner than all current and proposed federal, state, and local standards (see section "Coal Technology").

The forecasted capital investment of the project was $275 million, with AES holding 100% of the economic interest. By the end of 1987, the project was beyond the planning stage and under construction. However, limiting carbon dioxide emissions had not been incorporated into the project planning or original cost estimates. AES estimated that the Thames plant would emit over 15 million tons of carbon over its expected 40 year life.

The Independent Power Industry

Historically, electricity generating plants were constructed almost exclusively by regulated utilities, municipalities and rural electric cooperatives. In 1978, Congress passed the Public Utility Regulatory Policies Act of 1978 (PURPA) that fostered a new market of electricity generation produced by independent producers. The legislation required utilities to purchase power from independent power producers (IPP's) at a price at or below the utilities' "avoided" or incremental supply cost. By the late 1980's competition for these supply contracts was driving down the prices for electricity, making it difficult for small IPP's to compete. AES relied on its proactive environmental position as a means of setting it apart from its competitors.

In the *1987 AES Strategic Outlook,* the following statement summed up the state of competition in the independent power industry:

> Our best guess is that over the long-term, the utility industry will restructure towards competitive (deregulated) generation . . . When this happens we want to be the least cost (and most reliable) producers of electricity in order to survive in a deregulated market. Even in the near term, we are facing stiff competition from utilities and other IPP's in our bids to obtain electric contracts. We therefore need to lower our costs to obtain new electric contracts and maintain all of our plants profitably.

Coal Technology

Since World War I, over half of the electricity in the U.S. has been generated by coal-fired power plants. With the uncertainty of nuclear power and oil supply, coal-fired power plants in 1987 were expected to contribute up to 70 percent of electric power in the U.S. by the end of the century.[1]

The U.S. is estimated to have coal reserves for over 200 years, and long-term contracts can be arranged with coal producers. This economic advantage of locking in a low-cost fuel supply as an offset to fixed price electricity contracts has been a leading cause for the U.S. power producers to continue building coal-fired power plants.

Most coal-fired power plants are used for larger "base load" facilities, rather than "peak load" facilities. Base load power plants are used 24 hours a day, and shut down for maintenance only about every two years. Peak load facilities run during intervals of high usage, such as mid-day during the summer months when air conditioning loads are high. The variable operating costs drive the profitability of a base load plant; coal and nuclear power are the most common base load fuel because the fuel costs are so low.

Despite the fact that coal has long been a major source of U.S. electricity, coal has never been considered a very efficient fuel for power plants. Coal contains less energy per unit of weight than natural gas or oil; it is expensive to transport; and there are many hidden environmental costs to using it. Coal-burning plants generate emissions of sulfur dioxide, oxides of nitrogen, and carbon dioxide, gases which may fall back to the earth as acid rain or contribute to global warming. Of the various sources of air pollution in the U.S., coal-fired power plants account for about 70% of all sulfur dioxide emissions, 30% of all oxides of nitrogen emissions, and 35% of all carbon dioxide emissions.[2]

Development of new technologies for burning coal cleanly was a key issue during the 1980's for the utility industry and AES. Congress created a national initiative to demonstrate and deploy clean coal technologies to industry. Emission control systems accounted for as much as 40 percent of the capital cost of a new plant, and 35 percent of its operational costs.[3] Maintaining the lead in clean coal technology was inherent to AES's commitment to social responsibility. Creating the most energy efficient and low cost pollution controlled plants was also critical to maintaining their competitive advantage in the bidding process to win new electric contracts.

AES used a circulating fluidized bed (CFB) combustion technology to capture 90 percent or more of the sulfur released from coal during combustion while minimizing the formation of oxides of nitrogen by operating at a lower temperature. The advantages of this technology are its energy efficiencies and the flexibility for AES to purchase a range of coal qualities in the marketplace, reducing operating costs. In 1987, 78% of utilities were considering implementing the CFB combustion technology, making the technology less unique to AES and threatening their competitive cost advantage.[4] Thirty-six coal-fired cogeneration plants out of a total of 78 power plants were either under construction or planned through the year 2000 to satisfy a 1.5% to 3.6% forecasted growth in electricity demand.

Global Climate Change

The earth's temperature is a function of the rate at which the sun's rays reach the earth's surface and the rate at which the warmed earth sends infrared radiation back into the atmosphere. "Greenhouse" gases such as carbon dioxide and methane trap this infrared radiation in the lower atmosphere, resulting in warmer temperatures. Human activities during the last century have increased the concentrations of these naturally occurring greenhouse gases primarily through the burning of fossil fuels. Powerful new gases such as chlorofluorocarbons (CFC's) that are released through chemical processes have also intensified the "greenhouse effect" of the earth's lower atmosphere.

In 1987, the link between growing atmospheric concentrations of greenhouse gases and eventual global warming was becoming of greater interest world-wide to scientists and policy-makers. The Environmental and Energy

Study Institute, established by Congress and chaired by Roger Sant of AES, published a Special Report in 1987 summarizing the state of the global warming controversy:

> Recent studies support projections that the earth's surface temperature will climb in the next century by several degrees—to a level never experienced by humans. For virtually every effect, the amplitude, timing, and, in some cases, even direction of the projected changes are uncertain.[5]

Since scientists began measuring the mean global temperature over a hundred years ago, 1987 was the warmest year on record, and the 1980's the warmest decade on record.[6] Nevertheless, there were questions about the cause of leveling and slight downward trend of temperatures between 1940 and 1965, and the reliability of earlier measurements. Some scientists were also skeptical that these temperature trends represented simply a normal fluctuation from the thirty-year climate average rather than any link to the greenhouse effect.

The Department of Energy created climate models that estimated a 1.5 to 4.5 degrees Celsius (3 to 8 degrees Fahrenheit) increase in average global temperatures over the next 75 to 150 years using current carbon dioxide emission rates, and potentially double that increase with the other greenhouse gases included.[7] However, both the magnitude and the timing of global warming remain uncertain, and many related determinants of future climate change are still inadequately understood. For instance, climate models cannot predict how the thermal inertia of oceans may slow any temperature changes caused by increased greenhouse gases over the next several decades.

Roger Sant at AES thought the linkage between greenhouse gas buildup and global climate change was plausible. He also knew that carbon dioxide emissions were a primary contributor to the greenhouse gas buildup: global emissions of carbon dioxide in 1987 contributed to 57% of all greenhouse gas emissions. His research showed that the United States annually generated approximately 23% of global carbon dioxide emissions, and that U.S. energy producing plants alone generated over 6%.[8]

Although carbon dioxide emissions can be tied directly to industry smokestacks, they are also an integral part of virtually all natural and combustion processes. There is no single, identifiable source of carbon dioxide emissions, making the control of carbon dioxide through legislation particularly difficult.[9] Due to this fact, the Clean Air Act and its amendments never have included regulation of carbon dioxide emissions. By 1987 no legislation had been proposed to control carbon dioxide emissions, nor was there any expected to be considered in the near future.

Offsetting the Thames Plant Carbon Dioxide Emissions

Roger Sant presented the problem of carbon dioxide emissions from the Thames power plant and their possible relationship to global warming to Naill and Sturges. He asked them both to come up with some options to offset the carbon dioxide emissions for the next operating committee meeting in two weeks.

Neither Naill nor Sturges had a great deal of background knowledge on greenhouse gases nor the natural carbon cycle process. They did, however, know what kind of project would meet AES operational needs. Sitting in Naill's office, they developed the following criteria to evaluate the various alternatives:

a. **Cost of the alternative must not exceed 1% of capital cost of project (approximately $275 million).** If greater than this amount, the pool of investors would need to be advised and the electric sales contract would need to be modified. Such action would undermine AES's credibility and competitiveness.

b. **Carbon dioxide must be disposed of permanently.** For example, selling it to beverage companies to enhance to enhance the carbonation in their drinks would not permanently remove the carbon dioxide from the atmosphere.

c. **The alternative must be technologically feasible.** A solution is needed that solves the problem but maintains the viability of AES as a business.

d. **The alternative preferably has other positive social benefits aside from carbon sequestration.** The project itself is assured greater sustainability over the long-term and can be enhanced by financial leverage from other investor-related parties if it has further humanistic value than simply carbon sequestration.

The Alternatives

After developing these criteria, Naill passed the problem on to Sturges. After extensive investigation into the issue, Sturges came up with the following alternatives. The first three could be implemented for the Thames plant specifically, and then repeated for other coal-fired power plants. The last dealt with a strategy shift for AES, that would not only affect the carbon dioxide emissions but would drastically change the way AES does business.

1) Promote energy conservation of 180-megawatts per annum to offset the carbon dioxide emissions from the Thames plant. The Electric Power Research Institute estimated in 1986 that a 50,000-megawatt reduction in energy use was achievable during peak hours through industrial, commercial, and residential conservation and load management.[10] However, at that time, only a handful of utilities were focused on demand side energy conservation. Part of the problem of energy conservation programs was that, to assure project conservation goals were achieved, each individual user's old and new electricity utilization rates needed to be measured and aggregated. This made monitoring costs extremely high in relation to total conservation program costs.

Because utility companies had direct access to the residential market, their incremental cost of conservation marketing was minimal. AES did not have this access, so the company was limited to commercial and industrial sectors to target energy conservation. These sectors represented over 70% of all electricity end use in 1986.

A means of promoting conservation in these sectors was through "lighting retrofits." On average, one-third of commercial/industrial electricity costs were attributed to lighting. Lighting retrofits replaced short-lived fluorescent lights with longer life fluorescents that lasted up to ten years. The customer would not only save on operation costs for replacement of the lights, they would also save 30 to 40 percent on their electricity bills. In order to obtain 180 megawatts of conservation, AES would need to form partnerships with several utility and industrial companies to establish in excess of 100 lighting retrofit contracts with individual end-users. As well, a monitoring system would need to be implemented to guarantee that the end-users remain faithful to the lighting retrofits, the cost of which at this point was unknown, but thought to be very expensive.

2) Employ a technology that scrubs carbon dioxide from plant exhaust gases. Find a means to permanently remove them from the atmosphere. Carbon dioxide can be removed from smokestack emissions using liquid solvents or solid absorbents and converted into gas, liquid or solid blocks. A variety of new systems were available, at a very high cost, to perform this task. For instance, the Brookhaven National Laboratory uses the chemical solvent monoethanolamine to separate the carbon dioxide. The system, however, costs $50–300 million per plant in 1980 dollars. Also, extra energy capacity would be needed to run the removal system, lowering the overall efficiency of the plant. At the Shady Point plant currently operated by AES, the capital cost of 4% carbon dioxide removal was approximately $10 million.

A secondary market for carbon dioxide existed; however, the price of purified carbon dioxide kept the market small. The only potential market for captured carbon dioxide emissions that would not cause the emissions to be re-released into the atmosphere was enhanced oil recovery (EOR). This process injected carbon dioxide into rock formations during exploration and production of crude oil, pushing out excess crude otherwise unattainable. The carbon dioxide was then recycled by the oil company.

According to the authors of EPRI 4631 *Chemistry and Uses of Carbon Dioxide:*

> The [EOR] activity is intense; probably the only reason that more projects are not in place is the shortage of Carbon Dioxide. This has been a problem for years and awaits a solution.[11]

In developing a market for carbon dioxide, AES had three major considerations:

- the volume of carbon dioxide it would capture and resell could exceed the market demand.
- a sudden increase in carbon dioxide supply could drive current inflated prices down.
- the company had to be sure that the carbon dioxide would not be re-released into the atmosphere (criterion b).

An alternative to selling the carbon dioxide in the EOR market would be to store the gas deep in the bottom of the ocean so that it could never be re-released. The cost of this process, in addition to the carbon capturing technology installed in the plant, would be considerable.

3) Halt deforestation or encourage reforestation to increase amount of carbon removed from atmosphere by trees. AES determined that the Thames plant would emit 15.5 million tons of carbon over the plant's 40 year life. Rather than attempting to capture or conserve the carbon dioxide using man-made processes, this third option utilizes the natural carbon cycle to absorb or "sequestrate" the carbon dioxide emissions. The natural carbon cycle consists of plants/forests and oceans absorbing and emitting carbon particles as part of a natural process. The man-made portion (combustion processes, deforestation, etc.) represents only a small fraction of the carbon flows moving through this cycle. However, this intervention permanently affects the magnitude of the total process. By planting more trees or minimizing deforestation, for instance, the influence of the coal-fired combustion process can be minimized, returning the carbon process back to its more natural order.

Sturges came up with the following table to determine how many trees would need to be planted to offset the 15.5 million tons of carbon from the Thames plant. The numbers vary based on the type of tree (planting density and growth rates are critical factors), and the health of the soil being planted.

Area per 180-megawatt plant

Acres	32,400 to 127,800
Hectares	12,960 to 51,120
Square Miles	54 to 200

This table compares to nearly 410 million hectares (1 billion acres) of land that is currently recovering from "slash and burn" agricultural techniques in developing countries which could greatly benefit from reforestation work. Sturges also learned that trees in tropical areas grow more quickly thereby absorbing carbon more rapidly in the earlier years. Based on these figures, and discussions with various international development agencies, Sturges determined that the cost of such a project would be between $1.5 to $8.0 million in a tropical developing country, assuming that the reforested land would not need to be purchased. The development agencies believed that AES could leverage its financial input by collaborating with local groups that may provide cheap sources of labor or contribute to the funding of the reforestation project. The company could find land for reforestation near Connecticut, where the plant was to be located, however, the costs of the labor would be prohibitive. As it was, labor costs were projected to be 50% to 75% of the total project cost.

4) Reevaluate current strategy of coal-fired power plants as least cost technology. What are other long-term strategic options open to AES that may represent a least "social" cost?

Natural Gas

The most efficient technology for the natural gas fuel source in 1987 was combined cycle plants. These plants use combustion turbines which can burn natural gas, distillate, and residual oils allowing the risk of shortage or price variations to be spread across three products. The combustion turbines produced few or no sulfur dioxide emissions if the quality of the fuels burned is controlled. Nitrogen oxides are emitted, but could be mitigated through a secondary process of injecting water or steam into the system. Still, the amount of nitrogen oxide produced by natural gas is, per unit of energy, equal to or greater than that of coal. Carbon dioxide emissions from natural gas plants are approximately two-thirds that of coal.

Capital costs were approximately $600 per kilowatt for a combined cycle plant, as compared to $1000 per kilowatt for a coal-fired plant with CFB technology. However, fuel for the combined cycle technology was very expensive comparatively and subject to price swings; operating costs for natural gas ranged two to three times greater than that of coal. Also, plant profitability was at risk because the cost of the natural gas fuel could exceed the fixed price electric power sales contract developed by an independent power producer. Conservatively, the combined cycle option might add as much as 15% to AES real economic cost of doing business if gas price forecasts were to be realized.[12]

Renewables: Biomass, Wind, Hydro and Solar

Biomass refers to energy stored in plant and animal organic matter. The primary resources of biomass energy include wood wastes, agricultural residues, animal manures, the organic portions of municipal solid waste, landfill gas and sewage. Utilization of available biomass for energy production was estimated at only 25% in 1985.[13] However, biomass primarily provides energy for individual use rather than electricity sales. For instance, the lumber industry derives almost 75% of its energy from direct wood combustion and the pulp and paper industry derives 51% of its energy needs from wood.

The most promising biomass technology is waste-to-energy, which converts solid waste into aleable energy through incineration. Capacities typically of these plants are only 1 to 80-megawatts, with capita costs ranging from $500–$1600 per kilowatt. Most waste-to-energy projects must be developed through an alliance between a developer and municipality. The plants must also be located close to waste centers and to population centers, raising environmental concerns. Pollution from waste-to-energy plants varies based on the combustion method of the plant and the composition of the waste. However, little data exists as to the danger of the pollutants produced, and few regulatory standards have been established to monitor the emissions.

Wind energy is one of the fastest growing renewable technologies in the 1980's due to tax incentives passed in the Wind Energy Systems Act of 1980. However, these incentives expired during 1985, making wind energy production less appealing to investors. Over 95% of the U.S. development in wind energy production has been in California, in part due to state incentives. Wind is a clean, free and renewable source of energy with short lead times and few off-site environmental impacts. Major disadvantages are that wind is an intermittent energy source subject to unforeseen variations; it requires extensive land use potentially leading to land erosion, generates noise pollution for nearby home dwellers, and interrupts bird and wildlife migrations. The capital costs for wind technology range from $900 to $1200 per kilowatt, with most project size under 20-megawatts.

Hydropower harnesses the kinetic energy in falling water to produce electricity. The total capacity in the United States in 1985 was 79,000-megawatts or one-eighth of the nation's total generating supply. Because of the competing uses of rivers as water sources, and the depletion of available rivers for damming, most domestic development would need to be concentrated at existing dam sites with generating potential of 25-megawatts or less. In comparison with other renewable energy sources, hydropower's potential is limited due to its past high exploitation. A primary environmental advantage of hydropower is that it does not require combustion, therefore limiting any damage to air quality. However, the dams can have negative effects on wildlife, scenic river valleys and recreational uses of rivers, inhibiting future growth of hydropower. The process of obtaining a hydropower license has therefore become extremely expensive, arduous and time consuming.

Solar energy refers to technologies that convert energy from sunlight into thermal energy, which eventually becomes electricity. With tax incentives expiring year-end 1985, the solar industry could not maintain the financial support to continue growing as did the other renewables. As a result, capital costs of solar are higher than other renewable alternatives ($2000 to $3000 per kilowatt) and operating costs are burdensome. Most solar projects are under 30-megawatts of power.

The Operating Committee Meeting

Roger Sant had asked Naill and Sturges to present their recommendations at an upcoming operating committee meeting in October—two weeks away. Sturges knew that the operating committee members would be receptive to creative solutions that enhanced the company commitment to social responsibility. She also realized that the fourth option, changing the long-term strategy of AES from coal-fired power plants to natural gas or renewable energy could not be applied to the Thames plant which was already under construction. For the board meeting, she needed to present one of the first three options as a means to offset the carbon dioxide emissions.

Understanding the value structure at AES, she knew that eventually the company would need to reevaluate its least-cost strategy of coal-fired power plants to incorporate environmental externalities and generate a "total cost" strategy. For right now, she would have to leave that to later strategic planning meetings. Sturges turned to her computer and started working on the presentation of the alternative she knew was the right choice for the Thames plant and for AES.

B*

The Choice: The Guatemala Reforestation Project

With some trepidation, Sturges approached the 2:00 pm Operating Committee Meeting with her presentation materials. Sturges ran through the implications of the greenhouse gas buildup in the ozone and its potential link to global climate change. Then, she recommended that AES should fund a reforestation project in a tropical developing country to offset the carbon dioxide emissions that may be contributing to that buildup. She defended the project as being the most technically feasible, potentially coming under the 1% of capital costs of Thames, having positive social implications, and ensuring AES's position as the least cost supplier of clean coal-fired power plant energy. She paused to let the idea sink in, and was greeted with an exclamation from Dennis Bakke, President and Chief Operating Officer of AES: "Great idea Sheryl!"

The company asked The World Resources Institute (WRI) to advise them on the implementation of a reforestation, or tree-planting, program in a developing country. Over the next six months, WRI convened a panel of foresters

---

*Reprinted by permission of The Management Institute for Environment and Business. Copyright © 1992 by MEB.

and development experts to analyze various proposals from development agencies to implement the reforestation program. A project with CARE, an international relief and development organization, was chosen to help 40,000 smallholder farmers in Guatemala plant more than 52 million trees over a ten-year period. A total of 385 square miles of trees will be planted, one megawatt worth of carbon emissions for each two square miles planted. The forty year sequestration would amount to 19 million tons of carbon in the following manner:

35% Carbon mitigated by developing managed woodlots
- wood harvested would be used for building materials and firewood
- 15% new growth; 20% protecting existing forest
  60% Carbon mitigated by agro forestry planting
- trees help stabilize farm land, add nutrients to soil
- all 60% of mitigation is from protecting existing forests
  3% Carbon mitigated by preventing forest fires
  2% Carbon mitigated by adding carbon to soil

AES was able to leverage its $2 million grant into $14.5 million worth of funding from the following sources:

U.S. Peace Corps (labor value)	$ 7.5 million
U.S. AID (food aid)	$ 1.8 million
Guatemalan Government	$ 1.2 million
CARE	$ 2.0 million
AES	$ 2.0 million
Total	$14.5 million

WRI announced the project in a press release on October 11, 1988. Reaction to the carbon offset initiative was mixed. The *New Yorker* ran a cartoon depicting a sooth-sayer absolving a corporation of its pollution sins by telling the corporation how many trees to plant. On the other hand *Time* ran a short article calling the project "a healthy environmental equation." Two other publications, one an environmental advocacy magazine and the other an academic research journal, described the project in a very positive light and expressed a hope that the project would be emulated by other companies in the future. Because the feedback from the press was overall quite positive for AES, the small independent power producer in the United States gained international recognition, helping their eventual expansion overseas.

Investors in AES were worried and confused over the non-profit project, and the utilities, AES' primary customers, felt threatened that the initiative might force them to invest similarly to offset their carbon dioxide emissions. Some consumer groups where Thames was being built were also disappointed that the reforestation project would not involve their local community.

The company, and in particular Roger Sant, was not interested in the initiative as a public relations tool. Rather, Sant wanted to fulfill his commitment to the AES four corporate values (integrity, fairness, fun, and social responsibility) through the project. The total costs of the Guatemala project contributed approximately one-tenth of one cent per kilowatt to the cost of producing electricity at the Thames plant. AES' share was about one-seventh of that cost. Even in light of increased competition driving down the potential profitability in the independent power industry, the company took the risk and sponsored the project, maintaining its commitment to social and environmental responsibility.

The Sustainability Task Force

During the annual AES strategic planning process, the sustainability of coal-fired power plants, and its long-term viability in comparison with other fuel alternatives, was continually being analyzed. In early 1991, Roger Sant requested that Roger Naill spearhead a Sustainability Task Force that would extensively investigate alternate forms of fuel supply for AES new power plants. The company had not yet signed an electric contract to develop a new power plant since the Thames project, so the door was wide open to encouraging a realignment of AES basic business strategy of "least cost" through coal-fired power plants.

The charge of the task force was to find an energy fuel that was steady-state and 100% sustainable from an economic and environmental aspect. The task force, not surprisingly, found no fuel that would have both cost stability in the long-run (such as coal) and zero environmental externalities. What they did find is that the best means for AES to approach the sustainability issue would be to "hedge" their portfolio and begin looking into alternative fuels other than coal. In looking at a 50–100 year period, which includes the extended life of a power plant, it made sense to begin development of natural gas projects as well as coal. Incorporating this vision of a "total cost" strategy, the company is in fact now developing natural gas contracts both internationally and in the U.S.

Notes

1. Balzhiser, R. E., and Yeager, K. E., "Coal-fired Power Plants for the Future," *Scientific American*, vol. 257 (September 1987), pp. 100–107.

2. Corcoran, E. "Cleaning up Coal," *Scientific American*, May 1991, pp. 107–116.

3. Balzhiser, R. E., and Yeager, K. E., *supra* note 1.

4. "*1987 AES Strategic Plan*: Background Data and Issues," 1987.

5. Robock, A. "The Greenhouse Effect: Global Warming Raises Fundamental Issues," Environmental and Energy Study Institute Conference Special Report, September 1987.

6. "The Global Greenhouse Finally Has Leaders Sweating," *Business Week*, Aug. 1, 1988, p. 74.

7. Robock, A., *supra* note 5.

8. "The Looming Crisis in Electric Power Generation," April 4, 1989, Dennis P. Meany, Booz-Allen & Hamilton, Inc.

9. Peters, M. B. "An International Approach to the Greenhouse Effect: The Problem of Increased Atmospheric Carbon Dioxide Can Be Approached by an Innovative International Agreement," *California Western International Law Journal*, Winter 1989, pp. 67–89.

10. Keelin, T. W., and Gellings, C. W. *Impact of Demand-Side Management on Future Customer Electricity Demand*, Electric Power Research Institute Report EM-4815-SR, October 1986.

11. *Chemistry and Uses of Carbon Dioxide*, Electric Power Research Institute Paper 4631, 1987.

12. *1987 AES Strategic Plan*: Background Data and Issues.

13. Fenn S., Williams S., and Cogan D., *Power Plays: Profiles of America's Leading Renewable Electricity Developers*, Washington, DC: Investor Responsibility Research Center Inc. (1986).

Questions for discussion

1. Which alternative is the right one for the Thames plant?
2. What is the morally preferable strategy to take for future electricity generation?
3. How should AES proceed in the future?

• *Case Study* •

The Chainsaws of Greed:
The Case of Pacific Lumber*

LISA H. NEWTON

The bare facts of the Pacific Lumber Company chronicle are shortly told and widely known: once, there was a very traditional company, Pacific Lumber, based in its company town of Scotia in Humboldt County, California, home of the legendary 2000 year old Sequoia trees. And it took care of its workers, conserved its giant redwood trees, turned a modest but steady profit, planned for the long term, and, in brief, made none of the mistakes that all the short-sighted lumber companies made. A California Newsreel documentary, "Mad River: Hard Times in Humboldt County," made in 1982, excoriated the entire industry for its miscalculations of its market, its failures toward its workers and its destruction of its trees—but took time out to mention Pacific Lumber, as proof of the fact that good business and good citizenship could, with wise management, go hand in hand. Then came the villains, jetting in from Wall Street: the takeover artists, the sharks, Charles Hurwitz's Maxxam Inc, recently spun out of Federated, soon to be joined with MCO, who gobbled up the company's stock, bought off the management, threatened the workers' jobs and benefits, and immediately doubled the timber harvest to pay down the junk-bond-financed debt. Overtime pay fattened the workers' wallets but threatened long term security; environmentalists were horrified; state and national legislatures contemplated action but took none; the courts, to whom all resorted almost immediately, tentatively fumbled through new territory, not supporting any side consistently.

Despite, or because of, the fairytale quality of its story, Pacific Lumber crystallizes several of the most important ethical issues confronting American Business, in particularly poignant and understandable form: the company is small, the trees are large and well loved, the loggers are folk heroes, the financiers are folk villains, and covering it all, the press and the senators are highly articulate commentators and critics of the whole affair, a Greek Chorus with power of subpoena. From the materials available to us chronicling this case, we recognize five familiar issues, and the organization of this presentation will follow them in logical order:

1. At the outset: Is the traditional (paternalistic) American company worth preserving, as the traditional American Family Farm is held to be? Or is profit, return on investment to the shareholders, the only measure of good business practice?

2. Should "hostile takeovers" financed by "junk bonds" be outlawed, in light of the crime they invite and the injury they produce? Or are they just good business, working for the interests of the shareholders and the efficiency of the American economy?

3. What shall we do to save our national natural resources? Can we rely on business to protect them? Or is state regulation absolutely essential for anything of value? If the interests of a single state are not served by conservation, does the country as a whole have a right to dictate such policies?

4. In the present structure of the judicial branch and the corporate sector, it is entirely possible that resources might be irretrievably lost in the process of seeking legal means to protect them. Under the circumstances, are extreme and illegal tactics like those of Earth First! justified? How should a business deal with such tactics?

5. Who speaks for the worker? What courses are open to the employee in this confusion? To form a union? Join with management to drive out the environmentalists? Join with the environmentalists to drive out management? Or try to buy the company themselves?

1. Old Fezziwig vs. Ebenezer Scrooge: How to Run a Business

No one denies that Pacific Lumber Company was an exemplar of all the virtues traditionally professed by American Business. Founded a century ago, run from the turn of the century by one family, the firm undertook to protect equally the shareholders, the workers and the natural environment, and was doing very well at all of those tasks.

a. From the point of view of the shareholders, the firm had shown profits steadily since its founding, and stood to show profits steadily into the future. Financial statements for the years through 1984 show small cyclical adjustments to demand, but steady earnings on its outstanding shares.[1] Prudent management of its assets, 189,000 acres of the redwood forests of Humboldt County, California, including the largest virgin redwood stands still in private hands, ensured that no more was cut each year than grew, and avoided the boom-and-bust cycle endured by the rest of the lumber industry.

b. From the point of view of the workers, that policy worked out to steady employment; but PL was famous for employment policies that went far beyond the certainty of a job. The town of Scotia, in the center of the lumbering area, was one of the last of the company towns, wholly built and owned by PL; the houses were rented to the workers at rents that were low even for that area, and in hard times the company forgot to collect the rent. No one ever got laid off, or faced retirement or medical emergency without funds to cover them. A worker's children were assured jobs with the company, if that's what they wanted, or a full scholarship to college. Company loyalty came easy, and no union ever got a foothold in PL. "They always treated everyone so well, why rock the boat?" explained a former employee. "You knew you'd retire from there, and if your kids wanted to work there, they would. . . . People cared for the company and wanted to see it prosper."[2] We hear the echoes of Old Fezziwig, Ebenezer Scrooge's first employer in Charles Dickens' *A Christmas Carol,* who ran a business as a service for customers, employees, and the community at large; people came before profits in this operation.

Those employment policies can be examined from perspectives other than that of the workers. From the point of view of the share-holders, all that money paid out to meet the needs of the workers was money that could have been paid to the owners in dividends; on the other hand, in a shareholder-oriented climate, the workers would have joined a union, and paying union wages and union-obtained medical and other benefits might have been considerably more expensive; contractual obligations must be met before any owners get anything. From the point of view of the society at large, PL was a real bargain. When a worker is laid off, the company saves his wage, but the society has to pay unemployment; when a worker is too old or sick to work, if the company does not pay for him, we do, through our taxes. "Paternalism," the bygone policy of placing the company *in loco parentis* for the worker, at least where the satisfaction of his material needs were concerned, simply allocated a portion of all social welfare costs to the last company that employed the recipient of that welfare. Is that the proper role of the corporation? Is that an efficient way of allocating social costs? It may be, from the point of overall efficiency, that there is little to choose from between the paternalistic policy that picks up the costs for the worker and the new "lean and mean" company policy that lets the taxpayer pick up the tab. Some observations on the point, however, may be in order: (1) The company is closer to the worker and his situation than are the taxpayer and his hired agent, and is better able to meet real need and monitor for fraud; (2) Union officials have to be paid, and government agencies have to be paid a great deal; where companies administer these funds directly, there is no need to pay the middlemen, and those unproductive jobs in the bureaucracy are not added to the economy.

c. From the point of view of the environment, PL's record was excellent: not only was the selective cutting good for business in the long run, but it spared the hillsides the devastation wrought by clearcutting. Since the 1930's, it has been known that cutting all the trees on a hillside leads to the immediate dispersal or destruction of the wildlife, the erosion of the soil to the point where new trees will grow poorly or not at all, the consequent silting of the streams and the destruction of the fish, and, from the increasingly rapid runoff of the rain into the silted streams, the undermining of the downstream forests. The environmental deterioration proceeds quite without limit; and in the very steep and rainy forests of the Pacific Northwest, it proceeds very quickly. Most lumber companies in the area, in the rush to capitalize on the sudden demand for lumber for housing after the second World War, had moved to clearcutting as a more efficient way to get lumber out of the forest quickly, and had severely degraded their lands. PL had not done this; it stood as a living demonstration that prudent business practices equal sound labor relations equal sound environmental practices. Beyond sound conservationist cutting policy, PL had contributed substantially to the State Park system. Pursuant to an agreement with the Save-the-Redwoods League in 1928, PL set aside many of its most scenic groves for purchase by the State of California, for inclusion in the Humboldt Redwoods State Park. When the money was slow collecting, PL "held on to the land it had agreed to preserve, patiently paying taxes on it, letting people use it as if it were already a part of the park," until the money finally came through and the acquisition was complete—in the case of the last parcel, 40 years after the original agreement.[3]

• • •

So from the point of view of the usual list of "stakeholders" in the operations of any corporation, then, PL exemplified that "excellence," of which we made so much in the early 1980's, when the new breed of management consultants started writing their bestsellers.[4] But should management be working for "excellence?" The New Greed has driven anything approaching that description off the Bottom Line in fashionable circles. Scrooge's singleminded approach to business was not new in Dickens' time. Since Adam Smith, those who stand to profit from massive financial transactions have argued that capital is "most efficiently put to use" in that employment where it yields its highest monetary return in the shortest possible time, and that therefore the general welfare is best served by leaving financiers free to seek such a return.[5] Even the notion of the "stake-holder" is disagreeable to Scrooge's children, the defenders of the new business orientation: John Boland, writing in the *Wall Street Journal* in February, 1988, complains that shareholders have a right to protest the "diminished status" of "stakeholders" assigned to them by the community-oriented managers of the companies whose shares they hold; "the only direct, clear legal obligation of corporate fiduciaries (beyond obeying civil law and contractual constraints in general) is to corporate owners who pay them."[6] If return to shareholders can be significantly increased by management practices which are not to the advantage of the workers, or the community, or the natural environment, are the corporate fiduciaries—the officers of the corporation—obliged to adopt them?

Such a question is ordinarily academic: a company which has undertaken to consider the welfare of workers, community, forests and future, in all its decisions for a century and more, will not suddenly change to suit the new imperatives from the business Right. But in the Reagan-era climate of hands-off regulatory policies, there arose another way to direct cash into the shareholders' pockets: the hostile takeover. In the "takeover," for those who have been in the Amazonian jungle for the last ten years, a "raider" (elsewhere "shark") with truly astonishing amounts of cash, most of it borrowed at very high interest from investment banks that specialize in this sort of transaction, offers to buy up the stock of a corporation (the "target") at a level well above the market price. The shareholders of the moment get a much better price for their stock, should they tender it for sale, than they might have expected. Where the stock is held by institutional funds, and most outstanding stock is these days, the fund manager is under a fiduciary obligation to the fund's owners to get that price, and to tender the stock; loyalty to the company whose shares are in question is nowhere on the manager's possible list of obligations. Having (therefore) obtained a majority of the stock with rather little effort, the raider takes control of the company, then pays down the debt with the assets of the target. Of course, once in control, he can do anything else he likes with the assets. And the attractiveness of that control, especially where the assets are large and surely profitable, may tempt the raider to marginally legitimate means in pursuit of his ends. Such, at least, were the allegations in PL's case.

2. Shady Deals in the Canyons:
Michael Milken and the Sharks

In 1985, Pacific Lumber was debt-free, cash-rich (including a workers' pension fund overfunded by $50–$60 million), resource-rich beyond the knowledge of the Board of Directors (it had been 30 years since the last timber cruise, or inventory of its timber resources), and complacent in the knowledge that its practices were sound and well accepted by the community. Meanwhile, merger mania was in full swing, and Michael Milken was riding high at Drexel Burnham Lambert. On October 2, 1985, backed by Milken's "junk bonds"—the high-risk, high-yield notes that were Milken's specialty—the New York based Maxxam Group, led by Charles Hurwitz, an investor from Houston, Texas, made a tender offer of $38.50 per share for the company, almost $10 more than the then current market price of $29. PL's Board of Directors, led by CEO Gene Elam, obviously stunned by the attack, rejected the offer as not only "inadequate" but "unconscionable." Two weeks later, they accepted a Maxxam offer just 4% higher than the first, or $40 per share. Many analysts were surprised by the acceptance; they had reckoned the company as worth far more than that, and indeed, the entire increase from the first offer was funded, with change left over, from the pension plan. What had happened? Speculation turns on the following questions:

a. How was the Board of Directors taken by surprise? Were the infamous arbitragers Ivan Boesky and Boyd Jeffries involved with a scheme to "park" stock in friendly parking lots while the motives of all concerned were concealed from those who were charged with protecting the company? (How come, just as the deal got under way, Jeffries sold about 439,000 shares of PL stock to Maxxam at $29.10 per share, when the market was closing at about $33 per share?)

b. What kind of advice did they get? They hired Salomon Brothers to advise them, on a curious arrangement whereby Salomon would receive 2.25 million to keep PL independent but almost twice that if PL was sold at any bid higher than the $38.50 per share then offered. Maxxam was clearly willing to go higher; what incentive did Salomon Brothers have to oppose them?[7]

c. The major new provision in Maxxam's final offer of $40 per share included agreement to indemnify the Board of Directors against shareholder lawsuits, and to fund severence packages of up to two years' pay for 34 middle managers and "key people." When President Elam quietly left the company in June, 1986, he took with him $400,000 in such severence. Were all those people really thinking about the interests of the company when they hastily agreed to a friendly merger?[8]

Lawsuit after lawsuit challenged the takeover: from Stanwood (Woody) Murphy, grandson of the last CEO, and his brother and sister, contending that the supermajority required by the company charter (80% of shares) had not been obtained; from shareholders contending that the Board had been negligent in failing to inform itself of the true value of the company, and had sold out much too cheaply; from other shareholders, contending that Article 10 of the company charter required that the Board take into account the social, environmental and economic effects on the employees and the communities before accepting any merger agreement, and that no such determination had been made. In what is possibly a bureaucratic first, the SEC was petitioned, by the Northcoast Environmental Center, to submit an Environmental Impact Statement—since the terms of the merger were such that, if approved, it would inevitably lead to vastly accelerated logging practices, and thus would have a major impact on the environment. But the legal climate is as chilly to traditional companies as the Canyons of Wall Street; by the end of February, 1986, most of the claims had been rejected and the way was open for the merger to be completed.[9] (One remains open, and when the SEC investigation of Drexel Burnham Lambert advanced to consider the PL case, another was instituted, brought again by dissident stockholders; if they are successful, the acquisition will be declared illegal and the ownership of the company will have to be renegotiated.)

How does a financier run a lumber company? Everyone knew, by the time the last suit was settled, that Hurwitz would abandon the old careful schedule of cutting in order to raise cash. Of the $840 million he had spent for the company, $770 million was debt, of which $575 million was financed through Milken's junk bonds; that debt had to be paid, with predictable results for the workers and for the environment; see below. It is doubtful that even the Board of Directors foresaw the financial transformations that were to follow. For a start, Hurwitz terminated the employees' pension plan. Of the total $90 million in assets in the plan at the time of the takeover, Maxxam took $50 million for the debt and spent the remainder to buy annuities for the 2,861 plan participants. In a move that alarmed some of the executives covered by the plan, Hurwitz chose to buy those policies from the Executive Life Insurance Company of Los Angeles, which has, according to *New York Times* writer Robert Lindsey, "provided annuities to employees at several companies taken over with Drexel Burnham financing. According to investigators, that insurance company was chosen for the annuities contract despite missing a bidding deadline." The executives were alarmed because "a large proportion of its assets are in high-risk securities, among them a significant share of the bonds issued for Maxxam's takeover of Pacific Lumber."[10]

Sometimes a page of history is worth a volume of logic. Had anyone chosen to investigate, it would have been found that Hurwitz had an established career in controversial financial deals. "Indeed," chuckled *Barron's* in a review of the PL deals, "his career has been a bonanza for the legal fraternity: Everything he touches seems to turn to litigation."[11] Throughout the 1970's, his holding company—SMR Holding Corp.—had been involved with questionable and sometimes disastrous deals, and he had had to defend himself from charges of improper practice and civil fraud brought by the SEC, New York State, and the Texas Securities Board.[12] In the course of his acquisitions, he had picked up Federated Development, whose financial resources he employed to take over McCulloch Oil Co., which he restructured into MCO Holdings in order to buy United Financial Group and take over Simplicity Pattern, whose cash he raided for his next ventures. Through many of these dealings, Drexel Burnham Lambert had been the underwriter, making cash available for these extensive, and very profitable, transactions. From January 1985 through the summer of 1987, Hurwitz paid Drexel "more than $48 million in fees, expenses and commissions, some $46 million of that through Maxxam."[13] Bear, Stearns also figured in Hurwitz' financial history, managing a discretionary account with $44.6 million of Maxxam's money and acting as broker for its other accounts. As a matter of fact, Bear, Stearns and Hurwitz had been partners in a run at Alamito Company in March 1986.

So there were complaints when Hurwitz announced, late in the summer of 1986, that he intended to merge MCO holdings and Maxxam into one company, "in the best interests of both companies," and called in both Drexel and Bear, Stearns to help with the deal—there was, indeed, an immediate shareholder protest, arguing that the shares of Maxxam, supported by the enormous cash and resource holdings of Pacific Lumber, were worth between twice and three times what MCO was "offering" for them. It seemed to the angry shareholders that the merger was simply a device for funneling all that wealth into a shell holding company where Hurwitz could get at it more conveniently. Delaware law required that the "negotiations" for purchase be carried on by two "independent committees" of the two organizations, advised by separate investment banking firms. So such committees were formed, of the only members of the Boards of Directors of MCO and Maxxam not on the other Board or with other connections to Hurwitz, and Drexel Burnham Lambert and Bear, Stearns were retained by the "two parties" to determine whether the deal was "fair" to all. With Hurwitz the largest shareholder of both firms, and his long-term business associates advising on both sides of the table, fairness was rapidly determined all around. When, in the middle of all the dealings, Drexel (representing MCO) leaped across the table to help sell off a few pieces of Maxxam's PL holdings for about 50% more than their accepted evaluation, the appearance of conflict of interest—not to mention sheer double-dealing on the part of all parties—became overwhelming.[14] Despite legal protests, the merger went through—with disastrous effect on the Standard and Poor rating for Maxxam's takeover bonds.

For reasons beyond lay comprehension, and with consequences that will become evident in section 4 of this case, legal delays do not appreciably slow down business operations. Hurwitz explained to his public that the cash generated from the accelerated harvest was to be used to pay down PL's debt. But tremendous amounts of cash can be generated from an established company with uncounted timber resources, and the New Finance avoids such tedious uses as payment of debt when new opportunities present themselves. By early 1988, Hurwitz was on the move again, this time against KaiserTech (formerly Kaiser Aluminum), paying $224 million for a large portion of their stock. At least half that will be paid in cash, apparently (despite denials) straight from the coffers of Maxxam's biggest moneymaker, Pacific Lumber. Of course, if the shareholders' suits are successful, all that cash would be taken away from Hurwitz; but not if he spends it first. Plaintiffs in the suits were predictably outraged, but it is not clear what legal action is possible to block the payments.

3. Who Speaks for the Trees?
The Logger and the State

The Law has already figured largely in this case, as the vehicle for private parties to express, and attempt to validate, their conviction that their rights have been violated. There is another place for the law, of course: not as instrument of the remedial rights of offended private parties, but as creator of primary rights for the society as a whole, to protect what we value as our common inheritance and to provide for the common good in the future. Presumably our elected representatives are the authorized determiners of that public interest, and ultimate protectors of the resources of the nation. Presumably, to come to the point, when we are dealing with unique and irreplaceable resources like stands of 2000-year old redwoods, we might expect that the public authorities will determine what policy for those redwoods best serves the public, and private profit-oriented enterprises will operate within the guidelines set down in accordance with that policy.

That expectation is not generally fulfilled in a country dedicated to Free Enterprise. On the contrary, the presumption had been that anything that can be privately owned, like land, will be privately owned; and that whatever owners have traditionally been permitted to do with their land, like cut down trees and sell the lumber, the owners shall be permitted to do. The burden is on the public to prove that private control of the uses of land is so contrary to the public safety that the situation cries out for regulation and public control. On the question, who speaks for the trees?, the lumber industry has answered with a single voice: we do, and we need no public regulation and environmentalist criticism to teach us how to protect our resources.

This voice can be heard in the lumber industry's publications from the origins of the industry, and especially since 1970, when the nascent environmental movement descended upon logging operations with renewed energy. When Maxxam took over PL, with obvious plans to go after the older stands of timber protected by the old owners, the debate over the need for state protection of the lumber took on new urgency. An ecologist with the Northcoast Environmental Center, Andy Alm, summarized the areas of danger from the new practices: depletion of the timber supply, erosion of the watershed areas, increased sediment loads on area streams (endangering the fish, all species that depend on the fish, all species that depend on the streams), and the possible extinction of many endangered wildlife species such as the spotted owl.[15] A cautious scientist, Alm conceded that at that point, the projected impact on the environment "is speculative." More assertive was Earth First!'s Greg King, who advocates the complete cessation of harvest of old growth timber. The spokespersons for PL, predictably, immediately presented views in opposition to the environmentalists: statements from a consulting firm hired by Maxxam reassure that PL "could easily continue to harvest its timber at the current doubled rate for the next 20 years," and that "PL is just helping to fill in the gap left by the other companies whose capacity in production was reached shortly after World War II." The county should be happy, the consultant concluded ominously, that there was a company like PL who was "there to fill the gaps when other companies are not only dropping off production but laying off workers."[16] David Galitz, the company's manager of public affairs, was similarly reassuring, concluding on the familiar note:

> We're here to protect the land. Our resource is that land and we know it. The trees are a crop, and they keep coming back. If you want to meet a group of environmentalists, come within the Pacific Lumber Company . . . I think we practice more environmental protection methods and have more concern for the environment than the Greg Kings of this world.[17]

The dispute inspires reflection, to be conducted, very briefly, in three questions: First, where, if anywhere, does private enterprise get the right to speak for the trees? aren't they naturally suspect in such a case? Second, if the trees are to be guarded for the sake of the people, where do the people stand on the issue? and if the people are divided, do those on the spot have more right to vote than the others? Third, given that the California Department of Forestry is supposed to be appointed especially to speak for the trees, where is its position on the issue and why don't we just listen to it?

a. Private enterprise's claim derives from the ancient truth of Galitz's statement: "our resource is that land and we know it. The trees are a crop, and they keep coming back." We come from a long line of farmers and herdsmen—about 800 generations, probably. Only since the last century, three or four generations, has it become possible for any but a tiny percentage of us to live any other way. The imperatives of the farmer and herdsman are abundantly plain: conserve the land, the flock, the ability of the farm to produce more in future, or die. Owners and caretakers of property in land or livestock, whether or not they were the same persons, had interests in common, closely tied, on a daily basis, to obedience to those imperatives. Cultures which disobeyed the imperatives died out; cultures which obeyed them well flourished, and produced us, who carry the same commands by now in all our understanding of our cultural inheritance. For the best of economic reasons, then, in that inheritance, the property owner has properly been trusted with the care and preservation of his property, and barring a few municipal regulations to preserve residential peace and quiet, the legal system has incorporated few restrictions on how he may use that property.

But ancient truth does not mean present workability. The business community took note of the "separation of ownership and control" of the modern corporation earlier in this century, largely to call attention to the troubling fact that those who run the corporation (management) may, on occasion, reprehensibly deviate from the desires of the proper owners (shareholders). Of more interest to the environment, specifically to the owned land and livestock, is the fact that, once separated from control and daily management, the owners may have no interest at all in the care of the property, which will be consigned to hired stewards. Such stewardship has itself a long tradition, and becomes problematic only when the steward is given responsibility, not for land or stock or factory or corporation, but for a sum of money, or fund, which owns property only to use it to make more money. This is the position of the institutional funds, mentioned above, whose stewards must, on pain of breach of fiduciary responsibility, tender shares to raiders on evidence that they are likely to see no higher price. When the raider himself, as is usually the case, has no interest in the property except to drain it of cash for his next ventures, his own future welfare disappears from the imperatives above, and the property is no longer safe in its owner's hands. Ought we to take it away from him? Do we have the legal structure to do so? We know that under the doctrine of "eminent domain" we can seize the redwoods for a new park; but can we seize all that land just to continue a more conservative commercial logging operation? Or is that choice necessarily Owners' Option, a case of "different management philosophies and needs which need to be addressed," as David Galitz put it?[18]

b. What do the people want? Most of the people in the area are employees of Pacific Lumber. Almost by definition, they want their jobs, and they want wages as high as possible. The rest of the people are the shopkeepers, craftsmen and service personnel who take care of the employees and the towns in which the employees live. Their interests are as intimately tied to the company as those of the loggers. The very limited options of the loggers will be taken up in section 5 below; for the present, we may ask how the people affected by these policies see the issue, without taking specifics of employment into account. One indication of the will of the people turned up in May 1987, in the California State Legislature in Sacramento. State Senator Barry Keene had submitted a bill, SB1641, which would "limit sudden increases of timber harvesting and clear-cutting brought on by potential change of ownership of logging companies."[19] No one who favored, or opposed, the bill had any doubts about whose ownership was being discussed. PL's executive vice president was one of those who spoke against it, predicting a "whole new round of timber industry layoffs" should the bill be adopted. It was not; it had some support, especially from environmentalist groups like the Sierra Club, but was voted down in Committee.

Legislatures can be influenced, of course, by persistent popular effort. As is typical in such political exchanges, the corporations organized first: the sawmills, logging and trucking companies got their representatives to the May 1987 meetings and defeated the Keene bill. The environmental groups, all volunteer, organize much more slowly. As Summer turned to Fall, these groups got an unexpected publicity boost from the Congressional investigations into Maxxam's tangled financial history. By Spring of 1988, the country had begun to notice what was happening in Humboldt County. An article by Richard Lovett in the *Sacramento Bee* in February told the PL story to a statewide audience. "While the future of old-growth forests is very much in doubt, one thing is certain," Lovett concluded, "The Pacific Lumber takeover is a frightening cautionary tale—an example of how progressive business management can be replaced virtually overnight, with decades of conservationist practices likely to be erased in only a few years.[20] Alarm went nationwide with an article by Robert Lindsey, dramatically entitled "They Cut Redwoods Faster to Cut the Debt Faster," in *The New York Times* in March, citing not only the extensive environmental damage caused by the new logging policies, but also the dubious financial maneuvers behind the takeover.[21] And in April, Earth First! staged some very public demonstrations on PL land, getting themselves headlines in California newspapers.

By May, 1988, Byron Sher, Chairman of the Assembly Natural Resources Committee for the California State Assembly, was able to launch a campaign to get PL to stop clearcutting (at least) the remaining stands of virgin redwood (at least). The demand seems minimal; yet even this would have been impossible without the negative publicity of the last six months. Under those circumstances, he was able to muster enough clout (he thought) to enforce a reasonable agreement. Such an agreement was made, on May 26, 1988, and proudly announced by Sher, Assemblyman Dan Hauser of Humboldt County, and Pacific Lumber: "Pacific Lumber has agreed to stop clearcutting its remaining stands of virgin redwood. . . . This is the practice it followed for decades and earned it a reputation as a model timber company in the eyes of many Californians . . ."[22] Sher's office simultaneously released a hopeful statement on the agreement, as did PL's public relations office (". . . the agreement reflects the Company's sensitivity to concerns expressed by Assemblymen Sher and Hauser, as well as others, over the aesthetic effect of clear-cutting in virgin old growth redwood stands.") *The New York Times* found the agreement sufficiently newsworthy to record—and recorded also the scepticism of local environmentalists and Woody Murphy: "If the wolf tells you that he no longer wants to eat chickens, who are you going to believe?" Indeed, with time, the volunteers go home and the paid agents return to the saw. By January, 1989, Sher was sponsoring a new bill calling for the whole industry to stop clearcutting older trees or face $50,000 fines for each incident. "Pacific Lumber has reneged on last year's agreement," said Sher. "They are moving as quickly as they can to destroy the old-growth characteristic of their virgin redwood holdings." In hindsight, he regretted the May 1988 agreement that had ended his pursuit of similar legislation.[23]

Letters to local newspapers during the period in which it was pending overwhelmingly opposed the bill. One letter, chilling in its naivete, shows how much the new owners relied on the old for their early support:

> Inasmuch as the cutting of trees is the timber companies' main source of revenue, surely Senator Keene does not think that they would purposely shorten their own existence by clear cutting their timber without a definite re-forestation plan in mind. As far as the Pacific Lumber Company is concerned, they would not have been so attractive an acquisition were it not for the fact that, through careful timber management, they have built a solid reputation spanning a hundred years or more for good business practices which include long range goals benefiting both themselves and their community. In conclusion, I feel that we need to have enough faith in the experts of the timber industry to allow them to continue to make the necessary, intelligent decision regarding the future of the logging in this area.

This was four months before Hurwitz's move to merge Maxxam and MCO, stripping the cash from PL to feed more takeover attempts, was made public. Another, from the owner of a local sawmill that purchased logs from PL, pointed out that his sawmill would be out of business if PL stopped cutting, and that "there will be less jobs!" if the sales should stop. "Instead of kicking a good neighbor and generous community supporter, let's get behind Pacific Lumber and give them all the support we can." A third, to finish this quick sampling of local sentiment, had

> a few thoughts on the Barry Keene 'Maxxam-shutdown' bill. . . . As we all know by looking at a map of California, a majority of the land is owned by some form of government, i.e., national parks or state parks. Now that Maxxam owns The Pacific Lumber Company 'private land,' Maxxam should be able to use it in the way the present guidelines are set up. They were good enough for everyone else, why not Maxxam? We don't need government harassment in Humboldt County! The county has been hurting enough these past few years. Is the Barry Keene bill another 'land grab' by the government? By forcing Maxxam into bankruptcy, are they going to buy the land for yet another rotting park? I am really tired of government and their 'screw up of everything they touch' record. My only consolation is that when Pacific Lumber closes down, my family and I can mooch off the government instead of paying taxes, and I'll have a lot of time to get involved in demonstrations to shut down other private industries.

From a sociological perspective, that letter is a delight. All the notes of blue-collar conservatism are there: anti-parks, anti-welfare, anti-government in general, pro-private industry, above all pro-jobs. The next section of this paper discusses the environmental movement; this letter shows as clearly as may be shown the agenda that the environmentalists faced in their public education activities.

Simultaneously, the Fortuna Town Council convened a special meeting, ostensibly to debate the Keene bill, but actually (in the absence of any supporters) to denounce it and pass a resolution to that effect. The participants in the denouncing were not, significantly, employees of PL, but residents of the town and officers of local trucking companies and sawmills; the entire area's dependence on the logging industry, and on the freedom of that industry to bring in cash, could not have been more emphatically underlined.[24]

Yes, but what of all the *other* people, like me, here on the East Coast, or in the South, or anywhere at all except in Scotia, or Fortuna, Eureka, Arcata, or Humboldt County generally? Don't we have an interest in the redwoods? If the people of the area only want to speak for Maxxam, can't *we* speak for the trees? Whose are they, anyway? Can't our ownership, as Americans, be taken into account somehow? How should it be balanced against the need in Humboldt County for jobs, security, a steady economic and political setting in which to raise children and carry on communities with a hundred years and more of settled existence? Their interests are more immediate, but there are a lot more of us. Do we have a way to allot votes in such situations? Do we even have a candidate for a way?

c. Recognizing some years ago that redwoods were sort of special, California had passed legislation requiring the lumber companies to file Timber Harvest Plans (THPs) with the state, and charged its Department of Forestry (the CDF) with the task of reviewing these THPs for environmental soundness and compatibility with the long-term benefit of the industry and the state of California. This the Department had done, without much controversy, for years, until the takeover of PL.

• • •

The CDF makes an early appearance in the PL affair, as participant in the debate, quoted above, between Greg King and David Galitz on the wisdom of trusting private enterprise with the care of the trees. The CDF's position might surprise those accustomed to chilly relations between industries and the state agencies appointed to regulate them: "To date, the department has found no significant impacts to the various biological or environmental resources as a result of The Pacific Lumber Company timber harvesting. Whether it be clearcutting or selection, this harvesting has been ongoing since the turn of the century. Hopefully, it will continue on indefinitely into the future. The actions of The Pacific Lumber Company are not expected to deter this prospect." So said Tom Osipowich, the forest practice officer with the CDF. One wonders why Maxxam felt it had to hire private consultants to present its case.[25] When the new PL started submitting THPs, the issue revived. Shortly after the Keene bill failed in Committee, the Environmental Protection Information Center, one of numerous environmental organizations active in this case, brought suit against PL and the CDF to oppose state approval of some of those THPs. In company with other environmental organizations, EPIC was worried not only about the amount of timber that would be taken, but about the old-growth dependent wildlife that would be displaced. "You have specific species of wildlife that are dependent upon old-growth stands," explained John Hummel, a wildlife biologist attached to the California Department of Fish and Game to a public meeting on the THPs. "If their habitat is taken away from them you're going to lose a significant number of the population of certain species."[26] Specifically, EPIC wanted to send its own experts into the forests to see if matters were as the company said they were, and to see if damage to the environment would be as slight as the CDF said it would be. On that issue, Judge Frank Peterson of the Superior Court ruled in favor of the company: no independent experts traipsing through private property second-guessing the authorized foresters. But on the larger issue, of the methods used by the CDF to reach its determinations, the judge was unsparing:

> . . . one can conclude that no cumulative impact study or findings were adequately made and no alternative to clear-cutting was considered. It appears that the CDF rubber-stamped the timber harvest plans as presented to them by Pacific Lumber Company and their foresters. It is to be noted, in their eagerness to approve two of these harvest plans (230 and 241), they approved them before they were completed. . . . As to the effect on wildlife, there was no evidence presented except the conclusion of the Foresters that there were no *concerned* or endangered species affected. Both the Water Quality personnel and Fish and Game relied on the information provided by the professional foresters hired by Pacific Lumber and the Department of Forestry. Fish and Game's position was, if the forester saw something that needed their attention, he or she would inform them. That is not compliance with the law. That is not only naive, it was a total failure to exercise any discretion by those agencies who by law are to make findings and recommendations upon which the director is to base and exercise reasonable discretion. . . . What is most distressing to the Court is the position of the Water Quality and Fish and Game personnel, that any suggestions by them would not be considered by Forestry, and in fact Forestry would consider it to be ill advised. . . . In this case it is apparent that California Department of Forestry, the State Board of Forestry, its resource manager and director, as the *lead agency* does not want Fish and Game or Water Quality to cause any problems or raise any issues which would deter their approval of any timber harvest plan. Again it must be emphasized, this is not following the law; it is not only an abuse of discretion, but an absolute failure to exercise discretion, which the law demands. . . .[27]

The CDF was not a little miffed by the public scolding, but promised reporters that the whole matter would be straightened out soon: "We'll just change the documentation of what we do so the judge will have less difficulty in understanding it," said staff forester Harold Slack.[28]

• • •

The story of the CDF is familiar, almost a paradigm for American politics. Underfunded and understaffed, the CDF cannot monitor the forests it is supposed to monitor even if it wanted to, which it does not. Given the leg-hold restraints on its operation, it cannot keep the bright young idealists that periodically pass through its doors, but settles for career government men who know that satisfaction in life depends on not rocking the boat. The boat, of course, is the huge and rich industry that they minister to, source of colleagues, support in the legislature, and jobs when they retire from government work. As long as the industry is kept happy, the only threat to their existence is turf infringement by other government agencies in the same line of work. So we find the CDF, like any typical "regulatory" agency, dividing its time between pacifying its legislature (to avoid scandal), adjusting its delicate relationship with its industry (attempting to balance its eager cooperation with a show of control in the public interest), and fighting turf wars with other agencies, like Fish and Game and Water Quality.

Why did we ever expect anything better? When we set up task forces within a company to get a job done, we know enough to structure the incentives so that it will at least be to the interests of the task force members to do the job. But in the CDF, we have an agency, and again, not an unusual agency, whose employees are rewarded both in daily dealings and in long term career prospects for *not* doing their job: for ignoring what they are supposed to know, for concealing what they are supposed to reveal, for handing over for destruction what they are supposed to protect, and in general, for serving as advocate, not for the people, but for the industry the people hired them to control. Is there a better way to get the people's business done? What?

No doubt political pressure can help. The agencies, after all, have to maintain at least the public appearance of right-doing. Judge Peterson's opinion effectively tarnished that appearance. The following months, then, show signs of diligence. The following April, the State Department of Forestry, for the first time, actually turned down two THPs proposed by PL. Ross Johnson, a program manager for the Department, cheerfully admitted that their decision was due to pressure by environmentalists. "Because we've had so many lawsuits, we're being more thorough in our review of these timber harvest plans," he explained to a *Times-Standard* reporter. "I guess you could give credit to these environmental groups. If we keep getting beat up on, we'll continue to do a better job." And PL will continue to keep the pressure on from its side: the company immediately appealed the ruling to the State Board of Forestry, to which the Department reports, and the Board saw things the company's way, overturning the Department's decision and giving PL permission to carry through the original THPs. So EPIC went back into court to sue yet again to force the State to do its job.[29]

The unfairness of it all brings tears to the eyes. The state appointed and taxpayer bankrolled agencies openly admit that only public exposure and humiliation brought about by pressure from private groups will make them do their jobs; for the rest, they serve the industry. Let them actually be frightened into conscientious action for a change, and their action can be overruled by a taxpayer-financed but politically sensitive Board, well aware of where the votes are next election day. And so, having paid for the Board, and paid for the agency, to protect the trees, if we really want, after all, to save the trees, we must sue as private citizens the very same public servants, and pay the tab for the private litigation as well. There has to be a better method—a more direct and effective method.

4. Do Earth's Ends Justify Extra-Legal Means? Enter Earth First!

Who, then, speaks for the trees? Once, the lumber companies, but no more. Legitimately, the people, but with no single voice. Authoritatively, the California Department of Forestry, but not well. Yet the trees need protection now, immediately, not in some rosy future when we will have responsible business practices and an enlightened people and dedicated public agencies. Each day that goes by means that responsibility, enlightenment and dedication will arrive too late for yet more groves of redwoods. And a grove of redwoods is not like other things your bulldozer might accidentally run over. It's more like you.

Ordinarily we will stop the bulldozer if you are in front of it. The reason we will stop it is complex: it is not just a matter of law, not just a matter of prudent use of resources, and certainly not just a matter of tender feelings for you—it is more a perception of the dignity of the unique in life, and some permanent injunction against destruction of that uniqueness, an injunction to be breached only prayerfully and in strict necessity. The point is worth examining further.

It is not just a matter of law. Law forbids me to chase you down the sidewalk with a bulldozer, or ram through your house on your lot. But if you should place some construction on my property, blocking the legal and appropriate work of my bulldozer, I will knock it down with no qualms at all. The law provides no protection at all for your stuff on my property against my will, and precious little formal protection for your body. What legal right you might have is easily removed by legal injunction, forbidding you to block my bulldozer with your body. Yet if you defy the injunction and show up in front of my bulldozer, I will stop. Why?

Certainly not because human beings are irreplaceable, or even endangered. On the contrary, they're replacing themselves faster than the biosphere can adapt, and we run the danger of flooding the surface of the earth with their bodies. No matter how many we run over, we can always grow more, and we could really do with less. Any cost-benefit analysis of the choice to stop or to keep going when you place your body in front of my bulldozer will yield an immediate solution: keep going.

I might decide to ignore the results of the cost-benefit analysis if I were particularly fond of you, of course. But what if I am not? Typically, the people that plant themselves in front of bulldozers are not the type that those bulldozer drivers would even like, let alone love. In the hardest case imaginable, that might be Charles Hurwitz in front of *my* bulldozer. Would I stop even for him? I probably would: the prohibition against placing the bulldozer in forward gear, opening the throttle, holding the steering levers in place until the human face disappears, first beneath the scoop, then beneath the treads, of the oncoming machine, goes beyond any feelings I may have. Where does it come from, then?

It seems to have something to do with respect for that which we cannot create, a totally unique center of life and spirit which, once gone, is gone forever. I can grow other human beings to replace you, of course, but they just won't be the same; there is no combination of individuals that will ever add up to, or duplicate you, do what you did or be what you were. This uncreatable uniqueness properly inspires in us reverence and respect, and leads us to agonize over every deliberate taking of human life, no matter how justified by law and conduct (witness, for instance, the extreme reluctance of the states to bring back capital punishment, and their even greater queasiness at applying it in an instant case).

Now, by this criterion, an old grove of redwoods has all the bulldozer-, or chainsaw-, stopping rights of a human being. (We will adopt as correct the environmentalists' assumption, that from the point of view of the environment, it is the ecosystem as a whole, not the individual tree, that is the viable unit, including all its soil mass, wildlife, water, air, even its insects, as well as flowers, moss, trees. By "grove," then, we will understand a stand of trees of sufficient size to support itself indefinitely, barring interference from outside.) It is unique and uncreatable, certainly uncreatable by us. We can plant redwoods, but we cannot plant 1000-year old redwoods. We can plant trees, but we cannot restore the soil that has been washed away after the last clearcutting, and therefore we cannot replace the floral ground cover, nor bring back the animals that lived on that assortment of plants dependent upon the shade and moisture of that grove. It is very difficult to create any ecosystem, let alone to recreate a particular ecosystem, and I think it could be argued that it is by definition impossible to recreate one that has been slowly coming to be over a millennium. When we are dealing with groves of this complexity and antiquity, we do not need to ask for the solution to a cost-benefit analysis, although some interesting analyses of the cost of extinction of species have been presented. We need only note that the grove in front of the saw can in no way be created or recreated by us, that it deserves our respect, and that we have no right to destroy it.

All of the above is by way of philosophical background to spikes in the trees. Earth First! (the punctuation is part of the name) is not one of your polite conservation-minded groups. Its specialty is "monkey-wrenching," tossing monkey wrenches into or otherwise fouling up any and all activities that destroy the environment. In addition to the usual suits and injunctions, the group's program includes burning billboards, pulling up developers' landmark stakes, and crippling bulldozers with nasty substances like maple syrup.[30] It should be noted that Earth First!'s actions on PL property were restricted to sitting in trees, talking to loggers, and occasionally serenading the company with guitar-accompanied renditions of "Where Are We Gonna Work When the Trees Are Gone," led by folk singer Darryl Cherney. (Cherney was at that time a candidate for the state legislature.) Occasionally arrested and sued at least once by the company, Earth First! quietly settled the suit and volunteered for community service instead of jail.[31] But they are not always so nonviolent. In their efforts to prevent other logging operations, their activities have been known to include spiking roads to cripple the logging trucks, and tree-spiking, driving a twenty-penny nail into a tree. The nail is easily concealed, and the operation doesn't hurt a living tree. But it does render the tree useless for lumber, because the nail chews up the blades of the saws. If the authorities are informed that a grove is spiked, and tells the logging company about it, a prudent company would not log that grove, until the spikes could be removed. If the spiking is sufficiently persistent, it may be impossible to log the grove.

Is this good environmentalist activity? "They are outlaws," says Jay Hair, President of the National Wildlife Federation, of Earth First!, "they are terrorists; and they have no right being considered environmentalists." "A terrorist organization," echoes Michael Kerrick, supervisor of the Willamette National Forest in Oregon; Cecil Andrus, former Secretary of the Interior, calls them "a bunch of kooks."[32] It is hard to find supporters for these tactics in the ranks of the traditional conservationist organizations, and even harder in the ranks of the government agencies charged with enforcing environmental regulation. But has anything else worked, for individual groves or ecosystems? Sometimes we can get tradeoffs—we agree not to press the matter on 15 or 20 acres of old-growth redwoods, and they will preserve some particularly desirable stretches in Alaska. But if it is a grove of trees more than a millennium old that is slated for destruction today, and the lumber company is in the hands of a Wall Street financier who wants only cash now, and local councils and legislatures are dominated by sawmill owners and the like, and the CDF approved the THP even before it was drafted, what other than terrorist tactics will work to preserve it? Perhaps the notion of a "tradeoff" is not entirely appropriate to the situation of the irreplaceable grove. If we trade off a grove for another today, what shall we trade tomorrow? For it is impossible to grow something of equal value to satisfy the appetite of the company. Only complete preservation will preserve the status quo ante, the balance that trades try to maintain. We do not, after all, always insist on tradeoffs in all matters, even in the political system. We never tried to get the Ku Klux Klan to lynch *fewer* Blacks, or only rural Blacks or Blacks in the Deep South states. Sometimes we had to endure lynchings, but the notion of a legal and accepted compromise on the numbers of lynchings never came up. It may just be that when we are dealing with fragile ecosystems, as when we are dealing with human beings, the rule of compromise, applicable elsewhere in environmental matters and in political matters generally, will have to be scrapped in favor of a rule of strict preservation, and no lobbying or legislative efforts should be spent in attempts to reach "compromise solutions." If this is the move of the future for the environmentalist community, we will owe, perhaps, more of a debt than we are willing to acknowledge to Earth First!

Meanwhile, how should a legitimate business react to terrorist tactics? If PL by now does not seem to be legitimate, the question can be raised about any other company or industry. How should we react to Pro-Life threats to smash all windows in the pharmacies that sell abortifacients? to Vegetarian threats to poison the cattle herds? to Muslim threats to firebomb the bookstores? The usual counsel, and indeed, *my* counsel, under all other circumstances, is to take the strongest possible measures to arrest and disable the terrorists, while conducting business as usual to show that terrorism is unavailing. Should that be our advice to Maxxam in its dealings with Earth First!?

5. Tell Me, Which Side Are You On?
The Tragic Options of the Loggers

While the well-oiled machines of finance whir on Wall Street, and the salvoes fly between environmentalists and the industry, what is the worker to do? The communications identifiably from loggers and their families in the local newspapers reveal above all a sense of loss for the destruction of the company they knew, and which they expected to take care of them until retirement and beyond. Above all, they want to preserve the lifestyle and security they had. But that, of course, is the one thing they cannot do. Beyond that loss, all other options lead to more loss.

a. Onward and Upward with Private Enterprise. They can side with the company, and applaud the wasteful acceleration of the logging. After all, it leads to plenty of work now, including overtime, and that feeds the wallet enough to block out that empty feeling in the soul when the clearcut hillside is finished and abandoned. Loggers prefer to drive pickup trucks; now the PL loggers drive new pickup trucks. It could be argued that the job, now so secure, will evaporate 20 years down the road, just as the jobs did at other companies, when the timber is gone. But 20 years is a long time; indeed, if you are a young father, raising four children between the ages of two and seven, 20 years is forever, or as long as you need, which is the same thing. In many respects, this is the most rational option for the logger, and certainly it was the one most taken. By June, 1988, PL employees had even founded a pro-industry anti-environmentalist newsletter, "a cooperative effort to gather support against radical environmentalists that are attempting, and in some cases succeeding, in halting our attempt to make a living." The editors maintained that the publication was "not company supported," inviting cynicism; the first accomplishment claimed for the effort was a successful letter-writing campaign to the State Board of Forestry, that brought about the approval of those THPs temporarily held up by the CDF.[33]

b. Save the Trees. The loggers can side with the environmentalists and try to get the trees, especially the old growth, preserved forever under some state umbrella. This course is not so immediately unlikely as it sounds; most loggers genuinely love the woods and streams among which they live, and enjoy outdoor recreation by choice. But it was never a real option for the PL loggers. First, there was the visceral hatred of the environmentalists: long-haired, dirty, foul-mouthed, middle class and instinctively contemptuous of workers, to all appearances Communist and drug-abusers, these hippies repelled the loggers from the day they bumped into town in their Volkswagens. Even Stanwood Murphy, their natural ally, found them repulsive. "I agree with them that the accelerated harvesting is the wrong way to go at it," he told *L.A. Times* staff writer Ilana DeBare, "But Earth First! is a radical group, and a lot of that I just can't associate myself with. [They look like] a bunch of college kids with ponytails. . . . You've got to look like the people you're trying to convince."[34] Second, and more enduringly important, saving the trees meant instant unemployment and the necessity of leaving the area for a very uncertain future elsewhere. The loggers were never for one minute unaware of this; as the sampling above indicates, PL spokespeople never opened their mouths without reminding the workers that if the environmentalists had their way, there wouldn't be any jobs. To a young head of a family, without any educational qualifications, such forced relocation is equivalent to suicide; environmentalism had very few friends among the ranks of the loggers.

c. Solidarity Forever. There had never been a union at Pacific Lumber. Was it worth a try after the takeover? One article, filed two weeks after the takeover was announced, reported that Local 3-98 of the International Woodworkers of America, AFL-CIO, was considering an organizing effort in response to a few requests from frightened workers. About all the union could do, its business agent conceded, was make sure that layoffs took place in an orderly manner, respecting seniority. Given the way the company had always been run, he foresaw a great deal of difficulty in convincing the workers of the need for a union: "The employees have to understand they can't deal with management as individuals anymore, particularly if they find themselves with an owner who lives thousands of miles away and doesn't know the lumber business. . . . They're going to have to deal with the company as a group with some power."[35]

Unions happened in America because men like Hurwitz took over industry from men like Stanwood Murphy. In the vast impersonality of the factory, reduced to an impersonal cog in an impersonal machine, laborers found support, identity and confirmation of their own worth, as well as political and economic power, in the union. Is it too late for PL workers to go that route? I suspect it is. I found no follow-up to 3-98's "consideration" of their case.

d. The Dream of Ownership. By September of 1988, the extent of the destruction of the timber lands was evident to everyone, and the workers had begun to talk about alternatives to unwavering support of present management. Could they take over the company? The ESOP, or Employee Stock Ownership Plan, was a new idea for the workers, but organizer Patrick Shannon assured them it was feasible. The appeal was undeniable: to be the boss, to be the owner, to be in control of one's destiny! Woody Murphy immediately came out in favor of it, but pointed out that with the large, and undiminishing, debt accumulated by Maxxam, there might not be enough money in the company any more to afford it. Hurwitz and William Leone, his CEO, immediately published an ad in the Eureka *Times-Standard,* insisting that the company was not for sale—but then, Shannon pointed out, it hadn't been "for sale" when Hurwitz and Maxxam acquired it in 1985.

It is not actually an ESOP that is contemplated; such plans are usually initiated by management and never give the workers actual control. Shannon is urging a hostile takeover by workers, requiring that they raise hundreds of millions of dollars to buy up shares on the open market until they have a majority. Is this even remotely possible? Hurwitz did it in 1985. But he had access to Drexel Burnham Lambert, and Boesky and Jeffries and Michael Milken and all of the creative financing of which Wall Street is capable. Above all, he had the assets of Pacific Lumber—the corporate headquarters in California, now sold, a valuable welding company, now sold, the extensive virgin timberlands, now stripped or soon to be so, and all the good will in the world—to serve as equity for those loans. "Employees who want to pursue the dream of an ESOP takeover have every right to do so," editorialized the *Times-Standard* in October, 1988, "Circumstances, however, suggest it's an impossible dream—one fraught with the potential for great disappointment and financial loss."[36]

6. Conclusion

Whatever facet of this case we have under consideration—the traditional company, with its rich inheritance of social responsibility and compassion for its workers and its land, the loggers, once secure in a relatively carefree existence, the community, once assured of a prosperous future, the financial institutions, once reliable custodians of conservative fiscal practices, or the giant redwoods themselves, that we always assumed would last forever—"great disappointment and financial loss" seem to be among the outcomes. At this point it is not clear whether criminal acts were involved in the takeover that opens our story, whether shameful betrayal is the correct characterization of the acts of the Board of Directors, whether the government agencies charged with regulating the timber industry are up to the job, whether the radical environmentalists are right in their employment of extreme measures, and whether, eventually, the workers will be able to get off the rollercoaster and take control of their situation. In these and other unclarities, the case raises questions about the conduct of a business in every one of its areas of constituent relations, and serves as a prism through which a multitude of issues may be seen in exemplar.

Notes

This paper was presented at the Eighth National Conference on Business Ethics, entitled "Business, Ethics, and the Environment," October 26 and 27, 1989, sponsored by the Center for Business Ethics at Bentley College, Waltham, Massachusetts. It [appeared] in slightly different form in *The Corporation, Ethics and the Environment,* editors W. Michael Hoffman, Robert E. Frederick and Edward S. Petry, Jr., (New York: Greenwood Publishing Group, 1990). Copyright © 1990 by Center for Business Ethics at Bentley College.

1. In the third quarter of 1984, for instance, less than a year before the takeover, PL reported that its net earnings rose 50 percent over the previous year ($11,337,000, or 47 cents per share, compared to $7,547,000, or 31 cents per share, for the third quarter a year ago). Sources include annual reports from the years 1981 through 1984.

2. Ilana DeBare, "Old Redwoods, Traditions Felled in Race for Profits," *Los Angeles Times* April 20, 1987.

3. The source for this statement is a brochure published by Pacific Lumber, no date visible.

4. See Thomas J. Peters and Robert H. Waterman, Jr., *In Search of Excellence,* New York: Harper and Row, 1982; Daddy of them all; then progeny, Terrence E. Deal and Allan A. Kennedy, *Corporate Cultures,* Reading: Addison Wesley, 1982; John Naisbitt and Patricia Aburdene, *Re-inventing the Corporation,* New York: Warner Books, 1985; Tom Peters and Nancy Austin, *A Passion for Excellence,* New York: Random House, 1985; Buck Rodgers, *The IBM Way,* New York: Harper and Row, 1986; Robert H. Waterman, Jr., *The Renewal Factor,* New York: Bantam Books, 1987.

5. The orthodox capitalist approach is possibly best captured by Milton Friedman in his oft-reprinted "The Social Responsibility of Business is to Increase its Profits," *The New York Times Magazine,* September 13, 1970.

6. *Wall Street Journal,* February 10, 1988.

7. Testimony of William G. Bertain, Attorney at Law, attorney of record for the Murphy great-grandchildren in the suit to retain control of the company, before Congress, on October 5, 1987; investigation of Drexel Burnham Lambert's major customers.

8. "Pacific Accepts Maxxam Bid," *The New York Times,* October 24, 1985; "PL agrees to buyout deal: New York firm's offer of $40-a-share accepted," *Times-Standard,* Eureka CA, October 23, 1985; "Money Talks," *Wall Street Journal,* November 13, 1985; "PL chief quits; gets $400,000," *Times-Standard,* June 10, 1986.

9. "PL-Maxxam merger hit by second lawsuit," *Times-Standard,* Eureka CA, November 1, 1985; "One PL suit dismissed, another filed locally," *Times-Standard,* November 2, 1985; "Pacific Lumber Bid Is Studied," *The New York Times,* November 8, 1985; "Ecology Interests question PL deal," *Times-Standard,* November 11, 1985; "Pacific-Maxxam Link Is Fought by a Family," *The New York Times,* November 11, 1985; "Maxxam Gets 60% Of Pacific's Shares," *The New York Times,* November 12, 1985; "Judge clears way for merger of Maxxam, PL," *Times-Standard,* February 13, 1986; "Another suit filed to block PL takeover, *Times-Standard,* February 23, 1986.

10. Robert Lindsey, "They Cut Redwoods Faster to Cut the Debt Faster," *The New York Times,* March 2, 1988. Attempts to secure PL comment on the allegations were unsuccessful; Mr. Hurwitz was "not available" for comment. The company lawyer, however, Howard Bressler, "said the company had complied 'meticulously' with all applicable laws in the merger," and that there was "nothing improper" about the handling of the pension plan.

11. Diana Henriques, "The Redwood Raider," *Barron's,* September 28, 1987, pp. 14 ff.

12. Ibid., p. 14.

13. Ibid., p. 34.

14. Ibid., p. 34.

15. Enoch Ibarra, "Pacific Lumber Timber Harvest Causes Concern," *The Humboldt Beacon* (Fortuna, California), January 27, 1987.

16. Ibid.

17. Ibid.

18. Ibid.

19. *Times-Standard,* Eureka, CA, May 5, 1987.

20. Richard A. Lovett, "The Real Costs—to All of Us—of a Corporate Buyout," *The Sacramento Bee,* February 21, 1988.

21. Robert Lindsey, "They Cut Redwoods Faster to Cut the Debt Faster," *The New York Times*, March 2, 1988.

22. Statement on Pacific Lumber Old-Growth Agreement, Governor's Press Conference Room State Capitol, May 26, 1988.

23. See also "Company Eases Its Policy on Logging of Redwoods," *The New York Times*, Friday May 27, 1988; PALCO news release, The Pacific Lumber Company, PO Box 37, Scotia, CA 95565, May 26, 1988; "Bill to Stop Clearcutting in the Works," *San Francisco Chronicle*, January 28, 1989; "Bill would restrict PL clearcutting of virgin redwoods," *Times-Standard*, Eureka, CA, January 31, 1989.

24. Letters to *Times-Standard*, May 5, May 13, and June 4, 1987. "Timber bill opposed," *Times-Standard*, May 2, 1987.

25. Enoch Ibarra, "Pacific Lumber Timber Harvest Causes Concern," *Humboldt Beacon*, January 27, 1987.

26. Greg King, "Fish and Game Says Pacific Lumber/CDF Eliminating Wildlife," *Humboldt News Service*, May 11, 1987.

27. Superior Court of the State of California for the County of Humboldt, case 79879, Ruling on Petition for Writ of Mandamus, Nov. 5, 1987.

28. See also "Judge sides with PL and CDF," *Times-Standard*, Eureka, CA, July 10, 1987; "Suit Against Pacific Lumber To Be Fought On PL Terms," *North Coast News*, July 16, 1987; "CDF won't appeal ruling," November 13, 1987, "CDF upset by court's decision," *Times-Standard*, November 15, 1987.

29. "Pacific Lumber Harvest Denied," *San Francisco Chronicle*, April 21, 1988; "P-L plans for cutting old growth under fire," *Times-Standard*, Eureka, CA, April 22, 1988; "PL temporarily blocked from harvesting old-growth again," *Times-Standard*, April 28, 1988; "Protecting Redwoods," *Los Angeles Times* editorial, April 26, 1988; "PL appeals ruling on timber harvests to forestry board," *Times-Standard*, Friday, May 6, 1988; "Judge lifts restraining order; PL allowed to log old growth," *Times-Standard*, June 3, 1988; "Environmentalists file new suit over PL logging plans," *Times-Standard*, June 16, 1988.

30. David Foreman, *Ecodefense: A Field Guide to Monkeywrenching*, 1985; cited in Jamie Malanowski, "Monkey-Wrenching Around," *The Nation*, May 2, 1987.

31. *Times-Standard*, Eureka, CA, April 8, 1988; May 1, 1988; *Times-Standard*, April 14, 1988 ("20 Arrested in Kneeland Anti-Logging Protest"); Publications from Darryl Cherney for Congress, PO Box 9, Percy CA 95467.

32. Malanowski, *op. cit.* p. 569.

33. Save The Employees Newsletter (Box 128 Scotia, CA 95565) June 13, 1988.

34. DeBare, *op. cit.*

35. Lewis Clevenger, "Local Union Considers Trying to Organize at Pacific Lumber," *Times-Standard*, Eureka, CA, November 8, 1985.

36. *Times-Standard*, Eureka, CA, October 11, 1988.

Questions for discussion

1. Ultimately, who is responsible for our natural resources?

2. Given the needs and demands of business, is it possible to manage our limited natural resources effectively?

3. Who are the real stakeholders, and what is really at issue in the Pacific Lumber case?

4. Is there a way to "save the trees" and "save the industry"?

5. Is it correct to assume that any harm to the environment is also a moral wrong?

• *Case Study* •
Exxon's Knee-Deep in the Big Muddy*

MICHAEL G. BOWEN • F. CLARK POWER

THE PREACCIDENT PERIOD

On Friday, March 13, 1968, a field containing an estimated 10 billion barrels of oil was discovered under the North Slope of Alaska at Prudhoe Bay. One year later, a consortium of seven oil companies, now named the Alyeska Pipeline Service Company, announced plans to construct an 800-mile-long underground pipeline to some point in southern Alaska where the crude oil could be transferred to tankers and shipped to refineries in the lower 48 states. The eventual choice for the oil terminal was an ice-free port, tucked away in the Chugach Mountains on the northern banks of Prince William Sound, that provided easy access to the Gulf of Alaska and shipping lanes to California: the town of Valdez.

The oil companies' original plans called for construction to begin on the trans-Alaskan pipeline in the following year (1970). They projected that the pipeline would be completed two years later. Approximately 2 million barrels of oil per day would be pumped from stations on the North Slope to Valdez Harbor, where tankers would carry the oil south. The companies, however, had not counted on the powerful reaction of environmental interest groups to their plans. Those groups forced Alyeska into protracted legislative and court battles.

Over the next four years, the environmental and economic effects of the proposed pipeline were subject to intense scrutiny. There was little substantive disagreement on the purely economic issues: The oil companies, the state of Alaska, and many Alaskans would make a great deal of money if the pipeline were built. Many other benefits would directly result from the pipeline project. Of these, perhaps the most important was the development of a major new domestic source of oil reserves which would reduce the United States' dependency on foreign energy sources. There was also surprisingly little disagreement on the environmental issues. The oil companies admitted that there was the possibility of accidents and spills, perhaps major ones. There was agreement that the permafrost along the pipeline would melt, that wildlife would be adversely affected, and portions of Alaska's wilderness and extraordinary scenery would be either defaced or destroyed.

There was substantial disagreement, however, on how to estimate the benefits and costs that would accrue from shipping oil across Alaska. How should the tangible benefit of economic development in the region be weighed against the intangible costs of defacing Alaska's pristine scenery; of disturbing

---

*"Exxon's Knee-Deep in the Big Muddy: Managerial Ethics and Decision Making During the 1989 Exxon Valdez Oil Spill," by Michael G. Bowen and F. Clark Power, University of Notre Dame. Copyright © 1990 Columbia University Graduate School of Business. All rights reserved. Reprinted with permission of Columbia University and the authors.

the habitat of the vanishing bald eagles, bears, and caribou; of poisoning fish and damaging the food chain?

The trans-Alaskan pipeline was approved, however, in 1973 when the U.S. Congress, reacting to the possibility of fuel shortages in this country and to the repeated assurances of oil industry and government experts that policies and procedures would be put in place to meet environmental contingencies, cut off the court challenges that had delayed construction. At a U.S. Department of the Interior hearing held in Anchorage in 1971, for example, Alyeska representatives pledged that the environmental effects of the pipeline operations would be minimal, promising prompt and effective handling of any land or sea spill. They announced that an oil response plan would be prepared so that operations at the Port of Valdez and in Prince William Sound would be the safest in the world. While the Alyeska consortium would shoulder responsibility to clean up any spills, the task of monitoring Alyeska's preparedness would be handled by the Coast Guard and the state of Alaska. Behind the scenes, Alyeska officials recognized (as can be documented in their actual cleanup plan) that it would be impossible for them to clean up a major spill.

Only Once in 241 Years

For the first couple of years after oil began flowing through the pipeline in 1977, Alyeska's performance at responding to oil spills, as reported by state of Alaska officials, was excellent. Detailed records were kept on the cleanup of even very minor spills, such as crankcase oil dripping underneath a parked automobile. No doubt part of this vigilance was due to the public uproar over the 1978 sinking of the supertanker *Amoco Cadiz* off the coast of France, which resulted in a spill six times larger than that of the *Exxon Valdez*.

Alyeska's safety record for the first decade of the pipeline's operation appeared remarkably strong. Although 25 percent of the oil pumped from the ground in the United States passes through the Port of Valdez, by the end of 1988, 400 reported spills had leaked only about 200 barrels into the Alaskan waters. In the three-month period from November, 1988 through January, 1989, however, 43 spills were reported in Alaskan waters—ranging in size from 10,000 to 2 million gallons—including a 1,700-barrel leak (efficiently contained and cleaned up) from a tanker docked at the Valdez terminal. In spite of this increase in accidents, Alyeska officials still seemed content that a major spill was not a realistic possibility.

Their confidence was based on an independent consulting report conducted for the oil company consortium and approved by the state, which concluded that a spill of between 1,000 and 2,000 barrels (46,000 to 92,000 gallons) was the most likely disaster that would occur in the projected 30-year lifetime of the Valdez terminal. Because the route from Valdez Harbor to the Gulf of Alaska was relatively easy to navigate, and because of the safeguards to be put in place before shipping began, a catastrophic spill like that of the *Exxon Valdez* was thought to be extremely unlikely—it may happen only once in 241 years. Nevertheless, when it was time for Alyeska and the state to negotiate a new three-year contingency plan, the state requested that Alyeska develop a scenario for dealing with a major spill. Alyeska balked, as it had whenever regulatory demands had been made. The compromise left Alyeska geared up to contain and clean up spills almost 175 times smaller than the one that occurred. Why did the state of Alaska ever agree to such a plan? What had happened to the oversight that the state and the Coast Guard had promised? From the moment the pipeline opened, the people of Alaska had benefited from the approximately $400,000 per hour in state revenues that have accrued. In the ensuing years, as the state became more and more financially dependent on oil monies and as no major spill had occurred, vigilance over the pipeline operation slowly began to relax.

Warnings?

The first warnings concerning the deterioration of state monitoring and Alyeska's ill-preparedness came from Dan Lawn, Alaska's Department of Environmental Conservation (DEC) Inspector in 1983, who detailed his charges in a 1984 memo. For all practical purposes they were ignored. In 1984, Alyeska failed to contain a relatively small (60-barrel) simulated loading spill in a state-administered test of Alyeska's response capability. In a 1986 test, Lawn judged that Alyeska failed again, although other judges rated Alyeska's performance as marginally passable. As Lawn became more critical, Alyeska officials resorted to calling him a "jerk and a trouble maker"; and George Nelson, the President of Alyeska, admits trying to get Lawn fired. Lawn persisted in his warnings, predicting only three months before the Valdez incident that the odds favored a major spill and that no one would be prepared.

Why wasn't anyone listening, especially at the state and federal levels? Three reasons appear obvious. First, the collapse of oil prices that occurred between 1984 and 1985 dropped the state's oil income from over $4 billion per year to under $2 billion per year. Alaska, which generated over 80 percent of its revenues from oil, was forced to cut services. Subsequently, the agency charged with monitoring Alyeska and the operations at the Valdez terminal, the DEC, cut staff to the point where there was no full-time state monitor of the oil terminal operations.

Second, the relative absence of serious trouble seemed to justify reductions in preparedness. With the safe passage of so many vessels through the Sound, the Coast Guard came to believe that it could responsibly reduce its inspections of tankers coming into and leaving Valdez Harbor. Over time, staffing of the Coast Guard monitoring station was cut back; around-the-clock supervision at the radar console was eliminated; and to reduce paperwork, the Coast Guard stopped manual plotting of ships' courses in and out of the channel in 1987. Further, the Coast Guard also judged proposals for an advanced radar system and an additional navigation monitoring system that would have tracked tanker traffic through the channel more effectively (and would have included a radar site on Bligh Island) to be too costly for the added safety.

Third, as public attention shifted to other environmental concerns, pressure to develop technology to prevent and clean up low-probability spills eased. For example, the federal government decided in 1987 to shut down the Oil and Hazardous Material Simulated Environmental Test Tank (OHMSETT) research facility in New Jersey.

Exxon

The relatively sudden, drastic drop in oil prices hit oil companies hard. In contrast to foreign competitors, the domestic companies in the industry had added pressure on them to become more productive and efficient in order to meet heavy short-term financial performance requirements coming from the U.S. investment community. What this meant in general was that companies had to curtail what could be identified as "unnecessary" expenditures within their organizations so that profitability would be stabilized at an acceptable level. Precautionary measures, such as putting double hulls around tankers—effectively reducing cargo area by 25 percent and dramatically increasing the cost of oil vessels—were simply ruled out as not cost-effective.

Unlike many of its competitors in the oil industry that had resorted to heavy cost cutting and organizational restructuring in the early to mid-1980s, the Exxon Corporation initially turned to a diversification strategy to bolster sagging performance. During this time, Exxon invested heavily in nonoil ventures such as office automation and electrical equipment, both later proving to be costly failures. More drastic internal changes began at Exxon in late 1986 only a few months before Lawrence Rawl, a long-time Exxon employee who was described by coworkers as blunt and arrogant, became chairman. Armed with a reputation as a heavy-handed "cost-cutter," Rawl directed Exxon's downsizing. Within two years, he had cut employment 30 percent to around 100,000, slashing away at layers of bureaucracy, consolidating operations, and selling off unprofitable businesses.

Efforts to become more productive at Exxon during this time often meant large changes in the way the company did business and worked with employees. In addition to layoffs, reassignments, and job restructuring, Exxon looked to implement any technological improvements which would lower its costs of doing business. This led to, among other things, taking the industry lead in constructing new, more highly automated oil tankers (such as the *Exxon Valdez*), which functioned with smaller crews.

To implement plans for higher efficiency within the company, managers were given some latitude in devising the desired productivity improvements. Some embraced the ideas of noted management expert W. Edwards Deming. The chief importer of modern Japanese management techniques, Deming stressed commitment to change, continuous innovation and quality improvement, and removal of communication barriers between workers and supervisors. Other managers subscribed to the Japanese practice of finding and achieving maximum productivity through pushing work systems to their productive limits (i.e., to the point where they start to crack and workers can no longer handle the load). While implementing these changes, management discovered, as have many companies that have been put through similar restructuring, that predictable problems arose: serious complaints of overwork, an erosion of management confidence, and sagging morale. "The problem with restructuring," Rawl later said, "is the human factor: Can people perform the job they're given? You can't test a person like a computer chip."

The changes that were made at the Exxon Corporation in those days did, however, seem to "work" for the company's shareholders. In 1987, for example, a leaner and meaner Exxon netted $375 million more than it had the previous year. In total, Exxon earned a net profit of $48,400 per employee that year: more than double the profit of key competitor Amoco and five times more than Mobil in the same period.

March 23, 1989

On Thursday night, March 23, 1989, no one was particularly worried about the *Exxon Valdez* or any of the other tankers taking on crude oil in Valdez Harbor. The Alaskan economy, although still depressed, was recovering from its deepest financial woes. Its officials, nevertheless, had not deemed it necessary to enhance vigilance of oil operations there. Perhaps no one from the DEC knew about or was concerned with the fact that Alyeska's single oil spill emergency barge was in dry dock for repairs.

For the leaders of the Exxon Corporation, this also seemed like just another quiet night. Exxon Chairman Lawrence Rawl spent the evening at home. For Captain Hazelwood, his officers, and the crew, it had been another exhausting day. Having put in long hours, the usual double duty, as the ship was loading, all were very tired. Even so, Hazelwood and two of his mates stopped by a local tavern for a few drinks. At 9:25 P.M. the supertanker left the terminal at Valdez Harbor loaded with 1,250,000 barrels of crude oil.

There was nothing out of the ordinary going on in Prince William Sound that evening, not even the free-floating icebergs drifting through the waters of the Sound. As had become the routine timesaving practice, Captain Hazelwood steered around them rather than following the safer procedure of slowing down and staying in his traffic lane. For members of the U.S. Coast Guard on duty in Valdez, this seemed to be an uneventful night just like all of the other nights since the port was opened to oil traffic 12 years earlier.

AT THE TIME OF THE ACCIDENT

Four minutes after midnight on March 24, 1989, about two and one half hours into their journey south, with an inexperienced third mate in command, the crew of the *Exxon Valdez* felt a sudden jolt and the ship begin to shudder, a sickening 10-second shudder. Eventually more than 240,000 barrels, or about 11 million gallons, of crude oil would gush into the surrounding waters. Captain Hazelwood later said,

> I knew we'd struck something; something major had happened to the vessel. I didn't know, but over the years you feel different things. I'd had engines blow up, other groundings, but it's an unhealthy feeling.

Afterward, Captain Hazelwood recalled his feelings, "You don't know if you want to cry, throw up, or scream all at the same time; knowing at the same time you've got a job to do." Despite these mixed feelings, or perhaps because of them, the captain rushed to the ship's bridge from his quarters below and went to work. With the supertanker listing on its right side—oil gushing from a 600-foot tear in its hull—and apparently balancing precariously on a narrow ledge, the *Exxon Valdez*'s chief mate James Kunkel told the captain that he feared for all of their lives and that he thought the supertanker would capsize if it came off the reef.

At 12:26 A.M., 22 minutes after striking the reef, Captain Hazelwood (as he tells it: "trying not to cry, and [trying to] be reasonably businesslike") matter-of-factly radioed the Coast Guard station at Valdez. He was later to be criticized by the state of Alaska for being so calm in his radio transmissions. In Valdez, the Coast Guard watchperson who took the call put down the paperwork he had been busy with, adjusted the radar so that the Exxon Valdez came into view, and confirmed that the supertanker was indeed aground on Bligh Reef. Several minutes later, the superintendent of operations at Alyeska's Valdez terminal was awakened with news of the accident. Following the "book" on such incidents, he told a subordinate to take charge and went back to sleep. When Coast Guard Vice Admiral Clyde Robbins was informed about the grounding, he responded, "That's impossible. We have the perfect system." As he watched the oil from his ship pouring into the water, Joseph Hazelwood thought, "My world as I had known it had come to an end."

At approximately 12:49 A.M., Captain Hazelwood radioed the Coast Guard that despite having a little trouble with the third mate, and the fact that the ship had been "holed," he was trying to get the ship off the reef and would get back in touch as soon as he could.

Exxon's Response

At 8:30 A.M. (4:30 A.M. Valdez time), the kitchen phone rang as Rawl was having breakfast in his Westchester County, New York home. He remembered asking the caller what had happened, if a rudder had broken, and if the ship had lost its engine.

> At that point I didn't even know what it hit. All I knew was that it hit something and it was holed pretty badly. . . . When you have a large ship on the rocks, and they tell you it's leaking oil, you know it is going to be bad, bad, bad.

To deal with the unfolding crisis situation, Rawl, deciding not to waste time driving to his New York City office, began setting up conference calls from his home while his wife canceled Easter plans with the family.

Right from the start, Rawl says he "knew" that human error was to blame for the accident. Later, hearing that blood alcohol tests on the ship's captain, administered more than 10 hours after the grounding, showed that the captain was legally drunk under Alaska law, Rawl said that he was not surprised. As events that day unfolded, he quickly began to deal with the corporate-level issues related to the growing disaster. Three critical policy questions had to be answered:

1. What should Exxon's official stance be on the grounding? Should the company assume responsibility for the accident?
2. Should he, as chief executive of the company that employed the tanker's crew and owned the ship and the oil pouring into Prince William Sound, immediately go to Alaska to take charge of the situation and demonstrate Exxon's concern for what was happening?
3. How should information about the spill and subsequent containment and cleanup efforts be disseminated?

Rawl and Exxon's other top managers decided that the company would immediately accept responsibility for the grounding and for cleaning up the damage. With regard to the second question, Rawl's initial instinct was to go to Alaska, but fellow managers later talked him out of the notion. They argued that if he went, he would probably just be in the way and that he could better serve the company's interests from his office in New York. It was a decision that, in light of subsequent intense criticism, he would later regret: "I wake up in the night questioning the decision to stay home."

His—Exxon's—decision to inform news organizations of events in Valdez on a "real time" basis was also a decision that he came to regret. Only Exxon employees in Valdez were to provide information as the information became available. Reacting to charges that Exxon had manipulated and suppressed information back in the oil shortage days after the Arab embargo in the mid-1970s, Rawl said that he just wanted to get the information out: "At least you can't be accused of distorting data or slicking it up before it's presented to the press." But his new strategy still left the media frustrated and suspicious. Phone lines to Alaska were constantly jammed, Exxon officials there were often unavailable for comment, and the news conferences that took place in the "real time" off-hours made it next to impossible for the media networks and newspapers to present timely reports. "It just didn't work," Rawl said in retrospect.

CONTAINMENT AND CLEANUP

From the beginning, attempts to contain and clean the oil slick from the waters and beaches of Prince William Sound were beset by many of the problems that often curse hastily assembled crisis organizations. There was even some confusion about who was in charge: Eighteen hours after the spill, Exxon took over control from Alyeska.

Technical, Legal, and Moral Issues

Alyeska's lack of preparedness and inability to cope with such a large spill almost immediately became the subjects of verbal sparring over technicalities in and interpretations of the cleanup contingency plan. When the *Exxon Valdez* ran aground, the oil spill emergency barge was unloaded and in dry dock; it took 12 hours (the plan called for 5) to mobilize and travel the 28 miles from port in Valdez Harbor to the site of the accident. Further complicating things, barges and pumps, which could have limited the spill by offloading the remaining oil from the stricken ship, were not immediately available. Because of these problems, Dennis Kelso, Commissioner of the Alaska Department of Environmental Conservation, called Alyeska's emergency plan "the biggest piece of maritime fiction since *Moby Dick*." An Alyeska official replied to this charge, "This was a joint plan. We did exactly what the state [and federal governments] wanted. We did not deceive anyone, and we responded very well."

As the spill spread, eventually fouling 1,200 miles of shoreline in the Sound, technological problems and questions plagued decision makers. Fears of legal liability also seem to have played a major role in hindering early cleanup efforts. Lawyers representing Exxon, Alyeska, the state of Alaska, and the Coast Guard, for example, all urged their clients not to risk taking the initiative in cleanup efforts because of potential for later liability claims. "The legal system crippled our ability to make decisions," Alaska's Governor Steve Cowper said at the time. "Protecting themselves [Exxon] from a lawsuit was more important than cleaning up oil." Exxon President Lee Raymond countered that the state had deliberately held up cleanup efforts to bolster its own legal case. "They have been preparing for litigation from day one," he charged.

Soon after the accident, in an apparent move to shift blame for the accident, Exxon released to the press private information regarding Captain Joseph Hazelwood's history of drinking problems, and then fired him. Rawl denied, however, that Hazelwood was fired for being drunk: "A lot of the public and press think we fired him because we thought he was drunk on the ship; but we never said that, and we have cautioned people not to assume it." Rawl clarified: "Hazelwood was terminated because he had violated company policies, such as not being on the bridge and for having consumed alcohol within four hours of boarding the ship." Hazelwood saw the situation differently; he asserted that it was a commonly accepted practice for a ship's captain to issue simple instructions to the crew and then leave the bridge. When asked why Exxon and the state of Alaska both attempted to focus the blame for the incident on him, he replied that he did not know, but then said,

> I could be a lightning rod, easy target, scapegoat to take the heat. I would say the same for the state of Alaska. They came after me, hammer and tong, figuring I'd fold like a cheap suit. I imagine they're a bit surprised I didn't.

The outcome of all of this sparring and legal wrangling was an expensive public relations war involving Exxon, the state of Alaska, and to some extent the former captain of the *Exxon Valdez*. More important perhaps than these, however, was the withholding of important scientific data about the effects of the spill, collected by the many scientists on the scene, which could not be shared until later used in court.

Problems with Cleaning Up the Oil

From the first day, Exxon argued that but for Alaska's bureaucratic fumbling it could have sprayed chemical dispersants (which reduce the surface tension of oil and allow it to break up into small droplets and scatter more easily into the water) on the spill that would have reduced subsequent damage. Not so, answers the state of Alaska, explaining that in the first few days after the spill when dispersants might have helped somewhat, Exxon had far too little chemicals available to do any good and the calm seas would have prevented the chemicals from mixing thoroughly enough to make them effective. There were also scientific questions raised about the toxicity of the dispersants and about their efficacy even under ideal conditions. The evidence shows that such chemically treated oil first scatters, then comes back together, sinks, resurfaces, and eventually washes ashore as tar balls: Even though the oil seems to disappear, it simply does not go away.

Another severe problem for those trying to contain the spill was that the physical properties of an oil slick change over time. While the most toxic parts of the oil evaporate within about 20 hours, the remainder mixes with the salt water and sea debris, creating after about 14 days a heavy, thick, reddish-brown mousse. As the mousse collects even more debris, however, that which does not amass on the beaches eventually can turn into an even thicker muck that will sink to the bottom.

The thickening of the oil made it very difficult for the 60 skimmer vessels to vacuum the mess from the surface of the water and pump it into barges. Exxon's water cleanup coordinator Jim O'Brien indicated that the cleanup operation was doomed from the start:

> There's an important thing people must realize in planning for a spill of this size: No amount of equipment will clean it all up, even if they give you a month's notice

to get ready. Look at the expanse of water involved, and figure the time it takes to deploy boats and skimmers and support vessels at 12 knots. Skimmers need barges to collect their oil. Crews need food, ships need fuel, and somebody has to collect the garbage. And nothing works if the weather's bad.

The sticky mousse that ended up on the shores of Prince William Sound filled the nooks and crannies along the jagged coastal areas, saturating the surface and subsurfaces of the beaches and pooling in some places to depths of over four feet. The strategy for cleaning these from the rocky beaches quickly focused on removing the gross oil and then letting the residue biodegrade over time. On the beaches of Prince William Sound, where 90 percent of the oil went ashore, this meant that the mousse had to be first scooped up, mopped, or blotted up before the rocks could be scrubbed semiclean. Once this was done, the scrubbing was often done by hand but more generally by high-pressure hoses. The hoses would shoot scalding water to loosen and then flush the oil that had by now weathered to a substance somewhat like asphalt back into the water, where cold water hoses would direct it to off-shore skimmers. Another technique called bioremediation, used experimentally in places, involved spraying a special nitrogen-phosphorus fertilizer mix onto the shore in an attempt to stimulate oil-eating bacteria. It was hoped that this would double the pace of nature's self-cleanup efforts.

Controversy raged over every step of the cleanup effort, with critics finding fault in every technique. Some believed that the hot water scrubbing, by killing fish and surviving micro-organisms, wreaked greater environmental havoc than the oil. Others complained that bio-remediation, although it seemed to work in the few areas in which it was tried, would leave unsightly, nontoxic asphalt hydrocarbons to stain the beaches and would induce undesirable plankton growth in the Sound. Still others protested that the debris and garbage created by the cleanup crews were in themselves ecological disasters. Health experts voiced concerns that the cleanup workers were poorly trained, ill-equipped (many did not have breathing masks), and exposed to oil for long periods of time. They warned that exposure to oil and its vapors can lead to nausea, breathing difficulties, rashes, kidney and nervous system damage, and cancer.

For many critics, the cleanup efforts served no other purpose than the public relations interests of the principals (Exxon, the state of Alaska, and the Coast Guard) responsible for the mess in the first place. Many experts believe that, beyond the initial wildlife kills and the temporary (an estimated three to six years) destruction of the scenery, the lasting effects of the spill on the environment will be minimal. The cleanup had little beneficial effect on the environment, possibly added to the adverse consequences, and as a practical matter amounted to nothing more than a (multi) billion-dollar public relations campaign to assuage the anger of the people of Alaska, environmentalists, the larger general public, and Congress. The oil industry, in particular, had a lot at stake in public opinion. They greatly feared the potential political damage that any adverse publicity would have on requests for future off-shore drilling rights and for permission to explore for gas and oil in other environmentally sensitive areas in Alaska and elsewhere in the United States. One of the great ironies of the cleanup effort is perhaps best expressed on the most popular T-shirt sold in Valdez during the summer of 1989: "Cleanup '89. It's not just a job, it's a —ing waste of time."

In all, Exxon paid out anywhere from $1 to $3 billion (there have been several different numbers reported), while employing approximately 11,500 people in the cleanup effort. In addition, Exxon compensated Alaskan fishermen some $200,000 for lost income due to the spill. There was no compensation for the 980 otters, 138 eagles, and 33,126 other birds killed, nor even a reliable way of estimating the value of loss.

As the cleanup operation shut down on September 15, 1989, in advance of the harsh Alaskan winter, Exxon publicized its accomplishments: 60,000 barrels of recovered oil, and 1,087 miles of oiled beach now environmentally stable. The state of Alaska countered that the cleanup had actually recovered less than 30,000 barrels of oil and that only about 118 miles of beaches were safe for wildlife and new vegetation growth. Despite their release of an ambiguously worded memo on July 19, 1989 that seemed to state that, the job being finished, the company would not return again in the spring to resume cleanup efforts— a memo that had generated enormous public outrage—Exxon returned to Prince William Sound on May 1, 1990 to do what was necessary, as established by Coast Guard recommendations, to make things right.

Sources

BEHAR, R. "Exxon Strikes Back: Interview with Lawrence Rawl." *Time,* March 26, 1990, pp. 62–63.

BYRNE, J. A. "The Rebel Shaking Up Exxon." *Business Week,* July 18, 1988, pp. 104–11.

"Conoco Alters Stand on Tankers." Associated Press report appearing in the *South Bend Tribune,* April 11, 1990.

DiIANNI, D. "The Big Spill," for *NOVA.* PBS air-date: February 27, 1990. 1990 WGBH Educational Foundation. Transcript by Journal Graphics, 267 Broadway, New York, NY 10007.

HODGSON, B. "Alaska's Big Spill: Can the Wilderness Heal?" *National Geographic,* January, 1990, pp. 2–43.

Interview with Joseph Hazelwood conducted by Connie Chung, telecast on "Saturday Night with Connie Chung," March 31, 1990.

SATCHELL, M., AND CARPENTER, B. "A Disaster That Wasn't." *U.S. News & World Report,* September 18, 1989, pp. 60–69.

SOLOMON, J. "Strategies for Handling the Arrest of an Employee." *Wall Street Journal,* March 29, 1990.

STIGLER, G. "What an Oil Spill Is Worth." *Wall Street Journal,* April 17, 1990.

SULLIVAN, A. "Exxon's Restructuring in the Past *Is* Blamed for Recent Accidents: Cost Cuts in '86 Helped Profit, but Did They Make Spills, Refinery Fire More Likely?" *Wall Street Journal,* March 16, 1990.

SULLIVAN, A. "Rawl Wishes He'd Visited Valdez Sooner: Exxon Chief Regrets Actions Right after Oil Spill." *Wall Street Journal,* June 6, 1989.

TOBIAS, M. "Black Tide," for the Discovery Channel, air-date: March 18, 1990.

TUTTLE, J. "Anatomy of an Oil Spill," for *FRONTLINE.* PBS air-date: March 20, 1990. 1990 WGBH Educational Foundation. Transcript by Journal Graphics, 267 Broadway, New York, NY 10007.

Wall Street Journal. "Oil Spill Cleanup's Still Protect Workers Poorly, Unions Say," April 10, 1990.

Wall Street Journal. "Review and Outlook: Cleaning Up Oil," March 30, 1990.

Questions for discussion

1. Did Exxon have an obligation prior to the accident to have a contingency plan in case of an accident?

2. No matter who is found at fault or responsible, how much cleanup is enough?

3. Should Exxon have supervised more closely the general conduct and action of Captain Hazelwood?

• FOUR •

Employee–Employer Relations

The relationship between employees and employers has undergone constant evolution. Today one would never see the kind of sign that was posted in a New York carriage shop in 1878, reading

> It is expected that each employee shall participate in the activities of the church and contribute liberally to the Lord's work . . . All employees are expected to be in bed by 10:00 P.M. Except: Each male employee may be given one evening a week for courting purposes . . .[1]

Today's employees are better educated and bring to the workplace a higher set of expectations than their counterparts in the nineteenth century. Old organizational habits are confronting new demands, and in turn, new ethical problems.

Many modern theorists insist that employers must modify their attitudes toward employees and be willing to grant an expanding and increasingly well-defined set of "employee rights." Among the rights that such theorists champion are:

1. The right of an employee to complain about dangerous products and practices without being penalized.
2. The right of an employee to participate in political and personal activities outside the workplace without being penalized.
3. The right of an employee to a hearing before being fired.
4. The right of an employee to refuse immoral orders without being penalized.

One of the most controversial employee-employer issues today is "whistle blowing." Whistle blowing is directly related to the first item in the list, since the right to "blow the whistle" is at bottom the right to complain about dangerous or immoral practices without being penalized. In other words, advocates of the right to whistle blowing argue that when employees write letters to local newspapers, or inform government authorities, or contact local television reporters in order to complain about company practices they believe are immoral, illegal, or dangerous, they should be protected from being fired or demoted as a consequence. Usually, the right to blow the whistle is assumed to cover only those who appeal to *external* media or authorities (ones outside the organization) and who have first attempted to use *internal* remedies (say, by reporting the problem to their superiors).

Since the issue of whistle blowing is related to that of freedom of speech, one may wonder why so much controversy surrounds a right that presumably is already protected under the First Amendment of the U.S. Constitution. The reason is that, although the First Amendment protects the right of persons to free speech without suffering either government reprisal or the use of force by others to suppress one's speech, it has not—at least traditionally—been interpreted to protect free speech from *employer* reprisal. Indeed, this is an important fact not only about the right of whistle blowing, but of all other purported employee rights as well. People are in one sense always "free" to blow the whistle or refuse immoral orders. The tough question is whether they are free to do these things *and* not be penalized by employers.

Employers who object to the notion of "employee rights" offer two principal criticisms. First, they say that implementing employee rights will harm organizational efficiency. Management's hands would be tied, they say and unable to respond effectively to a company's primary responsibility—maintaining and increasing profits. Not all persons who complain to outside media and authorities are sincere, for example. Many are merely disgruntled troublemakers. Management must remain free to make decisions that it thinks best. Second, employers point out that employees are free to quit their jobs at any time they wish; why, then, should employers not be free to terminate employees when *they* wish? Employers do not demand a "good reason" before allowing an employee to quit; their ability to do so is simply a matter of individual freedom. Why then should employers always be required to offer a "good reason" when firing or demoting?

Over the past two decades, the law has become increasingly protective of employee rights in the United States, especially in the area of whistle blowing. The doctrine of "employment at will," a common-law principle allowing an employer to fire for good reason, bad reason, or no reason, continues to dominate court decisions, but its influence has steadily diminished. A series of court decisions in the late 1960s and early 1970s held that employees could sue employers who fired them as retaliation for whistle blowing *when that whistle blowing occurred either in a government organization or in a profit-making organization that conducted a majority of its work with the government.* In the late 1970s and early 1980s, courts appeared to be extending such employee privileges farther into the sphere of mainstream private business, but—at least at the time of this writing—it is unclear what the final position of the courts will be.

Besides the proposed rights already innumerated, some employees have argued in behalf of four more, namely:

1. The right of an employee to be protected in the workplace from physical harm and infectious diseases.
2. The right of handicapped and chronically ill employees, who are able to fulfill their job requirements, not to be discriminated against because of their illness.
3. The right of worker participation and meaningful work tasks, as much as is possible, for every employee.
4. The right of an employee not to be discriminated against because of sexual identity or sexual orientation.

For those championing expanded rights for employees, there are two separate and distinct remedies available. One is to protect such rights through the law through tougher regulations and broader rights of access for employees to the judicial process. The other is to protect rights not through the law, but through internal managerial procedures, policies, and structures. Grievance committees, "open door" policies, quality circles, and employees' "bills of rights" are among the suggestions presently being tried by modern corporations. Those who take the former approach argue that business will never voluntarily police its own house; it must be forced by external pressures. Those taking the latter approach deny that corporations lack the potential for moral initiative, and they point to the obvious drawbacks of using laws and the courts to enforce moral standards: Doing so involves red tape, governmental confusion, and inefficiency.

The cases in this section raise an array of employee-employer issues. "AIDS in the Workplace" examines the issue of infectious diseases and handicapped employees in the workplace. The problems of free speech, whistle blowing, and employment at will are explored in "The DC-10's Defective Doors" and "The Case of the Willful Whistle-Blower." The "Hazards of the Enterprise" case is purely fictional. But sometimes fiction can highlight the facts of an issue better than actual facts. "Weber v. Kaiser Aluminum" addresses the complicated issue of affirmative action. "Aggressive Ad Agency" also deals with the issues of confidentiality and intellectual property rights. It brings into question the fine line drawn between sharing expertise and sharing privileged information. Finally "Management Dilemma" and "Vital Information at Complex" deal with the issue of how managers should respond to the complex employee problems involving trade-offs between employee rights and organizational goals.

Note

1. Quoted in David Ewing, *Freedom Inside the Organization* (New York: McGraw-Hill, Inc., 1977), p. 12.

• *Case Study* •

AIDS in the Workplace:
Options and Responsibilities*

AL GINI • MICHAEL DAVIS

Statistics indicate that, while few of us will experience AIDS in private or family life, many will experience AIDS in the workplace. AIDS raises at least three fundamental questions for a manager: How should an employee with AIDS be treated? How should other employees be informed about AIDS and their safety and morale insured? How should the legal, ethical, and human considerations involved be balanced against the needs of business? Such questions will become more pressing as the AIDS epidemic spreads.[1] This chapter considers possible options and strategies for answering them. Let us begin with a case.

Elaine's Cafeteria

Elaine Merkavich operates the cafeteria of Bunyun Hospital under a ten-year agreement, with nine years remaining. As long as she pays the (fixed) rent; maintains the physical plant; satisfies all applicable city, state, and federal laws; and provides full service twenty-four hours a day, she is free to run the cafeteria as if she owned it. Indeed, she insisted on that as a condition for taking over what had been a money loser. The cafeteria's employees, more than ninety of them, are her employees, not the hospital's.

It is one of those employees who concerns her now. Barry, thirty, is a cook she hired only nine months ago. His former wife brought bad news this morning. Barry, she told Elaine ("in confidence" and "out of concern for others"), has AIDS. Barry had been an above-average employee, so hard-working and reliable that Elaine was on the point of promoting him to head cook on the night shift.

Elaine wondered what she should do now. What do you do with such confidential information? How, for example, do you confirm it? The more she thought about that, the more she doubted the information would remain confidential for long. Barry's former wife would probably tell others as well. The news would soon be out. That thought suggested other questions. What effect would news of the disease have on other employees, especially those who work close to Barry or who have become his friends? What effect would the disease have on Barry's ability to manage the night shift, indeed, on his ability to continue to be a hard-working and reliable employee? What effect would news of a cook with AIDS have on customers?

That last question worried Elaine the most. Last year some hospital personnel had refused for a time to take care of patients with HIV. The administration had dealt with that refusal by saying, "Do the job or look for another." Elaine had no such power to get hospital employees to eat in the cafeteria. They were free to bring lunch from home or pay a little extra to go across the street rather than eat food prepared by someone with AIDS. Before Elaine took over the cafeteria, many had done just that because the food and service had been so bad. If many did it again because they feared her cook, the cafeteria would once again be a losing proposition. But this time it would be hers. She would have to do something. But what?

AIDS in Business

A recent study sponsored by Allstate Insurance Company and *Fortune* magazine found that, although a majority of U.S. corporate executives believe that AIDS is one of the major problems facing the country, most companies lack direction in dealing with the problem in the workplace. Only 29 percent of the executives in the 623 companies polled said that their companies have or are planning to formulate a written or unwritten policy on AIDS.[2] The Fourth International Conference on AIDS reported that only 8 percent of U.S. *Fortune* 500 firms and 25 percent of Canadian *Fortune* 500 firms have developed formal policies on AIDS.[3] Seemingly, most companies are unwilling, unable, or unprepared to handle the problem. They teeter between denial and procrastination. Why?

According to Cheryl Russell, editor-in-chief of *American Demographics,* of the 2 million Americans who died in 1987, AIDS victims accounted for only 14,000, less than 1 percent of total deaths. In contrast, heart disease killed 800,000 and cancer another 400,000. Pneumonia, suicide, and cirrhosis of the liver were also far more common causes of death than AIDS. In number of deaths, AIDS ranks with emphysema, kidney failure, and murder. Even if the estimates for AIDS deaths in 1991 were correct—54,000—this figure would account for less than 3 percent of all deaths that year.[4]

AIDS has killed about 180,000 Americans during its ten years in the United States. During the same period, more than 20 million Americans died. For the nation as a whole, AIDS is an insignificant disease in absolute number of deaths—a mere blip in our mortality statistics.[5] Applied to the workplace, these figures mean that in any given company only a relative handful of employees will have AIDS. For example, in 1983, Control Data Corporation conducted a self-study that predicted that, at most, 104 of its 34,000 employees would die of AIDS between 1983 and 1988—fewer than would die of any other major disease.[6]

So the question remains: Why the hesitance of so many corporations to formulate policies and procedures in regard to AIDS? A large part of the answer at both the human and corporate level is fear, fear fueled by irresponsible headlines and controversies in the press. No other disease in modern times has generated so much fear. In some ways, that is understandable. AIDS touches on many of the basic taboos of human life: sex, homosexuality, illness, suffering, and death. As Reverend Ann Showalter, a Mennonite minister and director of the Chicago-based AIDS Pastoral Care Network, has said, "There are really two epidemics—one of the disease and one of fear. And the fear is much more readily transmitted than the disease."[7] What corporations and individuals alike fear as much as the costs and suffering of the disease are the social stigma associated with it and the unknowns and the intangibles of contagion and cure.

Many social commentators believe that this fear, no matter how exaggerated or misplaced, has immobilized the corporate sector, diminishing its ability to handle a crisis that will not soon go away.

Ethical Issues

The AIDS epidemic raises at least three kinds of ethical issues: First, there are issues of *rights*, both human and civil. Two rights are of special importance here: the right to privacy and the right to work. The right to privacy grants a presumption of confidentiality in regard to health records, financial accounts, and job evaluations or performance records, a presumption operating against both government and private persons until they show a specific need to know. (Does Elaine in fact have a right to know whether Barry has AIDS?) The right to work includes the right not to be discriminated against in matters of hiring, firing, compensation, and terms, conditions, and privileges of employment on the basis of race, color, religion, sex, national origin, or disability. (Can Elaine legally take Barry's disease into account when deciding whether to promote him to head cook on the night shift?)

Second, there are issues of *public health*. Government has an obligation to protect the public from infectious and communicable diseases. This obligation extends to protecting employees in the workplace from disease and unnecessary physical hazards. (What responsibilities does Elaine have to customers and other employees to protect them from Barry?)

Third, there are issues of *social ethics*. What is our commitment to fair treatment and justice for all members of society, in particular political minorities, the young, the aged, and the mentally or physically disabled? (Does Barry's disease even count as a disability?)

Framing these issues, however, are two practical questions. One is factual: Is AIDS readily communicable in the workplace? The other is legal: What legal protections do employees with AIDS have? We must consider these issues first.

How Communicable?

Unlike most transmissible diseases (colds, flu, measles, etc.), AIDS is not transmitted through sneezing, coughing, or eating or drinking from common utensils, or merely through being around an infected person. All scientific evidence so far indicates that transmission is not possible through casual personal contact.

Because of the difficulty of transmission, AIDS is an easily avoidable disease. Risk of contagion is proportional to high-risk behavior. Except for health-care workers engaged in invasive procedures bringing them into contact with blood and other bodily fluids, employees, patients, and customers afflicted with AIDS do not present a health risk under normal working conditions.[8] One has about as much chance of catching AIDS in the workplace as of catching cancer or multiple sclerosis. Although AIDS is a health issue for business, as well as a legal and moral issue, it is not a contagion issue. Businesses should not allow fear and ignorance to disrupt the workplace.[9]

Legal Protection

For employees, the only thing worse than having AIDS is losing one's job because of it. Before 1987, AIDS victims had few legal rights or unambiguous remedies in regard to their status in the workplace. The doctrine of "employment at will" allowed most employees almost unlimited discretion to fire individuals for any reason or for no reason whatsoever. Only union contracts and specific legislative provisions limited this plenary authority.[10] Employers could solve their AIDS problem simply by firing those with the disease—or even those they feared might have or get the disease. As recently as June 1986, a United States Justice Department memorandum declared that "fear alone" was legitimate grounds for dismissal: "Acting on an irrational fear of contagion is," it reasoned, "not prohibited by law and thus not discriminatory."[11] The memorandum led to a surge of firings, particularly in smaller companies.

Many other employers dismissed employees with AIDS or those simply suspected of having AIDS because the employers feared the threat of reprisals from other workers more than they feared the disease itself. Protests and strikes over health and safety issues have long been sanctioned by the law. Under Section 7 of the National Labor Relations Act, employees have the right to engage in "concerted activity" for their "mutual aid and protection." This means that two or more employees have a right to withhold services to protect their wages or hours or the terms or conditions of their employment. In addition, Section 502 of the Labor Management Relations Act specifically protects the employee's right to stop working because of "a good faith belief" that abnormally dangerous conditions exist in the workplace. Employers had good reason to fear that if, because of health concerns, a group of employees refused to work with a person who had or was suspected of having AIDS, the National Labor Relations Board could view the refusal as a valid protest strike over a health and safety issue.[12]

Since 1987, the legal pendulum has swung to the side of AIDS victims. Employers must now deal with a new legal fact: under the Americans with Disabilities Act of 1991 (ADA), an employee with AIDS is considered disabled and is protected from discrimination just as are other disabled people. The ADA effectively preempts the plenary authority of "employment at will" with respect to AIDS (and HIV), negates the Justice Department's memorandum on fear of contagion, and therefore probably overrides any possible ruling by the National Labor Relations Board in regard to the unwillingness of fellow employees to work with a colleague suffering from AIDS.[13]

This complete turnaround began with the Supreme Court's ruling in *School Board of Nassau County v. Arline,* 480 U.S. 273 (1987). Arline, a Florida schoolteacher, suffered from recurring bouts of tuberculosis but claimed she was not contagious. She argued that her firing by the school district violated Section 504 of the Federal Rehabilitation Act of 1973. Imposing a duty on the federal government, employers with federal contracts, and employers who are recipients of federal assistance not to discriminate against handicapped persons, the act defines "handicap" as "a physical or mental impairment or infirmity which substantially limits one or more of a person's major life activities" but expressly extends coverage to those not only presently disabled, but who have a "record of such impairment" or are "regarded as having such an impairment."

Until *Arline,* appellate courts had applied Section 504 only to conditions such as heart disease, cancer, blindness, epilepsy, multiple sclerosis, diabetes, and dyslexia. The question of whether contagious diseases were covered had never been addressed. When the Supreme Court agreed with Arline and ordered her reinstatement, it effectively extended the act's protection to those with transmissible diseases.[14] Persons suffering from AIDS were (apparently) covered because the ability to fight off infection and preserve health is a "major life function."[15]

The Court did, however, announce in a footnote that it was leaving for another day the question whether persons infected with HIV but free of symptoms qualified for protection as a handicapped person under the 1973 federal act:

> The United States argues that it is possible for a person to be simply a carrier of a disease, that is, to be capable of spreading a disease without having a "physical impairment" or suffering from any other symptoms associated with the disease. The United States contends that this is true in the case of some carriers of the Acquired Immune Deficiency Syndrome (AIDS) virus. From this premise the United States concludes that discrimination solely on the basis of contagiousness is never discrimination on the basis of a handicap. The argument is misplaced in this case, because the handicap here, tuberculosis, gave rise both to a physical impairment *and* to contagiousness. This case does not present, and we therefore do not reach, the questions whether a carrier of a contagious disease such as AIDS could be considered to have a physical impairment, or whether such a person could be considered, solely on the basis of contagiousness, a handicapped person as defined by the Act.[16]

The Civil Rights Restoration Act of 1987 effectively closed this question. The act states that a person with a contagious disease or infection is disabled if he or she does not "constitute a direct threat to health or safety" and is able to "perform the duties of the job."[17] It was this understanding of disability that the ADA incorporated.

The ADA differs from earlier legislation primarily in extent of coverage. Earlier legislation protected the disabled from discrimination by government or government contractors. The ADA applies to any company with more than fifteen employees.

The legislative history of the ADA is relevant to Elaine's problem. The House of Representatives included an amendment to the (proposed) ADA to exempt "food handlers." This was done out of respect for the interests of the food industry, even though the courts had long ago repudiated the argument that customer preference could excuse otherwise impermissible discrimination. (Many who engaged in racial discrimination in employment had sought to justify their conduct as arising not from their own prejudice but from sound business judgment concerning the prejudices of their customers.)

For that reason, the Senate rejected the House's amendment, while trying to satisfy the legitimate interests of the food industry. The Secretary of Health and Human Services was to maintain a list of infectious and communicable diseases known to be transmitted through food handling (and of methods known to prevent their communication). The ADA permits employers to refuse to assign an employee to a job involving food handling if the employee has one of the diseases on the list and could handle the food in a way capable of transmitting the disease. HIV is *not* on the list.[18]

The ADA classifies all life-disabling, life-threatening, and contagious illnesses under the general heading of "disability" and protects against discrimination all "disabled" employees. The ADA thus closes the door on (legal) summary dismissal of employees with AIDS and provides a framework for dealing with such employees. This framework may be summarized in this way:

1. An employee may not be terminated or otherwise discriminated against solely because of a disability that does not interfere with the performance of the employ-

ee's job. An employee with AIDS may be terminated only when his condition sub-stantially interferes with his job performance.

2. While no company is legally obligated to hire workers with AIDS, a business cannot refuse to hire individuals because of their disease. A disability may be a reason to fire, or to refuse to hire, only if it renders the employee either intellectually or phys-ically unable to perform the job (even with reasonable accommodations) or the employee could (even with reasonable accommodations) present a direct threat to the health or safety of herself or others.

3. An employer must make reasonable accommodations for all disabled individuals. The exact accommodations necessary will depend on several factors, such as the nature of the work, the size of the organization, and the costs involved. In general, no radical changes are necessary. Accommodations might include offering flexible hours, part-time work, or transfer to a less taxing position.

4. Given the overwhelming evidence that AIDS is not transmitted from person to per-son in the ordinary workplace, the ADA implies that employers have *no* demon-strable interest that could justify using blood tests to screen for exposure to the AIDS virus. If the employee or applicant is currently capable of performing the job, the test cannot be used in making employment decisions. Any adverse action premised on the test would be unlawful.[19]

Options for Businesses

Given the ADA, what can businesses do? What should they do? There seem to be three major options: first, guarantee full salary and benefits if the em-ployee agrees *not* to return to work; second, develop no AIDS policy, on the as-sumption that general policies can handle all possible contingencies; and third, develop a specific AIDS policy, describing both benefits and protections available to an employee with AIDS (or HIV).

The first option, while perhaps within the letter of the law, does not con-form to its spirit. The legality of this option remains to be adjudicated. Nu-merous firms are still unwilling to deal with the personnel problems of an em-ployee with AIDS. They argue that no matter what experts say, retaining an em-ployee known to have AIDS, whether on the shop floor or in the executive offices, creates feelings of anxiety and unrest among a significant portion of their other employees, suppliers, and customers. To resolve the problem while addressing the needs of an afflicted employee, some firms continue to pay the employee's full salary and medical and retirement benefits on condition that the employee not return to work. The employee is, in effect, forced to take paid leave.

One vice-president for personnel management of a *Fortune* 500 firm ex-plained the policy in this way in a private conversation:

> Who are we hurting? For the guy who's got it—we're helping him pay his bills, keep his house, and get first-rate medical attention through our group coverage for as long as he needs it. And from the point of view of the people he worked with, well—I'm sure they're glad he's taken care of and I know they're relieved by his absence. Look, don't kid yourself, *even* if it isn't contagious, it's just not the same thing as working next to someone who has cancer or a heart condition. As far as I'm con-cerned, this is just as much of a morale issue as it is a moral one.

When asked about the possibility of civil litigation, the vice-president's answer was equally forthright.

Why would they sue? We haven't fired anyone. We don't even list them as being on leave, and we never put them on disability. They will still be getting full pay without losing any benefits. We'll even give them their annual raise when it comes up. So what could they sue us for—loss of meaningful work? That would be a tough one to win. And even if they did win, it could prove to be a hollow victory if it took longer than forty-eight months to get it through the courts.

I just don't see it happening. It's just not worth the effort and grief involved.

This variation of the first option seems to take advantage of the weak negotiating position of an employee with AIDS. The vice-president does not claim any legal right to force the employee to give up working, merely a practical ability to take (what he obviously considers) "the easy way out." Can an employer justifiably trample on the legal rights of an employee this way? The answer to that question depends both on the *moral* justification of the right and on the alternatives available. Our discussion of the other two options will shed light on both.

The second option seems to be the option of choice for most American businesses. They feel that adopting specific policies that deal solely with AIDS is not advisable for them for at least one of three reasons. First, they don't want to draw attention to the problem and unnecessarily alarm their employees. Second, current company policy on life-threatening illnesses probably covers the situation, and therefore there is no reason to treat AIDS explicitly. Third, a special AIDS policy might prove too restrictive; flexibility is needed because both scientific knowledge and law in this area are changing rapidly.[20]

The key element in this approach is "flexibility." The companies involved believe that each AIDS case is different and must be handled on an individual ad hoc basis. IBM is one of the companies that uses its basic policy on catastrophic illness to deal with "the handful" of AIDS patients among its four hundred thousand employees. If they're fit, they can work. If they want counseling, they can get it. If their coworkers want counseling, IBM offers that, too. The same rules apply to all workers whether they have AIDS or cancer, or have suffered a heart attack.[21]

The third option is to develop, publish, and implement a special policy on AIDS. So far, only a few major companies—including Syntex, Bank America, AT&T, Transamerica, Levi Strauss, Wells Fargo, and Pacific Telesis—have adopted specialized personnel policies to handle the problems that AIDS poses in the workplace.[22]

All such policies are formulated around a commitment to six underlying principles:

1. AIDS is a blood-borne virus that cannot be transmitted through casual social or workplace contact.
2. All human beings gain much of their self-identity and self-esteem from their work. Moreover, good health is often enhanced by working at one's regular job, no matter what the diagnosis. Because of this, all workers should be allowed to determine for themselves, within the limits of safety and physical ability, how long they want to continue to work.[23]
3. All companies have an absolute obligation to provide a safe working environment for all employees and customers. Every precaution must be taken to ensure that an employee does not present a health or safety threat to other employees and customers through loss of physical or mental abilities. As long as medical evidence indicates that persons with life-threatening illnesses do not represent threats to them-

selves or others, managers should be sensitive to their conditions and ensure that they are treated the same as other employees.

4. The basic posture of every AIDS policy in the workplace must be educational, because while AIDS is a disease that cannot be cured, it can be stopped. Information, training, and counseling should be the cornerstone of any response to AIDS, both for employees with AIDS and for their fellow workers.

5. Special care must be taken with all issues of confidentiality. Management's best course of action is a simple one: except when required by law to do so, never reveal any part of an employee's confidential medical record without that employee's written consent.

6. Any employee refusing to work with an AIDS-afflicted fellow worker is, after appropriate counseling and formal warnings, subject to discharge.

A number of companies have done much to inform themselves and their employees concerning AIDS. Taking the lead in this area is the Business Leadership Task Force, which consists of fifteen major employers based in northern California. These companies have pooled their resources to provide a comprehensive AIDS education program for employees and their families. The basic message of the Task Force is a simple one. They encourage all employers to address the issues of AIDS in the workplace as a means of avoiding hysteria and mistrust. Levi Strauss, for example, a leading member of the Task Force, has developed programs that include lectures for managers by experts on AIDS; resource and support classes for persons with AIDS, as well as for anyone who is related to or knows a person with AIDS; a video presentation that can be checked out for home viewing; and regular updates on AIDS published in the company newsletter. Pacific Bell, another Task Force member, provides AIDS seminars and publishes information on topics not normally covered in a company vehicle, such as sexual activity and sexuality. All of the Task Force members also discuss AIDS in regard to their existing employee benefits programs. This provides them with the opportunity to remind their employees of the protection being provided for them and to reassure them of continued protection.[24]

The real import of a carefully rendered AIDS policy is that it communicates a company's concern to provide a safe, healthful, and efficient work environment. It also demonstrates to workers, suppliers, and customers alike that management cares not only about the continued success of its business but also about the well-being of its employees and the people the company serves. Sadly, however, as BusinessWeek commentator Irene Pave has stated: "Most companies . . . have yet to come to grips with AIDS. But . . . no responsible employer can continue to duck the issue. The peace of mind of future AIDS patients and the stability of a company's work force depend on setting a fair policy without delay."[25]

Conclusion

We have not yet determined what Elaine should do, much less presented an argument for why she should do it. Our purpose here is to sort out issues, to clarify what is at stake, and otherwise to give some structure to what originally might seem overwhelmingly complex. We believe this to be a legitimate service that philosophers can perform for managers. In that spirit, we now make three concluding points:

1. Elaine does not in fact know whether Barry has AIDS. She has only the word of his former wife, who may or may not know what she is talking about. Asking Barry whether he has AIDS, or otherwise seeking to determine whether he does, has three disadvantages for Elaine. First, she would be inquiring into a disability legally irrelevant to his job. That itself is legally risky. Second, she risks causing Barry a good deal of embarrassment, whether he has AIDS or not. (Imagine how you would feel if your employer asked you whether you have AIDS!) And, third, her seeking such information would suggest that Barry's former wife is justifiably "concerned for others." Elaine would be feeding the very fear she should be trying to kill. She would have been better off if she had just told Barry's wife, "You needn't have told me this. It has nothing to do with me. As long as Barry can do his job, his AIDS is of no concern to me. He can't infect either his fellow employees or my customers. And when he can no longer work, he will go on disability, whether he has AIDS or not."

2. Elaine's competitors across the street are in exactly the same position she is. They too may have employees with AIDS, whether they admit it or not. The problem is to be sure that the hospital's employees understand that.

3. Barry's former wife has done Elaine a service, not by telling her about Barry in particular, but by giving her a push to begin planning for a problem that will be hers sooner or later. She might, for example, want to find out what, if anything, the hospital is doing to inform its employees about AIDS. If the hospital has an educational program, does it include anything about the lack of connection between AIDS and food handlers? Could it? Could her employees take the program?

For Elaine, AIDS in her cafeteria is (among other things) a problem in human relations or employee management. She will probably respond most effectively if she responds to it as she would to any other such problem. While management styles differ, there are certain clear constraints: moral minimums ("Don't lie," "Don't cheat," etc.), the law (e.g., the ADA), and organizational attitudes or traditions that go beyond the moral minimums and the law (e.g., a commitment to treating employees "with respect"). These have a place in every management decision, even one (like this) that may require considerably more sensitivity and inventiveness than most.

Notes

1. Nancy Merritt, "Bank of America's Blueprint for a Policy on AIDS," *Business Week* (March 23, 1987): 127.

2. Allison Kittrell, "Employers Lack AIDS Strategy: Study," *Business Insurance* (February 1, 1988): 3.

3. National Public Radio, "All Things Considered," June 15, 1988.

4. Cheryl Russell, "Fear of AIDS May Re-create the Virtuous '50's," In AIDS, ed. Lynn Hall and Thomas Modl, p. 199. (St. Paul, Minn.: Greenhaven Press, 1988).

5. Ibid.

6. S. Siwolop et al., "The AIDS Epidemic and Business," *Business Week* (March 23, 1987): 123.

7. "AIDS: Lending a Hand," *Company: A Magazine of the American Jesuits* (Winter 1987): 22–24.

8. Centers for Disease Control, "Recommendations for Prevention of HIV Transmission in Health-Care Settings," *Morbidity and Mortality Weekly Report* 36, no. 2S 35.

9. Merritt, "Bank of America's Blueprint," 127.

10. Patricia Werhane, *Persons, Rights and Corporations* (Englewood Cliffs, N.J.: Prentice Hall, 1985), pp. 80–93.

11. Gary Ward, *What a Manager Should Know About AIDS in the Workplace* (Chicago: Darnell Corporation, 1987), p. 4.

12. Victor Schacter and Susan Seeburg, AIDS: *A Manager's Guide* (New York: Executive Enterprises, 1986), p. 23.

13. Chai R. Feldblum, "Employment Protections," *Milbank Quarterly* 69 (suppl. 1/2 (1991)): 81–110, esp. 86, 102–104.

14. Stephanie Benson Goldberg, "The Meaning of 'Handicapped,'" *American Bar Association Journal* (March 1, 1987): 56–61.

15. Schacter and Seeburg, AIDS, pp. 40, 41.

16. *Arline,* 480 U.S. 273, 282 n. 7.

17. Lawrence O. Gostin, "Public Health Powers: The Imminence of Radical Change," *Milbank Quarterly* 69 (suppl. 1/2) (1991): 268–292, esp. 273.

18. Nancy Lee Jones, "Essential Requirements of the Act: A Short History and Overview," *Milbank Quarterly* 69 (suppl. 1/2) (1991): 25–54, esp. 45–46.

19. Jay Waks and Lori Meyers, "An Introduction to AIDS Coverage Under Corporate Policies on Infectious Diseases and Life-Threatening Illnesses," *Business Laws, Inc. (CPS)* (1987): 985–989.

20. Ibid., 986.

21. Irene Pave, "Fear and Loathing in the Workplace: What Managers Can Do About AIDS," *Business Week* (November 25, 1985): 126.

22. Elizabeth Younger and Linda Harris, "AIDS: Employer's Rights, Responsibilities and Opportunities," Washington Business Group on Health, 229   Pennsylvania Avenue SE, Washington, D.C. 20003, N.p., n.d.

23. A. R. Gini and T. Sullivan, "Work: The Process and the Person," *Journal of Business Ethics* 6 (1987): 249–260.

24. Younger and Harris, "AIDS."

25. Pave, "Fear and Loathing," 126.

Questions for discussion

1. Do you believe that there is sufficient scientific evidence to comfortably claim that AIDS is primarily a bloodborne disease and is not easily communicated to others?

2. How would you feel if a classmate or fellow worker announced that he or she was HIV positive or began to show various symptoms of AIDS?

3. Why do you think there is an almost xenophobic reaction against AIDS victims?

4. If AIDS affects only "a relative handful of any company's workforce," why do so many corporations hesitate to develop formal policies in its regard? What do they fear most: the disease; the costs involved; reprisals by other workers; or the social stigma associated with the disease?

5 Should AIDS victims be categorized as medically handicapped employees?

6. Is AIDS in the workplace a matter of civil liberties or of public health?

• *Case Study* •

The Case of the Willful Whistle-Blower*

SALLY SEYMOUR

When Ken Deaver, CEO of Fairway Electric, promoted me to vice president of the nuclear division, I was on top of the world. Now, just a month later, it feels like the world's on top of me. I'm used to having a team to share the problems, but now I'm on my own. At least Ken's door has always been open to me. He's been my mentor since I began at Fairway eight years ago, and he's really responsible for my success here. I owe him a lot. But when I think back over the last few weeks, I have to wonder whether I should have listened to him on this one.

It started the morning I walked into my office to find Jim Bower, one of my old teammates, waiting for me. He apologized for taking my time but said it was really important. I had worked with Jim for more than four years. If he says it's important, it's important.

"What's up?" I asked.

"Bob," he said, "I've run up against something I can't handle alone. I hate to dump this on you when you're just starting your new job, but it's the sort of thing I should take to my boss, and that's you now."

"Sure, Jim. Whatever it is, you've got my help."

He took a couple of deep breaths before he continued. "You know how we're cramped for space downstairs. Well, yesterday I asked my secretary to clear out any files over five years old. Before she left for the day, she stacked the old files on my desk so I could glance through them. And I couldn't believe what I found."

Jim pulled a red notebook from his briefcase.

"I found this report written 15 years ago by two engineers in the nuclear division. It's about a flaw in our design of the Radon II nuclear reactor. Apparently there was a structural problem in the containment unit that would show up as the power plant was being built. It wasn't a safety hazard, but it would hold up construction and cost a lot to fix. The report says that Fairway was going to rework the design. But listen to this memo from the head of the nuclear division." Jim opened the notebook and read from a sheet stapled to the inside cover.

"'The potential problems in the design of the Radon II are disturbing. They do not, however, present a safety hazard. It therefore would be counterproductive to discontinue sales of the design. If there are problems with fittings, they will show up as the plant is built, at which point the necessary corrections can be made. The need for retrofitting is not uncommon. Our experience has been that customers rarely complain about such extra costs.'"

Jim closed the notebook and looked up.

"This memo makes me sick, Bob. I can't believe Fairway would risk its reputation by selling plans they knew were flawed. Those customers bought the designs thinking they were the best on the market. But the Radon II took longer to build and cost a bunch more money than what Fairway told customers. That's misrepresentation. Maybe the reason the utilities never complained is because they could pass the cost on to the rate payers. But that's a real rip-off, and the top guys at Fairway knew about it."

Jim threw the notebook on my desk and looked at me, his face flushed. "Don't you think engineering ought to know about this?" he said.

I'd never seen Jim so steamed up. Of course, I was pretty upset myself. That report was new to me too. But I had a lot of faith in Fairway, so I wasn't going to leap to conclusions. I told Jim I'd ask some questions and get back to him by the end of the day.

I headed straight for Ken's office, recalling along the way everything I could about the Radon II reactor. I knew that we'd had problems with it, but it never occurred to me that our original designs were flawed. Jim was right that no one ever complained about the delays and costs of refitting. But I remembered one instance where a utility converted a Radon II to a coal-fired plant because of the cost overruns. In that case, the utility paid for the conversion and it didn't go into the rate base.

When I showed the report to Ken, he recognized it right away.

"How did Jim get ahold of this?" he asked.

"He discovered it by accident—cleaning out old files," I said. "He's pretty disturbed about it, and I can't say I blame him." Ken's office was suddenly very still.

"I thought this report was dead and buried," he said. "Have you read it?"

"Enough to get the drift," I said. "Apparently we sold a power plant design when we knew there were flaws in it."

"Yes, but you've got to understand the context. Back then we were in the middle of an energy crisis. Everyone was rushing to build nuclear power plants. We were under tremendous pressure to come up with a winning design, and Radon II was what we decided on. After a few plants went under construction, some problems surfaced, so we put a couple of engineers on it. But by the time they wrote this report, it was too late for us to go back to the drawing board. We wouldn't have had any customers left. We figured we'd solve the problem as soon as we could, but we'd sell the original design in the meantime. It was basically a very good one. And it was safe."

"I can't believe we would risk our reputation like that."

"I know it's not the way we usually operate, but that shows you the pressure we were under," Ken said. "The whole division would have gone down. There was no other way."

I was uncomfortable putting Ken on the defensive. I'd always trusted his judgment. Who was I to grill him about something that happened 15 years ago when I wasn't even around? Still, I needed to press the point.

"So what do I tell Jim?" I asked.

"Nothing. It's ancient history. The engineers who wrote that report are long gone. Look at it this way, the fact that we ordered a study of the problem shows that we care about quality. We eventually got the bugs out. Besides, it was never a question of safety. It was merely a matter of some extra work during construction."

"But what about all the cost overruns? If Fairway didn't swallow them, someone else must have—like the utilities or their customers."

"Look, Bob, what's past is past. What would we gain by bringing this into the open today? But I guarantee we've got a hell of a lot to lose. The regulators and some shareholders would love to blame us for all the exorbitant cost overruns. And the antinuclear groups would have a field day. We've got enough problems getting licenses as it is.

"We'd lost a lot of business, you know. I'm talking about hundreds of jobs here, and the very survival of this company. Maybe we're not perfect, but we're the most conscientious, quality-conscious corporation I know of."

"And what do I do with this report?" I asked.

"Deep-six it. As we should have done long ago. Tell Jim Bower what I told you, and explain why there's no reason to make an issue of it at this late date."

I nodded in agreement and headed back to my office. I found Jim waiting. He scowled when I reported Ken's reaction.

"So you're telling me to forget I ever saw the report? And I suppose that means you're going to forget I showed it to you."

"Look, Ken's got some good reasons for not wanting to make an issue of it. I may or may not agree with him, but he's running the show."

"Damn it, Bob!" Jim shouted. "If we go along with this, we're just as guilty as the people who sold those bad designs 15 years ago."

"Cool down, cool down. I know what you're saying, but Ken is just being realistic. After all, no one got hurt, the cost was spread over a lot of people, and the problem's been corrected. If this gets exposed, it could really hurt us."

"No, I won't cool down. Maybe it seems like ancient history to Ken, but unless we make a clean slate now, it could happen again. One of the reasons I took this job is because Fairway is a company I can respect. What am I supposed to think now?"

"I see your point," I replied, "but I also see Ken's. And he's the boss. Maybe you should talk to him."

"If I can't get through to you I don't see how I'll get through to him. So I guess that's it."

As it turned out, that wasn't it. When Jim left my office, he didn't go straight back to work. First he went to the newspaper, and the story appeared two days later.

> FAIRWAY SOLD DEFECTIVE REACTORS—
> REPORT WARNED OF HAZARD

Naturally, the reporter got it all wrong and blew the problem out of proportion. He didn't even have a copy of the report. I suppose we hadn't helped matters though. When the reporter called for a comment, Ken asked him to call back in a couple of hours. Then Ken and I met with our public relations officer, Amy Thine, to discuss how to handle the situation. Amy thought we should come clean—admit we made a mistake and stress the fact that our record for the past five years had been excellent. But Ken felt that the less we said, the sooner it would blow over. I went along with him. When the reporter called back, Ken's response was "no comment."

The article did say that the anonymous source still thought Fairway was a reliable builder of nuclear plants and that it was a good company with many skilled and highly principled employees. The source had gone to the newspaper because he felt it was his ethical duty to the consumers who had been forced to pay for Fairway's mistakes. But that part of the story was buried in the next-to-last paragraph.

Needless to say, the public outcry was intense. Antinuke activists went berserk, and politicians made holier-than-thou speeches. After a couple of days hearing phones ring off the hook, we realized that stonewalling was compounding our problems. So we made a clean breast of it. We drafted a statement to the press saying that Fairway engineers had in fact discovered design flaws in 1973 but that the company had corrected the problem within 14 months. Ken made himself available to answer questions, and he and Amy arranged to meet with community leaders. They even invited experts from the university to answer the technical questions. The thrust of these efforts was to assure the public that no flaws had been discovered since 1973 and that all Fairway's designs were safe.

Thanks to Amy and Ken, the controversy finally died down. I was proud of the way they handled things. I was also glad that Ken didn't fire Jim. At the height of the crisis, someone at headquarters had suggested that he "get rid of the troublemaker," but Ken thought that would only make matters worse. I didn't want to fire Jim either. I felt he was still a valuable employee. I knew he was committed to Fairway, and we sure needed his skills.

We weathered those difficult weeks with only a few outstanding lawsuits, but an ugly incident like that never has a simple ending. It keeps unraveling. Now we have another problem. Word got out that Jim was the whistle-blower, and now his life here is miserable. The feeling is that Jim can't be trusted. Last week, Lorraine Wellman, another former teammate, came to talk to me about the problem.

"You know, it's not that anyone hates Jim for what he did," she said. "It's just that no one can understand why he did it. They could understand it if someone had been hurt or killed because of a bad design, but that wasn't the case. In their minds, he risked their jobs for something that happened ages ago.

"Morale is pretty low in the trenches," she added. "One guy told me he used to be proud of where he worked. Now his neighbors razz him about 'Radongate' and 'Three-Mile Radon.' No one wants to work with Jim, and it's affecting our output."

I felt terrible for Jim. Unlike the others, I understood why he did what he did, and I respected his integrity. On the other hand, I wasn't surprised that his coworkers resented him. I just wished everyone would forget the whole thing and get on with their work. But the situation seemed to be getting worse instead of better.

Yesterday Ken came to see me about the mounting problems in Jim's department. He suggested that Jim might want to resign and that we could give him a very generous package if he did. I knew what Ken was driving at. He didn't want to stir up trouble by firing a whistle-blower, but he thought we could get around it by pressuring Jim to leave on his own. That would solve all our problems. Of course Ken just wanted what was best for Fairway, but I resisted the idea. I asserted that the problems were temporary, and threw in a few remarks about Jim's outstanding performance. I figured I should defend him.

After all, Jim had done the noble thing, and it didn't seem right that he should get the shaft. But Ken persisted. He was worried about meeting targets and didn't think one person should be allowed to make everyone else look bad. He asked me to talk to Jim.

Jim had been avoiding me since he showed me the report, and maybe I was avoiding him too. The worst thing about this whole situation is that it ruined our friendship. Still, he agreed to see me in my office. I tried to break the ice by extending my hand and saying that I missed seeing him. But he ignored the gesture and mumbled something about being busy. So I decided to jump right in.

"I've heard about the problems you've been having with the team. This thing is taking its toll—on Fairway, your department, and you."

"I can handle it. Or maybe that's not your point. Are you saying that the company doesn't want me around anymore?"

"Look Jim," I said, "I'm real sorry this happened. I hate to see you and your family suffering like this. Maybe a transfer to another office would be the best thing. There are other divisions that could use your talents."

"You just don't get it, do you, Bob? I haven't done anything wrong, and I'm the one who's suffering. People are blaming me for a report I didn't write and bad designs I didn't push on customers. And now I'm the one you want out. I figured the idea of firing me might occur to someone, but I can't believe you agreed to it. That's one I hadn't expected."

"No one has mentioned firing," I said. "I'm talking about a transfer. I see why you're angry about your teammates giving you a hard time, but why come down on me? I'm one of the few who understand your position, and I've tried to support you."

"You've tried to *support* me? Give me a break! I didn't want to get into this, but now that you've brought it up, I'm going to spell it out for you.

"I didn't ask to see that report. It fell into my hands. But once it did, I couldn't just pretend it wasn't there. What the company did was wrong—you know that and I know that. If someone didn't say something, Fairway could get away with it again.

"But I surely didn't figure you'd make me go this alone. I didn't expect you to run to the newspapers, but I did expect you to make a strong case to Ken for the company coming clean on this. And failing that, I expected you—as my supervisor—to take this off my shoulders by assuming the responsibility yourself.

"You've got more power than I have, and you certainly have more influence with Ken. But you acted like this whole thing had nothing to do with you—like you were just a messenger. You dumped Ken's answer in my lap and washed your hands of the whole affair.

"I never thought I'd say this, but it's beginning to look like you care way too much for your fancy new title and your tight relationship with Ken. Well, I won't quit and I won't transfer!"

Before I could respond, Jim was out the door. I don't know how long I sat at my desk in a daze. After a while I tried to get back to work, but I couldn't concentrate. The whole morning I kept going over what Jim had said. How could I defend Jim and the company at the same time? Was Ken wrong? Had Jim really done the noble thing after all?

Questions for discussion

1. Did Jim Bower really have a case to blow the whistle on?
2. Is there a statute of limitations on ineptitude, mistakes, or misconduct?
3. Was anything realistically accomplished by blowing the whistle in this case?
4. Could similar results have been achieved in another fashion?

• *Case Study* •

The DC-10's Defective Doors*

Barbara Himes • Tom L. Beauchamp • Cathleen Kaveny

The Douglas Company had always held the lead in commercial aviation until the Boeing Company captured a significant portion of the jet market in the late 1950s with its 707. (The 707 was actually similar to Douglas's DC-8, which was already in service.) The Douglas Company, keenly aware of new and stiff competition, hoped to manufacture a wide-bodied jet that would be attractive in international markets. Management viewed an "airbus" as crucial to long-term economic well-being (although no wide-bodies were actually produced for another ten years).[1]

Douglas was taken over by McDonnell Aircraft in 1967. By this time, pressure to produce a wide-bodied jet had intensified. The Boeing Company had already introduced its 747, and neither Douglas nor the Federal Aviation Administration (FAA) wished Boeing to have exclusive control over this aspect of the air travel market. The McDonnell Douglas firm then searched for a structural design subcontractor capable of sharing short-term financial burdens of a program building wide-bodied jets that would realize long-term profits. The Convair Division of General Dynamics was a subcontractor with an excellent reputation for structural design. The understanding between the two companies was that McDonnell Douglas had the primary authority to furnish design criteria and to amend design decisions. Convair's role was to create a design that would satisfy the stipulated criteria.[2]

In August 1968, McDonnell Douglas awarded Convair a contract to build the DC-10 fuselage and doors. The lower cargo doors became the subject of immediate discussion. These doors were to be outward-hinging, tension-latch doors, with latches driven by hydraulic cylinders—a design already adequately tested by DC-8 and DC-9 models. In addition, each cargo door was designed to be linked to hydraulically actuated flight controls and was to have a manual locking system designed so that the handle or latch lever could not be stowed away unless the door was properly closed and latched. McDonnell Douglas, however, decided to separate the cargo door actuation system from the hy-

---

*Copyright © 1989 by Tom L. Beauchamp. Reprinted with permission.

draulically actuated primary flight controls. This involved using electric actuators to close the cargo doors rather than the hydraulic actuators originally called for. Fewer moving parts in the electric actuators presumably made for easier maintenance, and each door would weigh 28 pounds less.

However, the Convair engineers had considered the hydraulic actuators critical to safety. They were not satisfied with these changes, and they remained dissatisfied after further modifications were introduced. As Convair engineers viewed the situation, the critical difference between the two actuator systems involved the way each would respond to the buildup of forces caused by increasing pressure. If a hydraulic latch was not secured properly, the latches would smoothly slide open when only a small amount of pressure had built up in the cabin. Although the doors would be ripped off their hinges, this would occur at a low altitude, so that the shock from decompression would be small enough to land the plane safely. By contrast, if an electric latch failed to catch, it would not gently slide open due to increasing pressure. Rather, it would be abruptly and violently forced open, most likely at a higher altitude where rapid decompression would dangerously impair the structure of the plane.

Convair's Director of Product Engineering, F. D. "Dan" Applegate, was adamant that a hydraulic system was more satisfactory. However, McDonnell Douglas did not yield to Convair's reservations about the DC-10 cargo door design.

Once a decision had been made to use an electrical system, it was necessary to devise a new and foolproof backup system of checking and locking. In the summer of 1969 McDonnell Douglas asked Convair to draft a Failure Mode and Effects Analysis, or FMEA, for the cargo door system. An FMEA's purpose is to assess the likelihood and consequences of a failure in the system. In August 1969, Convair engineers found nine possible failure sequences that could result in destruction of the craft, with loss of human lives. A major problem focused on the warning and locking-pin systems. The door could close and latch, but without being safely locked. The warning indicator lights were prone to failure, in which case a door malfunction could go undetected. The FMEA also concluded that the door design was potentially dangerous and lacked a reliable failsafe locking system. It could open in flight, presenting considerable danger to passengers.[3]

The FAA requires that it be given an FMEA covering all systems critical to safety, but no mention was made of this hazard to the FAA prior to "certification" of the DC-10 model. McDonnell Douglas maintains that no such report was filed because this cargo door design was not implemented until all defects expressed in the FMEA were removed. The FMEA *submitted*, they contend, was the *final* FMEA, and did not discuss past defects because they had been removed.[4]

As lead manufacturer, McDonnell Douglas made itself entirely responsible for the certification of the aircraft and, in seeking the certification, was expressing its position that all defects had been removed. Convair, by contrast, was not formally responsible because its contract with McDonnell Douglas forbade Convair from reporting directly to the FAA.

During a model test run in May 1970, the DC-10 blew its forward lower cargo door, and the plane's cabin floor collapsed. Because the vital electric and hydraulic subsystems of the plane are located under the cabin floor (unlike in the 747, where they are above the ceiling), this collapse was doubly incapacitating.[5]

A spokesperson at McDonnell Douglas placed the blame for this particular malfunction on the "human failure" of a mechanic who had incorrectly sealed the door. Although no serious design problems were contemplated, there were some ensuing modifications in design for the door, purportedly to provide better checks on the locking pins. As modified, the cargo door design was properly certified and authorities at McDonnell Douglas believed it safe. Five DC-10s were flight tested for over 1,500 hours prior to certification of the craft.

Certification processes are carried out in the name of the FAA, but the actual work is often performed by the manufacturers. As a regulatory agency, the FAA is charged with overseeing commercial products and regulating them in the public interest. However, the FAA is often not in an independent position. The FAA appoints designated engineering representatives (DERs) to make inspections at company plants. These are company employees chosen for their experience and integrity who have the dual obligations of loyalty to the company that pays them as design engineers and of faithful performance of inspections to see that the company has complied with federal airworthiness regulations. The manufacturers are in this respect policing themselves, and it is generally acknowledged that conflicts of interest arise in this dual-obligation system.[6]

During the months surrounding November 1970, a number of internal memos were written at both McDonnell Douglas and Convair that cited old and new design problems with the cargo door. New structural proposals were made, but none was implemented. McDonnell Douglas and Convair quarreled about cost accounting and about pinning fault for remaining design flaws. The FAA finally certified the DC-10 on July 29, 1971, and by late 1971 the plane had received praise for its performance at virtually all levels. Under rigorous conditions its performance ratings were excellent. The company vigorously promoted the new aircraft.

But on June 12, 1972, an aft bulk cargo door of a DC-10 in flight from Los Angeles to New York separated from the body of the aircraft at about 11,750 feet over Windsor, Ontario. Rapid cabin decompression occurred as a result, causing structural damage to the cabin floor immediately above the cargo compartment. Nine passengers and two stewardesses were injured. A National Transportation Safety Board (NTSB) investigation found that the probable cause of the malfunction was the latching mechanism in the cargo door and recommended changes in the locking system. The NTSB's specific recommendations were the following:

1. Require a modification to the DC-10 cargo door locking system to make it physically impossible to position the external locking handle and vent door to their normal locked positions unless the locking pins are fully engaged.
2. Require the installation of relief vents between the cabin and aft cargo compartment to minimize the pressure loading on the cabin flooring in the event of sudden depressurization of the compartment.[7]

The administrator of the FAA, John Shaffer, could have issued an airworthiness directive that required immediate repairs. He elected not to issue the directive, choosing instead a "gentleman's agreement" with McDonnell Douglas that allowed the company to make the necessary modifications and recommend new procedures to affected airlines. All actions by the company were to be voluntary.

Fifteen days *subsequent* to the blowout over Windsor (June 27, 1972), Dan Applegate wrote a stern memo to his superior at Convair that expressed his doubts about the entire project and offered some reflections on "future accident liability." The following excerpts from the memo reveal Applegate's anguish and concerns:[8]

> The potential for long-term Convair liability on the DC-10 has caused me increasing concern for several reasons.
>
> 1. The fundamental safety of the cargo door latching system has been progressively degraded since the program began in 1968.
> 2. The airplane demonstrated an inherent susceptibility to catastrophic failure when exposed to explosive decompression of the cargo compartment in 1970 ground tests.
> 3. Douglas has taken an increasingly "hard-line" with regards to the relative division of design responsibility between Douglas and Convair during change cost negotiations.
> 4. The growing "consumerism" environment indicates increasing Convair exposure to accident liability claims in the years ahead. . . .
>
> In July 1970 DC-10 Number Two was being pressure-tested in the "hangar" by Douglas, on the second shift, without electrical power in the airplane. This meant that the electrically powered cargo door actuators and latch position warning switches were inoperative. The "green" second shift test crew manually cranked the latching system closed but failed to fully engage the latches on the forward door. They also failed to note that the external latch "lock" position indicator showed that the latches were not fully engaged. Subsequently, when the increasing cabin pressure reached about 3 psi (pounds per square inch) the forward door blew open. The resulting explosive decompression failed the cabin floor downward rendering tail controls, plumbing, wiring, etc. which passed through the floor, inoperative. This inherent failure mode is catastrophic, since it results in the loss of control of the horizontal and vertical tail and the aft center engine. We informally studied and discussed with Douglas alternative corrective actions including blow out panels in the cabin floor which would accommodate the "explosive" loss of cargo compartment pressure without loss of tail surface and aft center engine control. It seemed to us then prudent that such a change was indicated since "Murphy's Law" being what it is, cargo doors will come open sometime during the twenty years of the use ahead for the DC-10.
>
> Douglas concurrently studied alternative corrective actions, in house, and made a unilateral decision to incorporate vent doors in the cargo doors. This "bandaid fix" not only failed to correct the inherent DC-10 catastrophic failure mode of cabin floor collapse, but the detail design of the vent door change further degraded the safety of the original door latch system by replacing the direct, short-coupled and stiff latch "lock" indicator system with a complex and relatively flexible linkage. (This change was accomplished entirely by Douglas with the exception of the assistance of one Convair engineer who was sent to Long Beach at their request to help their vent door system design team.)
>
> This progressive degradation of the fundamental safety of the cargo door latch system since 1968 has exposed us to increasing liability claims. On June 12, 1972 in Detroit, the cargo door latch electrical actuator system in DC-10 number 5 failed to fully engage the latches of the left rear cargo door and the complex and relatively flexible latch "lock" system failed to make it impossible to close the vent door. When the door blew open before the DC-10 reached 12,000 feet altitude the cabin floor collapsed disabling most of the control to the tail surfaces and aft center engine. It is only chance that the airplane was not lost. Douglas has again studied alternative corrective actions and appears to be applying more "band-aids." So far

they have directed to us to install small one-inch diameter, transparent inspection windows through which you can view latch "lock-pin" position, they are revising the rigging instructions to increase "lock-pin" engagement and they plan to reinforce and stiffen the flexible linkage.

It might well be asked why not make the cargo door latch system really "fool-proof" and leave the cabin floor alone. Assuming it is possible to make the latch "fool-proof" this doesn't solve the fundamental deficiency in the airplane. A cargo compartment can experience explosive decompression from a number of causes such as: sabotage, mid-air collision, explosion of combustibles in the compartment and perhaps others, any one of which may result in damage which would not be fatal to the DC-10 were it not for the tendency of the cabin floor to collapse. The responsibility for primary damage from these kinds of causes would clearly not be our responsibility, however, we might very well be held responsible for the secondary damage, that is the floor collapse which could cause the loss of the aircraft. It might be asked why we did not originally detail design the cabin floor to withstand the loads of cargo compartment explosive decompression or design blow out panels in the cabin floors to fail in a safe and predictable way.

I can only say that our contract with Douglas provided that Douglas would furnish all design criteria and loads (which in fact they did) and that we would design to satisfy these design criteria and loads (which in fact we did). There is nothing in our experience history which would have led us to expect that the DC-10 cabin floor would be inherently susceptible to catastrophic failure when exposed to explosive decompression of the cargo compartment, and I must presume that there is nothing in Douglas's experience history which would have led them to expect that the airplane would have this inherent characteristic or they would have provided for this in their loads and criteria which they furnished to us.

My only criticism of Douglas in this regard is that once this inherent weakness was demonstrated by the July 1970 test failure, they did not take immediate steps to correct it. It seems to me inevitable that, in the twenty years ahead of us, DC-10 cargo doors will come open and I would expect this to usually result in the loss of the airplane. [Emphasis added.] This fundamental failure mode has been discussed in the past and is being discussed again in the bowels of both the Douglas and Convair organizations. It appears however that Douglas is waiting and hoping for government direction or regulations in the hope of passing costs on to us or their customers.

If you can judge from Douglas' position during ongoing contract change negotiations they may feel that any liability incurred in the meantime for loss of life, property and equipment may be legally passed on to us.

It is recommended that overtures be made at the highest management level to persuade Douglas to immediately make a decision to incorporate changes in the DC-10 which will correct the fundamental cabin floor catastrophic failure mode. Correction will take a good bit of time, hopefully there is time before the National Transportation Safety Board (NTSB) or the FAA ground the airplane which would have disastrous effects upon sales and production both near and long term. This corrective action becomes more expensive than the cost of damages resulting from the loss of one plane load of people.

F. D. Applegate
Director of Product Engineering

If this memo had reached outside authorities, Applegate conceivably might have been able to prevent the occurrence of events that (to some extent) he correctly foresaw. However, this memo was never sent either to McDonnell Douglas or to the FAA. Applegate received a reply to his memo from his immediate supervisor, J. B. Hurt. By now it was clear to both Applegate and Hurt that such major safety questions would not be addressed further at

McDonnell Douglas. Hurt's reply to Applegate pointed out that if further questions were now raised, Convair, not McDonnell Douglas, would most likely have to bear the costs of necessary modifications. Higher management at Convair subsequently agreed with Hurt. Without taking other routes to express his grave misgivings about the DC-10, Applegate filed away his memo.

In July 1972, Ship 29 of the DC-10 line was inspected by three different inspectors at the Long Beach plant of McDonnell Douglas. All three certified that the ship had been successfully altered to meet FAA specifications. Two years later, Ship 29 was owned by Turkish Airlines. This ship crashed near Paris in 1974, killing all 335 passengers and 11 crew members—the worst single-plane disaster in aviation history. Experts agreed that the immediate cause of the crash was a blowout of the rear cargo door, at approximately twelve minutes after lift-off. Decompression of the cargo bay caused a collapse of the cabin floor, thereby severing control cables. It was alleged by Sanford Douglas, President of McDonnell Douglas, that the Turkish airline involved in the crash had attempted to "rework" the door rigging or latching mechanism, was working with an inadequately trained ground crew, and failed to follow specified procedures for proper latching. The Turkish airline denied the charges. Recovery of a flight recorder indicated that there was no explosion, fire, or evident sabotage, and that the cargo door blew because it was not securely sealed.

In 1980 the McDonnell Douglas Corporation issued a special report addressing the public's growing fears about the design of the DC-10. The facts presented in the corporation's report were aimed at proving "that the DC-10 meets the toughest standards of aerospace technology."[9] The report does not mention the problems with the cargo doors. This omission is perhaps understandable in that a cargo door malfunction did *not* cause the American Airlines DC-10 crash at Chicago's O'Hare Airport on May 25, 1979, which killed 275 people and was then the worst air disaster in U.S. history. Subsequent examination by the FAA revealed that this DC-10, whose floor-venting problems (mentioned by Applegate) had been corrected, suffered from different defects.[10]

Notes

1. This paragraph profited from three unpublished sources: Fay Horton Sawyier, "The Case of the DC-10 and Discussion" (Chicago: Center for the Study of Ethics in the Professions, Illinois Institute of Technology, December 8, 1976), mimeographed, pp. 2–3; correspondence with John T. Sant of the McDonnell Douglas Corporation's Legal Department in St. Louis; and correspondence with Professor Homer Sewell of George Washington University (see his article in footnote 5).

2. See Paul Eddy, Elaine Potter, and Bruce Page, *Destination Disaster: From the Tri-Motor to the DC-10* (New York: Quadrangle Books, New York Times Book Co., 1976); John Newhouse, "A Reporter at Large: The Airlines Industry," *New Yorker,* June 21, 1982, pp. 46–93.

3. Eddy, *et al., Destination Disaster;* see also Martin Curd and Larry May, *Professional Responsibility for Harmful Actions* (Dubuque, Iowa: Kendall/Hunt Publishing Co., 1984), pp. 11–21, and Peter French, "What Is Hamlet to McDonnell-Douglas or McDonnell-Douglas to Hamlet: DC-10," *Business and Professional Ethics Journal* 1 (Winter 1982), pp. 1, 5–6.

4. John T. Sant, personal correspondence.

5. See Homer Sewell, "Commentary," *Business and Professional Ethics Journal* 1 (Winter 1982), pp. 17–19.

6. Eddy, *et al., Destination Disaster,* pp. 180–81.

7. National Transportation Safety Board, Aircraft Accident Report no. NTSB-AAR-73-2 (February 28, 1973), p. 38.

8. Eddy, *et al.*, *Destination Disaster,* pp. 183–85.

9. McDonnell Douglas Corporation, *The DC-10: A Special Report* (Long Beach, Calif.: McDonnell Douglas Corporation, 1980).

10. Newhouse, "A Reporter," p. 89: *New York Times,* June 7, 1979, sec. B, p. 13, and June 19, 1979, sec. D, p. 19; see also "New Testing Methods Could Boost Air Safety," *Science* 205 (July 6, 1979), pp. 29–31.

Questions for discussion

1. Ethics aside, what were McDonald-Douglas's legal obligations once it knew of the faulty mechanism?

2. Regardless of the product or service involved, what are the ethical obligations of a seller to furnish full information regarding a product's safety?

3. What happens when ethical and legal obligations differ?

4. Should Applegate have made his memo public?

• *Case Study* •

The Hazards of the Enterprise*

JOHN HASNAS

Upon graduating from Middle State University's MBA program last year, you were pleased to be offered a position with Kirk Enterprises, an American based multinational conglomerate. Originally started in the 1950's, the company grew rapidly due to its ability to supply NASA with several of the synthetic materials required by the space program for the development of space suits and heat shields. As the company grew, its product line diversified with one of its major successes being the development of long-lasting batteries for use in both automated probes and manned spacecraft. As the technology developed for the space program was found to have widespread commercial uses, Kirk Enterprises was able to exploit its competitive advantages to grow into a conglomerate supplying the international demand for this technology.

For many years, the company has been one of the world's largest suppliers of long-lived, large-scale batteries. However, it has become increasingly difficult to retain this position. The requirements of the Clean Air Act and especially California's state legislation mandating zero emission automobiles by the turn of the century has stimulated demand for powerful, long-lasting batteries for use in electric cars. This has greatly increased the number of competitors vying with Kirk for this market. In addition, American environmental regulations have reduced Kirk's ability to compete with producers of low cost batteries located in other countries. This is because the process of manufacturing the batteries produces measurable quantities of both lead and mercury, substances whose discharge into the environment is strictly controlled in the United States. The cost of separating these materials from the other byproducts and disposing of them in accordance with Environmental Protection Agency regulations has put Kirk at a competitive disadvantage relative to manufacturers located in countries without such controls and regulations.

Last year, Kirk made a major commitment to winning the competition in the market for the new electric car batteries. Accordingly, Kirk organized a new subdivision known as Impulse Power, Inc. devoted exclusively to the manufacture of these batteries. In deciding where to locate the new plant it proposed to build for Impulse, Kirk considered several sites both within the United States and abroad. The most favorable location appeared to be in the South American country of Parador. This had three main advantages over the other candidates. The first was the low cost of labor. The second was the site's location on the Miramonie river which empties into the Pacific Ocean and would facilitate shipment of the finished batteries to California. The third was the likelihood of being able to negotiate favorable business conditions with the Paradorian government.

One reason Kirk Enterprises had been interested in hiring you was the reputation of Middle State's graduates as being prepared to deal with matters of international business. Accordingly, after spending your initial year at the main headquarters in Orgainia, Florida, it was decided that you could be of value in Parador. As a result, you became the assistant to Jordy LaForge, Impulse's chief negotiator with the Paradorian government. You have spent the last month working with LaForge amassing information concerning Parador's tax, labor, and environmental law and preparing your negotiating strategy. You have learned that there are practically no labor or environmental regulations in Parador beyond a minimum wage requirement of $.57 per hour. Accordingly, LaForge decided to devote his attention in the negotiations to the tax issue.

Over the same period of time, you have been studying the operation of the proposed plant according to the documents submitted to the Paradorian government. The industrial waste generated by the manufacturing process is to be dumped into the Miramonie river which will carry it into the Pacific. Apparently, the company has no plans to separate the mercury and lead out of this effluvium. The reason the discharge of these elements into waterways is banned in the United States is that fish ingest these elements which are then absorbed into their tissues. When the fish are caught and eaten by human beings, the mercury and lead are ingested as well. Both these elements are neurotoxins which attack the human central nervous system and lead, which is easily absorbed, is especially dangerous to children even at relatively low levels. You are concerned by this because you know that most of the native Paradorians who live along the coast make their living by fishing and that fish is a staple of the native diet.

The negotiating sessions began last week. LaForge has been extremely skillful at keeping the discussion focused on the issue of tax concessions. In the first session the only time environmental concerns came close to being addressed was when the Paradorian negotiator asked, "Is the plant safe?" to which LaForge replied, "Of course, perfectly safe."

This response bothered you and you discussed it with LaForge after the meeting adjourned. When you inquired whether he thought he had made a false representation concerning the plant's safety, he responded, "All I said was that the plant was safe. That statement can be interpreted in many ways. And besides, the plant is safe. We're not making explosives or nuclear weapons." Still unsatisfied, you pressed him by asking, "But what about the mercury and lead that will be dumped into the river?" At this point, LaForge became impatient with you and stated, "Look, this is not Sunday school. These negotiations concern big money. We're not hiding anything. Our proposed manufacturing processes and methods of waste disposal are a matter of public record. It's the Paradorians' job to protect their country's environment. If they are not concerned enough to do their homework, I'm certainly not going to do it for them. Besides, it's the EPA regulations back home that are undermining our position in the global market. Why do you think we're locating this plant in Parador, anyway?"

LaForge's last comment greatly disturbed you and you decided to speak to Diana Troy, the head of Impulse's development team and LaForge's immediate superior. You explained the situation to her and asked whether it was company policy to mislead the Paradorian negotiators and whether the reason Impulse was locating in Parador was to avoid American environmental regulations. Troy assured you that such was not the case and that company policy had always been to be forthright and above board in all negotiations. She thanked you for bringing the matter to her attention and assured you that she would talk to LaForge about it.

Although this set your mind at ease at first, as the negotiations continued, LaForge made no attempt to correct his statement about the plant's safety and seemed to you to be skillfully preventing the subject of the proposed plant's environmental impact from being discussed. After two weeks, you went to see Troy again. She seemed considerably less hospitable than at your last meeting, claiming that she was very busy and could only give you five minutes. Upon inquiring whether anything had been done concerning Impulse's negotiating posture with regard to environmental issues, she told you that she had raised the matter with William Riker, the Vice President of Kirk's battery subdivision who is to be the first CEO of Impulse. Troy claims that he instructed her that if the negotiations were going well, she should not "rock the boat," and that the matter was now out of her hands.

The negotiations have been going well and LaForge has been successful in obtaining several favorable tax concessions for the company. He has told you that he expects to wrap things up within two weeks and has scheduled the last negotiating session for October 29. When you asked him whether he intended to raise the issue of the plant's environmental impact before then, he responded, "Get serious," and then added jokingly, "You're not going to hand me any 'Save the Whales' literature are you?"

You realize that you have a limited amount of time to decide what action, if any, you should take with regard to this situation. What should you do?

Questions for discussion

1. Is it morally acceptable for Kirk to build the proposed plant in Parador?

2. What moral obligations do Kirk and its representatives have to the Paradorian government and citizens regarding the exact nature of their proposed manufacturing process?

3. Whose behavior in this case is morally acceptable? Unacceptable?

• *Court Decision* •

Weber v. Kaiser Aluminum and United Steelworkers

U.S. Supreme Court, 1979

Decision: Corporation's voluntary affirmative action plan, granting preference to black employees over more senior white employees in admission to in-
plant craft training programs, held not violative of 42 USCS §§ 2000e-2(a), (d).
[Title VII]

Summary

A union and a corporation entered into a master collective bargaining
agreement covering terms and conditions of employment at several of the corporation's plants. Among other things, the agreement contained an affirmative action plan designed to eliminate conspicuous racial imbalances in the corporation's almost exclusively white craft work force. After setting black craft
hiring goals for each plant equal to the percentage of blacks in the respective
local labor forces, the plan established on-the-job training programs to teach
unskilled production workers the skills necessary to become craft workers. At
one particular plant, where the craft work force was less than 2% black even
though the local work force was 39% black, the corporation established a training program and selected trainees on the basis of seniority, with the proviso
that at least 50% of the new trainees were to be black until the percentage of
black skilled craft workers in the plant approximated the percentage of blacks
in the local labor force. During the plan's first year of operation, the most junior black trainee selected had less seniority than several white production
workers whose bids for admission to the program were rejected. One such
white worker instituted a class action in the United States District Court for the
Eastern District of Louisiana alleging that the manner of filling craft trainee positions discriminated against him and other similarly situated white employees
in violation of §§ 703(a) and 703(d) of Title VII of the Civil Rights Act of 1964
[42 USCS §§ 2000e-2(a), (d)]. The District Court held that the plan violated
Title VII, entered a judgment in favor of the class of white employees, and
granted a permanent injunction prohibiting the corporation and the union
from denying members of the class access to on-the-job training programs on
the basis of race. . . . The United States Court of Appeals for the Fifth Circuit
affirmed, holding that all employment preferences based upon race, including those preferences incidental to bona fide affirmative action plans, violated
Title VII's prohibition against racial discrimination in employment. . . .
On certiorari, the United States Supreme Court reversed. In an opinion,
by BRENNAN, J., joined by STEWART, WHITE, MARSHALL, and BLACKMUN, JJ., it
was held that (1) the prohibition §§ 703(a) and 703(d) of Title VII against
racial discrimination does not condemn all private, voluntary, race-conscious
affirmative action plans, since any contrary interpretation of §§ 703(a) and
703(d) would bring about an end completely at variance with the purpose of

the statute, the inference that Congress did not wish to ban all voluntary, race-conscious affirmative action being further supported by its use only of the word "require," rather than the phrase "require or permit," in § 703(j) of Title VII . . . which provides that nothing in Title VII shall be interpreted to "require" any employer to grant preferential treatment to any group, because of that group's race, on account of a de facto racial imbalance in the employer's work force, and (2) the affirmative action plan under consideration, which was designed to eliminate traditional patterns of conspicuous racial segregation, was permissible under Title VII, especially in light of the fact that it did not require the discharge of white workers and their replacement with new black hires, did not create an absolute bar to the advancement of white employees, and was a temporary measure not intended to maintain racial balance but simply to eliminate a manifest racial imbalance.

BLACKMUN, J., concurring, expressed the view that while it would have been preferable to uphold the corporation's craft training program as a "reasonable response" to an "arguable violation" of Title VII, the court's reading of Title VII, permitting affirmative action by an employer whenever the job category in question is "traditionally segregated," was an acceptable one.

BURGER, CH. J., dissenting, expressed the view that the quota embodied in the collective-bargaining agreement discriminated on the basis of race against individual employees seeking admission to on-the-job training programs, such discrimination being an "unlawful employment practice" under the plain language of 42 USCS § 2000e-2(d) [i.e., Title VII].

REHNQUIST, J., joined by BURGER, CH. J., dissenting, expressed the view that the corporation's racially discriminatory admission quota was flatly prohibited by the plain language of Title VII, and furthermore was sanctioned by neither the Act's legislative history nor its "spirit."

POWELL AND STEVENS, JJ., did not participate.

Opinion of the Court

Mr. Justice Brennan delivered the opinion of the Court.

[1a] Challenged here is the legality of an affirmative action plan—collectively bargained by an employer and a union—that reserves for black employees 50% of the openings in an in-plant craft training program until the percentage of black craft workers in the plant is commensurate with the percentage of blacks in the local labor force. The question for decision is whether Congress, in Title VII of the Civil Rights Act of 1964 as amended, . . . left employers and unions in the private sector free to take such race-conscious steps to eliminate manifest racial imbalances in traditionally segregated job categories. We hold that Title VII does not prohibit such race-conscious affirmative action plans.

In 1974 petitioner United Steelworkers of America (USWA) and petitioner Kaiser Aluminum & Chemical Corporation (Kaiser) entered into a master collective-bargaining agreement covering terms and conditions of employment at 15 Kaiser plants. The agreement contained, inter alia, an affirmative action plan designed to eliminate conspicuous racial imbalances in Kaiser's then almost exclusively white craft work forces. Black craft hiring goals were set for each Kaiser plant equal to the percentage of blacks in the respective local labor forces: To enable plants to meet these goals, on-the-job training programs were established to teach unskilled production workers—black and white—the skills necessary to become craft workers. The plan reserved for black employees 50% of the openings in these newly created in-plant training programs.

[2a] This case arose from the operation of the plan at Kaiser's plant in Gramercy, La. Until 1974 Kaiser hired as craft workers for that plant only persons who had had prior craft experience. Because blacks had long been excluded from craft unions, few were able to present such credentials. As a consequence, prior to 1974 only 1.83% (five out of 273) of the skilled craft workers at the Gramercy plant were black, even though the work force in the Gramercy area was approximately 39% black.

Pursuant to the national agreement, Kaiser altered its craft hiring practice in the Gramercy plant. Rather than hiring already trained outsiders, Kaiser established a training program to train its production workers to fill craft openings. Selection of craft trainees was made on the basis of seniority, with the proviso that at least 50% of the new trainees were to be black until the percentage of black skilled craft workers in the Gramercy plant approximated the percentage of blacks in the local labor force. . . .

During 1974, the first year of the operation of the Kaiser-USWA affirmative action plan, 13 craft trainees were selected from Gramercy's production work force. Of these, 7 were black and 6 white. The most junior black selected into the program had less seniority than several white production workers whose bids for admission were rejected. Therefore one of those white production workers, respondent Brian Weber, instituted this class action in the United States District Court for the Eastern District of Louisiana.

The complaint alleged that the filling of craft trainee positions at the Gramercy plant pursuant to the affirmative action program had resulted in junior black employees receiving training in preference to more senior white employees, thus discriminating against respondent and other similarly situated white employees in violation of §§ 703(a) and (d) of Title VII. The District Court held that the plan violated Title VII, entered a judgment in favor of the plaintiff class, and granted a permanent injunction prohibiting Kaiser and the USWA "from denying plaintiffs, Brian W. Weber and all other members of the class, access to on-the-job training programs on the basis of race." A divided panel of the Court of Appeals for the Fifth Circuit affirmed, holding that all employment preferences based upon race, including those preferences incidental to bona fide affirmative action plans, violated Title VII's prohibition against racial discrimination in employment. . . . We reverse.

We emphasize at the outset the narrowness of our inquiry. Since the Kaiser-USWA plan does not involve state action, this case does not present an alleged violation of the Equal Protection Clause of the Constitution. Further, since the Kaiser-USWA plan was adopted voluntarily, we are not concerned with what Title VII requires or with what a court might order to remedy a past proven violation of the Act. The only question before us is the narrow statutory issue of whether Title VII forbids private employers and unions from voluntarily agreeing upon bona fide affirmative action plans that accord racial preferences in the manner and for the purpose provided in the Kaiser-USWA plan. That question was expressly left open in McDonald v. Santa Fe Trail Trans. Co., . . . (1976) which held, in a case not involving affirmative action, that Title VII protects whites as well as blacks from certain forms of racial discrimination.

Respondent argues that Congress intended in Title VII to prohibit all race-conscious affirmative action plans. Respondent's argument rests upon a literal interpretation of §§ 703(a) and (d) of the Act. Those sections make it unlawful to "discriminate . . . because of . . . race" in hiring and in the selection of apprentices for training programs. Since, the argument runs, McDonald v. Santa Fe Trans. Co., . . . settled that Title VII *forbids* discrimination against whites as well as blacks, and since the Kaiser-USWA affirmative action plan operates to discriminate against white employees solely because they are white, it follows that the Kaiser-USWA plan violates Title VII.

[1b,2] Respondent's argument is not without force. But it overlooks the significance of the fact that the Kaiser-USWA plan is an affirmative action plan voluntarily adopted by private parties to eliminate traditional patterns of racial segregation. In this context respondent's reliance upon a literal construction of §§ 703(a) and (d) and upon McDonald is misplaced. . . . It is a "familiar rule, that a thing may be within the letter of the statute and yet not within the statute, because not within its spirit, nor within the intention of its makers." Holy Trinity Church v. United States, . . . (1892). The prohibition against racial discrimination in §§ 703(a) and (d) of Title VII must therefore be read against the background of the legislative history of Title VII and the historical context from which the Act arose. . . . Examination of those sources makes clear that an interpretation of the sections that forbade all race-conscious affirmative action would "bring about an end completely at variance with the purpose of the statute" and must be rejected. . . .

Congress' primary concern in enacting the prohibition against racial discrimination in Title VII of the Civil Rights Act of 1964 was with "the plight of the Negro in our economy." 110 Cong Rec 6548 (remarks of Sen. Humphrey). Before 1964, blacks were largely relegated to "unskilled and semi-skilled jobs. . . ." at 6548 (remarks of Sen. Humphrey). Because of automation the number of such jobs was rapidly decreasing. As a consequence "the relative position of the Negro worker [was] steadily worsening. In 1947 the non-white unemployment rate was only 64 percent higher than the white race; in 1962 it was 124 percent higher." (remarks of Sen. Humphrey). See also id., at 7204 (remarks of Sen. Clark). Congress considered this a serious social problem. As Senator Clark told the Senate:

> The rate of Negro unemployment has gone up consistently as compared with white unemployment for the past 15 years. This is a social malaise and a social situation which we should not tolerate. This is one of the principal reasons why this bill should pass.

Congress feared that the goals of the Civil Rights Act—the integration of blacks into the mainstream of American society—could not be achieved unless this trend were reversed. And Congress recognized that that would not be possible unless blacks were able to secure jobs "which have a future." As Senator Humphrey explained to the Senate:

> What good does it do a Negro to be able to eat in a fine restaurant if he cannot afford to pay the bill? What good does it do him to be accepted in a hotel that is too expensive for his modest income? How can a Negro child be motivated to take full advantage of integrated educational facilities if he has no hope of getting a job where he can use that education?
> Without a job, one cannot afford public convenience and accommodations. In-

come from employment may be necessary to further a man's education, or that of his children. If his children have no hope of getting a good job, what will motivate them to take advantage of educational opportunities?

These remarks echoed President Kennedy's original message to Congress upon the introduction of the Civil Rights Act in 1963.

> There is little value in a Negro's obtaining the right to be admitted to hotels and restaurants if he has no cash in his pocket and no job.

Accordingly, it was clear to Congress that "the crux of the problem [was] to open employment opportunities for Negroes in occupations which have been traditionally closed to them," (remarks of Sen. Humphrey), and it was to this problem that Title VII's prohibition against racial discrimination in employment was primarily addressed.

It plainly appears from the House Report accompanying the Civil Rights Act that Congress did not intend wholly to prohibit private and voluntary affirmative action efforts as one method of solving this problem. The Report provides:

> No bill can or should lay claim to eliminating all of the causes and consequences of racial and other types of discrimination against minorities. There is reason to believe, however, that national leadership provided by the enactment of Federal legislation dealing with the most troublesome problems *will create an atmosphere conducive to voluntary or local resolution of other forms of discrimination.* 88th Cong, 1st Sess (1963) (emphasis supplied.) . . .

[1c] Our conclusion is further reinforced by examination of the language and legislative history of § 703(j) of Title VII. Opponents of Title VII raised two related arguments against the bill. First, they argued that the Act would be interpreted to *require* employers with racially imbalanced work forces to grant preferential treatment to racial minorities in order to integrate. Second, they argued that employers with racially imbalanced work forces would grant preferential treatment to racial minorities, even if not required to do so by the Act. See 110 Cong Rec (remarks of Sen. Sparkman). Had Congress meant to prohibit all race-conscious affirmative action, as respondent urges, it easily could have answered both objections by providing that Title VII would not require or *permit* racially preferential integration efforts. But Congress did not choose such a course. Rather, Congress added § 703(j) which addresses only the first objection. The section provides that nothing contained in Title VII "shall be interpreted to *require* any employer . . . to grant preferential treatment . . . to any group because of the race . . . of such . . . group on account of" a de facto racial imbalance in the employer's work force. The section does *not* state that "nothing in Title VII shall be interpreted to *permit*" voluntary affirmative efforts to correct racial imbalances. The natural inference is that congress chose not to forbid all voluntary race-conscious affirmative action.

The reasons for this choice are evident from the legislative record. Title VII could not have been enacted into law without substantial support from legislators in both Houses who traditionally resisted federal regulation of private business. Those legislators demanded as a price for their support that "management prerogatives and union freedoms . . . be left undisturbed to the greatest extent possible. . . ." Section 703(j) was proposed by Senator Dirksen to allay any fears that the Act might be interpreted in such a way as to upset this compromise. The section was designed to prevent § 703 of Title VII from being interpreted in such a way as to lead to undue "Federal Government interference with private businesses because of some Federal employee's ideas about racial balance or imbalance." 110 Cong Rec, (remarks of Sen. Miller). . . . Clearly, a prohibition against all voluntary, race-conscious, affirmative action efforts would disserve these ends. Such a prohibition would augment the powers of the Federal Government and diminish traditional management prerogatives while at the same time impeding attainment of the ultimate statutory goals. In view of this legislative history and in view of Congress' desire to avoid undue federal regulation of private businesses, use of the word "require" rather than the phrase "require or permit" in § 703(j) fortifies the conclusion that Congress did not intend to limit traditional business freedom to such a degree as to prohibit all voluntary, race-conscious affirmative action.

[1d] We therefore hold that Title VII's prohibition in §§ 703(a) and (d) against racial discrimination does not condemn all private, voluntary race-conscious affirmative action plans.

We need not today define in detail the line of demarcation between permissible and impermissible affirmative action plans. It suffices to hold that the challenged Kaiser-USWA affirmative action plan falls on the permissible side of the line. The purposes of the plan mirror those of the statute. Both were designed to break down old patterns of racial segregation and hierarchy. Both were structured to "open employment opportunities for Negroes in occupations which have been traditionally closed to them." 110 Cong Rec (remarks of Sen. Humphrey).

[1e] At the same time the plan does not unnecessarily trammel the interests of the white employees. The plan does not require the discharge of white workers and their replacement with new black hires. Cf. McDonald v. Santa Fe Trail Trans. Co., supra. Nor does the plan create an absolute bar to the advancement of white employees; half of those trained in the program will be white. Moreover, the plan is a temporary measure; it is not intended to maintain racial balance, but simply to eliminate a manifest racial imbalance. Preferential selection of craft trainees at the Gramercy plant will end as soon as the percentage of black skilled craft workers in the Gramercy plant approximates the percentage of blacks in the local labor force. . . .

We conclude, therefore, that the adoption of the Kaiser-USWA plan for the Gramercy plant falls within the area of discretion left by Title VII to the private sector voluntarily to adopt affirmative action plans designed to eliminate conspicuous racial imbalance in traditionally segregated job categories. Accordingly, the judgment of the Court of Appeals for the Fifth Circuit is reversed.

Mr. Justice Powell and Mr. Justice Stevens took no part in the consideration or decision of this case. . . .

Mr. Chief Justice Burger, dissenting.

The Court reaches a result I would be inclined to vote for were I a Member of Congress considering a proposed amendment of Title VII. I cannot join the Court's judgment, however, because it is contrary to the explicit language of the statute and arrived at by means wholly incompatible with long-established principles of separation of powers. Under the guise of statutory "construction," the Court effectively rewrites Title VII to achieve what it regards as a desirable result. It "amends" the statute to do precisely what both its sponsors and its opponents agreed the statute was not intended to do. When Congress enacted Title VII after long study and searching debate, it produced a statute of extraordinary clarity, which speaks directly to the issue we consider in this case. In § 703(d) Congress provided:

> It shall be an unlawful employment practice for any employer, labor organization, or joint labor-management committee controlling apprenticeship or other training or retraining, including on-the-job training programs, to discriminate against any individual because of his race, color, religion, sex, or national origin in admission to, or employment in, any program established to provide apprenticeship or other training.

Often we have difficulty interpreting statutes either because of imprecise drafting or because legislative compromises have produced genuine ambiguities. But here there is no lack of clarity, no ambiguity. The quota embodied in the collective-bargaining agreement between Kaiser and the Steelworkers unquestionably discriminates on the basis of race against individual employees seeking admission to on-the-job training programs. And, under the plain language of § 703(d), that is "an unlawful employment practice."

Oddly, the Court seizes upon the very clarity of the statute almost as a justification for evading the unavoidable impact of its language. The Court blandly tells us that Congress could not really have meant what it said, for a "literal construction" would defeat the "purpose" of the statute—at least the congressional "purpose" as five Justices divine it today. But how are judges supposed to ascertain the purpose of a statute except through the words Congress used and the legislative history of the statute's evolution? One need not even resort to the legislative history to recognize what is apparent from the face of Title VII—that it is specious to suggest that § 703(j) contains a negative pregnant that permits employers to do what §§ 703(a) and (d) unambiguously and unequivocally forbid employers from doing. Moreover, as Mr. Justice Rehnquist's opinion—which I join—conclusively demonstrates, the legislative history makes equally clear that the supporters and opponents of Title VII reached an agreement about the statute's intended effect. That agreement, expressed so clearly in the language of the statute that no one should doubt its meaning, forecloses the reading which the Court gives the statute today.

Arguably, Congress may not have gone far enough in correcting the effects of past discrimination when it enacted Title VII. The gross discrimination against minorities to which the Court adverts—particularly against Negroes in the building trades and craft unions—is one of the dark chapters in the otherwise great history of the American labor movement. And I do not question the importance of encouraging voluntary compliance with the purposes and policies of Title VII. But that statute was conceived and enacted to make discrimination against *any* individual illegal, and I fail to see how "voluntary compliance" with the nondiscrimination principle that is the heart and soul of Title VII as currently written will be achieved by permitting employers to discriminate against some individuals to give preferential treatment to others.

Until today, I had thought the Court was of the unanimous view that "discriminatory preference for any group, minority or majority, is precisely and only what Congress has proscribed" in Title VII. Griggs v. Duke Power Co., . . . (1971). Had Congress intended otherwise, it very easily could have drafted language allowing what the Court permits today. Far from doing so, Congress expressly prohibited in §§ 703(a) and (d) the discrimination against Brian Weber the Court approves now. If "affirmative action" programs such as the one presented in this case are to be permitted, it is for Congress, not this Court, to so direct.

It is often observed that hard cases make bad law. I suspect there is some truth to that adage, for the "hard" cases always tempt judges to exceed the limits of their authority, as the Court does today by totally rewriting a crucial part of Title VII to reach a desirable result. Cardozo no doubt had this type of case in mind when he wrote:

> The judge, even when he is free, is still not wholly free. He is not to innovate at pleasure. He is not a knight-errant, roaming at will in pursuit of his own ideal of beauty or of goodness. He is to draw his inspiration from consecrated principles. He is not to yield to spasmodic sentiment, to vague and unregulated benevolence. He is to exercise a discretion informed by tradition, methodized by analogy, disciplined by system, and subordinated to 'the primordial necessity of order in the social life.' Wide enough in all conscience is the field of discretion that remains. B. Cardozo, *The Nature of the Judicial Process* 141 (1921).

What Cardozo tells us is beware the "good result" achieved by judicially authorized or intellectually dishonest means on the appealing notion that the desirable ends justify the improper judicial means. For there is always the danger that the seeds of precedent sown by good men for the best of motives will yield a rich harvest of unprincipled acts of others also aiming at "good ends."

Mr. Justice Rehnquist, with whom the Chief Justice joins, dissenting.

In a very real sense, the Court's opinion is ahead of its time; it could more appropriately have been handed down five years from now, in 1984, a year coinciding with the title of a book from which the Court's opinion borrows, perhaps subconsciously, at least one idea. Orwell describes in his book a governmental official of Oceania, one of the three great world powers, denouncing the current enemy, Eurasia, to an assembled crowd:

> "It was almost impossible to listen to him without being first convinced and then maddened. . . .
> "The speech had been proceeding for perhaps twenty minutes when a messenger hurried onto the platform and a scrap of paper was slipped into the speaker's hand. He unrolled and read it without pausing in his speech. Nothing altered in his voice or manner, or in the content of what he was saying, but suddenly the names were different. Without words said, a wave of understanding rippled through the crowd. Oceania was at war with East-asia! . . . The banners and posters with which the square was decorated were all wrong! . . .
> "[T]he speaker had switched from one line to the other actually in mid-sentence, not only without a pause, but without even breaking the syntax." G. Orwell, *Nineteen Eighty-Four,* 182–183 (1949).

Today's decision represents an equally dramatic and equally unremarked switch in this Court's interpretation of Title VII.

The operative sections of Title VII prohibit racial discrimination in employment simpliciter. Taken in its normal meaning, and as understood by all Members of Congress who spoke to the issue during the legislative debates, . . . this language prohibits a covered employer from considering race when making an employment decision, whether the race be black or white. Several years ago, however, a United States District Court held that "the dismissal of white employees charged with misappropriating company property while not dismissing a similarly charged Negro employee does not raise a claim upon which Title VII relief may be granted." McDonald v. Santa Fe Trail Transp. Co., . . . (1976). This Court unanimously reversed, concluding from the "uncontradicted legislative history" that "Title VII prohibits racial discrimination against the white petitioners in this case upon the same standards as would be applicable were they Negroes. . . ."

We have never wavered in our understanding that Title VII "prohibits *all* racial discrimination in employment, without exception for any particular employees." . . . In Griggs v. Duke Power Co., . . . (1971), our first occasion to interpret Title VII, a unanimous court observed that "[d]iscriminatory preference, for any group, minority or majority, is precisely and only what Congress has proscribed." And in our most recent discussion of the issue, we uttered words seemingly dispositive of this case: "It is clear beyond cavil that the obligation imposed by Title VII is to provide an equal opportunity for *each* applicant regardless of race, without regard to whether members of the applicant's race are already proportionately represented in the work force." Furnco Construction Corp. v. Waters, . . . (1978) (emphasis in original).

Today, however, the Court behaves much like the Orwellian speaker earlier described, as if it had been handed a note indicating that Title VII would lead to a result unacceptable to the Court if interpreted here as it was in our prior decisions. Accordingly, without even a break in syntax, the Court rejects "a literal construction of § 703(a)" in favor of newly discovered "legislative history," which leads it to a conclusion directly contrary to that compelled by the "uncontradicted legislative history" unearthed in McDonald and our other prior decisions. Now we are told that the legislative history of Title VII shows that employers are free to discriminate on the basis of race: an employer may, in the Court's words, "trammel the interests of white employees" in favor of black employees in order to eliminate "racial imbalance." . . . Our earlier interpretations of Title VII, like the banners and posters decorating the square in Oceania, were all wrong.

As if this were not enough to make a reasonable observer question this Court's adherence to the oftstated principle that our duty is to construe rather than rewrite legislation, United States v. Rutherford, . . . (1979), the Court also seizes upon § 703(j) of Title VII as an independent, or at least partially independent, basis for its holding. Totally ignoring the wording of that section, which is obviously addressed to those charged with the responsibility of interpreting the law rather than those who are subject to its proscriptions, and totally ignoring the months of legislative debates preceding the section's introduction and passage, which demonstrate clearly that it was enacted to prevent precisely what occurred in this case, the Court infers from § 703(j) that "Congress chose not to forbid all voluntary race-conscious affirmative action."

Thus, by a tour de force reminiscent not of jurists such as Hale, Holmes, and Hughes, but of escape artists such as Houdini, the Court eludes clear statutory language, "uncontradicted" legislative history, and uniform precedent in concluding that employers are, after all, permitted to consider race in making employment decisions. It may be that one or more of the principal sponsors of Title VII would have preferred to see a provision allowing preferential treatment of minorities written into the bill. Such a provision, however, would have to have been expressly or impliedly excepted from Title VII's explicit prohibition on all racial discrimination in employment. There is no such exception in the Act. And a reading of the legislative debates concerning Title VII, in which proponents and opponents alike uniformly denounced discrimination in favor of, as well as discrimination against, Negroes, demonstrates clearly that any legislator harboring an unspoken desire for such a provision could not possibly have succeeded in enacting it into law.

Questions for discussion

1. Are Title VII protections against racial discrimination and Affirmative Action plans mutually incompatible? That is, are Affirmative Action plans racially discriminatory?
2. Does Affirmative Action obey both the letter and the spirit of the purpose of Title VII protections?
3. Is Affirmative Action an effective means by which to achieve diversity in the workplace?

• *Case Study* •

The Aggressive Ad Agency: Selling Experience or Confidential Information?*

JOHN R. BOATRIGHT

Rob Lebow was used to aggressive advertising agencies. As director of corporate communications for Microsoft Corporation, the giant computer software producer located in Redmond, Washington, Lebow helped to administer the company's $10 million advertising budget. So when it was announced in the fall of 1987 that Microsoft was conducting an agency review, putting its business up for grabs, he was prepared for a flood of calls and letters. One particular piece of mail that caught his eye was a specially-prepared flier from a small agency in Boston named Rossin Greenberg Seronick & Hill.

Under the leadership of its president, Neal Hill, this five-year-old advertising agency had accounts totaling $26 million and a growth rate of 65 percent for the past year. Although its business was concentrated in New England, RGS&H was attempting to become a national force by going after high-tech industries. As part of this strategy, the agency recruited two talented people who had worked on an account for the Lotus Corporation at another firm. Jamie Mambro and Jay Williams, who were creative supervisors at Leonard Monahan Saabye in Providence, Rhode Island, joined RGS&H on November 2.

A few days later, Neal Hill read a news story in a trade publication about the agency review by the Lotus-rival. Since Microsoft's new spreadsheet program, Excel, was competing directly against Lotus 1-2-3, the industry leader, this seemed to be an ideal opportunity for RGS&H.

The flier was sent by Neal Hill on November 20, after two previous letters and several telephone calls elicited no response from Microsoft. Included in the flier was a round trip airline ticket from Seattle to Boston and an invitation that read in part:

> You probably haven't thought about talking to an agency in Boston. . . . But, since we know your competition's plans, isn't it worth taking a flier? . . . You see, the reason we know so much about Lotus is that some of our newest employees just spent the past year and a half working on the Lotus business at another agency. So they are intimately acquainted with Lotus' thoughts about Microsoft—and their plans to deal with the introduction of Excel.

In order to do an effective job for a client, advertising agencies must be provided with a certain amount of confidential information that would be of value to competitors. Many companies include a confidentiality clause in their contracts with advertising agencies, and Lotus had such an agreement with its agency, Leonard Monahan Saabye. Even in the absence of a confidentiality clause, however, advertising agencies generally recognize an obligation to preserve the confidentiality of sensitive information.

On the other hand, offering the experience of employees who have handled similar accounts is an accepted practice in the advertising industry. As the president of one firm observed, "There's a thin line between experience and first-hand recent knowledge." But, he continued, "I can't imagine a new-business presentation in which the agency didn't introduce people who worked on the prospect's kind of business."[1]

Rob Lebow was left to wonder, was Neal Hill at RGS&H offering Microsoft the experience of two employees who had worked on the Lotus account, or was he offering to sell confidential information? In either event, what should he do?

If the new employees at RGS&H had information about Lotus's advertising strategy for countering the introduction of Excel, this could be of considerable value to Microsoft. Anticipating the moves of rivals is often critical to the success of a campaign. However, moving even a part of Microsoft's business to another agency—especially to a small, untested agency like RGS&H—would surely attract the attention of Lotus. And in the rumor-filled world of advertising, the presence of two employees who formerly worked on a Lotus account would not go unnoticed. Therefore, any information that RGS&H had might be "too hot to touch."

Rob Lebow recognized that he could decline the offer in different ways. He could merely ignore the flier, or he could return it with the reply "Thanks but no thanks." Another possibility was to forward the flier to Lotus. Even the rumor that Microsoft had communicated with RGS&H could be damaging to the company, and so being open with Lotus would provide some protection. However, Lotus has a reputation within the industry of being quick to sue, and considerable harm could be done to RGS&H—and to the two new employees, Jamie Mambro and Jay Williams, who might be unaware of the offer made in the flier.

Thus, any decision that Rob Lebow made was bound to have significant ethical, legal, and practical implications.

Note

1. Cleveland Horton, "Ethics at Issue in Lotus Case," *Advertising Age*, December 21, 1987, p. 6.

Questions for discussion

1. Was it morally acceptable for Neal Hill to send the letter to Rob Lebow?
2. What should Rob Lebow do about this letter?
3. Can the line be drawn between expertise and privileged information?

• *Case Study* •

Management Dilemma*

FRED E. SCHUSTER

Stan Fritzhill, Manager of the Data Analysis Department of Aerostar, Inc., a small research firm, pondered how he should utilize a salary increase budget of $18,700 (10% of total payroll) to reward the five semi-professional employees in his unit. He knew that he did not have to spend the full budget, but under no circumstances could he exceed it. In his opinion, all of these individuals were properly paid in relation to their relative performance and seniority one year (12 months) ago, when he last adjusted their compensation. The rate of inflation last year was 7%.

Fritzhill had assembled a summary of his performance appraisals (see Appendix I on the following page) and other pertinent data to assist in determining his recommendations, which he knew were needed immediately.

Questions for discussion

1. Is the information provided in the column titled "personal circumstances" relevant to Mr. Fritzhill's decision? Why or why not?
2. Is the information provided in the column titled "years in department" relevant to Mr. Fritzhill's decision? Why or why not?
3. If it appears that an employee has been unfairly denied raises in the past, should special "make-up" raises be given? Are there any employees in this case who appear to have been unfairly treated?
4. How should Fritzhill distribute the money? What role, if any, should inflation play in his deliberations?

*This case was prepared by Professor Fred E. Schuster of Florida Atlantic University as a basis for class discussion rather than to illustrate either effective or ineffective handling of an administrative situation. All names have been disguised. Salary amounts in the case have been adjusted upward to reflect more recent salary scales. Copyright © 1978 by Fred E. Schuster. Reprinted with permission.

APPENDIX I

Name	Present Salary	Title	Salary Grade	Years in Dept.	Performance	Personal Circumstances
John Mason	$52,000	Analyst	6	5	Acceptable quality; several important deadlines have been missed but may not be his fault.	Married. Large family dependent on him as sole support.
G. W. Jones	$46,000	Analyst	6	2	Outstanding. Sometimes a bit "pushy" in making requests and suggestions about the department.	Single. No dependents. Has no pressing need for money. Reported to lead a rather "wild" life outside the office
Jane Boston	$40,000	Junior Analyst	5	8	Consistently an excellent performer, though not assigned to the full range of duties of an analyst. Dependable. Often initiates improvements in work methods.	Married. Husband is a successful architect. Children in high school.
Ralph Schmidt	$53,000	Senior Analyst	7	15	Acceptable, but not outstanding. Few original contributions recently. Seems to be a "plodder." Content to get by with minimum performance and participation.	Married. Financially pressed because he has 2 children in college (one plans to go on to Med. School).
Hillary Johnson	$38,000	Junior Analyst	5	6	Acceptable volume of performance, but continues to make costly mistakes. Has repeatedly been warned about this over last years.	Single. Has a dependent mother who is chronically ill.

• *Case Study* •

Vital Information at Complex*

Thomas Donaldson

Martha Van Hussen, Regional Director of Sales at Complex Corporation, was feeling vaguely uneasy as she sipped her morning coffee and glanced again at the latest memo from corporate headquarters. The memo stressed once more the need to block absolutely any information leaks to competitors both about changes in Complex's rapidly evolving line of computer software products and about its latest marketing strategies. Complex found itself in the middle of one of the hottest and most competitive markets in the world. The software it handled was sold primarily to banks, savings and loans, and brokerage firms, and although in the beginning Complex had been virtually alone in the market, in recent years a number of increasingly aggressive competitors had slowly whittled away at Complex's market share. The difference between a sale and a lost sale was frequently only the difference between being able to boast or not of a minor software innovation. Martha reminded herself as she looked at the memo that great hopes were being attached to the company's new "Data-File" line of products to be publicly announced in three months. Already salespeople in the division had been briefed on the new line in behind-closed-doors sessions to prepare them for selling the new products effectively.

What worried her was not so much that one of her salespeople would *intentionally* provide information to competitors, as that someone might allow an *unintentional* leak. It was true, she confessed to herself, two members of her twenty member sales force had been disgruntled over recent salary decisions and had threatened to quit. But she doubted they would actually commit an act of outright sabotage. More problematic was the fact that one of her salespersons, Frank Wright, was married to an employee of one of Complex's major competitors. Because Frank's wife, Hillary, was a software designer, Martha knew that she could interpret any relevant information, even off-hand information offered in casual remarks, decisively.

Of course, Martha had no reason to question the conduct either of Frank or Hillary. Both seemed to be good, down-to-earth types, and she had especially enjoyed chatting with them at a recent dinner party. Frank, furthermore, had done well during his first three years with the company. To further complicate the overall problem, two other members of her staff had relatives working for competing firms. In one case the relative was an uncle, and in the other it was a cousin. She also knew that her sales staff met infrequently with other salespersons from rival firms at conferences and exhibits.

Martha reminded herself that she had already called her people together to emphasize the need to protect vital corporate information. She had also sent each employee a copy of a recent memo from corporate headquarters, and had reminded them of the item in the company's Code of Conduct that stipulated that disclosure of vital information was a cause for dismissal.

---

*Copyright © 1982 by Thomas Donaldson. Reprinted with permission.

The question nagging her now was: Is there something more I should do? Should I take specific actions in specific cases? If so, what? Was it fair to penalize a person simply because he or she had the misfortune to be related to a competitor's employee? As she pondered these issues, one fact stared her in the face with perfect clarity: any leaks, either now or in the future, could seriously jeopardize the company's well-being; and moreover, if any leaks were tracked to her division, *she* would be held responsible.

Two days later, Martha received a phone call from the Vice President in charge of her Division, Mr. John Sears. Mr. Sears informed her that evidence had emerged indicating that crucial product information had been leaked by a member of her department. Two things were known for certain: (1) that Complex information had been obtained by a major competitor, and (2) that some of the information leaked had been circulated only to Van Hussen's staff. Mr. Sears was reluctant to divulge more, but he did remark that he was doubtful that more information would be forthcoming to use in tracing the leak to a specific member of Van Hussen's department. He concluded the phone call by saying, "I want you to do whatever is necessary to stop this problem."

Questions for discussion

1. Should employees have the right not to be discriminated against on the basis of outside personal activities (for instance, by being denied the same access to information as their fellow workers)?

2. How should Martha Van Hussen respond to the problem of information leaks?

• FIVE •

Diversity in the Workplace

As one of the articles in this section points out, the single most important event in the American labor market in the second half of the twentieth century is the unprecedented entry of large numbers of women into the workforce.

In January 1985, in their "Sixth Annual Salary Survey of Women," the magazine *Working Woman* announced a major shift in the composition of the workforce. According to the U.S. Census Bureau, 1984 was the first year that the white male (the prototype of the American worker) did not make up the majority of the labor force. Women and minority-group men now hold over 50 percent of all jobs. More women are now working than ever. Fifty-five percent of all women represent 46 percent of the entire workforce. As recently as 50 years ago, the notion of an unfulfilled housewife was, for most women, unheard of. Prior to World War II, the managing of a house and the attendant tasks were, if not always fulfilling, at least a full-time occupation and a demonstrably necessary one. Only in recent years, when the quotidian tasks of meal making, cleaning, and clothing maintenance have become less than full-time occupations, do we see women not merely bored by housekeeping but viewed by large segments of the population as underemployed. For these women, fulfillment in work outside the home was for the first time possible and, for many, necessary. Besides making up 46 percent of the workforce, women hold two thirds of the 20 million jobs created in the past ten years. For the first time, the majority of women are seeking jobs not simply for personal "pin money" nor for the exclusive purpose of supplementing family income, but rather for the purpose of pursuing their careers. These new careerists are now beginning to define their worth and status by their degree of success in the workplace. Perhaps for the first time, men and women are defining their identity and sense of self-worth according to the same ground rules. A brief review of the literature indicates that the most compelling evidence about the centrality of work in life comes from the recent efforts of women to fill a void in their lives with a sense of identity derived from work. As some social critics have noted, the desire for what work brings to the individual is at the foundation of the women's liberation movement.

Clearly the advent of women in the workplace is one of the most critical factors in the changing of the workforce and the work ethic. The entrance of women into the workforce has necessitated a fundamental reevaluation of our ideas regarding sexual equality, sexual role modeling, the purpose and function of marriage, the responsibility of parenthood, and the logistics of child rearing. In effect, a major revolution has been taking place in American society, one that can affect virtually all of our domestic, social, and economic arrangements.[1]

Recent research now indicates that the second major revolution that has occurred in the labor market has been the rapid diversification of the workforce. Demographers report that the homogeneous myth of America (*White Anglo-Saxon Protestant*) is now in full retreat. America is not now, and never really was, a monoculture. Assimilation, while once the goal, is now giving way to the honest recognition that we are a plural, multicultural society made up of differing ages, ethnicities, genders, physical abilities/qualities, races, and sexual/affectional orientations.

Time Magazine (Fall, 1993) in its Special Issue on diversity reported that white males are a steadily declining part of the population and currently represent just 37 percent of the total. By the year 2050, *Time* claims that the population will undergo a fundamental reconfiguration. In 1990, census statistics showed a population made up of: Anglos 76 percent, African Americans 12 percent, Latinos 9 percent, Asians 3 percent. The projected figures for 2050: Anglos 52 percent, African Americans 16 percent, Latinos 22 percent, Asians 10 percent. To help further dramatize the "changing face of America," *Time* also pointed out that presently 32 million people in the United States speak languages other than English at home and that more than 100 different languages are spoken by students in the school systems of New York, Chicago, Los Angeles, and Fairfax County, Virginia.

These new statistics and changes in our national make-up make it obvious that the workforce of the twenty-first century will be categorically different than the workforce of the twentieth century. This will require us to develop new rules, new laws, and new mores to accommodate our growing diversity. It will require us, however, to do more than just simply recognize diversity, we must also learn to live with, accept, and respect it.

The essays and cases in this section try to address some of the issues raised by our two "Revolutions in the Workplace." Felice Schwartz's article, "Management Women and the New Facts of Life," has provoked an extraordinary debate, labeled by others as the "mommy track controversy." According to Schwartz, the purpose of the article was to urge employers to create policies that help mothers balance career and family responsibilities and to eliminate barriers to female productivity and advancement. According to her critics (Barbara Ehrenreich and Deirdre English, "Blowing the Whistle on the 'Mommy Track'"; Carol Kleiman, "How to Get 'Em On Track"; and many others), the two-track system is really a way of closing off the professional future of any woman unwise enough to choose or be selected for the "career and family track." They claim that in advocating a two-track system, Schwartz is selling women short and helping to perpetuate the age-old stereotypes of women as "only or primarily," no matter what their other obligations, wives, mothers, and housekeepers.

"Women's Work: Seeking Identity Through Occupation" is an analysis of women's overall attitudes toward work and the workplace's attitude toward them. It specifically examines the notion of occupation as a source of identity and the conflict between work and the family. The "Foreign Assignment" case focuses on how women are perceived on the job by colleagues and customers. "Gender Issues at *Your House*" by John Hasnas and the two notes on "Sexual Harassment" provide the reader with a working definition of sexual harassment, recent court rulings, and a realistic workplace scenario of what can happen when a sexual harassment charge is made.

The "Sexual Discrimination at Eastern Airlines" and "Oil Rig" cases address the issue of diversity from two highly different perspectives. "Eastern Airlines" is a complicated case involving gender identity, sexual preference, gender reassignment surgery, job performance, public perception, and an inflexible (non-diverse) corporate culture. The "Oil Rig" case asks the question: In a diverse workforce is it ever morally acceptable to treat employees of different ethnic and national backgrounds differently? Finally, the reader is encouraged to turn back to Section 4, *Employee–Employer Relations*, and reexamine the "Weber v. Kaiser Aluminum" court decision (p. 144) in order to compare and reflect on the allied issues of affirmative action and diversity.

Note

1. A. R. Gini, T. J. Sullivan, *It Comes With the Territory* (New York: Random House, 1989), pp. xii, xiii.

• *Essay* •

Management Women and the New Facts of Life*

FELICE N. SCHWARTZ

The cost of employing women in management is greater than the cost of employing men. This is a jarring statement, partly because it is true, but mostly because it is something people are reluctant to talk about. A new study by one multinational corporation shows that the rate of turnover in management positions is 2½ times higher among top-performing women than it is among men. A large producer of consumer goods reports that one half of the women who take maternity leave return to their jobs late or not at all. And we know that women also have a greater tendency to plateau or to interrupt their careers in ways that limit their growth and development. But we have become so sensitive to charges of sexism and so afraid of confrontation, even litigation, that we rarely say what we know to be true. Unfortunately, our bottled-up awareness leaks out in misleading metaphors ("glass ceiling" is one notable example), veiled hostility, lowered expectations, distrust, and reluctant adherence to Equal Employment Opportunity requirements.

Career interruptions, plateauing, and turnover are expensive. The money corporations invest in recruitment, training, and development is less likely to produce top executives among women than among men, and the invaluable company experience that developing executives acquire at every level as they move up through management ranks is more often lost.

The studies just mentioned are only the first of many, I'm quite sure. Demographic realities are going to force corporations all across the country to analyze the cost of employing women in managerial positions, and what they will discover is that women cost more.

But here is another startling truth: The greater cost of employing women is not a function of inescapable gender differences. Women *are* different from men, but what increases their cost to the corporation is principally the clash of their perceptions, attitudes, and behavior with those of men, which is to say, with the policies and practices of male-led corporations.

It is terribly important that employers draw the right conclusions from the studies now being done. The studies will be useless—or worse, harmful—if all they teach us is that women are expensive to employ. What we need to learn is how to reduce that expense, how to stop throwing away the investments we make in talented women, how to become more responsive to the needs of the women that corporations *must* employ if they are to have the best and the brightest of all those now entering the work force.

The gender differences relevant to business fall into two categories: those related to maternity and those related to the differing traditions and expectations of the sexes. Maternity is biological rather than cultural. We can't alter it, but we can dramatically reduce its impact on the workplace and in many cases eliminate its negative effect on employee development. We can accomplish this by addressing the second set of differences, those between male and female socialization. Today, these differences exaggerate the real costs of maternity and can turn a relatively slight disruption in work schedule into a serious business problem and a career derailment for individual women. If we are to overcome the cost differential between male and female employees, we need to address the issues that arise when female socialization meets the male corporate culture and masculine rules of career development—issues of behavior and style, of expectation, of stereotypes and preconceptions, of sexual tension and harassment, of female mentoring, lateral mobility, relocation, compensation, and early identification of top performers.

The one immutable, enduring difference between men and women is maternity. Maternity is not simply childbirth but a continuum that begins with an awareness of the ticking of the biological clock, proceeds to the anticipation of motherhood, includes pregnancy, childbirth, physical recuperation, psychological adjustment, and continues on to nursing, bonding, and child rearing. Not all women choose to become mothers, of course, and among those who do, the process varies from case to case depending on the health of the mother and baby, the values of the parents, and the availability, cost, and quality of child care.

In past centuries, the biological fact of maternity shaped the traditional roles of the sexes. Women performed the home-centered functions that related to the bearing and nurturing of children. Men did the work that required great physical strength. Over time, however, family size contracted, the community assumed greater responsibility for the care and education of children, packaged foods and household technology reduced the work load in the home, and technology eliminated much of the need for muscle power at the workplace. Today, in the developed world, the only role still uniquely gender related is childbearing. Yet men and women are still socialized to perform their traditional roles.

Men and women may or may not have some innate psychological disposition toward these traditional roles—men to be aggressive, competitive, self-reliant, risk taking; women to be supportive, nurturing, intuitive, sensitive, communicative—but certainly both men and women are capable of the full range of behavior. Indeed, the male and female roles have already begun to expand and merge. In the decades ahead, as the socialization of boys and girls and the experience and expectations of young men and women grow steadily more androgynous, the differences in workplace behavior will continue to fade. At the moment, however, we are still plagued by disparities in perception and behavior that make the integration of men and women in the workplace unnecessarily difficult and expensive.

Let me illustrate with a few broadbrush generalizations. Of course, these are only stereotypes, but I think they help to exemplify the kinds of preconceptions that can muddy the corporate waters.

Men continue to perceive women as the rearers of their children, so they find it understandable, indeed appropriate, that women should renounce their careers to raise families. Edmund Pratt, CEO of Pfizer, once asked me in all sincerity, "Why would any woman choose to be a chief financial officer rather than a full-time mother?" By condoning and taking pleasure in women's traditional behavior, men reinforce it. Not only do they see parenting as fundamentally female, they see a career as fundamentally male—either an unbroken series of promotions and advancements toward CEOdom or stagnation and disappointment. This attitude serves to legitimize a woman's choice to extend maternity leave and even, for those who can afford it, to leave employment altogether for several years. By the same token, men who might want to take a leave after the birth of a child know that management will see such behavior as a lack of career commitment, even when company policy permits parental leave for men.

Women also bring counterproductive expectations and perceptions to the workplace. Ironically, although the feminist movement was an expression of women's quest for freedom from their home-based lives, most women were remarkably free already. They had many responsibilities, but they were autonomous and could be entrepreneurial in how and when they carried them out. And once their children grew up and left home, they were essentially free to do what they wanted with their lives. Women's traditional role also included freedom from responsibility for the financial support of their families. Many of us were socialized from girlhood to expect our husbands to take care of us, while our brothers were socialized from an equally early age to complete their educations, pursue careers, climb the ladder of success, and provide dependable financial support for their families. To the extent that this tradition of freedom lingers subliminally, women tend to bring to their employment a sense that they can choose to change jobs or careers at will, take time off, or reduce their hours.

Finally, women's traditional role encouraged particular attention to the quality and substance of what they did, specifically to the physical, psychological, and intellectual development of their children. This traditional focus may explain women's continuing tendency to search for more than monetary reward—intrinsic significance, social importance, meaning—in what they do. This too makes them more likely than men to leave the corporation in search of other values.

The misleading metaphor of the glass ceiling suggests an invisible barrier constructed by corporate leaders to impede the upward mobility of women beyond the middle levels. A more appropriate metaphor, I believe, is the kind of cross-sectional diagram used in geology. The barriers to women's leadership occur when potentially counterproductive layers of influence on women—maternity, tradition, socialization—meet management strata pervaded by the largely unconscious preconceptions, stereotypes, and expectations of men. Such interfaces do not exist for men and tend to be impermeable for women.

One result of these gender differences has been to convince some executives that women are simply not suited to top management. Other executives feel helpless. If they see even a few of their valued female employees fail to return to work from maternity leave on schedule or see one of their most promising women plateau in her career after the birth of a child, they begin to fear there is nothing they can do to infuse women with new energy and enthusiasm and persuade them to stay. At the same time, they know there is nothing they can do to stem the tide of women into management ranks.

Another result is to place every working woman on a continuum that runs from total dedication to career at one end to a balance between career and family at the other. What women discover is that the male corporate culture sees both extremes as unacceptable. Women who want the flexibility to balance their families and their careers are not adequately committed to the organization. Women who perform as aggressively and competitively as men are abrasive and unfeminine. But the fact is, business needs all the talented women it can get. Moreover, as I will explain, the women I call career-primary and those I call career-and-family each have particular value to the corporation.

Women in the corporation are about to move from a buyer's to a seller's market. The sudden, startling recognition that 80% of new entrants in the work force over the next decade will be women, minorities, and immigrants has stimulated a mushrooming incentive to "value diversity."

Women are no longer simply an enticing pool of occasional creative talent, a thorn in the side of the EEO officer, or a source of frustration to corporate leaders truly puzzled by the slowness of their upward trickle into executive positions. A real demographic change is taking place. The era of sudden population growth of the 1950s and 1960s is over. The birth rate has dropped about 40%, from a high of 25.3 live births per 1,000 population in 1957, at the peak of the baby boom, to a stable low of a little more than 15 per 1,000 over the last 16 years, and there is no indication of a return to a higher rate. The tidal wave of baby boomers that swelled the recruitment pool to overflowing seems to have been a one-time phenomenon. For 20 years, employers had the pick of a very large crop and were able to choose males almost exclusively for the executive track. But if future population remains fairly stable while the economy continues to expand, and if the new information society simultaneously creates a greater need for creative, educated managers, then the gap between supply and demand will grow dramatically and, with it, the competition for managerial talent.

The decrease in numbers has even greater implications if we look at the traditional source of corporate recruitment for leadership positions—white males from the top 10% of the country's best universities. Over the past decade, the increase in the number of women graduating from leading universities has been much greater than the increase in the total number of graduates, and these women are well represented in the top 10% of their classes.

The trend extends into business and professional programs as well. In the old days, virtually all MBAs were male. I remember addressing a meeting at the Harvard Business School as recently as the mid-1970s and looking out at a sea of exclusively male faces. Today, about 25% of that audience would be women. The pool of male MBAs from which corporations have traditionally drawn their leaders has shrunk significantly.

Of course, this reduction does not have to mean a shortage of talent. The top 10% is at least as smart as it always was—smarter, probably, since it's now drawn from a broader segment of the population. But it now consists increasingly of women. Companies that are determined to recruit the same number of men as before will have to dig much deeper into the male pool, while their competitors will have the opportunity to pick the best people from both the male and female graduates.

Under these circumstances, there is no question that the management ranks of business will include increasing numbers of women. There remains, however, the question of how these women will succeed—how long they will stay, how high they will climb, how completely they will fulfill their promise and potential, and what kind of return the corporation will realize on its investment in their training and development.

There is ample business reason for finding ways to make sure that as many of these women as possible will succeed. The first step in this process is to recognize that women are not all alike. Like men, they are individuals with differing talents, priorities, and motivations. For the sake of simplicity, let me focus on the two women I referred to earlier, on what I call the career-primary woman and the career-and-family woman.

Like many men, some women put their careers first. They are ready to make the same trade-offs traditionally made by the men who seek leadership positions. They make a career decision to put in extra hours, to make sacrifices in their personal lives, to make the most of every opportunity for professional development. For women, of course, this decision also requires that they remain single or at least childless or, if they do have children, that they be satisfied to have others raise them. Some 90% of executive men but only 35% of executive women have children by the age of 40. The *automatic* association of all women with babies is clearly unjustified.

The secret to dealing with such women is to recognize them early, accept them, and clear artificial barriers from their path to the top. After all, the best of these women are among the best managerial talent you will ever see. And career-primary women have another important value to the company that men and other women lack. They can act as role models and mentors to younger women who put their careers first. Since upwardly mobile career-primary women still have few role models to motivate and inspire them, a company with women in its top echelon has a significant advantage in the competition for executive talent.

Men at the top of the organization—most of them over 55, with wives who tend to be traditional—often find career women "masculine" and difficult to accept as colleagues. Such men miss the point, which is not that these women are just like men but that they are just like the *best* men in the organization. And there is such a shortage of the best people that gender cannot be allowed to matter. It is clearly counterproductive to disparage in a woman with executive talent the very qualities that are most critical to the business and that might carry a man to the CEO's office.

Clearing a path to the top for career-primary women has four requirements:

1. Identify them early.
2. Give them the same opportunity you give to talented men to grow and develop and contribute to company profitability. Give them client and customer responsibility. Expect them to travel and relocate, to make the same commitment to the company as men aspiring to leadership positions.
3. Accept them as valued members of your management team. Include them in every kind of communication. Listen to them.
4. Recognize that the business environment is more difficult and stressful for them than for their male peers. They are always a minority, often the only woman. The male perception of talented, ambitious women is at best ambivalent, a mixture of admiration, resentment, confusion, competitiveness, attraction, skepticism, anxiety, pride, and animosity. Women can never feel secure about how they should dress and act, whether they should speak out or grin and bear it when they encounter discrimination, stereotyping, sexual harassment, and paternalism. Social interaction and travel with male colleagues and with male clients can be charged. As they move up, the normal increase in pressure and responsibility is compounded for women because they are women.

Stereotypical language and sexist day-to-day behavior do take their toll on women's career development. Few male executives realize how common it is to call women by their first names while men in the same group are greeted with surnames, how frequently female executives are assumed by men to be secretaries, how often women are excluded from all-male social events where business is being transacted. With notable exceptions, men are still generally more comfortable with other men, and as a result women miss many of the career and business opportunities that arise over lunch, on the golf course, or in the locker room.

The majority of women, however, are what I call career-and-family women, women who want to pursue serious careers while participating actively in the rearing of children. These women are a precious resource that has yet to be mined. Many of them are talented and creative. Most of them are willing to trade some career growth and compensation for freedom from the constant pressure to work long hours and weekends.

Most companies today are ambivalent at best about the career-and-family women in their management ranks. They would prefer that all employees were willing to give their all to the company. They believe it is in their best interests for all managers to compete for the top positions so the company will have the largest possible pool from which to draw its leaders.

"If you have both talent and motivation," many employers seem to say, "we want to move you up. If you haven't got that motivation, if you want less pressure and greater flexibility, then you can leave and make room for a new generation." These companies lose on two counts. First, they fail to amortize the investment they made in the early training and experience of management women who find themselves committed to family as well as to career. Second, they fail to recognize what these women could do for their middle management.

The ranks of middle managers are filled with people on their way up and people who have stalled. Many of them have simply reached their limits, achieved career growth commensurate with or exceeding their capabilities, and they cause problems because their performance is mediocre but they still want to move ahead. The career-and-family woman is willing to trade off the pressures and demands that go with promotion for the freedom to spend more time with her children. She's very smart, she's talented, she's committed to her career, and she's satisfied to stay at the middle level, at least during the early child-rearing years. Compare her with some of the people you have there now.

Consider a typical example, a woman who decides in college on a business career and enters management at age 22. For nine years, the company invests in her career as she gains experience and skills and steadily improves her performance. But at 31, just as the investment begins to pay off in earnest, she decides to have a baby. Can the company afford to let her go home, take another job, or go into business for herself? The common perception now is yes, the corporation can afford to lose her unless, after six or eight weeks or even three months of disability and maternity leave, she returns to work on a full-time schedule with the same vigor, commitment, and ambition that she showed before.

But what if she doesn't? What if she wants or needs to go on leave for six months or a year or, heaven forbid, five years? In this worst-case scenario, she works full-time from age 22 to 31 and from 36 to 65—a total of 38 years as opposed to the typical male's 43 years. That's not a huge difference. Moreover, my typical example is willing to work part-time while her children are young, if only her employer will give her the opportunity. There are two rewards for companies responsive to this need: higher retention of their best people and greatly improved performance and satisfaction in their middle management.

The high-performing career-and-family woman can be a major player in your company. She can give you a significant business advantage as the competition for able people escalates. Sometimes too, if you can hold on to her, she will switch gears in mid-life and re-enter the competition for the top. The price you must pay to retain these women is threefold: you must plan for and manage maternity, you must provide the flexibility that will allow them to be maximally productive, and you must take an active role in helping to make family supports and high-quality, affordable child care available to all women.

The key to managing maternity is to recognize the value of high-performing women and the urgent need to retain them and keep them productive. The first step must be a genuine partnership between the woman and her boss. I know this partnership can seem difficult to forge. One of my own senior executives came to me recently to discuss plans for her maternity leave and subsequent return to work. She knew she wanted to come back. I wanted to make certain that she would. Still, we had a somewhat awkward conversation, because I knew that no woman can predict with certainty when she will be able to return to work or under what conditions. Physical problems can lengthen her leave. So can a demanding infant, a difficult family or personal adjustment, or problems with child care.

I still don't know when this valuable executive will be back on the job full-time, and her absence creates some genuine problems for our organization.

But I do know that I can't simply replace her years of experience with a new recruit. Since our conversation, I also know that she wants to come back, and that she *will* come back—part-time at first—unless I make it impossible for her by, for example, setting an arbitrary date for her full-time return or resignation. In turn, she knows that the organization wants and needs her and, more to the point, that it will be responsive to her needs in terms of working hours and child-care arrangements.

In having this kind of conversation it's important to ask concrete questions that will help to move the discussion from uncertainty and anxiety to some level of predictability. Questions can touch on everything from family income and energy level to child care arrangements and career commitment. Of course you want your star manager to return to work as soon as possible, but you want her to return permanently and productively. Her downtime on the job is a drain on her energies and a waste of your money.

For all the women who want to combine career and family—the women who want to participate actively in the rearing of their children and who also want to pursue their careers seriously—the key to retention is to provide the flexibility and family supports they need in order to function effectively.

Time spent in the office increases productivity if it is time well spent, but the fact that most women continue to take the primary responsibility for child care is a cause of distraction, diversion, anxiety, and absenteeism—to say nothing of the persistent guilt experienced by all working mothers. A great many women, perhaps most of all women who have always performed at the highest levels, are also frustrated by a sense that while their children are babies they cannot function at their best either at home or at work.

In its simplest form, flexibility is the freedom to take time off—a couple of hours, a day, a week—or to do some work at home and some at the office, an arrangement that communication technology makes increasingly feasible. At the complex end of the spectrum are alternative work schedules that permit the woman to work less than full-time and her employer to reap the benefits of her experience and, with careful planning, the top level of her abilities.

Part-time employment is the single greatest inducement to getting women back on the job expeditiously and the provision women themselves most desire. A part-time return to work enables them to maintain responsibility for critical aspects of their jobs, keeps them in touch with the changes constantly occurring at the workplace and in the job itself, reduces stress and fatigue, often eliminates the need for paid maternity leave by permitting a return to the office as soon as disability leave is over, and, not least, can greatly enhance company loyalty. The part-time solution works particularly well when a work load can be reduced for one individual in a department or when a full-time job can be broken down by skill levels and apportioned to two individuals at different levels of skill and pay.

I believe, however, that shared employment is the most promising and will be the most widespread form of flexible scheduling in the future. It is feasible at every level of the corporation except at the pinnacle, for both the short and the long term. It involves two people taking responsibility for one job.

Two red lights flash on as soon as most executives hear the words "job sharing": continuity and client-customer contact. The answer to the continuity question is to place responsibility entirely on the two individuals sharing the job to discuss everything that transpires—thoroughly, daily, and on their own time. The answer to the problem of client-customer contact is yes, job sharing requires reeducation and a period of adjustment. But as both client and supervisor will quickly come to appreciate, two contacts means that the customer has continuous access to the company's representative, without interruptions for vacation, travel, or sick leave. The two people holding the job can simply cover for each other, and the uninterrupted, full-time coverage they provide together can be a stipulation of their arrangement.

Flexibility is costly in numerous ways. It requires more supervisory time to coordinate and manage, more office space, and somewhat greater benefits costs (though these can be contained with flexible benefits plans, prorated benefits, and, in two-paycheck families, elimination of duplicate benefits). But the advantages of reduced turnover and the greater productivity that results from higher energy levels and greater focus can outweigh the costs.

A few hints:

Provide flexibility selectively. I'm not suggesting private arrangements subject to the suspicion of favoritism but rather a policy that makes flexible work schedules available only to high performers.

Make it clear that in most instances (but not all) the rates of advancement and pay will be appropriately lower for those who take time off or who work part-time than for those who work full-time. Most career-and-family women are entirely willing to make that trade-off.

Discuss costs as well as benefits. Be willing to risk accusations of bias. Insist, for example, that half time is half of whatever time it takes to do the job, not merely half of 35 or 40 hours.

The woman who is eager to get home to her child has a powerful incentive to use her time effectively at the office and to carry with her reading and other work that can be done at home. The talented professional who wants to have it all can be a high performer by carefully ordering her priorities and by focusing on objectives rather than on the legendary 15-hour day. By the time professional women have their first babies—at an average age of 31—they have already had nine years to work long hours at a desk, to travel, and to relocate. In the case of high performers, the need for flexibility coincides with what has gradually become the goal-oriented nature of responsibility.

Family supports—in addition to maternity leave and flexibility—include the provision of parental leave for men, support for two-career and single-parent families during relocation, and flexible benefits. But the primary ingredient is child care. The capacity of working mothers to function effectively and without interruption depends on the availability of good, affordable child care. Now that women make up almost half the work force and the growing percentage of managers, the decision to become involved in the personal lives of employees is no longer a philosophical question but a practical one. To make matters worse, the quality of child care has almost no relation to technology, inventiveness, or profitability but is more or less a pure function of the quality of child care personnel and the ratio of adults to children. These costs are irreducible. Only by joining hands with government and the public sector can corporations hope to create the vast quantity and variety of child care that their employees need.

Until quite recently, the response of corporations to women has been largely symbolic and cosmetic, motivated in large part by the will to avoid litigation and legal penalties. In some cases, companies were also moved by a genuine sense of fairness and a vague discomfort and frustration at the absence of women above the middle of the corporate pyramid. The actions they took were mostly quick, easy, and highly visible—child care information services, a three-month parental leave available to men as well as women, a woman appointed to the board of directors.

When I first began to discuss these issues 26 years ago, I was sometimes able to get an appointment with the assistant to the assistant in personnel, but it was only a courtesy. Over the past decade, I have met with the CEOs of many large corporations, and I've watched them become involved with ideas they had never previously thought much about. Until recently, however, the shelf life of that enhanced awareness was always short. Given pressing, short-term concerns, women were not a front-burner issue. In the past few months, I have seen yet another change. Some CEOs and top management groups now take the initiative. They call and ask us to show them how to shift gears from a responsive to a proactive approach to recruiting, developing, and retaining women.

I think this change is more probably a response to business needs—to concern for the quality of future profits and managerial talent—than to uneasiness about legal requirements, sympathy with the demands of women and minorities, or the desire to do what is right and fair. The nature of such business motivation varies. Some companies want to move women to higher positions as role models for those below them and as beacons for talented young recruits. Some want to achieve a favorable image with employees, customers, clients, and stockholders. These are all legitimate motives. But I think the companies that stand to gain most are motivated as well by a desire to capture competitive advantage in an era when talent and competence will be in increasingly short supply. These companies are now ready to stop being defensive about their experience with women and to ask incisive questions without preconceptions.

Even so, incredibly, I don't know of more than one or two companies that have looked into their own records to study the absolutely critical issue of maternity leave—how many women took it, when and whether they returned, and how this behavior correlated with their rank, tenure, age, and performance. The unique drawback to the employment of women is the physical reality of maternity and the particular socializing influence maternity has had. Yet to make women equal to men in the workplace we have chosen on the whole not to discuss this single most significant difference between them. Unless we do, we cannot evaluate the cost of recruiting, developing, and moving women up.

Now that interest is replacing indifference, there are four steps every company can take to examine its own experience with women:

1. Gather quantitative data on the company's experience with management-level women regarding turnover rates, occurrence of and return from maternity leave, and organizational level attained in relation to tenure and performance.
2. Correlate this data with factors such as age, marital status, and presence and age of children, and attempt to identify and analyze why women respond the way they do.
3. Gather qualitative data on the experience of women in your company and on how women are perceived by both sexes.
4. Conduct a cost-benefit analysis of the return on your investment in high-performing women. Factor in the cost to the company of women's negative reactions to negative experience, as well as the probable cost of corrective measures and policies. If women's value to your company is greater than the cost to recruit, train,

and develop them—and of course I believe it will be—then you will want to do everything you can to retain them.

We have come a tremendous distance since the days when the prevailing male wisdom saw women as lacking the kind of intelligence that would allow them to succeed in business. For decades, even women themselves have harbored an unspoken belief that they couldn't make it because they couldn't be just like men, and nothing else would do. But now that women have shown themselves the equal of men in every area of organizational activity, now that they have demonstrated that they can be stars in every field of endeavor, now we can all venture to examine the fact that women and men are different.

On balance, employing women is more costly than employing men. Women can acknowledge this fact today because they know that their value to employers exceeds the additional cost and because they know that changing attitudes can reduce the additional cost dramatically. Women in management are no longer an idiosyncrasy of the arts and education. They have always matched men in natural ability. Within a very few years, they will equal men in numbers as well in every area of economic activity.

The demographic motivation to recruit and develop women is compelling. But an older question remains: Is society better for the change? Women's exit from the home and entry into the work force has certainly created problems— an urgent need for good, affordable child care; troubling questions about the kind of parenting children need; the costs and difficulties of diversity in the workplace; the stress and fatigue of combining work and family responsibilities. Wouldn't we all be happier if we could turn back the clock to an age when men were in the workplace and women in the home, when male and female roles were clearly differentiated and complementary?

Nostalgia, anxiety, and discouragement will urge many to say yes, but my answer is emphatically no. Two fundamental benefits that were unattainable in the past are now within our reach. For the individual, freedom of choice—in this case the freedom to choose career, family, or a combination of the two. For the corporation, access to the most gifted individuals in the country. These benefits are neither self-indulgent nor insubstantial. Freedom of choice and self-realization are too deeply American to be cast aside for some wistful vision of the past. And access to our most talented human resources is not a luxury in this age of explosive international competition but rather the barest minimum that prudence and national self-preservation require.

Questions for discussion

1. Is Schwartz suggesting that women or companies choose to enter the mommy track? Does it make a difference?

2. If Schwartz is wrong, what sort of ethical and legal alternatives do women have with regard to their careers?

3. While women must bear children, don't men have ethical obligations with regard to the rearing of children?

• *Essay* •

Blowing the Whistle on the "Mommy Track"*

BARBARA EHRENREICH • DEIRDRE ENGLISH

When a feminist has something bad to say about women, the media listen. Three years ago it was Sylvia Hewlett, announcing in her book *A Lesser Life* that feminism had sold women out by neglecting to win child-care and maternity leaves. This year it's Felice Schwartz, the New York-based consultant who argues that women—or at least the mothers among us—have become a corporate liability. They cost too much to employ, she argues, and the solution is to put them on a special lower-paid, low-pressure career track—the now-notorious "mommy track."

• • •

The "mommy track" story rated prominent coverage in the *New York Times* and *USA Today,* a cover story in *Business Week,* and airtime on dozens of talk shows. Schwartz, after all, seemed perfectly legitimate. She is the president of Catalyst, an organization that has been advising corporations on women's careers since 1962. She had published her controversial claims in no less a spot than the *Harvard Business Review* ("Management Women and the New Facts of Life," January-February 1989). And her intentions, as she put it in a later op-ed piece, seemed thoroughly benign: "to urge employers to create policies that help mothers balance career and family responsibilities."

Moreover, Schwartz's argument seemed to confirm what everybody already knew. Women haven't been climbing up the corporate ladder as fast as might once have been expected, and women with children are still, on average, groping around the bottom rungs. Only about 40 percent of top female executives have children, compared to 95 percent of their male peers. There have been dozens of articles about female dropouts: women who slink off the fast track, at age 30-something, to bear a strategically timed baby or two. In fact, the "mommy track"—meaning a lower-pressure, flexible, or part-time approach to work—was neither a term Schwartz used nor her invention. It was already, in an anecdotal sort of way, a well-worn issue.

Most of the controversy focused on Schwartz's wildly anachronistic "solution." Corporate employers, she advised, should distinguish between two categories of women: "career-primary" women, who won't interrupt their careers for children and hence belong on the fast track with the men, and "career-and-family" women, who should be shunted directly to the mommy track. Schwartz had no answers for the obvious questions: how is the employer supposed to sort the potential "breeders" from the strivers? Would such distinction even be legal? What about *fathers?* But in a sense, the damage had already been done. A respected feminist, writing in a respected journal, had made a case that most women can't pull their weight in the corporate world, and should be paid accordingly.

*Reprinted by permission of *Ms. Magazine* © 1989.

Few people, though, actually read Schwartz's article. The first surprise is that it contains *no* evidence to support her principal claim, that "the cost of employing women in management is greater than the cost of employing men." Schwartz offers no data, no documentation at all—except for two unpublished studies by two *anonymous* corporations. Do these studies really support her claim? Were they methodologically sound? Do they even exist? There is no way to know.

Few media reports of the "mommy track" article bothered to mention the peculiar nature of Schwartz's "evidence." We, however, were moved to call the *Harvard Business Review* and inquire whether the article was representative of its normal editorial standard. Timothy Blodgett, the executive editor, defended the article as "an expression of opinion and judgment." When we suggested that such potentially damaging "opinions" might need a bit of bolstering, he responded by defending Schwartz: "She speaks with a tone of authority. That comes through."

(The conversation went downhill from there, with Blodgett stating sarcastically, "I'm sure your article in *Ms.* will be *very* objective." Couldn't fall much lower than the *Harvard Business Review,* we assured him.)

Are managerial women more costly to employ than men? As far as we could determine—with the help of the Business and Professional Women's Foundation and Women's Equity Action League—there is no *published* data on this point. A 1987 government study did show female managerial employees spending less time with each employer than males (5 years compared to 6.8 years), but there is no way of knowing what causes this turnover or what costs it incurs. And despite pregnancy, and despite women's generally greater responsibility for child-raising, they use up on the average only 5.1 sick days per year, compared to 4.9 for men.

The second surprise, given Schwartz's feminist credentials, is that the article is riddled with ancient sexist assumptions—for example, about the possibility of a more androgynous approach to child-raising *and* work. She starts with the unobjectionable statement that "maternity is biological rather than cultural." The same thing, after all, could be said of paternity. But a moment later, we find her defining maternity as ". . . a continuum that begins with an awareness of the ticking of the biological clock, proceeds to the anticipation of motherhood, includes pregnancy, childbirth, physical recuperation, psychological adjustment, and continues on to nursing, bonding, and child-rearing."

Now, pregnancy, childbirth, and nursing do qualify as biological processes. But slipping child-rearing into the list, as if changing diapers and picking up socks were hormonally programmed activities, is an old masculinist trick. Child-raising is a *social* undertaking, which may involve nannies, aunts, grandparents, day-care workers, or, of course, *fathers.*

Equally strange for a "feminist" article is Schwartz's implicit assumption that employment, in the case of married women, is strictly optional, or at least that *mothers* don't need to be top-flight earners. The "career-and-family woman," she tells us, is "willing" and "satisfied" to forgo promotions and "stay at the middle level." What about the single mother, or the wife of a low-paid male? But Schwartz's out-of-date—and class-bound—assumption that every woman is supported by a male breadwinner fits in with her apparent nostalgia for the era of the feminine mystique. "Ironically," she writes, "although the feminist movement was an expression of women's quest for freedom from their home-based lives, *most women were remarkably free already* [emphasis added]."

But perhaps the oddest thing about the "mommy track" article—even as an "expression of opinion and judgment"—is that it is full of what we might charitably call ambivalence or, more bluntly, self-contradictions. Take the matter of the "glass ceiling," which symbolized all the barriers, both subtle and overt, that corporate women keep banging their heads against. At the outset, Schwartz dismisses the glass ceiling as a "misleading metaphor." Sexism, in short, is not the problem.

Nevertheless, within a few pages, she is describing the glass ceiling (not by that phrase, of course) like a veteran. "Male corporate culture," she tells us, sees both the career-primary and the career-and-family woman as "unacceptable." The woman with family responsibilities is likely to be seen as lacking commitment to the organization, while the woman who *is* fully committed to the organization is likely to be seen as "abrasive and unfeminine." She goes on to cite the corporate male's "confusion, competitiveness," and his "stereotypical language and sexist . . . behavior," concluding that "with notable exceptions, men are still more comfortable with other men."

And we're supposed to blame *women* for their lack of progress in the corporate world?

Even on her premier point, that women are more costly to employ, Schwartz loops around and rebuts herself. Near the end of her article, she urges corporations to conduct their own studies of the costs of employing women—the two anonymous studies were apparently not definitive after all—and asserts confidently ("of course I believe") that the benefits will end up outweighing the costs. In a more recent New York *Times* article, she puts it even more baldly: "The costs of employing women pale beside the payoffs."

Could it be that both Felice Schwartz and the editors of the *Harvard Business Review* are ignorant of that most basic financial management concept, the cost-benefit analysis? If the "payoffs" outweigh the costs of employing women—runny noses and maternity leaves included—then the net cost may indeed be *lower* than the cost of employing men.

In sum, the notorious "mommy track" article is a tortured muddle of feminist perceptions and sexist assumptions, good intentions and dangerous suggestions—unsupported by any acceptable evidence at all. It should never have been taken seriously, not by the media and not by the nation's most prestigious academic business publication. The fact that it was suggests that something serious *is* afoot: a backlash against America's high-status, better paid women, and potentially against all women workers.

We should have seen it coming. For the past 15 years upwardly mobile, managerial women have done everything possible to fit into an often hostile corporate world. They dressed up as nonthreatening corporate clones. They put in 70-hour workweeks; and of course, they postponed childbearing. Thanks in part to their commitment to the work world, the birthrate dropped by 16 percent since 1970. But now many of these women are ready to start families. This should hardly be surprising; after all, 90 percent of American women do become mothers.

But while corporate women were busily making adjustments and concessions, the larger corporate world was not. The "fast track," with its macho camaraderie and toxic work load, remains the only track to success. As a result, success is indeed usually incompatible with motherhood—as well as with any engaged and active form of fatherhood. The corporate culture strongly discourages *men* from taking parental leave even if offered. And how many families can afford to have both earners on the mommy track?

Today there's an additional factor on the scene—the corporate women who *have* made it. Many of them are reliable advocates for the supports that working parents need. But you don't have to hang out with the skirted-suit crowd for long to discover that others of them are impatient with, and sometimes even actively resentful of, younger women who are trying to combine career and family. Recall that 60 percent of top female executives are themselves childless. Others are of the "if I did it, so can you" school of thought. Felice Schwartz may herself belong in this unsisterly category. In a telling anecdote in her original article, she describes her own problems with an executive employee seeking maternity leave, and the "somewhat awkward conversations" that ensued.

Sooner or later, corporations will have to yield to the pressure for paid parental leave, flextime, and child care, if only because they've become dependent on female talent. The danger is that employers—no doubt quoting Felice Schwartz for legitimation—will insist that the price for such options be reduced pay and withheld promotions, i.e., consignment to the mommy track. Such a policy would place a penalty on parenthood, and the ultimate victims—especially if the policy trickles down to the already low-paid female majority—will of course be children.

Bumping women—or just fertile women, or married women, or whomever—off the fast track may sound smart to cost-conscious CEOs, but eventually it is the corporate culture itself that needs to slow down to a human pace. No one, male or female, works at peak productivity for 70 hours a week, year after year, without sabbaticals or leaves. Think of it this way. If the price of success were exposure to a toxic chemical, would we argue that only women should be protected? Work loads that are incompatible with family life are themselves a kind of toxin—to men as well as women, and ultimately to businesses as well as families.

Questions for discussion

See questions: "How to Get 'Em on Track."

• *Essay* •

How to Get 'Em on Track*

CAROL KLEIMAN

It's hard to take seriously Felice Schwartz's proposition in the *Harvard Business Review* that some women are career-minded, some are family-minded, and the two should be identified and separated, as the wheat from the chaff, by employers at the onset of women's professional lives.

But, suppose for one minimum-$4.65-an-hour moment that there really are such differences among the paid labor market's 53 million women (a figure that's going to climb onward and upward in the next decade; despite Catalyst's dire prediction of an erosion in women's commitment to the workplace, women continue to swell managerial ranks—which will, in fact, be swell for business). Good executives, even the few women among them, know that identifying work characteristics is a management job. So the smart ones probably are busily working on how to figure out which women are destined to be chief honchos and which—in their eyes—couch potatoes.

It's obvious that the best way to approach the problem is by giving a series of entry-level tests to all women applicants, from clerks to MBAs. It's too late to do anything about the Superwomen—the millions of working mothers who are at this very moment rushing frantically from home to work to family, trying to be all things to all people except themselves; they're much too busy to be tested anyway.

From now on, though, a blood test should be given the minute a woman walks into the personnel office. The blood analysis should be used to eliminate women with a high hormone count: clearly, when hormones rage, women will want to have sex, fulfill their biological destinies, and stay at home with them after they're born. No one would want to hire anyone so decadent, anyway.

Women with high levels of testosterone, the male hormone, should be given A-pluses for strong career tracks. Obviously, they will eschew feminine ways; even if they do have babies, they will leave them alone at home and continue a vigorous climb up the corporate ladder—just like men.

Of course, the fact that women have very little testosterone in their blood should not hinder such a serious researcher as Schwartz in identifying her victims.

Brain tests are another source of information. The usual examination of which side dominates, the right or left, and whether or not you can do math doesn't add up here. The criterion should be weight. Women whose brains are extremely heavy probably have heads filled with grand ideas of being treated equally, getting promotions they deserve, and never being sexually harassed. A few may even envision a workplace that accommodates the real responsibilities of working women, rather than disregarding almost half the labor force. These women should be dropped now to save a lot of trouble later, whether they ever have a family or not. Instead, lighter-brained women should be given every affirmative action opportunity: they're less likely to complain about the burden of having too much to do.

But workplace tests are not enough. Women should do self-examination on a monthly basis, preferably in the shower. They should check for any signs of biological destiny erupting on their bodies—scar tissue from worrying about quality care for their families; dark shadows under their eyes from staying late at work to finish the annual report. Women who find such symptoms should be honorable enough to turn themselves in to their supervisors as counter-productive to the male corporate culture. They should, as decent human be-ings, eliminate themselves from the workplace. These are likely candidates for disappearance behind 1950s' picture-frame windows to bolster the diminish-ing numbers of traditional U.S. nuclear families—now at an all-time low of on-ly 9 percent.

Probably no one will institute these serious tests; instead, management will just let women plod along, with yearnings for both family and career dogging them every step of the way. But the "mommy" joke ultimately is on manage-ment, which, in the next decade, will be pursuing women vigorously whether or not they pass the critical devotion-to-duty test. Demographics show that women will make up 51 percent of new entrants to the labor force, and 65 per-cent of employees filling new jobs, by the year 2000; employers will be com-peting for their services—by offering, among other things, child care, flexible hours, and paid maternity leave.

The genie is out of the bottle: women are going to work, blood-screening notwithstanding. Perhaps Catalyst's Schwartz could devote future efforts to as-certaining which male executives are good bets for top management spots in a more family-oriented workplace—and to eliminating early on those who are not.

By blood-testing their estrogen levels, of course.

Questions for discussion

1. If women were more costly to employ than men, would that be sufficient to justify disparate treatment?

2. Is family life a significant public good that ought to be upheld by any corporation?

3. Do employers have a duty to provide employees with time to spend caring for their offspring?

• *Essay* •

Woman's Work:
Seeking Identity through Occupation*

AL GINI • TERRY SULLIVAN

Introduction

In a recent issue of *The New Republic,* Barbara Ehrenreich commented that twenty years ago the stereotypical liberated woman was a braless radical, hoarse from denouncing the twin evils of capitalism and patriarchy. Today's stereotype is more often a blue-suited executive carrying an attache case and engaging in leveraged buy-outs—before transmogrifying into a perfect mother and seductive cook in the evenings, e.g., "I can bring home the bacon, fry it up in the pan . . ." (Ehrenreich, 1986). Neither stereotype is or ever was true, but they can both tell us a great deal about what women and men would like to believe. What is true is that the single most important change in the American labor market in the 20th Century is the unprecedented entry of large numbers of women into the work force:

> When the history of that last quarter of the 20th century in the U.S. is written, scholars may well conclude that the nation's most important social development has been the rise to positions of power and influence of its most vigorous majority: American women. So many women have come flocking into the labor force—fully 70% of all American women aged 25 to 54 are today at work for pay or actively seeking jobs—that more Americans are now employed than ever before. This is no less than a revolutionary change, one that has created profound shifts not only in the family and the workplace but also in basic U.S. economic policy making. (Taylor, 1986)

At the turn of the century, only 5 million of the 28 million Americans in the work force were women. One quarter of these were teenagers and only a very few were married. As recently as 1947, women accounted for fewer than 17 million of the 59 million employed. Since that time, however, six of every ten additions to the work force have been women, and, in the last ten years, ·women have represented two-thirds of the 20 million newly created jobs (Smith, 1979). According to the U.S. Department of Labor, 1984 was the first year in which the historical prototype of the American worker—the adult male—did not make up the majority of the labor force. Women and minority group men now hold 50% of all jobs. Fifty-three percent of all adult women now hold full-time jobs and make up 44% of the entire work force (U.S. Department of Labor, 1985). Some demographers estimate that by 1995 the percentage of employed women will rise to 57%–60% and that they may represent a simple majority of the work force early in the 21st Century (Borman, 1984). This extraordinary increase of employed women has been stimulated by the feminist movement and its impact on the social consciousness, by techno-logical advances in the information and communications industries, by the conversion to a service economy, by increased access to education, and by fair employment and affirmative action legislation. For these and perhaps other reasons, there are now 49 million women in the American Labor market—and the profile of the female employee has changed dramatically.

While single and divorced women have long had relatively high labor force participation rates, fewer than one in five married women with young children was working full-time in 1960. That number is nearly 50% today. As social com-mentator John W. Wright has pointed out:

> Another unmistakable sign of the social change going on all around us is the sig-nificant increase in the number of women who go back to work *immediately* after having a baby. In 1976 about 31 percent of women who gave birth sometime with-in the preceding twelve months returned to or entered the labor force, but by 1985 the proportion had soared to 48 percent. (Wright, 1987)

Recent estimates also suggest that only 23% of all American households now fit the pattern of a father employed outside the home and a mother at home caring for one or more children (Borman, 1984). Surveys conducted over a five-year period by the magazine *Working Woman* reveal that, in addition to in-creasing their numbers in the job market, women in significant numbers have begun to find employment outside the traditionally so-called "women's pro-fessions." While nurses, teachers, librarians, and clerical workers are still pre-dominantly women, the proportion of engineers, architects, physicians, and public officials who are women—while still small in whole numbers—has more than doubled since 1960. Typical law school classes are now often composed of 40% women, and nearly 50% of those working in sales, technical and ad-ministrative are women. The proportion of women in what are classified as management or "management-related" occupations increased from 39% to 45% in the years 1983–1985 alone (Bodger, 1985). While women are grossly overrepresented at the lower-paying end and entry level of the professions, it is clear that the once absolute distinctions between "woman's work" and "man's work" have begun to blur.

Fifty years ago, the notion of an unfulfilled homemaker was, for most women, unheard of. Prior to World War II, the maintenance of a house and, often, a large family was—if not every woman's dream of fulfillment—a full-time occupation and acknowledged as such. Only in recent years have the everyday tasks of meal-making and house and clothing maintenance become less than full-time jobs. This, and the decrease in family size, have left large numbers of women no longer merely bored by housekeeping but viewed by large segments of the population as underemployed. While contemporary women's grandmothers may or may not have found satisfaction employed sole-ly in their homes, they had little choice and were at pains to find time for em-ployment even had it been possible. Their daughters and grand-daughters, however, now find full-time work outside the home to be not only possible but, in many cases, financially necessary. For the first time, women are defining their worth and status by their degree of success in the work place. For the first time, men and women are beginning to establish their personal sense of iden-tity and self-worth using the same ground rules.

The personal meaning of work is as important as are its economic and social meanings. Where we live, how well we live, whom we see, what and where we consume and purchase, how we educate our children—all of these are dominated by the work we do (Yankelovich, 1979). While a great many—perhaps most—people are unhappy with their jobs, virtually all insist that they want to work because they are aware at some level that work plays a crucial and perhaps unparalleled psychological role in the formation of human character. Work is not simply a source of a livelihood, but one of the most crucial factors in defining a sense of self. It may very well be that working in the home has, over the course of the past two generations, changed until it no longer meets the definition of work to which most people subscribe. While the work was demonstrably necessary and clearly a full-time occupation, most women were able to forge a sense of self-worth from it, regardless of their capacity for more challenging occupations.

People simply need to work. They see in work the outlines of human definition. Sociologist Peter Berger has written that "to be human and to work appear as inextricably intertwined notions" (Lefkowitz, 1979). Karl Marx, in his earliest philosophical writings, defined man as a worker, acquiring self-definition through labor. He wrote:

> As individuals express their life [sic], so they are. What (individuals) are . . . coincides with their production, both with what they produce and with how they produce. The nature of individuals thus depends on the material conditions determining their production. (Marx, 1967, p. 409)

When psychiatrists and psychologists talk about "ego boundaries," they mean that well-balanced people have a clear perspective on the limits and outlines of their identities. For most of us, the primary source of life's labels and "ego boundaries" is our work. It allows us to develop a "coherent web of expectations" of the rhythm and direction of our lives. Nothing is quite so uniquely personal to people as their skills and works, and the more descriptive we can be about our work, the clearer our sense of self-definition. Theologian Gregory Baum calls labor the "axis of human self-making" (Baum, 1982).

Work molds our perceptions of ourselves; to work is to be shaped by the job, to become, in some sense, what we do. In America in the last quarter of the 20th Century, paid employment is the principal activity that is classified as work. And because of this, paid employment is the principal activity by which we define ourselves and others (Kahn, 1981).

Granting the general thesis that work—paid employment—is the primary factor in defining worth and sense of self, it is particularly interesting that, at the moment, men and women perceive the importance of work and impact on personal identity slightly differently. University of Kentucky researchers conducted a series of nationwide surveys to test assumed gender differences in attitudes toward work (Lacy *et al.*, 1983). Overall, the study found only minimal differences between women and men in their preferences of job attributes. Approximately half of each group named meaningfulness of the work as most important and ranked the other four attributes in the following order: promotion possibilities, annual income, job security, and hours. There were, however, statistically significant gender differences in two of the five attributes. Women were more likely than men to select meaningfulness of the work as a first preference, and men were more likely than women to select job security as a first preference. Marital status had no significant impact upon the preferences listed by men. Currently married women, and women who had never been married, however, chose meaningful work as the first choice more often than men or any other marital category of women.

Most interesting, perhaps, was the response to the question: "If by chance you inherited enough money to live comfortably without working, do you think you would work anyway?" Seventy-four percent of the men and 64% of the women said they would continue to work even when it had become unnecessary financially. The difference was directly related to marital status. Among unmarried men and women there seemed to be no significant differences. Married men were, however, more likely than married women to continue working and unmarried women were significantly more likely than married women to continue to work. These responses are consistent with the historical standard that men, regardless of marital status, derive primary status and identity from their occupations and that women do not. The most compelling conclusion is that while more and more women are seeking identity through occupation, women retain some avenues of social-cultural identity other than paid employment.

Gloria Emerson has pointed out, in her award-winning *Some American Men* (1985), that every 12-year-old boy in America knows what must be done to make it as a man: Money must be made—nothing is as masculine as this. She cites as the major difference between American men and women the expectation that men will work faithfully all of their lives, without interruption or openly wishing otherwise. While the "postfeminist" generation of women are now more likely to draw their status and define their work in terms of their occupation, this life sentence to career is not yet, at least for married women, the compulsion that it is and has been for men.

This most recent generation of working women has, as male generations have for years, responded to a stereotype—the image of a superwoman, working in a psychologically demanding career, maintaining an intimate relationship with a partner, and nurturing children. While many women have won the right to go off to the corporate citadel every morning, they have more often than not retained the obligation to bear most of the responsibility for the home. This may be a case of it being easier to *do* it all than it is to change both corporate life and home life at the same time. Whatever the reason, this attempt to emulate an unattainable stereotype is beginning to cause many women to reappraise their professional victories (Taylor, 1986). Women are now being forced to reexamine their roles and newly found public identities and popular literature is beginning to talk about the working woman's identity crisis.

Betty Friedan has said that many women think that there is something wrong with them if they cannot be a perfect corporate executive and a perfect wife and mother. At the same time many women, especially those over 30, who do not have a family report a sense of unhappiness and frustration stemming from their fear that their careers and the competitive energies necessary to succeed in them have robbed them of the opportunity of marriage and the possibility of children. Many of these women report that their careers are less fulfilling and more costly than they expected, and that the deficits in their personal relationships in many ways negate the success they have achieved on the job (Friedan, 1986).

Clearly the women of the 1980s are caught between two powerful images that have shaped the notion of what a successful woman should be. The myth of the Supermom managing a perfectly run home and a star in the office is fading fast, doomed by anger, guilt, and exhaustion that Susan St. James and Phylissia Rashad never seem to feel.

Ideally, postfeminist women would like to be able to strike a balance between the responsibilities of the job and the home. The reality is that more women are reporting that they are being forced by circumstances to choose between the two. This is partly the result of one of the real cultural phenomena of the baby boom generation—the large number of middle-class working women who spent years building careers before having children. The birth of the second child is—in the opinion of countless women, not the least of whom is Erma Bombeck—the moment when even the most dedicated career woman is sorely tried to keep everything in motion at once.

While there are significant numbers of men who are substantially more committed to sharing the responsibilities of home and children, this alone—even in the unlikely event that it were to become more widespread—will not solve the problem. The fact is that very few organizations operate, recognize, and behave as if half of their employees were women. Most businesses and government policies are geared toward a family model that has not been dominant since the early 1950s. Tied to this is the limited support available to working women for child care and home maintenance. Labor Secretary William Brock has said "It is just incredible that we have seen the feminization of the work force with no more adaptation than we have had. It is a problem of sufficient magnitude that everybody is going to have to play a role (in solving it): families, individuals, businesses, local government, and state government (A mother's choice, 1986). In the newly published *A Lesser Life: The Myth of Women's Liberation in America* (Hewlett, 1986), economist Sylvia Hewlett argues: "The lack of any kind of mandated benefits around childbirth is the biggest single reason why women are doing so badly in the workplace. Unless you support women in their role as mothers, you will never get equality of opportunity."

Jobs have always been important for men, and they have seen their work as honorable—even if only as an honorable burden—and as their primary means of acquiring status. Over the past twenty-five years, women have increasingly demanded the right to be measured by these same standards and have, at least to some extent, succeeded. The dilemma in which they now find themselves is that, while able to compete with men in the workplace, the presence of children presents demands that in many cases simply cannot be met unless something very firmly entrenched gives way. A poll conducted by the Gallup Organization for *Newsweek* reported that, of 1009 women surveyed, 37% say they have changed jobs or working hours after having children and 45% that they drastically cut back on career plans (A mother's choice, 1986). These are career changes that men have never had to consider—in fact men have generally become even more career oriented after the birth of children.

In the beginning, the Women's Movement simply seemed to ask for a piece of the pie. It now appears that some other pieces of the pie will have to be made smaller, or the ingredients will have to be changed, if American society wishes to have both successful, adult women and another generation of children. The ingredients will be flexitime, guaranteed maternity leave, parental leave (without loss of seniority), child care facilities or allowances, part-time professional employment—for both men and women—and job sharing. The maintenance of a home has eased enormously, the raising of children has not. And professional women are concluding that almost nobody can sustain a career and be Donna Reed at the same time. If women are to participate fully in corporate life and find meaning in both home and family, the work must change and families must be seen by everyone, including government and corporations, as the responsibility of both men and women. The solution will be nearer when a man can confidently take the morning off to attend a third grade play.

In an essay in the 10th anniversary issue of *Working Woman*, Betty Friedan (1986) stated that the real crisis of the "second stage of the women's movement" stems from a set of political problems, and the only way they can be solved is if some women come together and force change. Women have the right to work, she reports, but at the cost of being penalized by almost every American institution if they choose to work and have a family. Women have a right to seek identity through work as well as through parenthood—as men have always done. But the fact of the matter is that society is not yet structured for women to live this way. For the time being, many women resolve the issue by remaining childless and working under rules and expectations set for a work force of men with wives at home, or by opting out of their careers for long periods of time. At the same time, a group of new women entrepreneurs are emerging—seeking professional careers that allow them to manage their own time and commitments. Independence is, however, not possible for all women, just as it is not possible for all men. Most people will earn their living working for organizations. It is those few women who refuse to compromise, who insist on the right to meaningful work and the right to a family, who will have to push for changes in the work place just as hard as they had to push to gain admittance to the jobs in the first place (Friedan, 1986).

From the beginning, feminism declared that the personal is always political. So it is, suggests Friedan, and so it will always remain. But as feminism enters its next stage, it is clear that the political must now accommodate the personal.

References

BAUM, G. (1982). *The Priority of Labor.* New York: Paulist Press.

BODGER, C. (1985). Sixth annual salary survey. *Working Woman, 10*(1), 65–72.

BORMAN, K. M. (1984). Fathers, mothers and child care in the 1980s. In Borman, K. M., Quarm, D., & Gideonse, S. (Eds.), *Women in the Workplace: Effects on Families.* Norwood, NJ: Ablex Publishing Corp.

EHRENREICH, B. (1986). Strategies of corporate women. *The New Republic, 194*(4), 28–31.

EMERSON, G. (1985). *Some American Men.* New York: Simon & Schuster.

FRIEDAN, B. (1986). Where do we go from here? *Working Woman, 11*(11), 152–154, 251.

HEWLETT, S. A. (1986). In Goblitz, P. (Ed.) *A Lesser Life: The Myth of Women's Liberation in America.* New York: William Morrow.

KAHN, R. L. (1981). *Work and Health.* New York: Wiley.

LACY, W. B., BOKEMEIER, J. L., & SHEPARD, J. M. (1983). Job attribute preferences and work commitment of men and women in the United States. *Personnel Psychology, 36*, 315–328.

LEFKOWITZ, B. (1979). *Breaktime: Living Without Work in a Nine-to-Five World.* New York: Hawthorn Books.

MARX, K. (1967). The German ideology. In Easten, L., & Guddat, K. (Eds. and Trans.), *Writings of the Young Marx on Philosophy and Society.* New York: Doubleday.

A mother's choice (1986). *Newsweek,* March 31, pp. 47, 51.

SMITH, R. E. (Ed.). (1979). *The Subtle Revolution: Women at Work.* Washington, DC: The Urban Institute.

TAYLOR, A. (1986). Why women managers are bailing out. *Fortune,* August 18, pp. 16, 23.

U.S. DEPARTMENT OF LABOR. BUREAU OF LABOR STATISTICS. (1985). *Employment and Earnings,* 146. Washington, DC: U.S. Government Printing Office.

WRIGHT, J. W. (1987). *The American Almanac of Jobs and Salaries* (3rd ed.). New York: Avon Books.

YANKELOVICH, D. (1979). The meaning of work. In Rosow, J. M. (Ed.), *The Worker and the Job: Coping with Change.* Englewood Cliffs, NJ: Prentice-Hall.

Questions for discussion

1. How do women's new roles in the workplace affect their perceptions of themselves, their mates, and their families?

2. Does the ethos of work affect the ethics of the work?

3. While women must bear children, don't men have ethical obligations with regard to the rearing of children?

• *Case Study* •

Sexual Discrimination at Eastern Airlines?*

AL GINI

On December 28, 1983, a federal judge ordered Eastern Airlines to reinstate a pilot who had been fired following a sex-change operation in 1980. The pilot, who flew for the airline for 12 years as Kenneth Ulane, is now known as Karen Ulane. Before joining Eastern in 1968, Ulane had previously been an Army pilot and was decorated for valor in connection with missions flown in Vietnam.[1]

In 1979, following years of psychiatric consultation, Ulane took a leave of absence and underwent a sex-change operation in April 1980. When she returned to work, the airline would not reinstate her as a pilot. After refusing to accept other administrative positions, Eastern fired her on April 24, 1981. Ulane charged that her dismissal was a direct result of her sex-change operation and filed a sex-discrimination suit. "In terms of sexual discrimination," said one of her lawyers, "Karen Ulane was kind of a perfect control group. As a male pilot, Eastern's own witnesses acknowledge that she was one of their better pilots. When she changed her sex, she was all of a sudden not acceptable. Eastern was willing to retain one sex in their employ, but not willing to retain the other."[2] At the time, only two of Eastern's 4,200 pilots were women.

In an emotionally charged two-hour oral opinion, Judge John Grady found in favor of Ulane and berated Eastern for their "ostrich-like and contemptuous attitude toward transsexuals."[3] Grady based his decision on Title VII of the Civil Rights Act of 1964. This statute provides that

It shall be an unlawful employment practice for an employer to fail or refuse to hire or to discharge any individual or otherwise to discriminate against any individual with respect to his compensation, terms, conditions or privileges of employment because of such individual's race, color, religion, sex, or national origin.

The specific question before the court, Judge Grady suggested, is whether the phrase "because of the individual's sex" encompasses a person such as the plaintiff who alleges that she is a transsexual or, alternatively, that having gone through sex-reassignment surgery, she is now no longer a man but a woman. In other words, is a person's sexual identity a protected category under the Civil Rights Act?[4]

Judge Grady pointed out that this section of the Civil Rights Act had originally prohibited discrimination on the basis of race but not sex. An amendment introducing sex into the statute was offered by a southern senator who hoped that by this gambit he would prevent the bill's passage. His ploy obviously did not work, but neither was there much discussion at that time concerning the scope of the term *sex*. Grady therefore set himself the task of defining *sex* in the context of Title VII. He first distinguished between our understanding of the terms *homosexual* and *transvestite* on the one hand, and *transsexual* on the other. The later group, he argued, have problems relative to their sexual identities as men or women, while the former do not. He indicated that, while the statute in question cannot reasonably be extended to matters of sexual preference it is an altogether different matter as to whether the matter of sexual identity is included in our general understanding of the term *sex*.[5]

In his ruling, Grady interpreted the word *sex* to reasonably include the question of sexual identity. He said that, prior to his participation in this case, he would have had no doubt that the question of gender was straightforward. But after hearing the testimony, he realized that there is no settled definition in the medical community as to what we mean by *sex*. He argued that sex is defined by something more than the biological. It is also defined by society, because the way an individual is perceived by society plays a crucial role in a person's sense of sexual identity.[6]

Having concluded that the term *sex* in Title VII reasonably includes the question of sexual identity, Grady then considered whether Ulane was indeed a transsexual. The defendants argued that Ulane is really a transvestite and hence is not protected by the statute. Grady contended that both the Gender Identity Board of the University of Chicago Medical School and her own doctor had found Ulane to be a transsexual. The defense countered that the plaintiff had only managed to persuade these medical practitioners—through some retrospective distortion—that she is transsexual. Grady dismissed this claim, saying that Ulane knew as much as most psychiatrists about her condition and the possible risks of her operation, and that she could hardly have any ulterior motive in undergoing such a radical procedure. He contended that the fact of Ulane's operation argues for her being a true transsexual, since she must have been aware that transvestites have very poor prognosis after sex-reassignment surgery.[7]

Grady then considered the question of whether Ulane had been discharged because of her sex. The evidence presented at the trial indicated that Eastern began to develop their brief leading to Ulane's discharge just after her surgery. Prior to that time, Eastern had no complaints about her performance as a pilot.[8] Eastern's legal department drafted two separate discharge letters which contained seven essential arguments, each of which they felt represented independent "nondiscriminatory" reasons for dismissal.[9]

(1.) Eastern alleged that because of Ulane's "underlying psychological problem" her presence in the cockpit represented an unjustifiable safety hazard to passengers and crew. Grady argued that Eastern was prejudiced from the start and had invented all sorts of dangers that inhered in the so-called "underlying psychological problem." Furthermore, Eastern never gave Ulane a fair hearing on this issue or the opportunity to show that they were wrong or at least had no reason for concern in her particular situation.[10]

(2.) Eastern charged that Ulane's medical certification was not unconditional after her surgery. Here, Grady compared her case to that of alcoholic pilots, whose certificates are also conditional. The FAA had, in fact, indicated that Ulane was fit to fly, and had ordered her to undergo periodic counseling only in order to help her deal with any problems created by unfriendly co-workers.[11]

(3.) Eastern complained that sex-reassignment surgery does not solve the underlying psychological problem. Grady indicated that there was no evidence of change in the plaintiff's psychological adjustment profile. Ulane, therefore, would be no more dangerous in the cockpit than before her surgery. Moreover, the judge cited evidence that such surgery actually decreases the patient's anxieties and makes them more stable in regard to their own sense of self-esteem. Grady concluded that the fact of transsexuality does not in itself constitute a safety problem, any more than does, say, left-handedness.[12]

(4.) Eastern claimed that Ulane's presence in the cockpit would counteract its efforts to assure the public that airline travel is safe. Grady drew a parallel here between Eastern and those who at one time believed that black salesclerks or waiters would drive customers away. The American public, said Grady, is a lot smarter than Eastern gives them credit for, and rejected their contention as prejudicial.[13]

(5.) Eastern alleged that, by virtue of her operation, Ulane was no longer the same person they had hired, and that, knowing what they do now, they would not have hired her in the first place. According to Grady, Eastern reacted to the situation as a public-relations problem: "A transsexual in the cockpit? The public wouldn't accept it! We will be the laughing stock of the airline industry! We have got to do something about it!" Grady ruled that this line of argumentation was a virtual admission of discrimination based on sex.[14]

(6.) Eastern alleged that Ulane had failed to disclose to the company the medication and medical and psychiatric treatments she had received over the years for her condition. Grady pointed out that the drugs Ulane had taken were approved by the FAA as not being dangerous. Therefore, he concluded that her flying ability was not impaired by the medication she was taking. He again drew a parallel between Ulane and male pilots who were alcoholics. Alcoholic pilots rarely, if ever, disclose their problems to the company, but they are not fired for that, even though the dangers of alcohol are well known. Female hormones, on the other hand, have no known effects on flying ability. Grady contended that Eastern had not followed its normal procedure in this case as a result of its initial prejudice against Ulane. If one employee is fired for failure to disclose, all should be treated alike.[15]

(7.) Eastern alleged that Ulane had instigated publicity damaging to Eastern Airlines. Grady countered that the company must have known that this case would inevitably draw publicity even as it drew up its letters of discharge. Besides, Eastern had raised no similar fuss when some of its female employees were featured nude in *Playboy* magazine.[16]

Grady dismissed all of Eastern's justifications for firing Ulane as mere pretexts. He concluded that, but for her being a transsexual, Ulane would not have been discharged.

> I am satisfied from this evidence that while some transsexuals, just as some tall people and some left-handers, some fat people, and some Irishmen would not be safe airline pilots, it is true that some transsexuals would not be safe airline pilots. But it cannot be said with any rationality that all transsexuals are unsafe airline pilots. Neither can it be said with any rationality that it is impossible to make this determination of whether or not a safety hazard is really involved on an individualized basis.[17]

Grady ordered Ulane reinstated with back pay and seniority. The amount of the award was not set during the hearing, but was estimated at about $142,000. Ulane had been receiving an annual salary of $50,000 at the time of her dismissal in 1981.[18]

Eastern said it would appeal what it calls Judge Grady's "novel view of the law" and stated that "Eastern remains confident that its position in this case is correct under the law."[19] Grady indicated that if the U.S. Courts of Appeals rules that transsexuals are not protected under Title VII, he will reconsider the question of whether Ulane could claim discrimination because she is a woman. Ulane had originally contended that she was fired because she is a transsexual and a woman. Grady said he was unsure if he could rule that Ulane is a woman. "I don't think I can find the plaintiff is both a transsexual and a woman," he said. "She's either one or the other. . . ."[20]

In the end, Judge Grady saw Eastern's dismissal of Ulane as an attempt by the company to maintain its image at the expense of a good employee's career. But, according to labor-relations attorney Gerald Skoning, the basic premise behind Grady's decision—that sexual identity is defined by something more than the number of X and Y chromosomes present at birth—could have far more extensive implications.[21] Until now the courts have generally refused to grant employment protection for homosexuals under Title VII, saying that although it prohibits discrimination based on sex, it was not intended to prohibit discrimination based on "sexual preference." Many legal scholars believe, however, that if Grady's ruling is upheld on appeal, the decision may be used to try to win protection for homosexuals. Although other scholars are not sure Grady's decision can be extended that far, the ruling, if upheld, not only protects reassigned transsexuals, but all men who feel like a woman but have not undergone surgery.[22]

UPDATE
Transsexual Pilot Loses Job Appeal
Adrienne Drell, *Chicago Sun Times*, **August 3, 1984**

A federal appeals court ruled yesterday that Karen Ulane, a former Eastern Airlines pilot fired after undergoing a sex-change operation, is not entitled to regain her job.

The 7th Circuit Court of Appeals reversed a Dec. 28 decision by U.S. District Judge John F. Grady that Eastern had violated federal sex discrimination laws.

The 12-page opinion by a three-judge panel, written by Harlington Woods Jr., said *the law does not cover transsexuals or anyone with a "sexual identity disorder. . . ."*

The appellate court said federal law "implies that it is unlawful to discriminate against women because they are women and against men because they are men. . . . A prohibition against discrimination based on an individual's sex is not synonymous with a prohibition against discrimination based on an individual's sexual identity disorder or discontent with the sex into which they were born."

Ulane is entitled to any "personal belief about her sexual identity she desires," the opinion notes. "But even if one believes that a woman can be so easily created from what remains of a man, that does not decide this case."

Endnotes

1. *New York Times,* December 29, 1983, p. 18.
2. *Ibid.*
3. *Chicago Tribune,* January 1, 1984.
4. *Karen Frances Ulane* v. *Eastern Airlines, Inc., et al.,* No. 81 C 4411, U.S. District Court, Northeastern Illinois.
5. *Ibid.,* p. 5.
6. *Ibid.,* p. 6.
7. *Ibid.,* pp. 15, 16, 17.
8. *Ibid.,* p. 19.
9. *Ibid.,* p. 33.
10. *Ibid.,* p. 22.
11. *Ibid.,* p. 27.
12. *Ibid.,* p. 30.
13. *Ibid.,* p. 32.
14. *Ibid.,* p. 14.
15. *Ibid.,* p. 15.
16. *Ibid.,* p. 16.
17. *Chicago Tribune,* January 11, 1984, sect. 2, p. 8.
18. *Ulane* v. *Eastern Airlines,* p. 47.
19. *New York Times,* December 29, 1983, p. 18.
20. *Chicago Tribune,* January 11, 1984, sect. 2, p. 8.
21. *Chicago Tribune,* January 8, 1984, p. 1.
22. *Ibid.,* p. 10.

Questions for discussion

1. Do you believe that a person should be penalized or discriminated against because of his or her sexual preference or sense of sexual identity?

2. Was Eastern, in effect, saying that it was unwilling to hire and retain women as pilots or simply that it was unwilling to hire and retain transsexuals as pilots?

3. Given Ulane's prior outstanding performance as a pilot, if she had not undergone the reassignment surgery but rather had suffered a psychological breakdown or succumbed to a severe bout of alcoholism, do you think that Eastern would have been so eager to demote or fire her?

4. Was Eastern's decision based on fact or fear of public perception and reaction?

5. Does an employer's right to fire (employment at will) include the right to dismiss an employee because of his or her private or personal life-style decisions?

• *Case Study* •

The Oil Rig

This case focuses on one of the three exploratory rigs which have been drilling for several years along the coast of Angola, under contract to a major U.S. multinational oil company. All three rigs are owned and operated by a large U.S. drilling company.

The "Explorer IV" rig is a relatively small jack-up (i.e., with legs), with dimensions of approximately 200 feet by 100 feet, which houses a crew of 150 men. The crew comprises laborers, roustabouts (unskilled laborers), and maintenance staff, and 30 expatriot workers who work as roughnecks and drillers or in administrative or technical positions. The top administrator on the Explorer IV is the "tool pusher," an American expatriate, who wields almost absolute authority over matters pertaining to life on the rig.

The crew quarters on the Explorer IV were modified for operations in Angola. A second galley was installed on the lower level, and cabins on this level were enlarged to permit a dormitory-style arrangement of 16 persons per room. This lower level is the "Angolan section" of the rig, where the 120 local workers eat, sleep, and socialize during their 28-day "hitch."

The upper level houses the 30 expatriates in an area equal in square footage to that of the Angolan section. The Expatriate section's quarters are semiprivate with baths, and this section boasts its own galley, game room, and movie room. Although it is nowhere explicitly written, a tacit regulation exists prohibiting Angolan workers from entering the Expatriate section of the rig, except in emergencies. The only Angolans exempt from this regulation are those assigned to the highly valued positions of cleaning or galley staff in the Expatriate section. These few positions are highly valued because of the potential for receiving gifts or recovering discarded razors, etc., from the expatriates.

The separation of Angolan workers from Expatriates is reinforced by several other rig policies. Angolan laborers travel to and from the rig by boat (an eighteen-hour trip), whereas expatriates are transported by helicopter. Also, medical attention is dispensed by the British R.N. throughout the day but only during shift changes for the Angolans (except in emergencies). When there are serious injuries, the response is different for the two groups. If, for example, a finger is severed, expatriates are rushed to Luanda for reconstructive surgery, whereas Angolan workers have the amputation operation performed on the rig by the medic.

Angolan workers are issued grey coveralls and expatriates receive red coveralls. Meals in the two galleys are vastly different; they are virtually gourmet in the Expatriate galley and somewhat more proletarian in the Angolan section. The caterers informed the author that budgets for the two galleys were nearly equal (despite the gross disparity in numbers served).

Communication between Expatriates and Angolans is notable by its absence on the Explorer IV. This is principally because none of the expatriates speaks Portuguese and none of the Angolans speaks more than a few words of English. Only the chef of the Portuguese catering company speaks both English and Portuguese, and consequently, he is required to act as interpreter in all emergency situations. In the working environment, training and coordination of effort is accomplished via sign language or repetition of example.

From time to time, an entourage of Angolan government officials visits the Explorer IV. These visits normally last only for an hour or so but, invariably, the officials dine with the expatriates and take a brief tour of the equipment before returning to shore via helicopter. Never has an entourage expressed concern about the disparity in living conditions on the rig, nor have the officials bothered to speak with the Angolan workers. Observers comment that the officials seem disinterested in the situation of the Angolan workers, most of whom are from outside of the capital city.

The rig's segregated environment is little affected by the presence of an American black. The American black is assigned to the expatriate section and is, of course, permitted to partake of all expatriate privileges. Nevertheless, it should be noted that there are few American blacks in the international drilling business, and those few are frequently less than completely welcomed into the rig's social activities.

Questions for discussion

1. Is it morally acceptable to treat employees of different national or ethnic backgrounds differently? That is, is separate and unequal a morally viable course of action?

2. Should the owner(s) of the rig rely on the moral standards of their own culture, or those of the country in which they are operating?

• *Case Study* •

Foreign Assignment*

THOMAS DUNFEE • DIANA ROBERTSON

Sara Strong graduated with an MBA from UCLA four years ago. She immediately took a job in the correspondent bank section of the Security Bank of the American Continent. Sara was assigned to work on issues pertaining to relationships with correspondent banks in Latin America. She rose rapidly in the section and received three good promotions in three years. She consistently got high ratings from her superiors, and she received particularly high marks for her professional demeanor.

In her initial position with the bank, Sara was required to travel to Mexico on several occasions. She was always accompanied by a male colleague even though she generally handled similar business by herself on trips within the United States. During her trips to Mexico she observed that Mexican bankers seemed more aware of her being a woman and were personally solicitous to her, but she didn't discern any major problems. The final decisions on the work that she did were handled by male representatives of the bank stationed in Mexico.

A successful foreign assignment was an important step for those on the "fast track" at the bank. Sara applied for a position in Central or South America and was delighted when she was assigned to the bank's office in Mexico City. The office had about twenty bank employees and was headed by William Vitam. The Mexico City office was seen as a preferred assignment by young executives at the bank.

After a month, Sara began to encounter problems. She found it difficult to be effective in dealing with Mexican bankers—the clients. They appeared reluctant to accept her authority and they would often bypass her in important matters. The problem was exacerbated by Vitam's compliance in her being bypassed. When she asked that the clients be referred back to her, Vitam replied, "Of course that isn't really practical." Vitam made matters worse by patronizing her in front of clients and by referring to her as "my cute assistant" and "our lady banker." Vitam never did this when only Americans were present, and in fact treated her professionally and with respect in internal situations.

Sara finally complained to Vitam that he was undermining her authority and effectiveness; she asked him in as positive a manner as possible to help her. Vitam listened carefully to Sara's complaints, then replied: "I'm glad that you brought this up, because I've been meaning to sit down and talk to you about my little game-playing in front of the clients. Let me be frank with you. Our clients think you're great, but they just don't understand a woman in authority, and you and I aren't going to be able to change their attitudes overnight. As long as the clients see you as my assistant and deferring to me, they can do business with you. I'm willing to give you as much responsibility as they can handle your having. I *know* you can handle it. But we just have to tread carefully. You and I know that my remarks in front of clients don't mean anything. They're just a way of playing the game Latin style. I know it's frustrating for you, but I really need you to support me on this. It's not going to affect your promotions, and for the most part you really will have responsibility for these clients' accounts. You just have to act like it's my responsibility." Sara replied that she would try to cooperate, but that basically she found her role demeaning.

As time went on, Sara found that the patronizing actions in front of clients bothered her more and more. She spoke to Vitam again, but he was firm in his position, and urged her to try to be a little more flexible, even a little more "feminine."

Sara also had a problem with Vitam over policy. The Mexico City office had five younger women who worked as receptionists and secretaries. They were all situated at work stations at the entrance to the office. They were required to wear standard uniforms that were colorful and slightly sexy. Sara protested the requirement that uniforms be worn because (1) they were inconsistent to the image of the banking business and (2) they were demeaning to the women who had to wear them. Vitam just curtly replied that he had received a lot of favorable comments about the uniforms from clients of the bank.

Several months later, Sara had what she thought would be a good opportunity to deal with the problem. Tom Fried, an executive vice president who had been a mentor for her since she arrived at the bank, was coming to Mexico City; she arranged a private conference with him. She described her problems and explained that she was not able to be effective in this environment and that she worried that it would have a negative effect on her chance of promotion within the bank. Fried was very careful in his response. He spoke of certain "realities" that the bank had to respect and he urged her to "see it through" even though he could understand how she would feel that things weren't fair.

Sara found herself becoming more aggressive and defensive in her meetings with Vitam and her clients. Several clients asked that other bank personnel handle their transactions. Sara has just received an Average rating, which noted "the beginnings of a negative attitude about the bank and its policies."

Questions for discussion

1. What should Sara have done?

2. Is it justifiable for corporations with overseas operations to alter their moral standards when working in a significantly different culture?

3. Should one resist corporate or societal practices, even where the possibility for change is slim?

• *Case Study* •

Gender Issues at *Your House**

JOHN HASNAS

Dominique Francon

You are Dominique Francon, a senior account representative in the advertising department of the successful architecture magazine, *Your House.* In this position, you supervise the junior account reps who directly contact potential advertisers to sell advertising space. You and Peter Keating, the other senior account representative, are each responsible for half the staff, although your half consistently out-performs Keating's. Both of you report directly to Henry Cameron, the manager of the advertising department. Recently, you were excited to learn that Cameron will soon be promoted to the magazine's editorial board. Since by any performance standard your results are greatly superior to Keating's, you feel sure that you are slated to replace Cameron.

You think of yourself as a self-assured and assertive woman and have a strong desire to succeed in what you view as the male-dominated publishing industry. Accordingly, you behave in what you consider a professional manner at all times. Although somewhat demanding, you are never unfair to your subordinates; a combination that you believe helps account for your staff's superior bottom-line performance. You feel some regret that this posture prevents you from developing the kind of work-place friendships that others do, but you see this as part of the price you have to pay to make it as a woman manager. You keep a strict separation between your social and professional lives and would never consider pursuing a personal relationship with any of your co-workers. In addition, you are a hard worker, typically putting in many hours beyond the 40 per week required by your position.

You get along fairly well with everyone at the magazine except Ellsworth Toohey, one of the senior editors. Even before the run-in you had with him last year, you considered Toohey to be a typical "male chauvinist pig." Toohey, a man in his mid-fifties from Lubbock, Texas, habitually engages in behavior that you find offensive and demeaning to the women who work at the magazine. Regardless of their position, he typically addresses the women on the staff as "Honey" or "Dear" and refers to them collectively as the magazine's "fillies." In addition, he will invariably greet them with some comment on their appearance such as "Looking good today, Dear" or "Nice dress. I don't know how I'll keep my mind on my work while you're around, Honey."

Last year, after a private meeting in his office concerning the advertising budget, Toohey asked you to go out with him. You told him that since he was a superior of yours whose judgment could have an effect on your future career, you thought it would be inappropriate and that you had a personal policy of never dating co-workers. Rather than accept your refusal, Toohey responded to this by saying, "Oh, loosen up. People go out with co-workers all the time. Let your hair down. I guarantee you won't be disappointed." Although you found this to be both condescending and offensive, you retained your calm and said, "Mr. Toohey, you are putting me in a very awkward situation. I don't think it would be a good idea and I'd appreciate it if you would drop the subject."

A few days following this, you overheard two of the female secretaries discussing Toohey at lunch. Upon inquiring, you learned that he had propositioned many of the single women at the magazine, something that upset several of them. The final straw, however, came the following week when you were leaning over to take a drink from the water fountain. Toohey, who was passing by at the time, said, "Whoa, nice view!" and when you stood up, "Have you reconsidered my proposal of last week? You should get to know me better. I can really be of help to you in this business."

Following this incident, you went immediately to the manager of personnel, Howard Roark, to complain. Roark listened to your description of both incidents and your claim that other female employees had had similar experiences and told you he would look into it. Less than a week later, he came by your office to say that the problem had been taken care of and if you had any further trouble with Toohey to inform him immediately. Although you have no idea what action Roark took, it was clear something had been done. From that point on, Toohey never said a word to you that was not strictly business related. His manner toward you had become completely cold and formal, and he seemed to try to avoid you whenever possible.

This state of affairs suited you fine until today. Yesterday afternoon, you were shocked to learn that the editorial board had voted to promote Peter Keating to manager of the advertising department. The editorial board is made up of the senior managers and editors and is empowered to fill any opening at the managerial level by majority vote. The board presently has nine members, none of whom are women.

Upset, you had gone to Roark's office to ask why you had been passed over. He informed you that although the vote was as close as it possibly could be, the board elected to go with Keating because it was impressed with his "people skills." However, when you came in this morning, one of your account reps asked you what you had ever done to Toohey. When you asked her what she meant, she said that she had been talking to the secretary who had kept the minutes of yesterday's Board meeting, and she had said that Toohey really had it in for you. Before you could stop yourself, you heard yourself saying, "Why, that son of a bitch. I'll sue him for sexual harassment and the entire board for sex discrimination."

When you calmed down, you found yourself wondering whether this was, in fact, a case of sexual harassment or sex discrimination. You also found yourself wondering what would be the best steps for you to take in this situation. What should you do? (You may ask to meet with either Roark or Toohey or both in addition to any other action you deem appropriate.)

Ellsworth Toohey

You are Ellsworth Toohey, a senior editor of the successful architecture magazine, *Your House.* This position has both editorial and managerial responsibilities. As an editor, you both decide which articles will be printed in the magazine and make editorial recommendations regarding them. However, as a senior editor, you are also a member of the editorial board, which makes the important managerial decisions for the magazine. The board is comprised of the nine men who are senior managers or editors. It has responsibility for planning the magazine's budget, establishing editorial policy, and selecting those who are to be hired or promoted to managerial positions.

You were born in 1937 in Lubbock, Texas. Your family was extremely poor and you always had to work as a boy, but you managed to put yourself through college, getting a B.A. in English. Following graduation, you married your college sweetheart, got a position as a reporter for the Dallas *Morning News,* and began your career. By 1982, you had worked your way up to editor of the *Morning News.* At that time, you left Dallas to join the staff of *Your House,* then a new magazine just starting out. You were quite happy with your new position and things were going very well for you until your wife died 18 months ago. After a very rough 6 or 7 months, you began to put your life back together and have rededicated yourself to your work, perhaps in order to compensate for some of the emptiness in your personal life.

You think of yourself as a skilled professional, but one who has never forgotten the importance of a friendly demeanor that your Southern upbringing impressed upon you. Accordingly, you try to maintain an informal and friendly manner with your co-workers and subordinates. You will often chat with the male employees about sports or politics. You also try to make small talk with the female employees, although you find this more difficult since your upbringing and life experience seems to have left you ignorant of what subjects are of interest to women. You have a personal policy of attempting to greet all co-workers with a complementary comment in an effort to overcome the intimidating effect your high-level position can have on lower-level employees. Even when you don't know their names, you might greet an employee with a comment such as, "Nice suit, Son." or "Looking good today, Dear."

You believe you get along fairly well with everyone at the magazine except Dominique Francon, one of the two senior account representatives in the advertising department. A senior account representative supervises the junior account reps who directly contact potential advertisers to sell advertising space. Even before the run-in you had with her last year, you considered Francon to be an example of an "uptight, feminist bitch"; cold, aloof, and demanding. She had the reputation for driving the accounts reps under her unmercifully hard while hardly ever dispensing a "Nice job" or "Well done." Although her section usually sold the most advertising, in your opinion these results came at the expense of a happy workforce.

Last year, about six months after your wife's death, you made what you now consider some terrible errors in judgment. Seeking escape from your loneliness, you asked several of the single women at the magazine to go out with you. Since you had not asked a woman out in over 35 years, you were not particularly good at it and felt foolish and inept trying to do so.

One day last year, you were having a private meeting with Francon in your office concerning the advertising budget. It was one of those days when you were feeling particularly lonely and couldn't stand the thought of going home to an empty house again. As a result, you asked Francon to go out with you despite the negative impression you had of her personality. To your surprise, she did not turn you down directly, but simply stated that she had a policy against dating people from the office. At the time, you interpreted this to mean that she would like to go out with you, but was concerned with the appearance of impropriety. Rather than let the matter drop, you said something to the effect that she should not be so concerned with appearances and that people on the magazine's staff go out with each other all the time. However, Francon responded by saying that she thought it would create an awkward situation and that she would rather not.

A week later, Francon was getting a drink at the water fountain when you passed by. After saying hello, you said "Have you reconsidered my proposal of last week? I would really like to get to know you better. I know you're trying to make a career in publishing. I have a lot of experience in the field. Maybe I can be of some help to you." To your surprise, she just stormed off.

The next thing you knew, Howard Roark, the manager of personnel, was in your office telling you that Francon had complained to him that you were sexually harassing her as well as other women on the magazine's staff. Angry and extremely embarrassed, you admitted to Roark that you had been lonely since your wife's death and had asked several women out. You assured him that since these actions had apparently been misinterpreted, you would not do so again. Since then, although you still have endeavored to remain on friendly terms with most of the women at the magazine, you have never been familiar with Francon again. You have kept all your dealings with her on a formal and professional level.

Yesterday, the editorial board met to vote on who should be named manager of the advertising department now that the former manager, Henry Cameron, had been promoted to senior manager and member of the editorial board. Although four members of the board wanted to promote Francon because of her section's superior sales performance, Cameron, now a board member, recommended Peter Keating, the other senior account representative. Cameron stated that he thought Keating had more "people skills" than did Francon and would make a better manager. You certainly agreed with this and said so. In the end, the board voted 5–4 to promote Keating.

Today, you learned that upon hearing that Keating had been promoted rather than her, Francon had told one of her account reps that she was going to sue you and the magazine for sexual harassment and sex discrimination. Your initial reaction to this was to exclaim, "Isn't that just like the bitch." However, after you calmed down, you realized that this could present a damaging situation both for you and the magazine. What should you do? (You may ask to meet with either Roark or Francon or both in addition to any other action you deem appropriate.)

Howard Roark

You are Howard Roark, personnel manager at *Your House,* a successful architecture magazine. In this position, you are responsible for arranging the employee benefit package, overseeing hiring and promotion decisions below the level of senior management to ensure compliance with all legal requirements, and equitably resolving grievances involving members of the magazine's staff. The magazine is managed by the editorial board, which has responsibility for planning the magazine's budget, establishing editorial policy, and selecting those who are to be hired or promoted to managerial positions. The board is made up of all senior editors and managers and is presently comprised of the nine men who hold these positions. Your position is not a senior position and you are not a member of the board.

At present, you are greatly concerned by a situation involving Ellsworth Toohey, one of the senior editors, and Dominique Francon, a senior account representative in the advertising department. Toohey, a man in his mid-fifties, has been with the magazine since its inception ten years ago. Originally from Lubbock, Texas, his "good old boy" manner can strike people as either quaint and friendly or overly familiar and crude. He has a habit of greeting co-workers with comments concerning their appearance and often refers to them as "Son" or "Dear," something some of the women staff members resent. Although he went through some rough times following the death of his wife 18 months ago, recently he seems to have gotten back to his former gregarious self.

Francon, a woman in her early thirties, is one of the two senior account representatives whose job it is to supervise the junior account reps who directly contact potential advertisers to sell advertising space. Unlike Toohey, Francon is reserved in manner and can strike people as either highly professional or cold and aloof. She is quite demanding of the junior reps she supervises, which accounts for both the superior revenues generated by her section and her lack of personal friends among the staff.

Your present problem arises out of an incident that took place a year ago. At that time, Francon came to your office to complain about sexual harassment by Toohey. She claimed that Toohey had repeatedly asked her out, would not take "no" for an answer, had made a sexually offensive comment to her, and had offered to help advance her career if she went out with him. She further claimed that Toohey had also propositioned several other women at the magazine. When you confronted Toohey with Francon's accusations, he was obviously both angry and embarrassed. He admitted that he had been quite lonely since his wife's death and that he had asked Francon and some of the other women on the magazine's staff to go out with him. He vehemently denied exerting pressure on any woman, however, and stated that, "If Francon says that I offered to help advance her career, then she's a lying bitch." After he calmed down, he assured you that there would be no further incidents involving either Francon or any of the other women on staff. A few days following this meeting, you informed Francon that the problem had been dealt with and that if she had any further trouble with Toohey she should inform you immediately.

Until yesterday, you thought the matter had been successfully resolved. That's when the editorial board met to replace Henry Cameron, the manager of the advertising department who had just been promoted to senior manager and member of the editorial board. The only two candidates for the position were Francon and Peter Keating, the other senior account representative. Although not privy to the board's deliberations, you were told that the board voted for Keating 5–4 despite the fact that Francon's section consistently sold more advertising space than Keating's. Apparently, the board was impressed with Keating's "people skills." Somehow, Francon found out that Toohey had both voted and spoken out against her at the meeting. You have just learned that today she told one of her account reps that she intends to sue both Toohey and the magazine for sexual harassment and sex discrimination.

You realize that such a suit could be extremely damaging to the magazine and find yourself wondering whether your handling of things last year might be responsible for the present situation. What should you do? (You may ask to meet with either Toohey or Francon or both in addition to any other action you deem appropriate.)

Questions for discussion

1. Did Howard Roark handle the situation in a morally appropriate manner? Did Toohey? Did Francon? What should they do now?

2. How can one account for the vastly different perceptions of Francon's and Toohey's behaviors by each other?

3. What can be done to resolve the situation in a morally acceptable manner?

4. How would you feel in Francon's position? In Toohey's?

• *Essay* •
A Note on Sexual Harassment*

ANDREW WICKS

Sexual harassment has been receiving a lot of attention in the headlines recently because of the Clarence Thomas hearings, the resignation of Dr. Frances Conley, a prominent neurosurgeon at Stanford University, and a variety of other cases. The focus on issues of sexual harassment has led to a growing awareness of the extent of the problem.

According to surveys, sexual harassment is an alarmingly pervasive reality. A survey of federal-government employees concluded that more than two women in five experienced harassment on the job: 42 percent of the women who responded claimed that they had been harassed between May of 1985 and May of 1987, while 14 percent of men reported similar experiences. Perhaps even more surprising is that only 5 percent of those who said they were victims filed any form of formal complaint. The board that conducted the survey estimated that the problems linked to sexual harassment cost the federal government $267 million during the two-year span in question, as a result of paying sick leave, replacing employees who quit, and reduced productivity (9).

In addition, a recent study of the military indicates that two out of three women who are part of the U.S. armed forces have experienced some form of sexual harassment. Half of those who responded affirmatively maintained that they suffered some form of serious harassment—including touching, pressure for sexual favors, and rape. The other respondents said that they experienced milder forms such as cat calls, teasing, dirty looks, and lewd jokes. In addition, 17 percent of the males in the military reported similar treatment (from both male and female sources). The surveys did not inquire whether respondents had experienced "sexual harassment"; respondents were asked about specific actions and behaviors, which were then placed in the categories of sexual harassment by those who performed the survey. Recent estimates put the incidence of sexual harassment in the work force, against women alone, at 30–40 percent (6).

Numerous reasons can be cited for the surprisingly low incidence of reporting on the part of employees who are victims of sexual harassment. Most obviously, the subject creates a good deal of embarrassment for anyone making a claim because of the social stigma attached to it. The social stigma is a problem for both sexes—for women because they are often labeled troublemakers or perceived as tainted; for men because of the perception that they might have been dominated or controlled by someone else. In addition, fears of retribution, repercussions for one's family and friends, and the psychological difficulties that victims often find in taking formal action—all make coming forward extremely difficult for victims. Finally, all victims share a fear of not being believed when they come forward and of not receiving justice. As one commentator noted in light of the Clarence Thomas hearings, "In general in

*This case was prepared by Andrew Wicks, Research Assistant, under the supervision of R. Edward Freeman, Elis and Signe Olsson Professor of Business Administration. Copyright © 1992 by the Darden Graduate Business School Foundation, Charlottesville, VA.

our society, it is not the behavior of the harasser that has been questioned but that of the victim" (5).

When they do come forward, victims of harassment typically do so to gain an end to the conduct, help in overcoming the physical and psychological effects, and the chance to return to a productive and positive work environment. They do not generally want to hurt others or reap large monetary awards from a drawn-out and personally invasive trial.

Somewhat surprisingly, sexual harassment has only fairly recently gained acceptance as and been formally recognized as illegal conduct in the United States. The first court cases did not appear until the mid-1970s. The issue received increasing attention, and in 1980 the federal government (through the EEOC, the Equal Employment Opportunity Commission) issued guidelines on sexual harassment. The guidelines attempted to define sexual harassment, established parameters for employer liability, and made suggestions for programs in the workplace to cope with the problem (3).

DEFINING SEXUAL HARASSMENT

Two basic types of sexual harassment were defined by the EEOC and appear in the various Supreme Court cases on sexual harassment. The first, and most clear-cut, form is termed *quid pro quo* harassment. It occurs when an employer/superior requests sexual favors in exchange for tangible benefits (advancement, promotion, pay raise) or to avoid a tangible harm (losing one's job, preventing a pay raise or promotion). The second, and more complex, type of harassment is *hostile environment*. It can take many forms and is often difficult to prove. Quid pro quo is the more easily identifiable as harassment. Hostile environment claims can be made on the basis of "unwelcome sexual advances, requests for sexual favors, and verbal or physical conduct of a sexual nature" that "unreasonably interfere with an individual's job performance" or that might "create an 'intimidating, hostile, or offensive working environment'."

To constitute sexual harassment, two elements must be shown in the behavior. First, the conduct must be unwelcome. Second, one of three factors must be demonstrated:

1. submission to such conduct is made a term or condition of an individual's employment
2. submission to or rejection of such conduct is used as the basis for employment decisions affecting the individual
3. the conduct has the purpose or effect of unreasonably interfering with an individual's work performance or creating an intimidating, hostile, or offensive working environment (7, p. 81).

In guidelines issued in 1988, the EEOC specified several factors that affect the finding of hostile-environment harassment:

1. whether the conduct was verbal, physical, or both
2. how frequently it was repeated
3. whether the conduct was hostile and patently offensive
4. whether the alleged harasser was a co-worker or a supervisor
5. whether others joined in in perpetrating the harassment
6. whether the harassment was directed at more than one individual

The primary issue these factors are meant to determine is whether the conduct "unreasonably interferes with an individual's work performance" or "creates an intimidating, hostile, or offensive working environment." In general, isolated incidents are not considered sufficient to establish a hostile environment, whereas one instance of the quid pro quo variety is considered grounds for proving sexual harassment. However, the EEOC 1988 guidelines clearly state that a single incident *can* constitute hostile-environment harassment if it is unusually severe (7, p. 83).

LEGAL ISSUES

Meritor Savings Bank, FSB v. Vinson

The first case to introduce hostile-environment claims at the Supreme Court level was *Meritor Savings Bank, FSB v. Vinson*. In it, the Court clearly established that sexual harassment is illegal under Title VII of the Civil Rights Act of 1964 (which makes it "an unlawful employment practice for an employer . . . to discriminate against any individual with respect to his compensation, terms, conditions, or privileges of employment, because of such individual's race, color, religion, sex, or national origin") and established that the statute prohibits both quid pro quo harassment as well as a hostile work environment (which includes "unwelcome sexual advances, requests for sexual favors, and other physical conduct of a sexual nature") (8, p. 28).

The case was brought by Mechelle Vinson, who was employed as a teller-trainee by Meritor Savings Bank. She remained on the job for several years and received promotions, but after using large amounts of sick leave toward the end of her employment, she was discharged for "excessive use of that leave." After being fired, Vinson brought suit against the bank and her supervisor, Mr. Taylor, on charges of being constantly harassed by him. She claimed that she had complied with his requests for sex but did so only because she feared losing her job (although apparently he never made this threat explicit). Vinson alleged that "over . . . several years she had intercourse with [Taylor] some 40 or 50 times . . . [He] fondled her in front of other employees, followed her into the women's restroom when she went there alone, exposed himself to her, and even forcibly raped her on several occasions." Vinson asked the court for an injunction to protect her from Taylor and sought monetary compensation from both Taylor and the bank. Taylor denied all of her charges. The bank claimed that, even if the claims were true, the bank had no knowledge of these incidents—that the incidents were "unknown to the bank and engaged in without its consent or approval" (4, p. 511).

One of the key aspects of this case is that the issue of sexual harassment was not contingent on whether the participation by the victim was voluntary. Rather, the crucial issue for the Court was whether the advances were unwelcome. To be unwelcome, (1) the conduct must not have been solicited or incited by the victim, and (2) the victim must regard the conduct as offensive or undesirable (7, p. 82). The Court found that the conduct in this case met these criteria and that the severity and persistence of the actions against Vinson clearly constituted a hostile environment.

In terms of the liability of the bank, the Court adopted a middle position. It held that ignorance of the harassment was no excuse, nor would the mere presence of a stated policy and procedure for sexual-harassment claims in the workplace exempt the bank from liability. It also maintained, however, that Vinson's plea for strict or complete liability was unacceptable. The Court held that the degree of an employer's liability is directly connected to its voluntary actions to create internal policies that deal with sexual harassment, to educate the work force on these issues, and to develop a mechanism designed to encourage harassment victims to come forward (8, p. 29). In short, if such assertive and comprehensive policies are in place and carefully maintained, then an employer's liability will be minimized. When such policies are in place and incidents of harassment occur that the employer has no reasonable basis to know, a court could determine that the employer has no liability. The Court emphasized, however, that the determination of employer liability is made on the basis of the facts of each case (7, p. 85).

The Impact of Vinson

The Vinson case profoundly changed the legal landscape of sexual harassment. Subsequent decisions have raised several problems, however, stemming from the Vinson decision. One issue involves defining hostile environment claims and determining a threshold for the severity and pervasiveness of harassment to determine when a complaint is valid. Some decisions have held that visual and verbal assaults must be frequent and truly offensive and that they must typically generate complaints from more than one person (*Volk v. Coler; Scott v. Sears, Roebuck & Co.; Robinson v. Jacksonville Shipyards*).

The Vinson case also left unresolved the issue of whose point of view is to be used to judge what constitutes a hostile environment. Should the "reasonable person" standard be used (a standard that many have argued means a reasonable man), a "reasonable woman" standard, or the viewpoint of the victim of the harassment? Courts and women's groups have offered a range of opinions on the subject. Two recent court cases, one in the Ninth Circuit Court of Appeals in San Francisco (CA) and one from the federal district court in Jacksonville (FL), have used a reasonable-woman standard to determine the validity of hostile-environment claims. The judges maintained that the women in the cases were victims of conduct that the men perceived as "harmless locker-room antics or romantic advances," and that this difference reflected a significant variation in the experience of the sexes relating to sexual mores and the threat of unwelcome sexual conduct. Experts in the Jacksonville trial testified that 75 percent of men who were asked about their response to sexual advances in the workplace said they would be flattered, with only 15 percent claiming to feel offended. In contrast, 75 percent of women polled said they would feel offended (2).

In addition to this generally different perception of sexual conduct, other factors that lead proponents to support a woman-based standard include the large difference in the incidence of sexual assault and violence between the sexes, the history of sexual domination by men over women, and the prevalence of male judges.

A further area of difficulty is the extent to which sexual harassment and the hostile environment issue require that a pre-existing hostile/vulgar workplace be transformed. Is there an "assumption of risk" on the part of employees who enter a particular work force that has a reputation for antiwomen attitudes? A judge in one case held that a woman who enters a work environment where offensive antiwomen attitudes abound, in effect, "gets what she deserves" (*Rabidue v. Osceola Refining Company*) (1, p. 365). While this case has been criticized by many, it raises the question of the extent to which the law can expect to transform the workplace when the wider culture and the mass media still harbor sexist attitudes (to an extent that many would argue is both pervasive and offensive). The courts, the EEOC, and activist groups will likely struggle over this problem for many years.

References

1. Burstein, James, and Vandenberg, Wendy. "The Practical Labor Lawyer." *Employee Relations Law Journal*, Autumn 1987.
2. Hayes, Arthur. "Courts Concede the Sexes Think in Unlike Ways." *Wall Street Journal*, May 28, 1991, p. B1.
3. Lewin, Tamar. "Ruling on Pinups as Sexual Harassment: What Does It Mean?" *The New York Times*, February 8, 1991, p. B16.
4. Morlacci, Maria. "Sexual Harassment Law and the Impact of Vinson." *Employee Relations Law Journal*, Winter 1987–88.
5. *The New York Times*, October 20, 1991, p. L22.
6. Schmitt, Eric. "2 out of 3 Women in Military Study Report Sexual Harassment Incidents." *The New York Times*, September 12, 1990, p. A22.
7. Susser, Peter, and Jett, David. "Washington Scene." *Employment Relations Today*, Spring 1989.
8. Tidwell, Gary, and Abrams, Andrew. "Sexual Harassment and Pregnancy Leave." *B&E Review*, July–September 1987.
9. "Wide Harassment of Women Working for U.S. Is Reported." *The New York Times*, July 1, 1988, p. B6.

Additional Sources

ELLIOT, STUART. "Suit over Sex in Beer Ads Comes as Genre Changes." *The New York Times*, November 12, 1992, p. D22.

HIPP, E. "Now You See It, Now You Don't: The 'Hostile Work Environment' after Meritor." *American Business Law Journal*, vol. 26, 1988.

MARCUS, RUTH. "Courts Strain to Define Sexual Harassment." *Washington Post*, February 19, 1991, p. 1.

Questions for discussion

1. How should "hostile environment" sexual harassment be determined? By the reasonable person standard? The reasonable woman standard?

2. What can/should be done to minimize the occurrence of sexual harassment in the workplace?

3. Have the courts gone far enough or too far in defining and punishing incidents of sexual harassment?

• *Essay* •

A Note on Sexual Harassment Policy*

ANDREW WICKS

Why Have a Policy

Numerous reasons exist for businesses to have a comprehensive and well-monitored sexual harassment policy. The first, and most self-interested, reason is that creating a strong program will significantly reduce the potential for and extent of liability for incidents of sexual harassment. Second, such a policy is likely to lead to a decrease in harassment, which will save a company considerable time, money, and effort (recall the figures from "A Note on Sexual Harassment" on the cost incurred by the federal government because of harassment incidents) and reduce the likelihood that the company's image/credibility will be damaged if incidents do occur. Third, as parties interested in creating a positive working environment, employers have reason to support such a policy actively. Finally, as moral agents, companies should support these efforts as part of their concern about the integrity of their companies and the well-being of their employees.

How to Construct a Policy

A number of steps are needed to create a good and effective sexual harassment policy. First, the employer should make sure that a formal, written policy clearly states that the company does not tolerate sexual harassment, specifically details what constitutes such conduct, and includes stiff penalties for violating the policy. Second, the company should take time to educate all employees about the policy and about sexual harassment in general. As the statistics cited in "A Note on Sexual Harassment" indicate, a good deal of misunderstanding exists about what constitutes a hostile work environment, and education would go a long way in clarifying some of the uncertainties and ignorance surrounding the subject. This education might include discussion of particular situations/cases that bring to light the concept of a hostile environment and the general differences between men and women in perceiving what constitutes such an environment.

Third, safe, secure, and effective means of registering a complaint are vital. Employees should be able to seek out a number of potential superiors with whom to discuss incidents of harassment and have the option of talking to someone of the same sex. In addition, a means of protecting victims' identities and preventing any form of retribution against them should be available. Fourth, employers ought to provide confidential counseling services and other forms of support for victims of harassment.

These suggestions outline some of the basic and most important aspects of a sound sexual harassment policy. Numerous other factors, however, may be important to suit the needs/culture of a particular organization.

*This case was prepared by Andrew Wicks, Research Assistant, under the supervision of R. Edward Freeman, Elis and Signe Olsson Professor of Business Administration. Copyright © 1992 by the Darden Graduate Business School Foundation, Charlottesville, VA.

A Sample Policy

During the Clarence Thomas hearings, AT&T Chairman and CEO Robert Allen sent out AT&T's policy on sexual harassment through company computers and reiterated the policy's importance and the penalties for violating it (which include dismissal and personal legal and financial liability). The policy is considered well written as to clarity and specifics by many experts. The policy reads as follows:

> AT&T's sexual harassment policy prohibits sexual harassment in the workplace, whether committed by supervisory or non-supervisory personnel. Specifically, no supervisor shall threaten to insinuate, either explicitly or implicitly, that an employee's submission to or rejection of sexual advances will in any way influence any personnel decision regarding that employee's employment, wages, advancement, assigned duties, shifts, or any other condition of employment or career development. Other sexually harassing conduct in the workplace that may create an offensive work environment, whether it be in the form of physical or verbal harassment, and regardless of whether committed by supervisory or non-supervisory personnel, is also prohibited. This includes, but is not limited to, repeated offensive or unwelcome sexual flirtations, advances, propositions, continual or repeated verbal abuse of a sexual nature, graphic verbal commentaries about an individual's body, sexually degrading words used to describe an individual, and the display in the workplace of sexually suggestive objects or pictures. Sexual harassment in the workplace by any employee will result in disciplinary action up to and including dismissal and may lead to personal legal and financial liability. Employees are encouraged to avail themselves of AT&T's Internal Equal Opportunity complaint procedure if they are confronted with sexual harassment or any prohibited form of harassment. Such internal complaints will be investigated promptly, and corrective action will be taken where allegations are verified. No employees will suffer retaliation or intimidation as a result of using the internal complaint procedure.
>
> ROBERT E. ALLEN, Chairman

DuPont is another company with a highly regarded program. The company has established a telephone hotline through which employees can report incidents and learn about their options in an anonymous setting. Nearly 65,000 of DuPont's 100,000 employees in America have undergone a half-day training program on sexual harassment. Employees are told to report an incident of harassment to any supervisor or manager, who is then obligated to take action on the claim.[1]

Note

1. *The New York Times*, October 20, 1992, p. L22. For additional source material, see "A Note on Sexual Harassment."

References

RUBENSTEIN, MICHAEL. "Devising a Sexual Harassment Policy." *Personnel Management*, February 1991.
SEGAL, JONATHAN. "Safe Sex: A Workplace Oxymoron?" *HR Magazine*, June 1990.

Questions for discussion

1. Do these policies cover all of the relevant matters?
2. What effect do you think having a sexual harassment policy will have on the incidence of and punishment of sexual harassment?

• SIX •

Obligations to Stakeholders

Employees, Customers,
Community, and Stockholders

History reveals marked differences in the ways that cultures treat business obligations to consumers. The Code of Hammurabi, almost 4,000 years old, holds merchants to certain standards of fair dealing and product safety. Seventeenth-century France under the rule of Louis XIV maintained a complex set of regulations and procedures governing product quality. Yet with the dawn of the Industrial Revolution and the influence of laissez-faire economic theorists such as Adam Smith, there came a dramatic loosening of government restraints. Smith and others argued that efficiency is significantly impaired when government tries to guarantee consumer satisfaction and safety; in turn the doctrine of "caveat emptor," or "buyer beware," dominated the economic scene during the first chapter of U.S. history.

Since the mid-nineteenth century, however, there has occurred a gradual shift in product liability law away from caveat emptor and in favor of caveat venditor, or "seller beware." In 1850 U.S. law decreed that only those who could prove fraud or breach of warranty could collect damages in the event they were harmed by a defective product. Not only did consumers find it extremely difficult to satisfy the courts' strict concepts of "fraud" and "breach of contract" but they were also required to sue only those with whom they existed in a relationship of "privity." "Privity" referred to a direct commercial relationship; thus a consumer who purchased a toxic bottle of aspirin from a drugstore could only sue the owner of the drugstore (with whom he or she had privity), and *not* the maker of the aspirin. This was true even when it was the maker of the aspirin who through negligence had mislabeled the toxic substance.

By the turn of the century, courts had struck down the doctrine of privity and were forcing companies to compensate injured consumers in a variety of instances. And by the mid-twentieth century, courts were holding corporations liable according to a doctrine of "strict liability," a doctrine under which consumers can collect damages even when it is impossible to prove corporate negligence. This means that so long as the product is defective and causes damage (barring dramatic consumer negligence), the producer is liable for damages—even when the producer took all possible safety precautions in the production of the product. Thus, if a can of hair spray explodes in a consumer's hands, the manufacturer of the spray is liable regardless of safety precautions taken.

Judges have justified strict liability using some of the following reasons:

1. The burden for consumer damage is best shouldered by corporations, who have "deep pockets," or in other words, more substantial financial reserves than do individual consumers. Since producers will necessarily raise prices somewhat to cover the most of anticipated liability, it will be consumers, not corporations, who will shoulder the ultimate financial burden for liability protection. But it is more efficient to protect the general public in this way than to rely on individual consumers to purchase a complex package of individual insurance for hair spray liability, jet engine liability, cosmetic liability, and so on.

2. Producers hold themselves to be "experts" and hence offer an "implied warranty" that their products will perform their intended function without damaging the user. That is to say, few of us could be expected to know about the combination of steel and stress in the design of a lawnmower; yet we assume that the manufacturer does, and moreover that the lawnmower will mow grass without throwing its blade dangerously through the mower housing. If and when it throws its blade, then we can claim the violation of an implied warranty, and we can claim it even when unable to prove that the manufacturer was, in fact, negligent.

3. Finally, a policy of strict liability is seen as a deterrent to dangerous practices. If a manufacturer knows that any attempt to hide behind excuses will fail in court, then the manufacturer may well be prompted to take special precautions to insure that nothing goes wrong.

One must clearly distinguish, however, *legal liability* from either *criminal* or *moral responsibility*. Legal liability, for example, can occur when there is no criminal or moral responsibility. If a small child throws a rock through a neighbor's window, the parents may be legally liable; that is, they may be required to compensate the injured party financially. And yet the parents may not be morally or criminally responsible at all (unless, say, they were morally guilty by failing to raise the child properly or criminally responsible through ordering the child to throw the rock). Similarly, a corporation may be found financially liable for compensating an injured consumer without criminal or moral blame being attached.

The "Ford Pinto" case found in this section is a good example of this distinction. In a long series of trials, Ford was found financially liable time after time. It was required in turn to compensate the victims and relatives of victims of the Pinto's exploding gas tank. Thus in a short time the issue of whether Ford was liable was settled: Ford *was* financially liable. But the questions of criminal and moral responsibility remained. In the version of the Pinto case in this section, the emphasis is on the question of criminal and moral responsibility. It centers on the celebrated trial in which Ford Motor Company was charged with criminal homicide. No company in the United States, interestingly enough, had ever been found guilty of homicide. The "Dalkon Shield" case not only examines A. H. Robins legal liability but also deals with the question of its criminal and moral responsibility. The fact is, Robins produced a product that caused injury and harm to many women. The question is, did Robins conspire to misinform its customers about the health factors involved in the use of the Dalkon Shield?

The other pieces in this section deal with financial harm and various kinds of stakeholder obligations and responsibilities other than direct physical harm.

The "Dorrence Corporation Trade-Offs" case confronts the reader with a series of questions that can generally be applied to any company. What responsibilities does a CEO have to the investors, the employees, the customers, the company itself? What compromises can/should a CEO be willing to make? What's the "bottom line"? The "Sears" cases explore at least three critical issues in customer-employee relations. What happens when managers don't effectively monitor their policy decisions? How can managers stimulate employee productivity without generating unethical behavior? What happens to a company when it loses its "good name"? Clinton Oak's article "Roger Hixon: Let the Buyer Beware" exposes the tendency of many people to hide the truth when selling products or personal possessions. The case of "Commissions on Sales at Brock Mason Brokerage" further illustrates how good intentions can give way to the desire for profits in sales.

• *Case Study* •

The Ford Pinto*

W. MICHAEL HOFFMAN

I

On August 10, 1978 a tragic automobile accident occurred on U.S. Highway 33 near Goshen, Indiana. Sisters Judy and Lynn Ulrich (ages 18 and 16, respectively) and their cousin Donna Ulrich (age 18) were struck from the rear in their 1973 Ford Pinto by a van. The gas tank of the Pinto ruptured, the car burst into flames and the three teen-agers were burned to death.

Subsequently an Elkhart County grand jury returned a criminal homicide charge against Ford, the first ever against an American corporation. During the following 20-week trial, Judge Harold R. Staffeldt advised the jury that Ford should be convicted of reckless homicide if it were shown that the company had engaged in "plain, conscious and unjustifiable disregard of harm that might result (from its actions) and the disregard involves a substantial deviation from acceptable standards of conduct."[1] The key phrase around which the trial hinged, of course, is "acceptable standards." Did Ford knowingly and recklessly choose profit over safety in the design and placement of the Pinto's gas tank? Elkhart County prosecutor Michael A. Cosentino and chief Ford attorney James F. Neal battled dramatically over this issue in a rural Indiana courthouse. Meanwhile, American business anxiously awaited the verdict which could send warning ripples through board rooms across the nation concerning corporate responsibility and product liability.

II

As a background to this trial some discussion of the Pinto controversy is necessary. In 1977 the magazine *Mother Jones* broke a story by Mark Dowie, general manager of *Mother Jones* business operations, accusing Ford of knowingly putting on the road an unsafe car—the Pinto—in which hundreds of people have needlessly suffered burn deaths and even more have been scarred and disfigured due to burns. In his article "Pinto Madness" Dowie charges that:

> Fighting strong competition from Volkswagen for the lucrative small-car market, the Ford Motor Company rushed the Pinto into production in much less than the usual time. Ford engineers discovered in pre-production crash tests that rear-end collisions would rupture the Pinto's fuel system extremely easily. Because assembly-line machinery was already tooled when engineers found this defect, top Ford officials decided to manufacture the car anyway—exploding gas tank and all—even though Ford owned the patent on a much safer gas tank. For more than eight years afterwards, Ford successfully lobbied, with extraordinary vigor and some blatant lies, against a key government safety standard that would have forced the company to change the Pinto's fire-prone gas tank. By conservative estimates Pinto crashes have caused 500 burn deaths to people who would not have been seriously injured if the car had not burst into flames. The figure could be as high as 900. Burning Pintos have become such an embarrassment to Ford that its advertising agency, J. Walter Thompson, dropped a line from the ending of a radio spot that read "Pinto leaves you with that warm feeling."
>
> Ford knows that the Pinto is a firetrap, yet it has paid out millions to settle damage suits out of court, and it is prepared to spend millions more lobbying against safety standards. With a half million cars rolling off the assembly lines each year, Pinto is the biggest-selling subcompact in America, and the company's operating profit on the car is fantastic. Finally, in 1977, new Pinto models have incorporated a few minor alterations necessary to meet that federal standard Ford managed to hold off for eight years. Why did the company delay so long in making these minimal, inexpensive improvements?
>
> Ford waited eight years because its internal "cost-benefit analysis," which places a dollar value on human life, said it wasn't profitable to make the changes sooner.[2]

Several weeks after Dowie's press conference on the article, which had the support of Ralph Nader and auto safety expert Byron Bloch, Ford issued a news release attributed to Herbert T. Misch, vice president of Environmental and Safety Engineering at Ford, countering points made in the *Mother Jones* article. Their statistical studies significantly conflicted with each other. For example, Dowie states that more than 3000 people were burning to death yearly in auto fires; he claims that, according to a National Highway Traffic Safety Administration (NHTSA) consultant, although Ford makes 24 percent of the cars on American roads, these cars account for 42 percent of the collision-ruptured fuel tanks.[3] Ford, on the other hand, uses statistics from the Fatality Analysis Reporting System (FARS) maintained by the government's NHTSA to defend itself, claiming that in 1975 there were 848 deaths related to fire-associated passenger-car accidents and only 13 of these involved Pintos; in 1976, Pintos accounted for only 22 out of 943. These statistics imply that Pintos were involved in only 1.9 percent of such accidents, and Pintos constitute about 1.9 percent of the total registered passenger cars. Furthermore, fewer than half of those Pintos cited in the FARS study were struck in the rear.[4] Ford concludes from this and other studies that the Pinto was never an unsafe car and has not been involved in some 70 burn deaths annually as *Mother Jones* claims.

Ford admits that early model Pintos did not meet rear-impact tests at 20 mph but denies that this implies that they were unsafe compared to other cars of that type and era. In fact, its tests were conducted, according to Ford, some with experimental rubber "bladders" to protect the gas tank, in order to determine how best to have their future cars meet a 20 mph rear-collision standard which Ford itself set as an internal performance goal. The government at that time had no such standard. Ford also points out that in every model year the Pinto met or surpassed the government's own standards, and

> it simply is unreasonable and unfair to contend that a car is somehow unsafe if it does not meet standards proposed for future years or embody the technological improvements that are introduced in later model years.[5]

Mother Jones, on the other hand, presents a different view of the situation. If Ford was so concerned about rear-impact safety, why did it delay the federal government's attempts to impose standards? Dowie gives the following answer:

> The particular regulation involved here was Federal Motor Vehicle Safety Standard 301. Ford picked portions of Standard 201 for strong opposition way back in 1968 when the Pinto was still in the blueprint stage. The intent of 301, and the 300 series that followed it, was to protect drivers and passengers after a crash occurs. Without question the worst post-crash hazard is fire. Standard 301 originally proposed that all cars should be able to withstand a fixed barrier impact of 20 mph (that is, running into a wall at that speed) without losing fuel.
>
> When the standard was proposed, Ford engineers pulled their crash-test results out of their files. The front ends of most cars were no problem—with minor alterations they could stand the impact without losing fuel. "We were already working on the front end," Ford engineer Dick Kimble admitted. "We knew we could meet the test on the front end." But with the Pinto particularly, a 20 mph rear-end standard meant redesigning the entire rear end of the car. With the Pinto scheduled for production in August of 1970, and with $200 million worth of tools in place, adoption of this standard would have created a minor financial disaster. So Standard 301 was targeted for delay, and with some assistance from its industry associates, Ford succeeded beyond its wildest expectations: the standard was not adopted until the 1977 model year.[6]

Ford's tactics were successful, according to Dowie, not only due to their extremely clever lobbying, which became the envy of lobbyists all over Washington, but also because of the pro-industry stance of NHTSA itself.

Furthermore, it is not at all clear that the Pinto was as safe as other comparable cars with regard to the positioning of its gas tank. Unlike the gas tank in the Capri which rode over the rear axle, a "saddle-type" fuel tank on which Ford owned the patent, the Pinto tank was placed just behind the rear bumper. According to Dowie,

> Dr. Leslie Ball, the retired safety chief for the NASA manned space program and a founder of the International Society of Reliability Engineers, recently made a careful study of the Pinto. "The release to production of the Pinto was the most reprehensible decision in the history of American engineering," he said. Ball can name more than 40 European and Japanese models in the Pinto price and weight range with safer gas-tank positioning.
>
> Los Angeles auto safety expert Byron Bloch has made an indepth study of the Pinto fuel system. "It's a catastrophic blunder," he says. "Ford made an extremely

irresponsible decision when they placed such a weak tank in such a ridiculous location in such a soft rear end. It's almost designed to blow up—premeditated."[7]

Although other points could be brought out in the debate between *Mother Jones* and Ford, perhaps the most intriguing and controversial is the cost-benefit analysis study that Ford did entitled "Fatalities Associated with Crash-Induced Fuel Leakage and Fires" released by J. C. Echold, Director of Automotive Safety for Ford. This study apparently convinced Ford and was intended to convince the federal government that a technical improvement costing $11 per car which would have prevented gas tanks from rupturing so easily was not cost-effective for society. The costs and benefits are broken down in the following way:

Benefits

Savings:	180 burn deaths, 180 serious burn injuries, 2,100 burned vehicles
Unit Cost:	$200,000 per death, $67,000 per injury, $700 per vehicle
Total Benefit:	180 × ($200,000) + 180 × ($67,000) + 2,100 × ($700) = $49.5 million.

Costs

Sales:	11 million cars, 1.5 million light trucks
Unit Cost:	$11 per car, $11 per truck
Total Cost:	11,000,000 × ($11) + 1,500,000 × ($11) = $137 million

Component	1971 Costs
Future Productivity Losses	
Direct	$132,000
Indirect	41,300
Medical Costs	
Hospital	700
Other	425
Property Damage	1,500
Insurance Administration	4,700
Legal and Court	3,000
Employer Losses	1,000
Victim's Pain and Suffering	10,000
Funeral	900
Assets (Lost Consumption)	5,000
Miscellaneous	200
TOTAL PER FATALITY	$ 200,725

(Although this analysis was on all Ford vehicles, a breakout of just the Pinto could be done.) *Mother Jones* reports it could not find anybody who could explain how the $10,000 figure for "pain and suffering" had been arrived at.[8]

Although Ford does not mention this point in its News Release defense, it might have replied that it was the federal government, not Ford, that set the figure for a burn death. Ford simply carried out a cost-benefit analysis based on that figure. *Mother Jones*, however, in addition to insinuating that there was industry-agency (NHTSA) collusion, argues that the $200,000 figure was arrived at under intense pressure from the auto industry to use cost-benefit analysis in determining regulations. *Mother Jones* also questions Ford's estimate of burn injuries: "All independent experts estimate that for each person who dies by an auto fire, many more are left with charred hands, faces and limbs." Referring to the Northern California Burn Center which estimates the ratio of burn injuries to deaths at ten to one instead of one to one, Dowie states that "the true ratio obviously throws the company's calculations way off."[9] Finally, *Mother Jones* claims to have obtained "confidential" Ford documents which Ford did not send to Washington, showing that crash fires could be largely prevented by installing a rubber bladder inside the gas tank for only $5.08 per car, considerably less than the $11 per car Ford originally claimed was required to improve crash-worthiness.[10]

Instead of making the $11 improvement, installing the $5.08 bladder, or even giving the consumer the right to choose the additional cost for added safety, Ford continued, according to *Mother Jones*, to delay the federal government for eight years in establishing mandatory rear-impact standards. In the meantime, Dowie argues, thousands of people were burning to death and tens of thousands more were being badly burned and disfigured for life, tragedies many of which could have been prevented for only a slight cost per vehicle. Furthermore, the delay also meant that millions of new unsafe vehicles went on the road, "vehicles that will be crashing, leaking fuel and incinerating people well into the 1980s."[11]

In concluding this article Dowie broadens his attack beyond just Ford and the Pinto.

> Unfortunately, the Pinto is not an isolated case of corporate malpractice in the auto industry. Neither is Ford a lone sinner. There probably isn't a car on the road without a safety hazard known to its manufacturer . . .
>
> Furthermore, cost-valuing human life is not used by Ford alone. Ford was just the only company careless enough to let such an embarrassing calculation slip into public records. The process of willfully trading lives for profits is built into corporate capitalism. Commodore Vanderbilt publicly scorned George Washington and his "foolish" air brakes while people died by the hundreds in accidents on Vanderbilt's railroads.[12]

Ford has paid millions of dollars in Pinto jury trials and out-of-court settlements, especially the latter. *Mother Jones* quotes Al Slechter in Ford's Washington office as saying: "We'll never go to a jury again. Not in a fire case. Juries are just too sentimental. They see those charred remains and forget the evidence. No sir, we'll settle."[13] But apparently Ford thought such settlements would be less costly than the safety improvements. Dowie wonders if Ford would continue to make the same decisions "were Henry Ford II and Lee Iacocca serving 20-year terms in Leavenworth for consumer homicide."[14]

III

On March 13, 1980, the Elkhart County jury found Ford not guilty of criminal homicide in the Ulrich case. Ford attorney Neal summarized several points in his closing argument before the jury. Ford could have stayed out of the small car market which would have been the "easiest way," since Ford would have made more profit by sticking to bigger cars. Instead Ford built the Pinto "to take on the imports, to save jobs for Americans and to make a profit for its stockholders."[15] The Pinto met every fuel-system standard of any federal, state or local government, and was comparable to other 1973 subcompacts. The engineers who designed the car thought it was a good, safe car and bought it for themselves and their families. Ford did everything possible quickly to recall the Pinto after NHTSA ordered it to do so. Finally, and more specifically to the case at hand, Highway 33 was a badly designed highway, and the girls were fully stopped when a 4,000-pound van rammed into the rear of their Pinto at at least 50 miles an hour. Given the same circumstances, Neal stated, any car would have suffered the same consequences as the Ulrich's Pinto.[16] As reported in the *New York Times* and *Time,* the verdict brought a "loud cheer" from Ford's Board of Directors and undoubtedly at least a sigh of relief from other corporations around the nation.

Many thought this case was a David against a Goliath because of the small amount of money and volunteer legal help Prosecutor Cosentino had in contrast to the huge resources Ford poured into the trial. In addition, it should be pointed out that Cosentino's case suffered from a ruling by Judge Staffeldt that Ford's own test results on pre-1973 Pinto's were inadmissible. These documents confirmed that Ford knew as early as 1971 that the gas tank of the Pinto ruptured at impacts of 20 mph and that the company was aware, because of tests with the Capri, that the over-the-axle position of the gas tank was much safer than mounting it behind the axle. Ford decided to mount it behind the axle in the Pinto to provide more trunk space and to save money. The restrictions of Cosentino's evidence to testimony relating specifically to the 1973 Pinto severely undercut the strength of the prosecutor's case.[17]

Whether this evidence would have changed the minds of the jury will never be known. Some, however, such as business ethicist Richard De George, feel that this evidence shows grounds for charges of recklessness against Ford. Although it is true that there were no federal safety standards in 1973 to which Ford legally had to conform and although Neal seems to have proved that all subcompacts were unsafe when hit at 50 mph by a 4,000-pound van, the fact that the NHTSA ordered a recall of the Pinto and not other subcompacts is, according to De George, "*prima facie* evidence that Ford's Pinto gas tank mounting was substandard."[18] De George argues that these grounds for recklessness are made even stronger by the fact that Ford did not give the consumer a choice to make the Pinto gas tank safer by installing a rubber bladder for a rather modest fee.[19] Giving the consumer such a choice, of course, would have made the Pinto gas tank problem known and therefore probably would have been bad for sales.

Richard A. Epstein, professor of law at the University of Chicago Law School, questions whether Ford should have been brought up on criminal charges of reckless homicide at all. He also points out an interesting historical fact. Before 1966 an injured party in Indiana could not even bring civil charges against an automobile manufacturer solely because of the alleged "uncrashworthiness" of a car; one would have to seek legal relief from the other party involved in the accident, not from the manufacturer. But after *Larson v. General Motors Corp.* in 1968, a new era of crashworthiness suits against automobile manufacturers began. "Reasonable" precautions must now be taken by manufacturers to minimize personal harm in crashes.[20] How to apply criteria of reasonableness in such cases marks the whole nebulous ethical and legal arena of product liability.

If such a civil suit had been brought against Ford, Epstein believes, the corporation might have argued, as they did to a large extent in the criminal suit, that the Pinto conformed to all current applicable safety standards and with common industry practice. (Epstein cites that well over 90% of U.S. standard production cars had their gas tanks in the same position as the Pinto.) But in a civil trial the adequacy of industry standards is ultimately up to the jury, and had civil charges been brought against Ford in this case the plaintiffs might have had a better chance of winning.[21] Epstein feels that a criminal suit, on the other hand, had no chance from the very outset, because the prosecutor would have had to establish criminal intent on the part of Ford. To use an analogy, if a hunter shoots at a deer and wounds an unseen person, he may be held civilly responsible but not criminally responsible because he did not intend to harm. And even though it may be more difficult to determine the mental state of a corporation (or its principal agents), it seems clear to Epstein that the facts of this case do not prove any such criminal intent even though Ford may have known that some burn deaths/injuries could have been avoided by a different placement of its Pinto gas tank and that Ford consciously decided not to spend more money to save lives.[22] Everyone recognizes that there are trade-offs between safety and costs. Ford could have built a "tank" instead of a Pinto, thereby considerably reducing risks, but it would have been relatively unaffordable for most and probably unattractive to all potential consumers.

To have established Ford's reckless homicide it would have been necessary to establish the same of Ford's agents since a corporation can only act through its agents. Undoubtedly, continues Epstein, the reason why the prosecutor did not try to subject Ford's officers and engineers to fines and imprisonment for their design choices is because of "the good faith character of their judgment, which was necessarily decisive in Ford's behalf as well."[23] For example, Harold C. MacDonald, Ford's chief engineer on the Pinto, testified that he felt it was important to keep the gas tank as far from the passenger compartment as possible, as it was in the Pinto. And other Ford engineers testified that they used the car for their own families. This is relevant information in a criminal case which must be concerned about the intent of the agents.

Furthermore, even if civil charges had been made in this case, it seems unfair and irrelevant to Epstein to accuse Ford of trading cost for safety. Ford's use of cost-benefit formulas, which must assign monetary values to human life and suffering, is precisely what the law demands in assessing civil liability suits. The court may disagree with the decision, but to blame industry for using such a method would violate the very rules of civil liability. Federal automobile officials (NHTSA) had to make the same calculations in order to discharge their statutory duties. In allowing the Pinto design, are not they too (and in turn their employer, the United States) just as guilty as Ford's agents?[24]

IV

The case of the Ford Pinto raises many questions of ethical importance. Some people conclude that Ford was definitely wrong in designing and marketing the Pinto. The specific accident involving the Ulrich girls, because of the circumstances, was simply not the right one to have attacked Ford on. Other people believe that Ford was neither criminally nor civilly guilty of anything and acted completely responsibly in producing the Pinto. Many others find the case morally perplexing, too complex to make sweeping claims of guilt or innocence.

Was Ford irresponsible in rushing the production of the Pinto? Even though Ford violated no federal safety standards or laws, should it have made the Pinto safer in terms of rear-end collisions, especially regarding the placement of the gas tank? Should Ford have used cost-benefit analysis to make decisions relating to safety, specifically placing dollar values on human life and suffering? Knowing that the Pinto's gas tank could have been made safer by installing a protective bladder for a relatively small cost per consumer, perhaps Ford should have made that option available to the public. If Ford did use heavy lobbying efforts to delay and/or influence federal safety standards, was this ethically proper for a corporation to do? One might ask, if Ford was guilty, whether the engineers, the managers, or both are to blame. If Ford had been found guilty of criminal homicide, was the proposed penalty stiff enough ($10,000 maximum fine for each of the three counts = $30,000 maximum), or should agents of the corporation such as MacDonald, Iacocca, and Henry Ford II be fined and possibly jailed?

A number of questions concerning safety standards are also relevant to the ethical issues at stake in the Ford trial. Is it just to blame a corporation for not abiding by "acceptable standards" when such standards are not yet determined by society? Should corporations like Ford play a role in setting such standards? Should individual juries be determining such standards state by state, incident by incident? If Ford should be setting safety standards, how does it decide how safe to make its product and still make it affordable and desirable to the public without using cost-benefit analysis? For that matter, how does anyone decide? Perhaps it is putting Ford, or any corporation, in a catch-22 position to ask it both to set safety standards and to competitively make a profit for its stockholders.

Regardless of how the reader answers these and other questions it is clear that the Pinto case raises fundamental issues concerning the responsibilities of corporations, how corporations should structure themselves in order to make ethical decisions, and how industry, government, and society in general ought to interrelate to form a framework within which such decisions can properly be made in the future.

Notes

1. *Indianapolis Star,* March 9, 1980, sec. 3, p. 2.
2. Mark Dowie, "Pinto Madness," *Mother Jones,* Sept/Oct, 1977, pp. 18 and 20. Subsequently Mike Wallace for "Sixty Minutes" and Sylvia Chase for "20-20" came out with similar exposés.
3. Ibid., p. 30.
4. Ford News Release (Sept. 9, 1977), pp. 1–3.
5. Ibid., p. 5.
6. Dowie, "Pinto Madness," p. 29.
7. Ibid., pp. 22–23.
8. Ibid., pp. 24 and 28. Although this analysis was on all Ford vehicles a breakout of just the Pinto could be done.
9. Ibid., p. 28.
10. Ibid., pp. 28–29.
11. Ibid., p. 30.
12. Ibid., p. 32. Dowie might have cited another example which emerged in the private correspondence which transpired almost a half century ago between Lammot du Pont and Alfred P.

Sloan, Jr., then president of GM. Du Pont was trying to convince Sloan to equip GM's lowest-priced cars, Chevrolets, with safety glass. Sloan replied by saying: "It is not my responsibility to sell safety glass. . . . You can say, perhaps, that I am selfish, but business is selfish. We are not a charitable institution—we are trying to make a profit for our stockholders." Quoted in Morton Mintz and Jerry S. Cohen, *Power, Inc.* (New York: The Viking Press, 1976), p. 110.

13. Ibid., p. 31.
14. Ibid., p. 32.
15. Transcript of report of proceedings in *State of Indiana v. Ford Motor Company,* Case No. 11-431, Monday, March 10, 1980, pp. 6202–3. How Neal reconciled his "easiest way" point with his "making more profit for stockholders" point is not clear to this writer.
16. Ibid., pp. 6207–9.
17. *Chicago Tribune,* October 13, 1979, p. 1, and sec. 2, p. 12; *New York Times,* October 14, 1979, p. 26; *Atlanta Constitution,* February 7, 1980.
18. Richard De George, "Ethical Responsibilities of Engineers in Large Organizations: The Pinto Case," *Business and Professional Ethics Journal,* vol. 1, no. 1 (Fall 1981), p. 4. *New York Times,* October 26, 1978, p. 103, also points out that during 1976 and 1977 there were 13 fiery fatal rear-end collisions involving Pintos, more than double that of other U.S. comparable cars, with VW Rabbits and Toyota Corollas having none.
19. Ibid., p. 5.
20. Richard A. Epstein, "Is Pinto a Criminal?" *Regulation,* March/April, 1980, pp. 16–17.
21. A California jury awarded damages of $127.8 million (reduced later to $6.3 million on appeal) in a Pinto crash where a youth was burned over 95% of his body. See *New York Times,* February 8, 1978, p. 8.
22. Epstein, p. 19.
23. Ibid., pp. 20–21.
24. Ibid., pp. 19–21.

Questions for discussion

1. Evaluate from a moral perspective the "cost-benefit" analysis conducted by Ford.
2. Did Ford "knowingly and recklessly choose profit over safety in the design and placement of the Pinto's gas tank"?
3. How might Ford alter its policies to avoid a similar disaster in the future?

• *Case Study* •

A. H. Robins: The Dalkon Shield*

AL GINI • TERRY SULLIVAN

On August 21, 1985, A. H. Robins of Richmond, Virginia—the seventeenth largest pharmaceutical house in America and corporately rated as number 392 in the Fortune 500—filed for reorganization under Chapter 11 of the 1978 Federal Bankruptcy Code. On the surface, Robins seemed to be a thriving company. Its popular products, including Robitussin cough syrup, Chap Stick lip balm, and Sergeant's flea and tick collars for cats and dogs generated record sales in 1985 of $706 million with a net income in excess of $75 million. Robins' petition for protection under Chapter 11 stems directly from the "blitz of litigation" over a product it has not produced since 1974, the Dalkon Shield intrauterine birth control device. At the time it filed for bankruptcy Robins had been deluged with more than 12,000 personal injury lawsuits charging that the Dalkon Shield was responsible for countless serious illnesses and at least 20 deaths among the women who used it.

In many ways this bankruptcy petition mimes and mirrors (Johns-) Manville's unprecedented request for reorganization in 1982. Manville, the nation's, if not the world's, largest producer of asbestos, claimed that it was succumbing to a "blitz of toxic torts" and therefore could not carry on with business as usual. In August 1982 Manville was facing 16,500 suits on behalf of people who claimed to have contracted cancer and other diseases caused by asbestos and the asbestos-related products that the company produced.

Like Manville, A. H. Robins is defending and explaining its actions by claiming that it simply cannot go on and fulfill its immediate and potential obligations to its stockholders, customers, employees, and litigants (claimants) unless it takes dramatic financial action. In filing for Chapter 11 Robins has won at least temporary respite from its legal woes. Although the company will continue operating during the reorganization, all suits now pending are frozen and no new suits can be filed. While the company develops a plan to handle its liabilities, it is up to the bankruptcy courts to deal with all present claims as well as to establish guidelines for the handling of any future claims.[1] Whatever the final results, the Dalkon Shield case may well turn out to be the worst product liability nightmare that a U.S. drugmaker or major corporation has ever suffered.[2]

The A. H. Robins company is essentially a family owned and operated organization. The original company was founded by Albert Hartley Robins, a registered pharmacist, in 1866 in Richmond, Virginia. His grandson, E. Claiborne Robins, built and directed the company into a multinational conglomerate which was able to obtain Fortune 500 status by the middle of the twentieth century. While E. Claiborne Robins remains Chairman of the Board, E. Claiborne Junior is now the firm's president and CEO. Both the family and the company are much liked and respected in their home state. Generations of employees have repeatedly claimed that E. Claiborne Senior was at his worst a "benevolent despot" and at his best a kind and gentle man sincerely interested in quality control as well as his employees' well being. By all reports E. Claiborne Junior seems to be following in his father's footsteps. Moreover, the family's kindness has not been limited to its employees. In 1969 E. Claiborne Senior personally donated over $50 million to the University of Richmond. Since then the Robins family has given at least $50 million more to the university, and additional millions to other universities and to diverse other causes. In December 1983 *Town and Country* magazine listed Claiborne Senior among the top five of "The Most Generous Americans."

Both the family and the company take pride in having "always gone by the book" and always giving their customers a good product at a fair price. In its 120 years of operation the company had done business without having a single product-liability lawsuit filed against it. Critics now claim that Robins has been involved in a directly ordered, prolonged institutional cover-up of the short-

and long-term effects of the use of the Dalkon Shield. Moreover, many critics claim that more than just stonewalling the possible side effects of the Shield, Robins is guilty of marketing a product they knew to be relatively untested, undependable, and therefore potentially dangerous. Robins is accused of having deceived doctors, lied to women, perjured itself to federal judges, and falsified documentation to the FDA. According to Morton Mintz, Robins' most outspoken critic, thousands, probably tens of thousands of women who trusted the doctors who trusted A. H. Robins paid a ghastly price for the use of the Dalkon Shield: chronic pelvic infections, impairment or loss of childbearing capacity, children with multiple birth defects, unwanted abortions, recurring health problems, and chronic pain.

IUDs are among the most ancient forms of contraception, known for more than two thousand years. Exactly how an IUD prevents conception is not known. It may interfere with the fertilization of the eggs, but most experts believe that when inserted into the uterus it prevents pregnancy by making it difficult for a fertilized egg to attach itself to the wall of the uterus. Over the centuries the materials used in the fabrication of IUDs include ebony, glass, gold, ivory, pewter, wood, wool, diamond-studded platinum, copper, and plastic.[3] The Dalkon Shield was developed by Dr. Hugh J. Davis, a former professor of obstetrics and gynecology at the Johns Hopkins University, and Irwin Lerner, an electrical engineer. In 1970 they sold their rights to the Shield to Robins, who agreed to pay royalties on future sales and $750,000 in cash. Between 1971 and 1974 Robins sold 4.5 million Dalkon Shields around the world, including 2.85 million in the United States.

By the late 1960s large numbers of women had become concerned about the safety of the Pill. These women formed an ever-growing potential market for an alternative means of birth control. Many of these women switched to "barrier" methods of birth control, particularly the diaphragm, which, when used with spermicidal creams or jellies, can be highly effective, though inconvenient. Others turned to IUDs, which, although convenient, previously had been considered unsafe—causing pelvic infections, irregular bleeding, uterine cramps, and accidental expulsion. Robins leapt at an opportunity to develop a new market with their product. The company's task was to convince physicians that the Shield was as effective as oral contraceptives in preventing pregnancies and that it was safer, better designed, and afforded greater resistance to inadvertent expulsion from the uterus than other IUDs.[4]

In January 1971 Robins began to sell the Dalkon Shield, promoting it as the "modern, superior," "second generation" and—most importantly—"safe" intrauterine device for birth control. The Shield itself is a nickel-sized plastic device that literally looks like a badge or a shield with spikes around the edges and a thread-sized "nylon tail string," which allowed both the wearer and the physician a means to guarantee that the device had not been expelled. The Shield was relatively inexpensive. The device itself sold for between $3.00 and $4.50 (its production costs were an incredibly low figure of $.25 a Shield). The only other cost associated with the Shield was the doctor's office fee for insertion and a recommended yearly pelvic examination. Dr. Hugh Davis claimed that the Dalkon Shield was the safest and most effective IUD because it is "the only IUD which is truly anatomically engineered for optimum uterine placement, fit, tolerance, and retention."[5] Davis was able to persuade a large number of physicians of the effectiveness of the Shield in an article he published in the "Current Investigation" section of the *American Journal of Obstetrics and Gynecology* in February 1970. The article described a study conducted at the Johns Hopkins Family Planning Clinic involving 640 women who had worn the Shield for one year. His analysis was based on 3,549 women-months of experience. Davis cited five pregnancies, ten expulsions, nine removals for medical reasons, and three removals for personal reasons. His startling results: tolerance rate (non-expulsion), 96 percent; pregnancy rate, 1.1 percent. The A. H. Robins Company reprinted no fewer than 199,000 copies of the Davis article for distribution to physicians.[6]

While various executives strongly recommended that other studies be commissioned to validate Davis' results, in January 1971 Robins began to market and sell the Shield on the basis of Davis' limited analysis. Robins' decision to produce and sell the Shield based on Davis' statistics may not coincide with the highest standards of scientific research, but it did not violate any FDA statutes and was therefore perfectly legal. At the time Robins produced the Shield, the FDA had no regulatory policies in force regarding IUDs of any kind. While the FDA had the authority to regulate the production, testing, and sales of all new prescriptions, it could only *recommend* testing on new medical devices. It could not monitor, investigate, or police a device unless charges of lack of effectiveness, injury, or abuse were formally leveled against the device or the producer.

In December 1970 Robins commissioned a major long-term study to reinforce Davis' results. The study concentrated on ten clinics, seven in the United States and one each in continental Canada, Nova Scotia, and British Columbia. Between December 1970 and December 1974 (six months after Robins suspended domestic sales) 2,391 women were fitted with the Shield. The first results came out in November 1972, and only about half of the women enrolled in the study. The statistics showed a sixteen month pregnancy rate of 1.6 percent. The Robins home office was more than pleased and immediately communicated this information to its sales staff. Thirteen months later, with all the women now participating in the program, less happy figures began to show up. The pregnancy rate after six months was 2.1 percent; after twelve months, 3.2 percent; after eighteen months, 3.5 percent; and after twenty-three months, 4.1 percent. In a final report published as a confidential internal document in August 1975 the final figures and results were even more devastating. The pregnancy rate after six months was 2.6 percent; after twelve months, 4.2 percent; after eighteen months, 4.9 percent; and after twenty-four months, 5.7 percent. Two of the scientists involved in this project submitted a minority report claiming that the Shield was even less effective than these already damaging figures indicated. They claimed that the pregnancy rate during the first year was much higher: after six months, 3.3 percent; and after twelve months, 5.5 percent. This twelve-month pregnancy rate is exactly five times *higher than* the rate Robins advertised and promoted—1.1 percent—to catapult the Shield to leadership in the IUD business.[7] This minority report was never disclosed to the medical community by Robins. Nor did Robins communicate these results to its own sales force. It did report some of these findings to the FDA in July 1974, but only after the company had suspended domestic sales earlier that June.

Soon after the Shield entered the marketplace, independent research results began to appear in both national and foreign journals of medicine. In 1970 and 1971 Dr. Mary O. Gabrielson, working out of clinics in San Francisco and Oakland, did an eighteen-month study on 937 women with results that

Robins would not want to advertise. The rate of medical removals was 26.4 percent; the pregnancy rate, 5.1 percent. In 1973 the *British Medical Journal* published a study showing a 4.7 percent pregnancy rate in Shield users.[8] Again because there was no law requiring disclosure of this new research information, Robins did not rush to inform the general public, the medical community, or the FDA.

At the same time that the Robins Company was receiving research results pointing to poor statistical effectiveness of the Shield, they also began to receive more and more "single physician experience" reports warning and complaining about some of the medical consequences from using the Shield. These physician's reports plus the statistics generated from controlled clinical reports began to portray the Shield as neither effective nor safe.

The primary cause of concern for Shield users proved to be a much higher incidence of uterine/pelvic bacterial infections. PID (pelvic inflammatory disease) is a highly virulent and very painful, difficult to cure, life threatening infection, which more often than not impairs or destroys a woman's ability to bear children. Of those women who conceived with the Shield in place (approximately 110,000 in the United States), an estimated 60 percent of them miscarried after suffering severe bacterial infections (PID). In 1974 the FDA reported that over 245 women in their fourth to sixth month of pregnancy suffered the relatively rare bacterially-induced miscarriage called septic spontaneous abortions. For fifteen women, these septic abortions were fatal.[9] Moreover, hundreds of women throughout the world who had conceived while wearing the Shield gave birth prematurely to children with grave congenital defects, including blindness, cerebral palsy, and mental retardation.[10]

Scientists now believe that the systemic cause for these virulent forms of bacterial infection is the nylon tail of the Shield itself. The Dalkon Shield tail string runs between the vagina, where bacteria are always present, and the uterus, which is germ free. It then passes through the cervix, where cervical mucus is the body's natural defense against bacterial invasion of the uterus. Robins claimed that cervical mucus would stop all germs from entering and infecting the uterus. To the naked eye, the Dalkon Shield tail string is an impervious monofilament, meaning that bacteria on it could not get into it. Actually, however, it is a cylindrical sheath encasing 200 to 450 round monofilaments separated by spaces. While the string was knotted at both ends, neither end was actually sealed. Therefore, any bacteria that got into the spaces between the filaments would be insulated from the body's natural antibacterial action while being drawn into the uterus by "wicking," a phenomenon similar to that by which a string draws the melting wax of a candle to the flame. Scientists believe that the longer the Shield and its string/tail is in place, the greater the chances for its deterioration and infiltration, thereby inducing infection in the uterus. Scientists now also contend that the "syndrome of spontaneous septic abortions" that occurred to women who had the Shield in place in the early second trimester of their pregnancy was caused by the tail string. That is, radical and sudden infection occurred with the uterus expanded to the point where it tended to pull the tail string into itself thereby bringing on instant, often lethal, contamination.[11]

In the summer of 1983 the Centers for Disease Control in Atlanta and the FDA recommended that all women still using the Shield should contact their physicians and have it immediately removed. The Agencies found that women using the Shield had a fivefold increase in risk for contracting PID as compared to women using other types of IUDs. No change in contraceptive practice was recommended for women using any other type of IUD.[12] In April 1985 two studies funded by the National Institute of Health announced yet another dire warning. These studies showed that childless IUD wearers who have had PID run a higher risk of infertility if their devices were Shields than if they were other makes.[13]

Throughout all of this, A. H. Robins officials appeared to be unaware of, or at best indifferent to, the issues, facts, and effects of their product. The company assumed the position of complete denial of any intentional wrongdoing or any malicious intent to evade full public disclosure of pertinent medical information about the safety and effectiveness of the Shield. On numerous separate occasions both in public forums and under oath, E. Claiborne Robins, Senior, has claimed near ignorance of Robins' sixteen-year involvement with the Dalkon Shield. At a series of depositions taken in 1984, Robins Senior swore that he was unable to recall ever having discussed the Shield with his son, the company's chief executive officer and president. When asked, "You certainly knew, when you started marketing this device, that PID was a life-threatening disease, did you not?" Robins testified: "I don't know that. I never thought of it as life-threatening." Did he know it could destroy fertility? "Maybe I should, but I don't know that. I have heard that, but I am not sure where." Carl Lunsford, senior vice-president for research and development, swore he could recall no "expression of concern" by any company official about PID, and he didn't remember having "personally wondered" about the toll it was taking. He had not tried to find out how many users had died. He had not "personally reviewed" *any* studies on the Shield's safety or effectiveness. When asked if he had "any curiosity" regarding the millions of dollars the company had been paying out in punitive damages to settle lawsuits, his answer was, "No."[14] The case of William Forrest, vice-president and general counsel of A. H. Robins, further strains belief. He has been described by E. Claiborne Junior as one of the company's "two most instrumental" persons in the Dalkon Shield situation. He was in effect in charge of all Shield matters and related legal issues for over a decade. In a trial proceeding, Forrest testified that his wife had worn a Shield until it was surgically removed. She had also had a hysterectomy. Although IUD removals and hysterectomies were frequently connected and simultaneous events for many infected Shield wearers, Forrest steadfastly denied any connection in his wife's case and gave vague and widely differing dates for the two events. He and his wife, he explained, did not discuss such matters in detail. Indeed, Forrest gave a series of confusing accounts of his wife's hysterectomy and its possible relationship to the Shield she had worn.

Q: Did her doctor advise her that her hysterectomy was in any way related to the Dalkon Shield?

A: Not that I know of, no, sir.

Q: Did you ever ask her that?

A: I don't recall. I may have asked her that. I don't recall the doctor telling her that. . . .

Q: . . . Are you telling the ladies and gentlemen of the jury that you and your wife have never had a discussion concerning whether or not the Dalkon Shield played a part in her hysterectomy?

A: Well, certainly, as I indicated to you, we have very general discussions. Now, if I asked her whether that played a part, I don't recall specifically if I did. If I did, to my knowledge, there was no indication that it did.[15]

The company's response to all claims of faulty product design and limited testing procedures has been counter assertions or counter claims regarding the faulty or improper use of the product by the user or the physician. The company has steadfastly maintained that there were no special dangers inherent in the device. In a report to the FDA they stated: "Robins believes that serious scientific questions exist about whether the Dalkon Shield poses a significantly different risk of infection than other IUDs." Their continuous theme has been that doctors, not the device, have caused any infections associated with the Shield. The company was committed to the notion that pregnancy and removal rates could be kept extremely low by proper placement of the Shield. They also contended that user abuse played a part in the Shield's supposed malfunctioning. They defined user abuse as poor personal hygiene habits, sexual promiscuity or excessive sexual activity, or physical tampering with the device itself.

According to three different independent investigative reports,[16] the company's public face of calm denial and counterargument masked an internal conspiracy to conceal information from the public, the court system, and the FDA. These reports (books) claim documented evidence of the multilevel cover-up. They claim that Robins quashed all documentation debating and contesting Dr. Hugh Davis' celebrated pregnancy rate of only 1.1 percent, and that Robins knew of the real significance and traumatic effect of the wicking process of the tail string but did nothing about it. Not only did the company know that the nylon cord used on the tail could degenerate and cause infection, but as early as the summer of 1972 the company was warned in writing by one of its chief consultants, Dr. Thad Earl, that pregnant women should have the Shield immediately removed to avoid "abortion and septic infection." These reports also contend that on at least three separate occasions executives and officials of Robins lost or destroyed company files and records specifically requested by the Federal Appellate Courts and the FDA.

By May 1974 Robins could no longer avoid the evidence presented to it by the FDA implicating the Shield in numerous cases of spontaneous septic abortions and in the death of at least four women as a result. These findings were disclosed in a letter sent by the company to 120,000 doctors. In June 1974 Robins suspended the U.S. distribution and sale of the Shield. In January 1975 Robins called back and completely removed the Shield from the market. The company termed the action a "market withdrawal," not a recall, because it was undertaken voluntarily and not at the direct order of the FDA. In September 1980 Robins again wrote the medical community suggesting as a purely precautionary measure that doctors remove the Shield from their patients. In October 1984 Robins initiated a $4 million television, newspaper, and magazine advertising campaign warning and recommending that all women still wearing the device have it removed at Robins' expense. In April 1985 Robins publicly set aside $615 million to settle legal claims from women who had used the Shield. This reserve is the largest provision of its kind to date in a product liability case. In May 1985 a jury in Wichita, Kansas, awarded nearly $9 million to a woman who had charged that the use of the Shield caused her to undergo a hysterectomy. The award was the largest ever made in the history of litigation involving the Shield. Officials of the Robins Company felt that adverse decisions of this magnitude could mean that their $615 million fund would prove to be inadequate. On August 21, 1985, Robins filed for Chapter 11 protection, citing litigation relating to the Shield as the main cause for its actions. Company spokesmen said that it hoped that the Federal Bankruptcy Court in Richmond would set up a payment schedule that would enable it to survive while insuring that victims "would be treated fairly." E. Claiborne Robins, Jr., called it "essential that we move to protect the company's economic viability against those who would destroy it for the benefit of a few."[17] The intriguing financial irony in all of this is that when Robins filed for Chapter 11 it had already spent, at a conservative estimate, $500 million in settlements, litigation losses, and legal fees for a product it had only manufactured for three years and from which it had only realized $500,000 in real profits![18]

In all candor it must be remembered that Robins' actions are not without danger. To the extent that Robins is using Chapter 11 as a shelter against the rush of product-liability litigation, the company is nevertheless taking a gamble. Robins must now operate under the eye of a federal bankruptcy judge, and as Lawrence King, Professor of Law at NYU, has said in regard to the Manville case, "Once you file, there is always a risk of liquidation."[19] For example, as part of their reorganization arrangement with the court, Robins agreed to a class action procedure in which they would begin a 91 nation advertisement campaign to announce to all former users their right to file a claim for compensation for any health problems that may have been caused by the Shield. All potential claimants are given a case number and sent a questionnaire to determine if they qualify for a financial settlement. As of June 1986 more than 300,000 claims have been filed against Robins![20] Numbers such as these may completely overwhelm the bankruptcy court's ability to reorganize and reestablish the company on a sound financial basis.

Given all of this data, perhaps there is only one thing we can say with certainty in regard to Robins' production of the Dalkon Shield: "In the pharmaceutical world, products that fail can cripple companies as well as people."[21]

AN UPDATE

Since filing for Chapter 11 in 1985 A. H. Robins has received at least three serious takeover bids. Two of these bids were made by the Rorer Group of Philadelphia and Sanofi the Paris-based pharmaceutical and cosmetics house. Both were rejected primarily because of their inability or unwillingness to guarantee the $2.475 billion escrow fund that the court has mandated be established for the payment of all possible liability and injury claims now pending against Robins.[22] On July 26, 1988, however, Judge Robert R. Merhige approved a plan for the acquisition of Robins by American Home Products of New York. Under this plan, American Home would pay Robins' shareholders about $700 million in American Home stock and provide for most of the Dalkon Shield trust fund with Aetna Life and Casualty Co. contributing $425 million. The judge decreed that since 94 percent of the Shield claimants and 99 percent of the Robins' stockholders approved of the plan, the reorganization, pending appeal, would become final on August 25, 1988.[23]

Yet even in an era of corporate raiders and mergers, why would so many major organizations want to take over a company bogged down in bankruptcy proceedings?

The answer lies in such mundane but popular items as Robitussin and Dimetapp cold medicines, Chap Stick lip balm and Sergeant's flea-and-tick collars. These are among the products that make Robins one of the most profitable bankrupt companies in history. In the first three quarters of 1987, Robins earned $60 million on sales of $621 million, compared with profits of $55 million on revenues of $579 million during the same period of 1986.[24]

Nevertheless, as Guerry Thorton Jr., a lawyer for the Dalkon Shield Victims Association, has pointed out, "the plans confirmation was a phenomenal success story. It has set a precedent by not allowing Robins to escape liability by filing for bankruptcy."[25]

Notes

1. Al Gini, "Manville: The Ethics of Economic Efficiency?" *Journal of Business Ethics,* 3 (1984), p. 66.
2. *Time,* September 2, 1985, p. 32.
3. Morton Mintz, *At Any Cost* (New York: Pantheon Books, 1985), p. 25.
4. Ibid., p. 29.
5. Ibid., p. 82.
6. Ibid., pp. 29–31.
7. Ibid., pp. 86–88.
8. Ibid., pp. 81, 82.
9. *FDA Consumer,* May 1981, p. 32.
10. Morton Mintz, "At Any Cost," *The Progressive,* November 1985, p. 21.
11. *At Any Cost,* pp. 131–48 and 149–72.
12. *FDA Consumer,* July–August 1983, p. 2.
13. *Wall Street Journal,* April 11, 1985, p. 1.
14. Mintz, "At Any Cost," *The Progressive,* p. 24.
15. Mintz, *At Any Cost,* p. 111.
16. Mintz, *At Any Cost* (New York: Pantheon Books, 1985). Sheldon Engelmayer and Robert Wagman, *Lord's Justice* (New York: Anchor Press/Doubleday, 1985). Susan Perry and Jim Dawson, *Nightmare: Women and the Dalkon Shield* (New York: Macmillan Publishing, 1985).
17. *New York Times,* August 22, 1985, pp. 1, 6.
18. *Time,* November 26, 1984, p. 86.
19. Gini, "Manville: The Ethics of Economic Efficiency?" p. 68.
20. *Wall Street Journal,* June 26, 1986, p. 10.
21. *U.S. News and World Report,* September 2, 1985, p. 12.
22. *Time,* January 11, 1988, p. 59.
23. *New York Times–National Edition,* July 27, 1988, p. 32.
24. *Time,* January 11, 1988, p. 59.
25. *New York Times–National Edition,* July 27, 1988, p. 32.

Questions for discussion

1. Is A. H. Robins telling the truth about its knowledge of the health factors involved in the use of the Dalkon Shield? Is it true that they had no awareness of the connection between PID and spontaneous septic abortions and the nylon tail of the Shield? Or is it the case, as many of their critics contend, that they have conspired for more than 16 years to both deny and cover up any knowledge of the short- and long-term effects of wearing the Shield?

2. Even if Robins is not guilty of conspiring to misinform its customers, why didn't simple prudence lead the company to go public immediately when "single physician experience" and the results of their own and outside testing procedures indicated from the beginning that there were serious drawbacks, limitations, and dangers inherent in the product? Moreover, after suspending production in 1974 because of FDA findings, why did Robins wait until 1984 to recommend that all women still wearing the Shield have it removed?

3. Is the 1978 Federal Bankruptcy code a proper and valid means of seeking relief from immediate and possible future liability?

• *Case Study* •

Dorrence Corporation Trade-offs*

HANS WOLF

Arthur Cunningham, Chief Executive Officer of the Dorrence Corporation, was reflecting on the presentations by the various divisions of the company of their operating plans and financial budgets for the next three years, which he had heard during the past several days. A number of critical decisions would have to be made at tomorrow's meeting of the nine senior executives who formed Dorrence's Corporate Operating Committee. Although Dorrence's tradition was one of consensus management, Cunningham knew that he was expected to exercise leadership and would have the final word, as well as the ultimate responsibility for the subsequent performance of the company.

Dorrence, a large U.S.-based pharmaceutical company with sales and operations throughout the world, had achieved an outstanding long-term record of growth in sales and profits. The company had not incurred a loss in any year since 1957 and profits had increased over the prior year in 28 out of the past 32 years. During the past 10 years, sales had grown at an average compound rate of 12% per year and profits had increased at a 15% average annual rate. Dorrence's profit as a percent of sales was considerably higher than that of the average U.S. industrial concern.

This growth had produced a huge increase in the value of Dorrence's stock. There are approximately 30,000 Dorrence shareholders, but as with many large American corporations, about 65% of Dorrence shares are held by a relatively small number of pension funds, mutual funds, university endowments and insurance companies. Dorrence grants stock options to its executives and permits employees in the U.S. and several other countries to purchase

*Reprinted by permission of the author, Hans Wolf, Columbia University Graduate School of Business. Copyrighted © by Hans Wolf 1990. This material may not be produced without written permission. Names and data have been disguised.

Dorrence stock through the company's savings plan. Dorrence executives own about 2% of the company's shares and all other employees about 1%. Thus, directly and indirectly, Dorrence is owned by millions of people who are affected to some degree by the market place of Dorrence shares.

Dorrence's fine record of growth had also brought benefits to the company's customers, employees and the communities in which the company had operations. Dorrence had steadily expanded its research expenditures at a greater rate than its sales growth and had developed important new products that extended life and improved the quality of life for millions of people. Because of its profitability, Dorrence was able to pay higher than average salaries to its employees, pay sizeable incentive awards to middle and upper management and bonuses to all employees based on the success of the company. Dorrence's growth also had provided unusual opportunities for career growth to many of its people. The company prided itself on being a good citizen in the communities in which its laboratories and factories were located. It contributed to local charities and encouraged its employees to work constructively in community organizations.

Cunningham felt that 1989 was however, a very disappointing year. The company fell short of the goals management had established at the start of the year.

Growth in sales and profits was far below the rate of recent years and below the levels achieved by several of Dorrence's peers in the pharmaceutical industry. Management incentive awards and employee bonuses were, therefore, about 5% smaller than those distributed for 1988. The value of Dorrence stock was about 20% below its high point.

Consequently, Cunningham considered it important that Dorrence achieve at least a 13% profit growth in 1990, and higher rates in the two years beyond that. He recognized that such a goal would not be easy to reach. It would not only require the best efforts of the entire organization, but also force some tough decisions.

The 1990 budgets proposed by the divisions added up to a growth rate of only 8% in profit-after-taxes, five percentage points below what Cunningham considered a minimum acceptable level. As a rough rule of thumb he calculated that each percentage point increase in the profit growth rate required about $8 million additional profit-before-taxes. Thus, each percentage point improvement could be achieved in a number of ways: $13 million additional sales volume accompanied by normal incremental costs, or $8 million additional revenue from price increases, or $8 million reduction in expenditures. During the course of the three days of presentations he had identified several possibilities for such improvements about which decisions would have to be made. In his notes he had summarized them as follows.

1. Size of the research budget: Dorrence's total expenditures for research and development had climbed annually, not only in absolute dollars but also as a percent of sales. During the current year they totaled about 17% of sales, one of the higher levels in the pharmaceutical industry. The proposed budget included a further increase and Cunningham knew that many promising projects required additional funding if the company were to demonstrate the safety and efficacy of important new drugs in a timely manner.

Cunningham was keenly aware that pharmaceutical research and development was a very risky activity. The failure rate was high. Many years of effort were required before the success or failure of a new product could be known. Typically, it took seven to ten years from the identification of a potential new drug to receiving the approval to market it from the Food and Drug Administration and its sister bodies in other countries. On average, a pharmaceutical company brought to successful conclusion only one new drug development program for each $100 million of R&D expenditures.

Clearly, there was a trade-off between investing for future growth and achieving acceptable profits in the short run. On Cunningham's list of possible changes in the proposed 1990 budget was a $10 million reduction in the amount of money requested for R&D.

2. *Export sales:* The International Division had presented an opportunity for a $4 million sale to the Philippine government which was not included in the 1990 budget because of lack of product availability. It was for Savolene, a new Dorrence injectable drug for the treatment of serious viral infections, including measles. The drug was difficult and expensive to manufacture and had been in very short supply since its introduction.

A large lot, costing about $1 million, had been rejected for the U.S. market on the basis of a very sensitive new test for endotoxins recently required by the U.S. Food & Drug Administration in addition to another test that had been the FDA standard for many years. The new test had shown a very low level of endotoxins on this batch of Savolene, even though no endotoxins has been revealed by the older test.

Cunningham had asked whether this ruled out shipping the batch to the Philippines. The company's chief medical safety officer had answered, "Officially the Philippines and a lot of other countries still rely only on the old test. It always takes them a while to follow U.S. practice, and sometimes they never do. Endotoxins might cause a high fever when injected into patients, but I can't tell you that the level in this batch is high enough to cause trouble. But how can we have a double standard, one for the U.S. and one for Third World countries?"

However, when Cunningham asked Dorrence's export vice president the same question, she said, "It's not our job to over-protect other countries. The health authorities in the Philippines know what they're doing. Our FDA always takes an extreme position. Measles is a serious illness. Last year in the Philippines half the kids who had measles died. It's not only good business but also good ethics to send them the only batch of Savolene we have available."

3. *Capital investments:* Among the capital investments that had been included in the proposed budgets was a $200 million plant automation program for Dorrence's Haitian chemical plant. The purpose of the investment was to permit a dramatic reduction in the cost of Libam, Dorrence's principal product whose U.S. patent would expire in a couple of years. Patent protection had already ended in most other countries and chemical manufacturers in Italy, Hungary, and India were selling Libam's active ingredient at very low prices. Once there was no longer patent protection in the U.S. these companies, and others, could capture a large share of Dorrence's existing sales unless Dorrence could match their low prices. Automating the Haitian plant was essential to achieving such lower cost. Successful implementation of the new technology would enable the plant to achieve the required output with far fewer people than currently employed at the plant. What to do about these surplus workers presented a difficult problem for which no solution had yet been worked out.

Dorrence was currently earing about 9% interest on its surplus funds. The proposed automation project would use up $200 million of those funds and thus reduce the interest income earned by the company. The 1990 impact of such a reduction was about $9 million. If the automation program were stretched out over a longer period, almost half of that interest income reduction would be postponed a year, thus adding $4 million to 1990 profits. The risk was that the automated plant would not be in operation in time to meet the expected competition.

4.Employee health insurance costs: Like all U.S. companies Dorrence was experiencing rapid escalation in the cost of its employee health insurance program. Dorrence paid 100% of the premium for its employees and 80% of the premiums for their dependents. After meeting certain deductibles, employees are reimbursed 80% to 90% of their medical and dental costs. The company's cost of maintaining the plan was budgeted to increase 22%, or $12 million in 1990. An important issue, therefore, was whether the plan should be changed to shift all or a portion of that cost increase to the employees through reducing the share of the premiums paid by the company, or increasing the deductibles, or reducing the percent reimbursement, or some combination of those changes.

5. Closing Dorrence's plant in Argentina: Dorrence had purchased a small pharmaceutical company in Argentina in the early 1950s when prospects for growth in the local market seemed excellent. However, in most years since then Argentina has been plagued by hyper-inflation. With rapidly rising wage rates and other local costs on the one hand, and strictly controlled selling prices for pharmaceuticals on the other hand, Dorrence's Argentine subsidiary had consistently lost money. The 1990 budget projected a loss of $4 million.

For the past year Dorrence had tried to find a buyer for its Argentine subsidiary who would utilize the existing Dorrence 120-person sales force and continue to operate Dorrence's Buenos Aires factory with its 250 employees. No such buyer had been found, but recently a local company had offered to purchase the rights to Dorrence's product line. It would manufacture them in its underutilized plant and distribute them through its own sales force. If Dorrence accepted this offer, the 370 Dorrence employees in Argentina would be laid off. Dorrence had already created a financial reserve for the government-mandated severance payments. Thus if Dorrence decided to end its operations in Argentina, corporate profits would improve by $4 million in 1990.

6. Price increase on principal product sold in the U.S.: The budget proposed by Dorrence's U.S. pharmaceutical division already assumed a 5% price increase on all its current products at the end of the first quarter of the year, producing a $40 million increase in sales revenues. A substantially higher price increase on Libam, its largest selling product, could probably be implemented without adversely affecting sales volume. For example, if the budgeted price increase were 10% instead of 5%, an additional $12 million would be generated. Alternatively, if two 5% price increases were implemented six months apart, Dorrence would earn $4 million above the proposed budget. Libam is used by chronically ill patients, many of them elderly.

In most countries pharmaceutical prices are controlled by the government. The United States is one of the few countries in which pharmaceutical companies are free to decide what prices to charge for their drugs. Physicians generally prescribe the drug which they feel will be most beneficial to their patients regardless of price. Unless the patent on a drug has expired and a generic equivalent is available, the demand for a prescription drug is not very sensitive to its price. Consequently, drug prices in the United States are substantially higher than in most other countries.

Cunningham was, however, very conscious of the growing public concern about health care costs. Although drugs constitute only a small fraction of the nation's total health care bill, drug prices are an easily identified target and drug companies were becoming increasingly under attack for their price increases.

7. New Costa Rican manufacturing plant: $10 million in sales of a new lifesaving drug developed by Dorrence had been removed from the budget because of an unexpected problem at the new plant that had been constructed to produce the product.

Three years earlier Dorrence had chosen a small town in Costa Rica after evaluating various possible sites for the plant. The town had won the competition for the new plant because of the availability of inexpensive land, relatively low wages, certain tax concessions, and a promise by the local government to build a new municipal waste treatment facility by the time the plant would be completed. In addition Dorrence felt it would be fulfilling its social responsibilities by providing jobs in an area of high unemployment.

A few days before Dorrence's budget meeting the company had learned that the completion of the municipal waste treatment plant was delayed at least a year. Although Costa Rica's environmental regulations are less stringent than those of industrialized countries, local law does prohibit the discharge of untreated factory waste water into streams. Without a means of disposing of its waste water, the Dorrence plant could not operate.

A message from the Dorrence plant manager received yesterday seemed to solve the problem. The city sanitation commissioner had given Dorrence a special exemption which would allow it to discharge its waste water into a stream behind the plant until the city's waste treatment facility was completed. Cunningham had immediately asked for a fuller report on the situation. The plant manager had sent the following additional details:

> The stream is used to irrigate sugar cane fields and small vegetable plots on which people in this area depend. There is, therefore, a chance that substances in the waste water would be absorbed by the crops that people are going to eat. I wonder if that is acceptable. On the other hand, I fear that all the good we have accomplished here will go down the drain if we don't begin manufacturing operations. Construction of the plant was completed on schedule three months ago. Building our own waste treatment facility now would add $5 million to the cost of the plant and would take at least 12 months. I've already hired over 100 workers and have given them extensive training. We obviously can't pay the workers for a year to sit around in an idle plant. Losing their jobs would be devastating to them and the

whole community. Besides, there is no other Dorrence facility or plant of another company which could accomplish the synthesis required for this new product. Lots of people in the United States are anxiously waiting for this new drug.

8. Pricing of an important new product: Finally, there was the issue of what price to charge for another new Dorrence drug, Miracule, which was expected to be introduced late in the year. In most cases patients for whom Miracule was prescribed would require the drug for the rest of their lives, unless an even more effective drug became available. The budget had assumed a price which would result in a daily cost of $1.75 (including wholesaler and drug store markups) for the average patient. A price of $2.50 would yield an additional $8 million profit to Dorrence during 1990 and far greater sums in subsequent years.

Despite the difficulties surrounding each of the issues Cunningham had identified, he felt it was critical that the 1990 budget be improved to call for 13% profit growth over 1989. He believed that a second year in a row of below average profit growth would be viewed very negatively by the investment community, be demoralizing to the company's management, and could result in a substantial drop in the value of the company's stock as investors switched to pharmaceutical companies with better 1990 results. He also recognized that large institutional investors, such as pension funds, were taking a more active role in demanding better performance from the managements of the companies in which they invested the funds entrusted to them.

Questions for discussion

1. What should Cunningham do to obtain his 13 percent goal? Cut costs? Raise prices?

2. What responsibilities does Cunningham have to the investors? The employees? The customers? The suppliers? The company itself?

3. Do the stockholders' interests take priority over those of everybody else involved?

• *Case Study* •

Sears Auto Shock*

RONALD M. GREEN

"There's a saying, 'You Can Count on Sears.' I'm here to tell you in auto repair you cannot."

—JIM CONRAN, director, California
Department of Consumer Affairs,
press conference, June 13, 1992.[1]

A

For most of his life, Michael J. Stumpf considered himself a walking advertisement for Sears, Roebuck & Co. "We had an all-American relationship with Sears," said Stumpf, a 32-year-old industrial video producer who lives in San Francisco. But when his fiancée brought their 1987 Ford to a local Sears Automotive Center for an advertised $89.99 strut job, she ended with a $650 repair bill instead.[2]

Ruth Hernandez had a similar experience. In October 1991, she went to a Sears Automotive Center in Stockton, California, to buy new tires for her 1986 Honda Accord. The mechanic who worked on the care told her that she also needed new struts, at a cost of $419.95. Hernandez, 53, sought a second opinion. Another auto-repair store told her the struts were fine. Furious, Hernandez returned to Sears, where the mechanic admitted his diagnosis was wrong. "I kept thinking," she adds, "how many other people has this happened to?"[3]

Apparently it happened to many others. On June 10, 1992, California's Bureau of Automotive Repairs (BAR) moved to revoked the operating permits of 72 Sears auto service centers in the state. Announcing the results of an 18-month-long undercover investigation into repair practices at 33 Sears auto centers throughout the state, BAR accused Sears automotive operations in California of fraud and willful departures from accepted trade standards.

BAR launched its unprecedented sting operation in December of 1990 after receiving 250 consumer complaints about Sears—enough to suggest a pattern of abuse. During this period Sears advertised brake service specials ranging from $48–$58 that had attracted many customers. Between December 1990 and December 1991, state workers posing as motorists took unmarked state cars for brake inspections 48 times at 27 Sears outlets. Before taking the cars in, state mechanics took apart the brakes and suspension, inspected and marked the parts, and had them photographed and catalogued. Worn brake pads were purposely placed on most of the cars.

The cars were then trailered to a few blocks from the targeted Sears outlet and driven there by the undercover employee. According to BAR investigators, in 42 out of 48 runs Sears employees recommended and performed unnecessary service or repairs. The highest overcharge occurred at the San Bernadino store, where the bill came to $550. On average, according to the state, consumers were bilked $250 each. Many of the replaced parts were nearly new.

On several occasions, BAR officials said, the cars emerged from Sears in worse or unsafe condition, with loose brakes or improperly installed parts. According to state investigators, Sears service personnel were not above using scare tactics to up the bill. According to Jim Schoning, BAR's chief, one of the undercover operators was told that the front calipers on his car were so badly frozen that the car would fishtail if the brakes were applied quickly. "The calipers were in fine working order," Schoning said.[4]

The investigation was a serious blow to Sears, whose auto service business was the largest in California. Nationwide, Sears's $3 billion service and parts business was also threatened by similar investigations being launched in New Jersey, New York, and Florida. Overall, auto repair and service accounted for $2.8 billion or 9% of the retail giant's $31.4 billion in revenues in 1991.

What led a company that was once regarded as one of the nation's most enlightened retailers into such difficulties? One factor, in the minds of some observers, was a change of compensation policies in Sears auto service and some of its other retail businesses. In 1990 mechanics, who had previously been paid at an hourly rate, were told that commissions would replace a part of their compensation. A manager formerly earning, say, $15 an hour would now receive $12 an hour and was told to make up the difference through increased sales of services and parts.

Investigators at BAR found that Sears also instructed employees to sell a certain number of repair or services during every eight-hour work shift, including a specified number of alignments, springs, and brake jobs. Employees were pressured to sell a specified number of shock absorbers or struts for every hour worked. If they failed to meet their goals, Sears employees told investigators, they often received a cutback in hours or were transferred to other Sears departments.[5] One Sears mechanic described his experience under this system as "pressure, pressure, pressure to get the dollars"[6]

Changes in compensation policies were part of Sear's overall effort to improve its sagging profit posture. During the late 1980s Sears had been hurt by a national recession and new competition from discount outlets and an emerging industry of specialized mail order businesses. In 1990, Sears announced a 40% drop in earnings and a $155 million write-off. Its Merchandise group, which includes auto centers and appliance sales, dropped 60%. During this period Sears Roebuck's new Chairman Edward A. Brennan scrambled to shake up the retail giant, slashing costs by $600 million in 1991. Brennan began renovating the company's 868 lackluster stores, and pushed new low prices. His overall thrust was to make every employee, from the sales floor to the chairman's suite, focus on profits.[7]

Caught off guard by news of the California investigation, the company's response was angry and defensive. Saying it would fight the allegations in court, Sears blasted the investigation as "incompetent, very seriously flawed." In a press statement the company said the investigation "simply does not support the allegations." Pointing out that Sears has offered automotive repair for more than 60 years, the statement went on to say that "we have a hard-earned and outstanding reputation for trust with our customers."[8] The company suggested there may have been political motives behind the charges, a case of a state agency trying to gain support at a time when it was threatened by severe budget cuts.

Perry Chlan, a company spokesman, denied that a quota system existed in Sears' 850 auto service centers nationwide. "We have sales goals, but that in no way affects what we recommend in service to a customer's car."[9] Other Sears spokesmen said that the company routinely audits the performance of its sales advisors and mechanics and surveys customers to see that service is satisfactory. Because the company believes in preventive maintenance, they pointed out, some of the problems may have resulted from overzealous efforts on the part of individual mechanics or sales personnel to serve customers. But Roy Liebman, a deputy Attorney General in California, disagreed. Sears's behavior, he charged, shows that "there was a deliberate decision by Sears management to set up a structure that made it totally inevitable that the consumer would be oversold."[10]

Whoever is right, the controversy was clearly something Sears did not need at this difficult moment in its history. With each day's headlines reporting new investigations into its auto business, Sears executives and employees struggled to manage an escalating corporate crisis.

B

On June 15, Sears chairman Edward F. Brennan called a press conference in Chicago as his company struggled to contain a widening crisis. Less than week before, the state of California had charged Sears with improper sales practices in its California auto service centers. Since then, New Jersey, Florida, and Alabama had announced similar investigations and hundreds of new complaints had been lodged against the company in California.

The day before, the company began a national campaign featuring full-page advertisements in *USA Today*, *The Wall Street Journal* and 25 large metropolitan newspapers. An "Open Letter to Sears Customers" signed by Brennan claimed the company would never violate customers' trust, and that in repairing more than 2 million vehicles annually in the state, "mistakes may have occurred." [See Exhibit 1 for a copy of this ad.]

By addressing customer concerns, the Sears campaign represented a change in course from the company's initial response to the crisis, which insisted on the company's legal innocence and denied that Sears had done anything wrong. According to Charles Ruder, Sears vice president for public affairs, chairman Brennan had played an integral role in developing the ad campaign. The weekend before, after canceling a business trip, he had worked on the advertisements with members of management, the company's advertising agency, Ogilvy & Mather, and several unnamed public relations advisors.

Ruder explained that a decision had been made not to hold a news conference with Mr. Brennan or to ask the chairman to appear on television programs to address the charges being leveled at the company. "We thought it was appropriate for Ed to be part of the process of putting the ad together, but we did not think it was necessary to take it to a higher level of escalation," Mr. Ruder said.[11]

EXHIBIT 1
An Open Letter to Sears Customers

On June 10th, the California Bureau of Automotive Repair made charges concerning the practices of Sears Auto Centers in California.

With over 2 million automotive customers services last year in California alone, mistakes may have occurred. However, Sears wants you to know that we would never intentionally violate the trust customers have shown us for 105 years.

You rely on us to recommend preventive maintenance measures to help insure your safety, and to avoid more costly future repairs. This includes replacement of worn parts, when appropriate, before they fail. This accepted industry practice is being challenged by the Bureau.

Our report policy is to:

1. Consult with you before the repair.
2. Prepare a written estimate.
3. Perform only repairs you authorize.
4. Guarantee all work performed.

Sears has been providing Customer Satisfaction in auto repairs for over 60 years. In addition to our own extensive training program, our technicians have over 14,000 Automotive Service Excellence (ASE) certifications.

Sears's hallmark has always been Satisfaction Guaranteed or Your Money Back. If you have any doubt or question about service performed on your car, we urge you to call or stop by your local Sears Auto Center.

I pledge we will do our utmost to resolve any concern you may have,

ED BRENNAN
Chairman and Chief Executive Office
Sears, Roebuck and Co.

C

By late 1992 Sears chairman Edward Brennan and other senior managers could start to believe that they had put behind them the serious embarrassment and legal threat posed by a California investigation of practices at Sears auto centers in that state.

Sears's handling of the crisis had been marked by several changes in course. Following an initial response based on legal issues, the company had shifted attention to its customers, launching an advertising campaign that conceded mistakes, but denied that the company had intentionally sought to violate its customers' trust. This ad was apparently met with a measure of skepticism by many of its readers. [See Exhibit 2 for one such response.]

EXHIBIT 2
"A Little Searing Commentary" (Excerpts)
by Tony Kornheiser

By now you've undoubtedly seen the full-page ad Sears has placed in newspapers around the country. It begins. "You may have heard recent allegations that some Sears Auto Centers in California and New Jersey have sold customers parts and services they didn't need."

They say, "You may have heard . . ." as though it is some sort of wild rumor that is circulating, like a sighting of bigfoot by some toothless man in a trailer park.

In fact, the reason you may have heard about this is that California consumer affairs officials, after an extensive investigation, have charged Sears with "organized planned fraud." Between December 1990 and August 1991, investigators made 38 visits to 27 Sears Auto Centers with cars that needed minor brake repair, but had no other mechanical problems, and in 34 cases—34 out of 38, mind you, a higher percentage than might be attributable to, say, "wind shear"—Sears mechanics performed work that was unnecessary. That's like going to a doctor's office for a cholesterol test and coming out without a gall bladder . . .

How many Sears mechanics does it take to change your oil?

Fourteen. One to change the oil, and 13 to rebuild your engine as "preventive maintenance."

I knew I was in trouble when I went to a Sears Auto Center for a routine change of fluids, a $29 job, and they looked under the hood and said I needed a new washer.

"No big deal," I said.

When I came back, they handed me a bill for $795.

"What's this for?" I asked.

"Your new washer," they said. And they pointed to the open trunk where they had installed a deluxe Kenmore with three rinse cycles. . . .

There are a number of priceless lines in this ad. One of my favorites is: "As always, no work will ever be performed without your approval."

Oh sure, they get your approval beforehand. They get it by saying, "I don't want to alarm you, but I just thank God you came in when you did. Because if you don't have your froindoid adjusted, and that's this small set of rings underneath your engine block—it's an essential component of the reverse tramiclater—if you don't do this, and again, believe me, I don't want to do anything that isn't absolutely necessary, I want you to keep coming back, but if you don't do this, well, you won't get five blocks from here without your car exploding like a can of Right Guard in a microwave, and you and your beautiful children dying in a fiery wreck, and I don't want to be responsible for that. So, like I said, it's up to you."[12]

Less than a week later, with sales in its auto centers down 15% nationally and 20% in California, Sears chairman Edward F. Brennan held a news conference in Chicago. While continuing to deny that Sears had intentionally wronged its customers, Brennan conceded that the company's incentive compensation program and sales goals had created an environment where mistakes occurred.

Stating that the mistakes "may have been the result of rigid attention to goals, or . . . the result of aggressive selling," Brennan said that the company now realized that the incentive systems were an error. He announced that they would be replaced by a noncommission program intended to reward service personnel for high customer-satisfaction levels. "We want to eliminate anything that could even lead to the perception that our associates could be motivated to sell our customers unneeded repairs."[13] Brennan added that Sears would eliminate sales goals for specific products and would hire an independent organization to perform shopping audits of Sears auto centers. The aim was to insure that company policies and standards were being met.

Over the next few months, Sears sought to put its legal difficulties behind by arriving at out-of-court settlements with state officials and the many individual customers who had joined together in class action suits against it. In July, Sears settled an investigation in New Jersey by paying $3,000 in penalties and $200,000 to set up an Auto Repair Industry Reform Fund. Late in October, the company announced a settlement in California by agreeing to pay $8 million to end a consolidated class-action against it, and by providing $3.5 million to finance auto repair training programs at the state's community colleges.

In November Sears announced a final aspect of its settlement effort: a yearlong nationwide offer of $50 coupons, redeemable for any Sears product or service, to any customer who bought one or more of the five commonly sold Sears auto parts between August 1, 1990 and January 31, 1992. Given the nearly 1 million eligible for the coupon, Sears could pay out as much as $46.7 million, although it expected to pay out far less.[14]

As the year ended and Sears top managers turned their attention back to the company's long-term struggle back to profitability, it was not clear what impact the auto center flap would have. In that struggle against new competitors, Sears had one major asset: its century-old reputation for quality and integrity. Ian Mitroff, co-director of the University of Southern California Center for Crisis Management, put the problem facing the company succinctly: "If I put my trust in you and you betray me, that creates a very deep response."

Notes

1. Judy Quinn, "Repair Job," *Incentive* (October 1992), 40.

2. Julia Flynn, Christina Del Valle, and Russell Mitchell, "Did Sears Take Other Customers for a Ride," *Business Week*, August 3, 1992, 24.

3. Kevin Kelly and Eric Schine, "How Did Sears Blow This Gasket?" *Business Week*, June 29, 1992, 38.

4. UPI, June 11, 1992.

5. Lawrence M. Fisher, "Sears's Auto Centers to Halt Commissions," *The New York Times*, June 23, 1992, D5.

6. Flynn et al., "Did Sears Take Other Customers for a Ride," 25.

7. Kelly and Schine, "How Did Sears Blow This Gasket?" 38.

8. John Schmeltzer and Jim Mateja, "Sears Auto Centers Charged with Fraud; California Probe 'Flawed,' Retailer Says," *Chicago Tribune*, June 12, 1992, 1.

9. Ibid.

10. Flynn et al., "Did Sears Take Other Customers for a Ride," 24.

11. Richard W. Stevenson, "Sears Crisis: How Did It Do?" *The New York Times*, June 17, 1992, D4.

12. *Washington Post*, July 28, 1992, Style, 1.

13. Fisher, "Sears Auto Centers to Halt Commissions," D1.

14. Quinn, "Repair Job," *Incentive* (October 1992), 41.

Questions for discussion

1. Do you think that responsibility for the alleged wrongdoing in Sears Auto Repair Centers lies with their individual employees, or with the company itself?

2. Are commission sales always to the detriment of the customer?

3. What should Sears do as a result of the charges leveled against the company?

4. What can happen when a company loses its "good name"?

• *Case Study* •

Commissions on Sales at Brock Mason Brokerage*

TOM L. BEAUCHAMP

James Tithe is Manager of a large branch office of a major midwestern brokerage firm, Brock Mason Farre Titmouse. He now manages forty brokers in his office. Mr. Tithe used to work for E. F. Hutton as a broker and assistant manager, but when that firm merged with Shearson-Lehman/American Express, he disliked his new manager and left for Brock Mason. He knew the new firm to be aggressive and interested primarily in limited partnerships and fully margined common stock. He liked the new challenge. At Hutton his clients had been predominantly interested in unit investment trust and municipal bonds, which he found boring and routine forms of investment. He also knew that commissions are higher on the array of products he was hired to sell at Brock Mason.

Although bored at Hutton, James had been comfortable with the complete discretion the firm gave him to recommend a range of investments to his clients. He had been free to consult at length with his clients, and then free to sell what seemed most appropriate in light of their objectives. Hutton of course skillfully taught its brokers to be salespersons, to avoid lengthly phone calls, and to flatter clients who prided themselves on making their own decisions; but the firm also did not discourage the broker from recommending a wide variety of products including U.S. government bills, notes, and bonds, which averaged only a $75 commission on a $10,000 investment.

This same array of conventional investment possibilities with small commissions is still available to him and to his brokers at Brock Mason, but the firm has an explicit strategy of trying to sell limited partnerships first and fully margined common stock second. The reason for this strategy at the brokerage house is that commissions on a $10,000 investment in a limited partnership run from $600 to $1000, and commissions on a $10,000 investment in fully margined common stock average $450.

James has been bothered for some time by two facts: The first fact is that in the brokerage industry the largest commissions are paid on the riskiest and most complicated forms of investment. In theory, the reason is that these investments are the most difficult to sell to clients. Real estate and oil and gas drilling partnerships, for example, typically return between 4 percent and 8 percent to sellers—although lately most have been arranged to return the full 8 percent. Some partnerships actually return more than 8 percent because they rebate management fees to any securities firm that acts as a participant in the partnership. The second fact is that James trains brokers to make recommendations to clients based on the level of commission returned to the broker and the firm. He is therefore training his brokers to sell the riskiest and most complicated forms of investment. Although Brock Mason, like all brokerage firms, advertises a full range of products and free financial planning by experts, all salespersons dislike financial planning per se because it carries zero commission.

James has long appreciated that there is an inherent conflict of interest in the brokerage world: The broker is presumed to have a fiduciary responsibility to make recommendations based on the best financial interest of the client; but the broker is also a salesperson who makes a living by selling securities and who is obligated to attempt to maximize profits for the brokerage house. The more trades made, the better for the broker, although this rule seldom works to the advantage of the client. Commissions are thus an ever-present temptation in the way of presenting alternatives or making an entirely objective recommendation.

Brock Mason does have a house mutual fund that is a less risky form of investment—the Brock Mason Equity-Income Fund. But the return to brokers and to the firm is again substantial. The National Association of Securities Dealers (NASD) allows a firm to charge up to an 8.5 percent commission or "load" on a mutual fund, and Brock Mason charges the full 8.5 percent. As an extra incentive, an additional percentage of the commission on an initial investment is returned to a broker if he or she can convince the client to automatically reinvest the dividends rather than have them sent by mail. Brock Mason also offers a fully paid vacation in Hawaii for the five brokers who annually sell the largest number of shares.

The firm has devised the following "piggy-back" strategy: Brokers, as we have seen, are trained to sell limited partnerships first and fully margined stock accounts second. In the latter accounts an investor is allowed to purchase stock valued at up to twice the amount of money actually deposited in the account. The "extra" money is a loan from the brokerage firm. Twice the normal stock entails twice the normal commission on the amount of money in the account. In addition, salespersons are given a small percentage of the interest earned on the loan made to the client.

Brock Mason, like most brokerage firms, is now suffering because a stock market slump has caused business to fall off sharply. In the last six months, business has been off 24 percent, and Brock Mason is encountering difficulty paying for the sophisticated electronic equipment that sits on each broker's desk. James's superiors are pressuring him to place pressure on his brokers to aggressively market limited partnerships as a solid form of investment during a period of instability in stocks.

Last year the average annual commission brought into a firm by a broker in the U.S. brokerage industry was $249,500. Each broker personally takes home between 25 percent and 50 percent of this amount, depending on the person's contract and seniority. James's own take-home earnings last year amounted to $198,000—35 percent more than he had ever earned at Hutton. A friend of his began his own financial planning firm last year and now retains 100 percent of his commissions, making $275,000 last year. His friend rejected the idea that he charge a *flat fee* or a percentage of *profits* in lieu of commissions for his recommendations and services. In his judgment, flat fees would have cost him more than 30 percent of his earnings.

Securities firms are required by law to disclose all commissions to clients. However, James and his brokers are aware that limited partnerships are generally easier to sell than straight stock and bond purchases, because the statistics on fees are buried beneath an enormous pile of information in a prospectus that most clients do not read prior to a purchase. Most clients do not even obtain the prospectus until after the purchase, and there is no report of a dollar figure for the commission. Brokers are not required to disclose commissions orally to clients and rarely do; moreover, it is well known that clients virtually never ask what the commission is. James has been instructed to tell his brokers to avoid all mention of commissions unless the subject is explicitly raised by the client.

The Securities and Exchange Commission (SEC) does not set ceilings on commissions and does not require a broker to receive a written consent from a client prior to a purchase. The SEC does occasionally determine that a markup is so high at a brokerage house that the commission amounts to fraud. It is here that James has drawn his own personal "moral line," as he calls it: He has tentatively decided that he will market any product that has passed SEC and NASD requirements. Only if the SEC is considering a judgment that a markup is fraudulent will he discourage his brokers from marketing it.

But James wonders about the prudence and completeness of these personal guidelines. He has been around long enough to see some very unfortunate circumstances—they are *unfortunate* but not *unfair*, in his judgment—in which unwary clients bought unsuitable products from brokers and had to live with the consequences. Recently one of his brokers had steered a 55-year-old unemployed widow with a total account of $380,000 (inherited upon the death of her husband) into the following "diversification": 25 percent in limited partnerships, 25 percent in dividend-paying but margined stocks, 25 percent in bonds yielding 9.8 percent, and 25 percent in the mutual fund. But the woman had not appreciated at the time of purchase how low-paying the dividends are on the stocks and the mutual fund. She now has far less annual income than she needs. Because she cannot sell the limited partnerships, she must now sell the stock for a high dividend-paying instrument.

James and his broker have been modestly shaken by this client's vigorous protest and display of anger. James decided as a result to take the case to the weekly staff meeting held on Wednesday mornings, which all brokers attend. There was a lively discussion of the best form of diversification and return for the widow. But James's attempt to introduce and discuss the problem of conflict of interest during this session fell completely flat. His brokers were not interested and could not see the problem. They argued that the brokerage industry is a free-market arrangement between a broker and a client, who always knows that fees are charged. Disclosure rules, they maintained, are well established, even if particular percentages or fees are sometimes hidden in the fine print. They viewed themselves as honest salespersons making a living through a forthright and fair system.

James walked away from this meeting thinking that neither the widow nor the broker had been prudent in making decisions, but again he viewed the outcome as unfortunate rather than unfair. He had to agree with his brokers. No client, after all, is forced to make any purchase.

Questions for discussion

1. Does a salesperson have a duty to disclose all relevant information regarding a product to a customer?
2. Does one's duty to be forthright in interpersonal dealings extend to those who are ignorant of the subject or to those who ought to know as well?
3. Is it possible to be a successful salesperson without sometimes stretching the truth?

• *Case Study* •

Roger Hixon: Let the Buyer Beware*

CLINTON L. OAKS

What obligation, if any, does a vendor have to point out to a prospective buyer the flaws or defects in his product? Roger Hixon, a former executive with a national firm and now a teacher of business policy at a western college, raised this question with respect to the remarks of a guest speaker in a previous class period. The speaker had talked about various levels of business ethics among the salesmen for companies with whom he dealt regularly. He had concluded that while some companies had a very strict policy calling for honesty and complete disclosure, many did not.

During the ensuing discussion, one student commented, "I hear all these platitudes being mouthed about how 'complete disclosure is always good business practice.' How many of you practice complete disclosure in your personal business dealings? I am sure I don't." At this point, just as the discussion was beginning to get a little heated, the instructor noted that the class period was

---

nearly over. He invited several of those who were participating most actively in the discussion to write up a specific incident for discussion the next time the class met.

Joan Stullard

"My parents, who live in a small college town in the northern part of the state, decided a year ago last spring to try to sell their home and move into a condominium. Since my father is pretty close to retirement, they tried to sell the place themselves rather than going through a real estate agent. The real estate market up there, unlike that in many urban areas, was quite slow. By late August, they had only had one potential buyer who had shown enough interest to come back several times.

"One of the nicest features of our home was its large backyard. A huge cottonwood tree standing in one corner of the yard provided the entire house and yard with shade against the late afternoon sun. The tree was very large—its trunk had a circumference of nearly fifteen feet. The only problem with it was that it was dying. While it looked healthy and green from our house, our neighbors behind the tree could see many dead and potentially dangerous branches. A violent storm would often litter their yards and prompt them to call us and demand that we cut down the tree.

"The prospective buyer who had shown the greatest interest in the place was standing on the patio one afternoon with my father. 'That sure is a nice, big tree,' he said. I was standing at the door, and overheard his remark. His comment wasn't one that required an answer. I found myself wondering what, if anything, my father would say."

Mark Bascom

"My brother is working as a used car salesman at Clark Motors. He tells me that the manager of the used car lot keeps a folder on every car in stock. Everything that is known about the car is recorded in the folder. This would include information about the previous owner, any major body or engine repairs, the mechanic's evaluation at the time the car came on the lot, etc.

"Before school started, my brother got permission to borrow a Buick Estate Wagon for several days to take a short vacation. He said he and his wife really enjoyed the car but they were appalled at the gas mileage—less than eight miles per gallon on the open road. When he returned the car, he made a note of this in the car's folder. He also talked to one of the mechanics about it. 'I'm not surprised,' the mechanic commented. 'As you know, we clean the carburetor, put in new plugs and points, adjust the timing and so forth whenever we get a car—but that particular model always was a gas hog.'

"A few days later, a young couple who were looking at cars on the lot expressed a great deal of interest in this car. They asked my brother a lot of questions and he, having had some personal experience with the car, was able to answer them in greater detail than was normally the case. He was also able to point out some of the features of the car that might have otherwise been overlooked. The longer they talked, the more enthusiastic the couple became. Almost the only question they didn't ask was about the car's mileage. They had to leave at 4:30 to pick up their child at the babysitter's but made an appointment to come back at 9:30 the next morning to work out the details of the sale.

"That night my brother came over to talk about a deal we were working on together. While he was there he told me about what had happened and said, 'As you know, things have been really tight for Jean and me since we took that trip, and the commission on this sale would really help us right now.' I have always tried, as a matter of policy, to answer honestly any question that a prospective buyer raises. If I were to tell this couple about the gas mileage on that car, however, I'm pretty sure they would back out of the sale. I don't intend to try to deceive them, but do I have any obligation to tell them about it if they don't ask?'"

Jeff Moyer

"My wife and I live approximately thirty-five miles away from the university. She teaches school in a district that is also about thirty miles from where we live, but in the opposite direction. As you can imagine, transportation is a big item in our budget. Neither of us has been successful in finding a car pool. Fortunately, my wife's parents have graciously allowed us to continue to use the car my wife drove before we were married. We own an older car, and with the two cars we have been able to get by up to now.

"When my wife accepted the teaching position we knew the travel involved would be both time consuming and expensive. However, our projections on costs were painfully underestimated. Not only have gas and oil prices increased sharply, but we hadn't realized that both cars would need new tires. Because we drive as far as we do, we have had to have tune-ups on both cars more frequently than anticipated. In addition to all this, we have had to have work done on our own car's distributor, muffler and lights—all of which has cost us well over two hundred dollars. Just recently we had more trouble requiring a mechanic's examination. His diagnosis was 'You need a valve job.'

"While I was trying to figure out where I could borrow the projected $240 for the valve job, the mechanic said, 'The engine block is pitted and needs to be ground down. If you are going to do that you might as well overhaul the whole engine.'

"'How much will that be over the $240,' I asked, bracing for the shock.

"'About $360,' the mechanic replied.

"Fighting the churning feeling in my stomach, I asked what would happen if he didn't grind down the block. I was told that the engine head and block might not seal when put back together after the work was done on the valves. 'Just try to get it to seal,' I told him knowing our budget was already dripping with red ink.

"The mechanic put the engine back together and I crossed my fingers. Evidently it sealed because the car is running now. I suspect that with all the miles that it travels weekly it may need the overhaul before long. I can't begin to afford that. Both my father and father-in-law have given me the same advice. 'Get rid of the car while it is still running.'

"I checked on the Blue book value of this model and it ranged from $1600 to $2300. I was pretty sure that if I were to tell the buyer about the engine block, I would have more difficulty in selling it and I would probably have to knock $400 to $800 off the going price.

"I try to think of myself as an honest person, and I don't think I could lie about it if someone asked me whether or not the car engine needed an overhaul. But suppose they didn't ask? Am I obligated to tell them anyway?

"Suppose I were to trade in the car on another car at an auto dealership. A dealer will almost always have a mechanic check out the car before he makes you an offer. Do I need to say anything in a situation like that? If I said anything I am sure it would lower the offer the dealer would make to me, but I am not at all sure, based upon my past experience, that the dealer would pass this information and a lower price on to another customer. In such a transaction isn't there almost a mutual understanding that everyone is governed by the old merchant's law of 'Let the buyer beware'?

"Having decided not to keep the car, I felt my choices were: (1) tell whoever buys the car about the engine; (2) tell whoever buys the car about the engine only if he or she asks if I know of any mechanical flaws; (3) tell about the engine only if I sell the car myself instead of trading it in; and (4) don't tell anyone about the engine even if asked. What should I have done?"

Don Case

"Just after I turned sixteen, I spent a summer working with my best friend on his dad's used car lot. Our job was to 'clean-up' and 'recondition' cars before they were put on the sales lot. We were to make them presentable so they could be shown to prospective buyers.

"Some of the things we had to do were what you might expect. We washed and waxed the body, scrubbed the seats and door interiors and shampooed the rugs. We also tightened any loose screws and repositioned the carpet, tightening down the carpet edges.

"My friend's dad taught us how to do a lot of other things as well. We were to use a powerful grease cutting detergent to wash the engine and eliminate the dirt, oil and grease that had accumulated on it. 'A buyer is always impressed with a clean engine,' he told us, 'and besides he won't be alarmed by any evidence that oil is leaking from the engine.' We were also shown how to use a spray shellac on all the rubber hoses so that they would look like they were new.

"If the car was burning any oil, we were told to add a can of STP. If the blue smoke coming out of the back end was heavy we would add two cans and sometimes three.

"Rust had often eaten through the steel from the wheel well and would show around the fenders. With the help of a steel brush and can of spray paint this was easily hidden and the rust would not show through the paint again for at least a month.

"Sometimes the carpets were too stained with grease and dirt to be cleaned. A coat of dark spray coloring hid the stains and would make the carpets look nice for at least a week or two after the car was purchased.

"I was young enough at the time and grateful enough to have a job that I don't ever remember even questioning the rightness or wrongness of the things we did. My friend's dad's conscience must have troubled him a little, however, because he was always telling us that there wasn't anything wrong or illegal about what we were doing. He told us that every used car lot did the same thing and he had to do it to remain competitive. 'We never turn back an odometer,' he said. 'That is illegal. The buyer expects that a used car lot will do everything possible to make a used car look good—and part of his job as a buyer is to check out anything that might be wrong.'

"Two or three years later, I had a used car of my own to sell. Without thinking about it, I gave it some treatment we used to give cars on the lot, including the addition of two cans of STP. I put a 'For Sale' sign in the window and parked it on our curb. The next night, a girl about my age who evidently didn't know much about cars, came by to ask me how much I was asking for it. After I told her, she asked, 'Is the car in good condition? Do you know of any problems that I am likely to have with it?' What should I have said?"

Ned Oborne

"At the end of last spring semester, one of my roommates transferred to a school down in Texas. Before he left, he turned over to me two pairs of skis, both virtually new. He said, 'There isn't any market for these right now but they should be easy to sell in the fall. Why don't you keep them for me until then?'

"Knowing that he wasn't much of a skier, I asked him, 'Where did you get them?' He replied, 'One of the guys I run around with gave them to me. I don't know for sure, but I wouldn't be surprised if he picked them up off an unlocked ski rack on a car parked in front of the motel where he used to work. At any event there aren't any identifying marks on them. I checked in the local ski shops around here and both pairs retail for around $300. Sell them for whatever you can get and you keep half of it.' Before I had any chance to protest, he took off.

"Those skis stood in my closet for nearly six months. Late in the fall, we got a little cramped for room and I decided I had better do something with them. I was half tempted to just turn them over to campus security and tell them that they had been left in my apartment and I didn't know whose they were.

"One day when I was trying to rearrange some of the things in the closet, I had both pairs of skis out on my bed. A friend of another roommate saw them and said, 'You wouldn't like to sell a pair of skis, would you? I am really in the market and they look just like what I have been looking for.'

"Without stopping to think about it, I asked, 'What will you give me?' He said, 'I'll give you $150.00 for the pair on the right.'

"What should I have done? My textbooks that fall had cost me about twice what I had estimated and I was really strapped for cash. I hadn't stolen the skis—in fact I didn't know for sure they had been stolen. I could truthfully say that a roommate had left them with me to sell and let it go at that. Was I obligated to tell a prospective purchaser that they might have been stolen? I can imagine what effect that might have had on the reputation of those of us living in the apartment.

"If the skis were stolen, it was extremely unlikely that the rightful owners could ever be located. In view of this, what difference did it make whether or not they had been stolen? If I turned them over to campus security, they would probably just keep them for a while and then sell them at an auction. If the end result would be the same—that is, that the skis would end up with some third party who didn't know who the original owner was and who could care less— why shouldn't I pick up a few dollars to cover my 'costs of handling'?"

Questions for discussion

1. Should Joan's father disclose to prospective buyers the status of the cottonwood tree?
2. How should Mark respond to his brother?
3. Which of Jeff's four strategies should he adopt?
4. How should Don respond? Does the fact that an action is a customary industry practice make a moral difference?
5. Should Ned sell the skis?

• SEVEN •

Multinationals

The cases in previous sections have dealt with ethical issues in domestic contexts. In this section we move beyond national boundaries to confront issues arising in different cultures, traditions, and economic systems. It is easy to lose our footing. When we step beyond a nation's borders we abandon two practical guides to behavior: the system of laws that govern a country, and the rough moral consensus that characterizes a national culture. When asking whether bribery in a foreign culture is acceptable, or whether a woman should be treated in business dealings exactly as a man is, even in a culture that endorses marked sexual differences, we ask questions that defy simple ethical analysis.

Many ethical issues arise regarding the multinational corporation. The multinational shares the global limelight with the nation state. By definition, it is a single company operating in two or more nations, with one of its parts exerting at least partial control over the other parts. Even though the multinational is *multi*-national by virtue of operating in many countries, it remains *uni*-national in many other respects. Its upper management is usually dominated by nationals of a single country, its stock is usually owned largely by residents of a single country, and its charter is authorized by a single country.

The multinational has experienced explosive growth, almost all of which has occurred since World War II. Indeed, for many writers the question is not whether the multinational has sufficient power, but whether it has *excessive* power. Its power often exceeds even that of nation states, and its effect on culture is pervasive. It is an exporter of dreams as well as of products, and it serves to communicate an ideal of material life even to those who lack the money to achieve it. At the same time, it benefits developing economies in many ways. It often provides examples of organization and technology desperately needed in fledgling economies. And because its global operation requires political and economic coordination, many believe that it promotes international understanding and world peace.

A plethora of ethical issues surround multinational corporations, including those of bribery and sensitive payments, employment issues, marketing practices, impact on the economy and development of host countries, effects on the natural environment, cultural impacts of multinational operations, relations with host governments, and relations with the home countries. Few writers applied explicit ethical criteria to multinationals prior to the late 70s. It was then that moral philosophers and business academics began exploring global issues in detail. Since then writers have tended to split into two camps over the issue of whether multinationals should adhere merely to a minimum level of ethics or whether they should go beyond that minimum. One may be called the "minimalist" camp, and the other the "maximalist." The "minimalist" camp argues that a multinational's moral responsibilities are tied directly to its economic purposes: i.e., to make profits for its investors and products or services for the public. Minimalists deny it is the responsibility of the corporation to help the poor, encourage the arts, or contribute to social causes—except insofar as doing such things is consistent with its more fundamental mission. They argue that multinationals have moral responsibilities, but that these are largely subsumable under the heading of "not harming" and not directly violating the rights of others. In contrast, the maximalist believes that corporations are unique in their level of organization and ability to control wealth, and that, in turn, they have the duty to reach out and help others. If housing and water supplies are substandard in the local area, then the company should work toward their improvement. And if malnutrition is a serious problem, the multinational should both develop nutrition programs and facilitate their implementation. Both minimalists and maximalists agree that multinationals should meet minimal ethical standards in conducting their business, but what they disagree about is whether multinationals should exceed this minimum.

One of the key challenges posed by the cases in this section, then, is *What are the minimum ethical standards applying to a particular case?* The cases raise many issues of minimal standards, including ones of environmental activities (in "Tropical Plywood Imports"), of product safety (in "H. B. Fuller in Honduras"), wages (in "Three Scenarios: No Wage Out"), the issue of divided loyalty (in "Ethics and International Business Consulting"), and the ambiguity of cultural relativism (in "The Project at Moza Island"). When you read the cases in this section, you will do well to ask yourself whether minimal standards can be identified that are relevant to the case. Another case in this section ("Merck & Co., Inc.") raises the further question of *going beyond the minimum.* Should multinational companies, at least sometimes, go beyond a minimal level of good citizenship to give positive help to less fortunate groups? To provide medicine even when customers cannot pay for it? Should it do this even when it may cost the company significant profits?

• *Case Study* •

Ethics and International Business Consulting: The ERCI Episode*

Peter Madsen

The following interchange between Senator David Pryor (D., Arkansas) and Ms. Donna R. Fitzpatrick, Assistant Secretary for Management and Administration, Department of Energy, took place during a subcommittee hearing of the Senate Governmental Affairs Committee, November 6, 1989.

PRYOR: Let me move to another issue. How would you respond if I asked if it is a proper role for a private contractor to monitor the nuclear non-proliferation policy of our country?

FITZPATRICK: Well again, we are into the question of what exactly do we mean by "monitor"? And I am not—

PRYOR: Have you heard of a firm ERCI?

FITZPATRICK: ERCI?

PRYOR: ERCI.

FITZPATRICK: I am not sure that I have.

PRYOR: All right. They do a lot of business with your Department.

FITZPATRICK: Okay.

PRYOR: ERCI had a major contract with the Department of Energy to assist in the U.S.–Japan nuclear non-proliferation treaty. One area of concern was to help get this treaty passed in Congress. ERCI has clients not only in the United States, this is their own annual report, but they work for Tokyo Electric Power and the Japanese Ministry of International Trade and Industry. The Department of Energy has hired this firm to assist in securing the passage of the U.S.–Japan nuclear non-proliferation treaty. Is this a conflict?[1]

This was the first public mention of the ERCI episode in which ERC International, Inc. and its affiliates, both past and present, were caught up in troublesome questions about their delivery of consulting services to international and domestic clients. The questions raised issues involving foreign relations, Washington politics, the dangers of terrorists stealing weapons-grade plutonium, the threat to the environment by a major nuclear accident, and the nature of the stakes in international business dealings. ERCI managers found they had to wrestle with these issues as they sought to provide answers to their questioners.

Business consulting in general, and international consulting in particular, are growth industries. They can be expected to continue to increase their reach and importance. With more firms offering consulting services, their managers will, at the least, need codes of professional ethics. The widespread publicity given to the ERCI episode may instruct consulting managers of the problems and dangers inherent in their business.

MBA students have been choosing consulting in ever larger numbers, especially since a Wall Street career has lost its former luster, before the junk bond market began to unravel. The editors of *Money* magazine reported that a 1989 survey found that more business school graduates went into consulting than into any other field.[2] Such a choice was not surprising—since the recent, swift economic changes in Eastern Europe, the coming of the European common market (scheduled for 1992), and the industrial emergence of the Pacific Rim, including Japan, as major world producers and traders, the demand for international consultants had never been higher. With more and more people finding positions in consulting firms, both they and their managers may need to examine how socialization will proceed—how they will establish and learn the norms and codes of the profession. How and to whom should consultants give their loyalties, if any? What obligations do they have to their home governments, if such can be identified, and what responsibilities do they have to their clients?

The ERCI episode developed out of government efforts to implement the U.S.–Japan Peaceful Nuclear Cooperation Agreement (see Exhibit 1, "Chronology of Events").

Background: The U.S.–Japan Plutonium Connection

In the 1950s and early 1960s, the U.S. enjoyed a virtual world-wide monopoly in the market for nuclear reactor fuel. Its government sought nuclear nonproliferation agreements with various European countries and with Japan. They gave the U.S. direct control and oversight over the uses any foreign government might make of the fuel sold to it. The U.S. included safety restrictions on reprocessing and shipping the fuel. For example, the 1968 agreement with Japan stipulated that any shipment of nuclear fuel from the U.S. would be approved on a case-by-case basis.

As the Japanese planned for and developed an increasingly sophisticated network of reactors for the production of electricity, it needed a more regular, assured procedure approving the transport and shipping of nuclear fuel. In 1982, responding to that need, the U.S. government offered to negotiate changes in the 1968 agreement. The negotiators agreed to a 30-year blanket approval for shipping nuclear fuel. It would allow Japan to import the fuel from the U.S. and then to reship spent fuel for reprocessing in France and Great Britain. The Americans feared that if changes were not made in the 1968 agreement, the Japanese would turn to other sources of nuclear fuel. Such a development would lose the U.S. nuclear program large sales and also tend to worsen the trade balance with Japan. The terms of the new agreement made good business sense, and they contributed to better relations with Japan.

A draft agreement was completed in 1987, after five years of negotiations. Upon publication of its terms, it met criticism from environmentalists and other public interest groups, supported by Congressional spokespersons and sympathetic media reporters. The critics focused on the security risks that they perceived the new agreement would create. Spent Japanese nuclear fuel, reprocessed in Europe, meant shipping plutonium and other dangerously radioactive materials long distances around the world. They argued that such global transportation of weapon-grade plutonium was both dangerous to the environment, but more alarming, an invitation to terrorists who might contrive to intercept a shipment, diverting it for their own mad uses.

The Nuclear Control Institute, a Washington-based interest group opposed to the proliferation of nuclear weapons, estimated that the new agreement would allow the U.S. to ship up to 45 tons of plutonium to Japan by 2000, and a total of 400 tons during its 30-year duration. That total would amount to more than twice the plutonium stockpiled by *both* the U.S. and the U.S.S.R. Anyone who might secure even a small part of the total—15 pounds—and have access to a reasonably sophisticated technology could produce a crude nuclear device. The bomb that destroyed Nagasaki, after all, required only 13 pounds of plutonium.

The debate between advocates of the draft agreement and its critics intensified when U.S. officials proposed that the nuclear fuel could be shipped by air as well as by sea. They first proposed that flights might be made from Europe to Japan over Canada, with a refueling stop in Alaska. State officials in Alaska immediately expressed concern about the potential threat such shipments held for the pristine environment, should a plane carrying the fuel crash within the state's boundaries. They emphasized that plutonium is one of the most poisonous materials ever created. Governor Steve Cowper protested the flight route, in a letter sent in April 1987, to Secretary of State George Shultz. He argued that flying highly radioactive plutonium over his state could have "tremendous consequences for the health and safety of Alaskans as well as for the state's environment."[3] Later that year Alaska brought suit to require the U.S. government to perform a full environmental impact statement before shipments began. The Canadian government also made its concerns clear to Washington; its officials were not ready to support the arrangements Washington had worked out with Japan. They reserved the right to block any flights in which nuclear fuel was transported through Canadian air space.

Alaskan grassroots opposition to flights carrying nuclear fuel over the state was strong. Twenty-one local groups formed the Alaska Coalition Against Plutonium Shipments; it included such diverse organizations as the Alaska Academy of Trial Lawyers, SANE-Alaska, and the state's AFL-CIO. Both the state senate and assembly unanimously passed a resolution expressing opposition to any flights, carrying nuclear fuel, across Alaskan territory. Michele Brown, Assistant Attorney General, expressed the feeling of many Alaskans when she declared, "A tiny amount of plutonium can kill half a million people, which is about all we have here. It's frightening something this big can be authorized without public scrutiny."[4]

Environmentalists became even more concerned when they learned that Japan wanted to ship reprocessed fuel from Europe in powdered plutonium-oxide form. The Nuclear Control Institute warned that a crashed shipment of 500 pounds of the deadly powder could translate into tens of millions of cancer doses. There was also speculation that, depending upon particle size and weather conditions that if a plane carrying the fuel crashed, the poisonous particles could suspend in the air, and long remain airborne, traveling hundreds and even thousands of miles.

Senators raised the issues of both security and safety in committee hearings where the agreement was examined. In December 1987, the Senate Foreign Relations Committee voted 14–3 against it, and then asked the administration to renegotiate its terms. As presented to the committee, most of the members believed the risks involved were too great; further, its terms might also be in violation of the Atomic Energy Act of 1954. Senator Jesse Helms (R., North Carolina) ranking minority member of the committee and a staunch administration supporter was among those who joined in the request. The next month, 23 members of the House Foreign Affairs Committee sent a letter to the White House, also requesting new terms under the agreement. Congress could reject the agreement, however, only if both houses passed a resolution of disapproval.

A handful of influential Senators made their opposition even more public and attempted to organize support for a resolution of disapproval. Among the most vocal were John Glenn (D., Ohio) and Alan Cranston (D., California). Glenn, who had the distinction of being the author of the 1978 Nuclear Nonproliferation Act, argued that the draft agreement would lead to unnecessary proliferation of nuclear material. "By loosening U.S. control for 30 years over international commerce in plutonium, the agreement would condone the widespread use of this deadly material," he warned in December 1976.[5] Cranston was prepared to move the whole matter into a courtroom, if necessary, to block the administration's implementation of the agreement.

Congressional critics were not alone in voicing their objections. Within the administration there were indications of uneasiness over some of the agreement's terms. Initially, officials in the Department of Defense (DOD) had expressed major reservations. The Secretary of Defense, Caspar Weinberger, had written to the Secretary of State in April, saying that in his opinion the accord was not consistent with sound nonproliferation practices. When Frank Carlucci succeeded Weinberger, however, DOD about-faced and offered its support. Carlucci had already given his support to the agreement in his former capacity as head of the National Security Council.

Members of the Nuclear Regulatory Commission (NRC) also had expressed their reservations. These included concerns about the potential for "accounting errors" on the part of Japanese firms managing breeder reactors in which the plutonium would be used. Breeders produce more fuel than they consume, but precise measurement of the amounts consumed and produced are not easy to make during and after reprocessing the spent fuel, since the plutonium is mixed with a variety of radioactive elements. Cass Peterson, a reporter for *The Washington Post,* cited NRC documents to support his assertion that "As much as 200 pounds of plutonium a year could be 'unaccounted for' in a facility of the size contemplated by Japan, even if current international safeguards and inspection requirements were applied."[6] He also pointed out that Mr. Landow Zech, Jr., chair of the NRC, expressed his opposition to the draft agreement, in a letter to the President.

Criticism of the agreement appeared in the press. In September 1988, *The Los Angeles Times* published an editorial opposing it, urging Congress to reject its terms and maintain the case-by-case review process. The nationally syndicated columnists, Jack Anderson and Dale Van Atta, also made clear their opposition. They referred to the agreement as "Japan's Risky Plutonium Shipment Plan" and condemned it as "an engraved invitation to piracy for any number of terrorist groups or militaristic Third World despots."[7] They also belittled Japan's capacity and ability to protect fuel shipments.

In December 1987, the Senate Foreign Relations Committee heard testimony from Richard Kennedy, U.S. Ambassador at Large and Special Adviser on nonproliferation and nuclear energy to the Secretary of State. He had become the chief administration spokesperson for the draft agreement. He argued, "The agreement will help ensure the continuation and growth of U.S. nuclear exports to Japan including enrichment services with an annual average value of more than $250 million and component exports whose value is also very substantial."[8] He also tried to allay the fears of those who feared a possible environmental disaster. "The agreement will not have a significant impact on the human environment. A great deal of concern has been voiced, most notably in Alaska and Canada, that such flights might pose a potential risk to the populations and natural environments of the areas that might be transited or overflown. Such concerns are quite understandable, but they are also, the administration is convinced, unwarranted."[9]

The widespread criticism required the administration to offer changes in the agreement's terms to avoid an outright rejection by Congress. The most important of these had to do with the routings of shipments by air. In March 1988, the administration announced that commercial 747 cargo planes would be used to transport spent and reprocessed fuel, as well as virgin plutonium, on polar routes that would cross neither Canada nor Alaska. Only in the case of emergencies would such flights stop in the U.S., and then only at remote military bases far from populated areas.

The change was sufficient to win the Congressional battle. The Senate considered a resolution of approval, March 21, 1988, introduced by both the Senate's majority and minority leaders. Senator Cranston led the opposition to the agreement, anticipating that he would have the support of 65 to 70 Senators. He was wrong. Thirteen Senators upon whom he had counted were among seventeen absent for the Monday vote. After a limited debate over the agreement—in which Cranston and other critics were not able to participate—the vote for approval was 53–30. The result was a surprise to both sides.

The vote did not quiet the critics, and the administration decided it had to do more. It issued a policy statement May 26, 1988, in the form of a letter to Rep. Stephen J. Solarz (D., New York), who had been a vocal opponent in the House. The Deputy Secretary of State, John C. Whitehead, wrote that the U.S. would reserve the right to suspend the agreement unilaterally "to prevent a significant increase in the risk of proliferation or threat to its national security." Solarz, for one, found this policy interpretation to his liking, declaring that "Even those who had deep concerns about the agreement can rest easier."[10] The U.S.–Japan Peaceful Nuclear Cooperation Agreement formally took effect July 17, 1988. Shipments of plutonium via a polar air route from Europe were scheduled to begin in 1992.

Japanese officials then began to be concerned that they would not be able to meet the requirements for crash-proof plutonium containers by that date. In September 1988, they requested that negotiations be reopened to allow possible sea shipments, in case air transport was not feasible. The State Department agreed. It sent notice to Congress on September 15 that it had renegotiated a provision, permitting Japan latitude to ship plutonium on the high seas. Rather than submitting the changed provision as an amendment to the original agreement, State characterized it as a "subsequent arrangement clause."

Congress has 90 days to consider an amendment, but only 15 in which to review a subsequent arrangement clause. Obviously the latter would lessen the likelihood of public debate, there being less time for critics to mobilize.

Furthermore, State submitted the clause to Congress during the hectic, final days of the 1988 session; it received little attention by either news reporters or critics of the overall agreement. The 15-day period passed unchallenged by either, and approval was pro forma. Afterwards critics denounced State's submission as a tricky ploy, charging the administration with catering to Japanese interests, who all along had wanted the right to transport nuclear fuel by ship as well as air.

Allegations Against ERCI

The issue of plutonium shipments re-emerged 13 months later in November 1989, when Senator David Pryor conducted hearings as chair of the Senate Governmental Affairs Subcommittee on Federal Services, Post Office and Civil Service. He was investigating the international consulting activities of ERCI as part of a more general examination of the executive branch's widespread use of outside consultants in government and the influence such consultants had on the formulation of policy and practices.

The subcommittee had found the Department of Energy (DOE) to be a promiscuous user of consultants. Pryor was concerned about departmental use of consultants in ways that tended to generate conflicts of interest. The same people—or the same firms—were often involved in formulating policy or preparing testimony for Congress and in performing routine operations as well as special operations affecting arms control and transfer of nuclear technology. The subcommittee's staff had raised questions about ERCI's relationship with DOE: Had it been engaged in improprieties when it helped or influenced the departmental presentation to Congress in support of the administration's case for the U.S.–Japan Peaceful Nuclear Cooperation Agreement?

DOE had awarded a contract, in September 1986, to IEAL (International Energy Associates Limited), a subsidiary of ERCI. In a 1988 reorganization IEAL became a part of a firm incorporated as ERC Environmental and Energy Services Company (ERCE).[11] Besides serving DOE, ERCE had consulting contracts with the Nuclear Regulatory Commission, the U.S. Army and Navy, the Environmental Protection Agency, the National Aeronautics and Space Administration and the Tennessee Valley Authority, as well as many state and local governments or their agencies. A number of foreign governments and international energy agencies were also ERCE clients. In a promotional brochure ERCE boasted that its "early involvement in providing high-level consulting in energy supply, use and consumption makes us a leader in the energy field, both domestically and internationally."

Pryor cited IEAL/ERCE's widespread involvement in international consulting on energy issues as problematic when it also acted as a consultant to American policy makers. In serving both the DOE and Japanese utility firms at the same time, on issues closely related, for example, the possibility of a conflict of interest could not be avoided. In a letter to the President, dated March 23, 1990, Pryor asked whether ERCI (through IEAL/ERCE) had not compromised Congressional action when it "had played a key role" in the administration's campaign of defending the U.S.–Japan Peaceful Nuclear Cooperation

Agreement, while at the same time it was advising Japanese utility companies on how they might be affected by the agreement. He feared that ERCI's technical advice to DOE, upon which its recommendations to Congress were based, was tainted rather than impartial and objective. It may have contaminated its expertise in helping DOE marshal arguments in support of the draft agreement, since it was not a disinterested party; the Japanese utility firms, who were also clients, stood to benefit by Congressional approval of the agreement.

ERCI had certainly not hidden its services to either the DOE or the Japanese utility firms. The subcommittee staff had discovered the "conflict of interest" by reading through the company's annual reports. From DOE's own submissions and documents, including billing letters, it found that the company had provided the department with draft analyses of the draft agreement and had offered specific language for inclusion in DOE analyses for submission to Congress. ERCI's subsidiary had also provided whole sections of possible use in the draft agreement, along with an analysis of the arguments advanced against the agreement.

Pryor's concerns provided material for a lengthy article in *The Wall Street Journal*. John Fialka examined the charges of possible conflict of interest in a story published March 27, 1990.[12] He reported that IEAL (ERCI's subsidiary) had been providing confidential newsletter reports to a group of Japanese utility executives and to a quasi-governmental agency, the (Japan) Power Reactor and Nuclear Fuel Development Corporation. While IEAL was providing DOE with analyses of the draft agreement, it was supplying the Japanese with reports on the plutonium agreement, whose implementation would be worth billions to the utilities using the nuclear fuel. Fialka concluded that IEAL's reports had the effect of keeping "the prime beneficiaries of the deal—the Japanese utility executives—ahead of the game"; they passed "valuable inside information" along to the Japanese utility managers, for the confidential reports contained what Fialka considered to be "well-informed discussion about secret documents."

As an example of inside information, Fialka reported that in August 1987, when Alaskan officials and public interest groups were voicing their opposition to plutonium flights over their state, DOE needed an environmental impact assessment quickly. ERCI's IEAL provided an analysis of the possible consequences should a plane, loaded with plutonium, crash in Alaska, finding no significant risks involved. In the meantime IEAL, in its reports to the Japanese utility executives, had "predicted" that the U.S. government would not find any serious environmental problems in any scenario of the crash of a plane carrying plutonium. Fialka wrote:

> As global economic relations grow closer, the consultants that help shape U.S. policy are in greater demand than ever. A stack of proprietary reports for IEAL's clients, obtained by *The Wall Street Journal*, show how easily such consulting firms can play both sides of an issue.[13]

Fialka shared the reports with Senator Pryor, who characterized the situation they revealed as a "brazen conflict" and "a classic example of working both sides of the street." The consulting firm's undisclosed two-hatted role, Pryor said, may have tainted Congress' whole understanding of the agreement with Japan. As required by Public Law 95-39 and Public Law 95-70, the department has a rigorous process to identify and resolve conflicts of interest in which those doing business with it may be involved. In his article Fialka suggested that IEAL had not warned DOE of a possible conflict of interest when it signed its consulting contract with the department. He intimated that IEAL had not disclosed its business with the Japanese utilities. He quoted Peter Brush, acting assistant secretary, DOE, who "promoted the IEAL contract" as being unaware of IEAL's newsletter reports to the Japanese utility executives. "Had I known about this newsletter, I probably would have taken it down to our procurement people," Brush said.

Fialka also suggested that IEAL in fact was not just serving two masters, but actually was engaged in lobbying on behalf of the Japanese utilities. One of the newsletters reports a direct approach made by IEAL officials to a House committee staff member in an attempt to head off a General Accounting Office report questioning the legality of the Japanese plutonium deal. He offered no specific details about the incident, but raised the question, was IEAL involved in more than just a technical consultant for DOE? Senator Pryor requested further investigations to determine if ERCI had illegally not registered as a lobbyist for a foreign agent; ERCI may have placed its own proprietary interests ahead of those of the U.S. government. Senators Glenn and Pryor, seeking to reopen the debate over U.S.-sourced plutonium shipments raised the issue publicly in an article in *The Washington Post,* May 9, 1990.

> When the United States enters into agreements with other nations covering future uses of U.S.-origin bomb-grade nuclear materials, the American people have a right to expect that such agreements will be concluded to serve the national security interests of the United States, not the corporate interests of business enterprises . . .[14]

ERCI Responses

ERCI managers rejected the charges made by Fialka, Pryor, and Glenn. They did not formally respond in public although they granted press interviews in which they made short comments of denial. In an interview, June 20, 1990, Harold D. Benglesdorf,[15] vice president and general manager of ERCE's International Division, discussed the relationships the company had had with both DOE and the Japanese. The work performed for DOE was under a support contract, providing time-urgent technical analysis. The department, not IEAL, defined the tasks to be performed, and thus IEAL could have taken any initiative in defining policy *only to the degree it was asked.* The service rendered was through technical analyses in the form of talking papers, detailing possible environmental consequences of the draft agreement's terms, *after* they had been negotiated—after what Benglesdorf declared it "was a done deal." "We were not part of the negotiation team. We were not on the inside shaping policy. And we did not influence the agreement."

IEAL employed a project team to provide the technical advice it offered DOE. A typical team had a project manager and various professionals whose expertise in a given area matched the needs of the client. Additional associate consultants were hired from the outside, as necessary to fill any gaps in needed proficiency. Benglesdorf served as the project manager on both the DOE and the Japan utility teams. Both included professionals with specialties in health physics, transportation, engineering, and law. At least two and sometimes three of the same professionals were assigned to both teams. Nevertheless, Bengelsdorf maintained, there was "absolute compartmentalization" of the two teams. As project manager for both, he took great pains to ensure no transfer between them of information that would involve a conflict of interest.

"The Japanese did not at all know the scope of our work for DOE," he pointed out, and insisted that a review of the newsletter reports could verify this claim. The newsletter mentioned the draft agreement only once, in a speculative comment that in IEAL's opinion that despite congressional questions there would not be a full-blown environmental impact statement required. Moreover, Bengelsdorf asserted, the opinion was offered to the Japanese "three or four months prior to our DOE assignment."

Thomas Lippman in *The Washington Post* agreed with Bengelsdorf, writing that "no evidence has come to light that IEAL influenced its [draft agreement's] contents." He further wrote:

> Energy Department General Counsel Stephen Wakefield said yesterday that "there is no reason to think there was anything untoward" in the dual client relationship. He said that, "if we had known then what we know about the relationship of the contractor to some Japanese utilities, we might have made some further inquiries," but he said there was "no suggestion" that IEAL's work for the Energy Department was compromised by its work for the Japanese.[16]

There was no foundation for the charge of a conflict of interests, Bengelsdorf insisted, because IEAL had complied with all the laws and regulations that require disclosure of actual or potential conflicts. "There was wide understanding about our Japanese contacts and we were used by DOE because of those contacts." Its client relationships with the Japanese demonstrated IEAL's unique expertise and qualification.

Not only had IEAL revealed its service to the Japanese utilities, as required by law, but it also reviewed the potential for conflict with DOE while the company was working with DOE. "Every Japanese report was shared with DOE in a four or five hour meeting. They complimented us for doing so." DOE apparently never perceived any conflict of interest, though IEAL "was ready to stand down if DOE thought there was a problem." "We consulted in spades" on the conflict of interest question, Bengelsdorf said. Thus ERCI managers were surprised to read the allegations in *The Wall Street Journal.*

In an internal document, responding to them, ERCI declared that the article had "mischaracterized the role our company played in providing technical and analytical support to the Department of Energy. . . ." The memo went on to charge that the article contained distortions and implications not warranted by the facts. Since company managers had given both time and care in responding to Fialka's questions, when he interviewed them, they were perplexed at the omissions in his story and the false impression thereby created. Since the reporter had worked closely with Senator Pryor's staff, they thought it strange that he failed to note the subcommittee's own report which quoted a DOE official as saying that the department was aware of ERCI's Japanese affiliation.

In its response to Fialka's article, the internal memo explained IEAL's relationship to DOE:

> The Journal article also alleges that there was much well-informed discussion about secret documents in our reports to our Japanese clients. We found this aspect of the article to be particularly egregious since we neither passed to our clients classified information, nor did we transmit to them non-public information obtained

from DOE by virtue of our technical support of that agency. In fact, our access, through our contracts with DOE, to non-public information was very limited.

For ERCI managers the charge of failing to keep confidentiality was most disturbing. The ability of an international consulting firm to keep secrets is an essential ingredient of success. Should its employees be perceived as indiscrete in the use of shared information its reputation could be seriously damaged. The ERCI internal memo declared that its managers found "any implication that we may have leaked classified information to foreign parties to be simply intolerable."

Bengelsdorf denied that IEAL had in any way acted as a foreign agent. The firm had been a passive consultant, offering only analyses and information to the Japanese, not representing their interests, either in Japan or in the U.S. "We were not on retainer and we were not their lobbyists," he said. The firm's legal advisers told him that it was not necessary to register either as a lobbyist or as a foreign agent. IEAL was serving the federal government as a kind of resource by providing technical expertise, not lobbying it. With no underlying conflict of interest, there was no way in which IEAL could have tainted its reports to DOE, and thus it could not have compromised the consideration Congress gave of the draft agreement. In its internal memo ERCI managers complained:

> We feel that it is unfair to imply that either their [DOE's] handling or our handling of the matter impaired the integrity of the process.

If their complaint was justified, then why had ERCI been criticized? Bengelsdorf's answer was that it had been caught in the middle of a political struggle between the critics of the draft agreement and its supporters.

> This issue can't be looked at without looking at the players and their motivations. Senator Glenn and Senator Pryor led the fight against the agreement and lost the fight. They have made it clear that they will do whatever they can to reopen the case. This was a transparent—not very fastidious—attempt to use ERCI to make the agreement look bad.

The charges against the company were part of political in-fighting, during which an innocent victim had been hurt. ERCI's internal memo summed up the episode:

> We respect the right of those who oppose the U.S.–Japanese Agreement to state their view. We also respect the efforts of Senator Pryor to tighten up governmental procurement procedures. However, from our perspective, we provided DOE with high quality technical support when we were asked to do so by the Agency on an urgent basis and did so only after full discussions with DOE on the implications of doing so. We also believe that DOE itself operated in a careful way in the process. We were pleased to provide this assistance and we resent any implication that our objectivity was tainted because we have some Japanese clients.

Bengelsdorf admitted that the episode had been a painful and damaging experience for ERCI. He had few doubts that the negative publicity would hurt the company. He had learned that doing business in an international forum was risky. "One is not immune from unfounded allegations. The question is: 'Are you willing to take those risks?'" What a firm actually does and what it is perceived as doing can be quite different. "Because there are political agendas, there is a difference between real ethics and allegations. We need to be more careful about appearances. Optics are important."

EXHIBIT 1
Chronology of Events

1987

January: American and Japanese officials complete draft of U.S.–Japan Peaceful Nuclear Cooperation Agreement after five years of negotiating. Department of State presents the draft to the President for interagency review.

March: The Nuclear Control Institute issues a report highly critical of the Agreement and recommends its disapproval.

April: Governor Cowper, Alaska, sends a letter to Secretary of State, George Shultz, requesting environmental impact studies before the implementation of the Agreement.

April: Secretary of Defense, Caspar Weinberger, expresses his opposition to the Agreement in a letter to the Secretary of State.

October: The State of Alaska files suit against the federal government, requesting that the court order environmental impact studies before the Agreement is approved.

November: Agreement is signed and Congress has 90 days to block its implementation.

1988

February: General Accounting Office issues a report with the conclusion that the Agreement may be illegal.

March: The Administration announces a polar air route for any plutonium shipments, eliminating any overflights of either Canadian or Alaskan territory.

March: Senate resolution disapproving the Agreement fails in a 53–30 vote.

May: Japan agrees to fly a polar route, thus avoiding Canadian and American soil, in line with the Administration's announcement, March 1988.

July: Agreement formally goes into effect.

September: Administration submits "subsequent arrangement clause" to Congress, the effect of which would allow either sea or air transport of plutonium under the Agreement. After 15 days and in the closing moments of the Congressional session, the clause becomes effective, without any Congressional action.

Notes

1. Hearing before the Subcommittee on Federal Services, Post Office, and Civil Service of the Committee on Governmental Affairs of the United States Senate, November 6, 1989, *Congressional Record,* Washington, D.C.: U.S. Government Printing Office, p. 14.

2. Timothy Aeppel, "Shipping Plutonium to Japan; Proposed US—Japan Plan Raises Safety Concern," *The Christian Science Monitor,* June 3, 1987, p. 3.

3. Robin Epstein, "It's a Bird, It's a Plane, It's Plutonium," *The Progressive,* vol. 52, no. 2, February 1988, p. 23.

4. Michael R. Gordon, "U.S. Ready to Tell Japan It Will Proceed With a Nuclear Cooperation Pact," *The New York Times,* January 13, 1988.

5. Cass Peterson, "U.S. to Allow Unrestricted Transfer of Plutonium; Critics Call Pact With Japan Dangerous," *The Washington Post,* April 22, 1988.

6. Jack Anderson and Dale Van Atta, "Japan's Risky Plutonium Shipment Plan," *The Washington Post,* February 2, 1989, p. DC15.

7. Epstein, p. 22.

8. Epstein, p. 24.

9. Cass Peterson, "Controls Added to Pact With Japan," *The Washington Post,* June 6, 1988, p. A19.

10. ERCE was a diversified company, headquartered in Fairfax, Virginia, with offices in Nashville and San Diego, offering consulting, engineering, and technical services in the rapidly-growing environmental and energy fields. ERCE reported earnings of $62.8 million in 1988, and $72.3 million the next year. ERCI owned 69 percent of ERCE's outstanding stock.

11. John J. Fialka, "Consultant Doubled as Adviser to Japanese Firms and to the US, Playing Its Dual Role With Ease," *The Wall Street Journal,* March 27, 1990, p. A22.

12. Fialka, *The Wall Street Journal,* March 27, 1990.

13. Thomas Lippman, "Did Tainted Advice Guide DOE on Plutonium Pact?" *The Washington Post,* May 9, 1990, p. A25.

14. Benglesdorf had formerly served in the U.S. Department of State and was the senior IEAL executive who oversaw the consulting arrangements with both the Japanese utility executives and DOE.

15. Lippman.

16. Lippman.

Questions for discussion

1. What are the issues of loyalties that international consultants must confront?

2. What recommendations would you make to ERCI's managers to help them avoid the charge of a conflict of interest?

3. If a consulting firm's actions are judged not in violation of the law, has its responsibilities been fulfilled? Does such a firm have national loyalties, beyond the law, that transcend its own proprietary interests?

• *Case Study* •

Tropical Plywood Imports, Inc.*

LaRue Tone Hosmer

The tropical forests of the world are being destroyed at a rate that is far greater than the annual losses earlier reported by government agencies. Recent surveys taken by satellite reveal that each year 40 million acres[1] of rain forest simply disappear, with the marketable trees cut for timber while the remaining species are so severely damaged by the logging operations that they cannot recover. The whole forest may be destroyed shortly afterwards by the "slash and burn" agricultural practices of the inhabitants of the area, who follow the logging roads and trails into cut-over areas. The World Resources Institute, in cooperation with the United Nations, prepared a recent report, based upon satellite surveys. It showed that in the nine largest tropical countries, accounting for 73 percent of the total measured destruction, the actual annual losses of tropical forest acreage were four times greater than the 1985 estimates of government officials in those countries. (See Table 1.)

TABLE 1
Estimated Versus Actual Losses in Tropical Forest Acreage

	Annual Acreage Losses Estimated during 1981—1985	Annual Acreage Losses Revealed by 1988 Satellite Survey
Brazil	3,657,000	19,768,000
Cameroon	198,000	247,000
Costa Rica	160,000	306,000
India	363,000	3,707,000
Indonesia	1,482,000	2,224,000
Myanmar (Burma)	254,000	1,673,000
Philippines	227,000	353,000
Thailand	437,000	981,000
Vietnam	161,000	427,000
Total	6,939,000	29,686,000

Source: World Resource Institute, reported in *The New York Times,* June 8, 1990, p. A10.

The satellite surveys revealed that in some countries tropical forests officially classified as state or national preserves and parks were in fact treeless. In a particularly telling comment, the report explained that the figures on actual losses might have been undercounted because smoke from burning brush and logging debris obscured some of the satellite photos; only areas that could be clearly seen to be deforested were included in the official reports. Officials at the World Resource Institute, members of the U.S. Congress, and international economists were dismayed at the newly reported totals. James Speth, chair of the World Resource Institute said, "Tropical deforestation is an unparalleled tragedy. If we don't reverse the trend now, it will soon be too late."[2] Senator Patrick Leahy, chair of the Agriculture Committee, U.S. Senate, declared, "This is the first reliable data we've had on tropical deforestation in 10 years. A situation we knew was bleak is now shown to be truly horrendous."[3]

Scientists were even more appalled, if that were possible. Sara Oldfield, writing in *The New Scientist,* warned that

> The destruction of tropical forests is one of the worst ecological disasters of the 20th century. It is the key to the most serious environmental problems: mass extinctions, global warming, shortages of natural resources, and the displacement and suffering of the tribal people who live in the forest.[4]

There are three reasons the destruction of the tropical forests can be described with such strong adjectives. The first is the possibility of global warming and the greenhouse effect. Green plants absorb carbon dioxide, and through photosynthesis (the action of sunlight upon chlorophyll) convert carbon dioxide and water into carbohydrates that are basic to the growth of all living organisms, both plants and animals. Trees are the largest green plants and consequently are among the earth's most important plant sinks for carbon dioxide; and among trees, those in tropical forests are exceedingly effective absorbers, since they receive maximum sunlight, heavy rainfall, and grow the year around.

Carbon dioxide is formed as the result of burning fossil fuels, such as lignite, coal, and oil or natural fuels, such as wood or straw, as well as by the weathering of carbonate rocks and volcanic eruptions. The amount of carbon dioxide in the atmosphere has, of course, increased significantly since the beginning of the industrial revolution[5] and the great burning of fossil fuels. Atmospheric carbon dioxide reflects infrared radiation from the earth's surface, much as greenhouse glass does, increasing surface temperatures and changing weather patterns.

Scientists are not sure of the exact relationship of atmospheric carbon dioxide and the greenhouse effect. Separating long-term trends of global temperature from daily, seasonal, and yearly variations is not at all easy or simple. Surface temperatures are affected by topography, wind streams, cloud patterns, rainfall, and solar radiation, all interacting in complex, poorly understood ways. Increases in surface temperatures can be definitely established for some regions, but they seem to be at least partially offset by decreases in other regions. Further, global temperatures have varied in the past, as evidenced by the successive ice ages, and those changes are not likely to have been caused by human activity.

The greenhouse effect has not been proven. The concern of many atmospheric scientists and meteorologists is that when it can be proven, which may not be for another two decades when adequate data will have been accumulated, it will be far too late to take remedial action. The amount of carbon dioxide in the atmosphere might be irreversible if the tropical forests no longer exist. If current rates of cutting and burning continue, only scattered remnants in the higher and more inaccessible region may be left.

The possibility of irreversible global warming is only one of the adverse effects of the destruction of the rain forests. The second is the extinction of plant and animal species. Tropical rain forests originally accounted for less than 7 percent of the earth's surface, yet they may have held more than half of all the earth's living species. Many of those still surviving have not been identified, and few of these have ever been studied. Many biologists believe that some of the many species, particularly among the plants, may possess materials and substances of great value to human health and well-being.

The third adverse impact of the destruction of the rain forests is the increased poverty of the tropical nations that will come with the final depletion of this resource. The nine nations listed in Table 1, with the exception of Brazil, are Third World countries: poor, underdeveloped, and overpopulated. The export value of tropical hardwood timber was reported to be $7 billion per year in the early 1980s;[6] it was expected to decline to $2 billion by the year 2000 and become negative in 2010. "Become negative" means that the tropical economies will have to import timber for building and other local uses by that year.

The last, and perhaps the most serious, *proven* and pernicious effects of destroyed rain forests are the ruined cultural life and, often, living conditions inflicted upon indigenous peoples, who have long lived in the forests. The forests have not been unpopulated. They provided a rich environment for people as well as for plants and animals. Tribes living in small groups or communal villages thrived on fish, game, wild fruits, and small cleared plantations of root crops such as sweet potatoes, in the Amazon basin, or manioc, in southeast Asia. Such a life is not possible after deforestation.

Native residents have usually been either forcefully removed from the land prior to cutting or are economically forced to move after the logging operations end. A particularly poignant aspect of the forced movement was the attitude of the indigenous peoples. Commonly they assume that the forests are, and should be, communal property, owned by all for the benefit of all. The communal belief was reflected in the national law of most tropical countries. Forests were legally owned by the government for the benefit of its citizens. Typically, land could not be sold to timber companies. Instead, "concessions" or rights to cut the timber for a limited number of years were sold. Consequently, "concessionaires," the formal title for timber companies operating in Southeast Asia, had no long-term interest in preserving the forests as a national resource. Their most profitable action was to cut all the marketable trees, drag the logs by tractor to the nearest road, and leave.

When they left, the land rapidly deteriorated even if it were not burned for agricultural use. Tropical forests are not similar to those in the more temperate Northern Hemisphere. The nutrients that support the vegetation of the forests are not found in the soil; instead they are contained in the "bio-mass" or the decaying debris of plants, vines, and trees that lays upon the forest floor. This debris decays rapidly, helped by the heat, the water, the insects, and fungi common in the tropics. After trees are cut down, the remaining forest debris is easily washed away by heavy rainfalls, leaving a raw clay that will support little except coarse grass.

Many environmentalists favor "selective logging," taking only a few of the mature trees per acre and leaving the rest to regenerate. Selective logging is also known as "sustained yield" forestry. If a timber concessionaire were to take out only selected trees during the first cutting, it would then be able to recut the land on a 25-year or 40-year cycle harvesting the cumulative growth each time. Harvesting costs, of course, are higher than those of clear cutting, where all the trees in an area are cut at once.

Selective cutting and sustained yield forestry are widely practiced in northern Europe and the southeastern United States, but the practices are not easily transferred to the tropics. First, the timber of the temperate forests is predominantly softwood—pine, spruce, and fir—growing to a merchantable size in 30 to 50 years. The valuable timber in the tropical rain forests is exclusively hardwood—mahogany, rosewood, and teak—and grows much more slowly.

Second, the timberlands in northern Europe easily reproduce themselves through seeding. Timberlands in the tropics contain a much wider variety of species. It is estimated that Indonesia is the home of 700 different trees that grow large enough to be harvested, yet only 20 of those trees produce lumber with the grain, color, and "workability" needed for export. A few of the remaining trees have some value for local construction, but many are commercially useless except for pulp, and few pulp and paper mills have been built in the developing countries. When the desired trees are selectively logged, there often are not enough specimens left for natural seeding in the complex, highly competitive ecological environment of tropical forests.

Third, in a tropical forest, the desired, mature trees tend to be huge. They are often encumbered by vines and creepers, connecting and tying them to their various neighbors. When felled, they generally flatten a considerable section of surrounding trees. The logs, of course, are also large and heavy. In mountainous regions—and much of the southeastern Asian tropical landmass is mountainous—large, powerful tractors have to be used to drag them to the nearest road for trucking. Sledding big, massive logs down steep slopes destroys much vegetation. Photographs of tropical forests that allegedly have been selectively logged show a wasted landscape, with broken tree stubs, crushed undergrowth, and churned-up soil that may not be a hospitable seedbed for regenerating another forest.

There is one further reason, seldom discussed at international conferences though well known, why selective logging and sustained growth forestry have not been successful in the tropical rain forests: economic exploitation and political corruption. Profits in logging the concessions offered by the national governments can be immense. The *Far Eastern Economic Review*[7] estimated that a concessionaire in the Philippines, after meeting all reasonable costs and paying all expected taxes, would make a net profit of P100,000 (US $4,673) per hectare.[8] The *Review* also reported that one concessionaire on the island of Palawan, Philippines, had been awarded cutting rights on 168,000 hectares (c. 263 square miles). Simple mathematics converts this award to a potential profit, over the five years of the grant, of $785,000,000. Profits of such a magnitude have been known to fund political influence in industrialized countries, as well as in Third World countries. A writer for the *Review* complained that

> Palawan is being plundered. Its destruction, spurred by a lack of the political will to stop it and administrative neglect, has set the stage for a last-ditch struggle by conservationists. The fight over Palawan's resources contains in miniature the structure and workings of Philippine politics: the interlocking interests of politicians, government officials, military officers and the businessmen who control the province's economy.[9]

Local residents were unable to stop the private destruction of the public forests. The *Review* reported that the concessionaire on Palawan "maintains a considerable number of private security guards and has an intemperate reputation."[10]

The combination of profits, politics, government, and the military was said in 1989 to have defeated an attempt to convert to sustained yield forestry in Thailand. Many villages in the southern portion of that country had been carried away by flash floods in November 1988, or had been buried in mud and logs washed down from hillsides denuded by recent logging, with a resulting loss of 3,500 people. A government report on the causes blamed a "complete failure in the entire system of forestry protection."[11]

> ... there were 301 logging concessions throughout country, most of which were granted in 1972. All carried a 30-year lease. Adverse environmental impact would have been minimal if the logging procedures had been strictly observed. Each of the concessions was divided into 30 plots; the concessionaires were to fell systematically only the large trees on one-year-per-plot basis whereby at the end of the lease, smaller trees in the initially logged plots would have grown enough for relogging. But because of rampant corruption among forestry and other local officials, the scientific logging procedures were ignored.[12]

Selective logging and sustainable forestry have not been successful in the past; unfortunately, there is little hope that these scientific practices for the sound utilization of the forest resources can be successful in the future:

> Corruption, commercial pressures, the high rate of return expected on capital, the ravages of heavy machinery all make sustainable logging a pipedream. . . . The

tragedy of the rain forests is that they are being managed neither in the traditional manner, by hunters and shifting cultivators making their livings from the forests
without destroying them, nor by strong state forest agencies or large commercial
companies willing and able to adopt strategies for the long-term management of a
sustainable resource.[13]

In a last-ditch effort to save the tropical forests, it has been suggested by
environmental groups that the industrialized nations should simply refuse to
import tropical hardwoods from areas that have been improperly logged. The
suggestion has been strongly rejected by both exporting and importing companies.

Spokespersons for exporting countries argue that such a refusal would be
an attack upon national sovereignty, upon nations' right to manage their own
resources in their own way for their own way, for their own interests. Delegates
from exporting countries are occasionally willing to acknowledge political corruption as an element in wasteful forest exploitation, but they maintain that
the overall results have been beneficial to them, if not to the world. Critics
should recognize, they say, that harvesting the tropical rain forests creates rural jobs, increases export earnings and tax revenues, and provides the additional, cleared agricultural land needed for a growing population.

> "I worry about the greenhouse effect too," says one of the Brazilian delegates to
> the ITTO (International Timber Trade Organization) meeting. But why is it the
> tropical forest countries that have to pay the price to try to do something about
> it. . . . Environmentalists are always talking about our moral duty, but our people
> can't live on moral duty.[14]

A Filipino professor, visiting a U.S. university, told the case writer:

> Environmentalists from Western Europe, the United States, and Japan have already
> cut down their forests for economic development and to provide the land needed
> for agricultural use. Now they want to keep us from doing exactly the same thing.

Managers of importing companies maintain that they are not the cause of
the problem. They are merely buying commodity products at market prices,
thereby generating domestic employment and foreign exchange for the host
countries while providing needed products for retail and industrial consumers
in their home countries.

Tropical Plywood Imports, Inc.[15] is an American importing company. It
was recently formed in Seattle, Washington to import meranti plywood from
Indonesia. Meranti is a tropical hardwood very similar to mahogany; it is a
strong, dense wood without growth rings that can be cut into very thin veneer
and then laminated into plywood sheets that are   inch thick. American soft-
woods such as Douglas fir and southern pine cannot be cut into such thin ve-
neers because of growth rings. The veneer tears at the soft inner portion of the
ring wood. Consequently all plywoods produced in the United States are a minimum of   inch thick. It would be possible to produce   inch plywood from
the strong and dense American hardwoods, such as birch, maple, cherry, or
walnut, but those woods are very expensive and are reserved for fine furniture.

The meranti plywood is ideal for concrete forms. It is much less costly than
American plywood used for this purpose, in part because it is thinner and uses less wood and in part because it can more easily be sawn, drilled, and nailed
without danger of splitting. Meranti plywood is also used in manufacturing
kitchen cabinets and paneling for travel trailers and mobile homes.

Tropical Plywood Imports, Inc. sells approximately $375 million worth of meranti plywood annually to lumber yards and industrial firms throughout the U.S. In an interview with the local newspaper, the founder of the company was quoted as saying that

> Cutting the meranti trees helps provide jobs and income for the Indonesian people, as well as a useable product for the American market. The meranti trees have to be at least 20 inches in diameter, and the timber is harvested in a selective logging method in which smaller trees are left to be cut 35 years from now. Environmentalists disagree with us, of course; they say that you should let the large trees stay there and rot.

The founder admitted, however, that he had never visited the logging sites in Indonesia where the meranti was harvested; he relied upon assurances from the concessionaire and government officials.

Notes

1. Or 62,500 square miles, equal to a block 250 miles on each side.

2. James Speth, Chairman of World Resource Institute, *The New York Times,* June 8, 1990, p. A10.

3. Patrick Leahy, Chairman of the Agricultural Committee of the U.S. Senate, *The New York Times,* June 8, 1990, p. A10.

4. Sara Oldfield, "The Tropical Chainsaw Massacre," *New Scientist,* September 23, 1989, p. 55.

5. The atmospheric concentration of CO_2 has risen about 30 percent since the 1850s. See "CO_2 Rise May Favor Trees Over Grassland," *The New York Times,* January 15, 1991.

6. *Futures,* October 1985, p. 451.

7. *Far Eastern Economic Review,* November 24, 1990, p. 50.

8. A metric surface measure equal to 2.471 acres.

9. Ibid, p. 49.

10. Ibid, p. 50.

11. *Far Eastern Economic Review,* January 12, 1989, p. 40.

12. The article continues to describe the actions by which the land, in essence, was denuded of all vegetation. Ibid, p. 40.

13. *New Scientist,* Sept. 16, 1989, p. 43.

14. *Far Eastern Economic Review,* January 12, 1989, p. 41.

15. The company's name is disguised.

Teacher's Guide
Tropical Plywood Imports, Inc.

I have never taught "Tropical Plywood Imports, Inc.," since I have just completed the case for the contest sponsored by the Ethics in Business Program, Graduate School of Business, Columbia University. However, let me explain some of the means I would use when teaching the case to draw out the main points and major lessons. I assume that the case will be used in a class on International Business, not on Business Ethics, so that the students will have limited acquaintance with philosophic concepts and moral reasoning.

I would start with a video. Most students have very limited experience in forestry and have never seen the havoc caused by chain saws and logging tractors. Surprisingly, there are no good videos that focus solely on the destruction of the tropical rain forests—at least I have not been able to find them, if they do exist—but there are two that do portray it as part of a larger threat to the environment. I would show excerpts from the first of these tapes, though the second is also useful.

Our Threatened Heritage (19-minute videotape): Shows scenes of the destruction of the tropical rain forests at the start of the tape. Available for $25.00 from the National Wildlife Federation, 1400 Sixteenth Street NW, Washington, D.C. Mention the "Corporate Council" in your correspondence; the National Wildlife Federation has a wide range of activities and many of the volunteers who staff the switchboards or mailroom do not seem to know of this tape.

What Is the Limit? (23-minute videotape): Examines world population growth and the effect of that growth on natural resources. Good scenes on logging in tropical forests about halfway through the video. Available for $25.00 from the National Audubon Society, 801 Pennsylvania Avenue SE, Washington, D.C. Mention "Population Program" in your correspondence; that will help to get you through to the proper people.

I would suggest discussion of applications of various ethical principles. If you are not fully comfortable with talking about these principles in class, let me suggest either Homer, *The Ethics of Management,* Irwin, 2nd edition, 1990, or Velasquez, *Business Ethics,* Prentice Hall, 2nd edition, 1989; both are short, explicit, no-nonsense paperbacks. There are four principles I would at least mention in an early class on the ethics of international business.

Personal virtues: The basic source is Aristotle's *Nicomachean Ethics,* and the principle is that there are ways of acting that can be said to be "good." Aristotle lists 14 virtues (ways of acting that lead to personal excellence); they include courage, truthfulness, etc. They are often summarized in the statement, "Be proud of what you do, and the way in which you do it." Can the founder of Tropical Plywood Imports be proud of what he or she is doing? Only, I would think, if he or she is absolutely certain that the forests in the region are being properly cut by the concessionaire. Does the founder have a duty to go and see for himself or herself? Aristotle would say, "Yes, that it is a very basic duty of being a member of society never to lie to others."

Utilitarian benefits: The basic source is Bentham's *Introduction to the Principles of Morals and Legislation* and Mills's *Utilitarianism.* The principle is that there are outcomes of actions that can be said to be "good." Analogies with cost-benefit analysis can be made, selecting the alternative with the greatest net benefit. Bentham was interested in the benefits to society, however, not merely the net benefits to particular individuals or to a company. The benefits almost surely are probabilistic and difficult to quantify.

Universal rules: The basic source is Kant's *Groundwork of the Metaphysics of Morals.* The principle is that there are personal duties that can be said to be "good." The rule is well known: If it is "right" for one person to take a certain action, then it has to be right for everyone, faced with approximately the same situation, to take the same action.

Social contract: The original source is Hobbes's *Leviathan,* but the argument has been modernized in Rawls's concept of Distributive Justice and Nozick's idea of Personal Liberty. The principle is that there are ways of deciding that can be said to be "good." The rule is to remove self-interest and to presuppose a situation in which people did not know what their interests would be. If members of the class did not know, when they left the room, whether they would be an Indonesian concessionaire (with a probable profit in the hundreds of millions), a Seattle importer (with a sizeable and—we must assume—profitable business), or citizens of Indonesia, or forest dwellers whose environment will be drastically altered immediately, how would they decide?

I suggest that you do not express your own opinion. Students feel much more comfortable with ethical issues when they are allowed to decide and no one answer is declared to be "correct." I often take a vote, record those votes on the blackboard, and end the class early so that members of the class have time to talk about the problem further, out in the corridor, among their friends.

Questions for discussion

1. Is it ethically and environmentally right for Tropical Plywood Inc. to purchase tropical woods?

2. What duties do multinational corporations (MNCs) have regarding the use of natural resources in foreign countries?

• *Case Study* •

H. B. Fuller in Honduras:
Street Children and Substance Abuse*

Norman Bowie • Stefanie Ann Lenway

In the summer of 1985 the following news story was brought to the attention of an official of H. B. Fuller Company in St. Paul, Minnesota.

Glue Sniffing Among Honduran Street Children Honduras: Children Sniffing Their Lives Away

An Inter Press Service Feature
By Peter Ford

Tegucigalpa July 16, 1985 (IPS)—They lie senseless on doorsteps and pavements, grimy and loose limbed, like discarded rag dolls.

Some are just five or six years old. Others are already young adults, and all are addicted to sniffing a commonly sold glue that is doing them irreversible brain damage.

Roger, 21, has been sniffing "Resistol" for eight years. Today, even when he is not high, Roger walks with a stagger, his motor control wrecked. His scarred face puckers with concentration, his right foot taps nervously, incessantly, as he talks.

Since he was 11, when he ran away from the aunt who raised him, Roger's home has been the streets of the capital of Honduras, the second poorest nation in the western hemisphere after Haiti.

Roger spends his time begging, shining shoes, washing car windows, scratching together a few pesos a day, and sleeping in doorways at night.

Sniffing glue, he says, "makes me feel happy, makes me feel big. What do I care if my family does not love me? I know it's doing me damage, but it's a habit I have got, and a habit's a habit. I can not give it up, even though I want to."

No one knows how many of Tegucigalpa's street urchins seek escape from the squalor and misery of their daily existence through the hallucinogenic fumes of "Resistol." No one has spent the time and money needed to study the question.

But one thing is clear, according to Dr. Rosalio Zavala, Head of the Health Ministry's Mental Health Department, "these children come from the poorest slums of the big cities. They have grown up as illegal squatters in very disturbed states of mental health, tense, depressed, aggressive."

"Some turn that aggression on society, and start stealing. Others turn it on themselves, and adopt self destructive behavior . . ."

But, he understands the attraction of

the glue, whose solvent, toluene, produces feelings of elation. "It gives you delusions of grandeur, you feel powerful, and that compensates these kids for reality, where they feel completely worthless, like nobodies."

From the sketchy research he has conducted, Dr. Zavala believes that most boys discover Resistol for the first time when they are about 11. Some children as young as five are on their way to becoming addicts.

Of a small sample group of children interviewed in reform schools here, 56 percent told Zavala that friends introduced them to the glue, but it is easy to find on the streets for oneself.

Resistol is a contact cement glue, widely used by shoe repairers, and available at household goods stores everywhere . . .

In some states of the United States, glue containing addictive narcotics such as toluene must also contain oil of mustard—the chemical used to produce poisonous mustard gas—which makes sniffing the glue so painful it is impossible to tolerate. There is no federal U.S. law on the use of oil of mustard, however . . .

But even for Dr. Zavala, change is far more than a matter of just including a chemical compound, such as oil of mustard, in a contact cement.

"This is a social problem," he acknowledges. "What we need is a change in philosophy, a change in social organization."

Resistol is manufactured by H. B. Fuller S.A., a subsidiary of Kativo Chemical Industries, S.A. which in turn is a wholly owned subsidiary of the H. B. Fuller Company of St. Paul, Minnesota.[1] (See Appendix I for an organization chart of Kativo Chemical Industries S.A.) Kativo sells more than a dozen different adhesives under the Resistol brand name in several countries in Latin America for a variety of industrial and commercial applications. In Honduras the Resistol products have a strong market position.

Three of the Resistol products are solvent-based adhesives designed with certain properties that are not possible to attain with a water-based formula. These properties include rapid set, strong adhesion, and water resistance. These products are similar to airplane glue or rubber cement and are primarily intended for use in shoe manufacturing and repair, leatherwork, and carpentry.

Even though the street children of each Central American country may have a different choice of a drug for substance abuse, and even though Resistol is not the only glue that Honduran street children use as an inhalant, the term *Resistolero* stuck and has become synonymous with all street children, whether they use inhalants or not. In Honduras Resistol is identified as the abused substance.

Edward Sheehan writes in *Agony in the Garden*:[2]

Resistol. I had heard about Resistol. It was a glue, the angel dust of Honduran orphans. . . . In Tegucigalpa, their addiction had become so common they were known as los Resistoleros.

Honduras[3]

The social problems that contribute to widespread inhalant abuse among street children can be attributed to the depth of poverty in Honduras. In 1989, 65 percent of all households and 40 percent of urban households in Honduras were living in poverty, making it one of the poorest countries in Latin America.[4] Between 1950 and 1988, the increase in the Honduran gross domestic product (GDP) was 3.8 percent, only slightly greater than the average yearly increase in population growth. In 1986, the Honduran GDP was about U.S. $740 per capita and has only grown slightly since. Infant and child mortality rates are high, life expectancy for adults is 64 years, and the adult literacy rate is estimated to be about 60 percent.

Honduras has faced several economic obstacles in its efforts to industrialize. First, it lacks abundant natural resources. The mountainous terrain has restricted agricultural productivity and growth. In addition, the small domestic market and competition from more industrially advanced countries have prevented the manufacturing sector from progressing much beyond textiles, food processing, and assembly operations.

The key to the growth of the Honduran economy has been the production and export of two commodities—bananas and coffee. Both the vagaries in the weather and the volatility of commodity markets have made the foreign exchange earned from these products very unstable. Without consistently strong export sales, Honduras has not been able to buy sufficient fuel and other productive input to allow the growth of its manufacturing sector. It also had to import basic grains (corn and rice) because the country's traditional staples are produced inefficiently by small farmers using traditional technologies with poor soil.

In the 1970s the Honduran government relied on external financing to invest in physical and social infrastructures and to implement development programs intended to diversify the economy. Government spending increased 10.4 percent a year from 1973. By 1981, the failure of many of these development projects led the government to stop financing state-owned industrial projects. The public sector failures were attributed to wasteful administration, mismanagement, and corruption. Left with little increase in productivity to show for these investments, Honduras continues to face massive budgetary deficits and unprecedented levels of external borrowing.

The government deficit was further exacerbated in the early 1980s by increasing levels of unemployment. By 1983, unemployment reached 20–30 percent of the economically active population, with an additional 40 percent of the population underemployed, primarily in agriculture. The rising unemployment, falling real wages, and low level of existing social infrastructure in education and health care contributed to the low level of labor productivity. Unemployment benefits were very limited, and only about 7.3 percent of the population was covered by social security.

Rural-to-urban migration has been a major contributor to urban growth in Honduras. In the 1970s the urban population grew at more than twice as fast a rate as the rural population. This migration has increased in part as a result of a high birth rate among the rural population, along with a move by large landholders to convert forest and fallow land, driving off subsistence farmers to use the land for big-scale cotton and beef farming. As more and more land was enclosed, an increasing number of landless sought the cities for a better life.

Tegucigalpa, the capital, has had one of the fastest population increases among Central American cities, growing by 178,000 between 1970 and 1980, with a projected population of 975,000 by the year 2000. Honduras's second largest city, San Pedro Sula, is projected to have a population of 650,000 by 2000.

The slow growth in the industrial and commercial sectors has not been adequate to provide jobs for those moving to the city. The migrants to the urban areas typically move first to cuarterias (rows) of connected rooms. The rooms are generally constructed of wood with dirt floors, and they are usually windowless. The average household contains about seven persons, who live together in a single room. For those living in the rooms facing an alley, the narrow passageway between buildings serves both as sewage and waste disposal area and as a courtyard for as many as 150 persons.

Although more than 70 percent of the families living in these cuarterias had one member with a permanent salaried job, few could survive on that income alone. For stable extended families, salaried income is supplemented by entrepreneurial activities, such as selling tortillas. Given migratory labor, high unemployment, and income insecurity, many family relationships are unstable. Often the support of children is left to mothers. Children are frequently forced to leave school, helping support the family through shining shoes, selling newspapers, or guarding cars; such help often is essential income. If a lone mother has become sick or dies, her children may be abandoned to the streets.

Kativo Chemical Industries S.A.[5]

Kativo celebrated its fortieth anniversary in 1989. It is now one of the 500 largest private corporations in Latin America. Financial information for October, 1988–September 30, 1989 on Kativo Chemical Industries S.A. is presented in Appendix IV. In 1989, improved sales in most of Central America were partially offset by a reduction of its sales in Honduras.

Walter Kissling, chairman of Kativo's board and senior vice president for H. B. Fuller's international operations, has the reputation of giving the company's local managers a high degree of autonomy. Local managers often have to respond quickly because of unexpected currency fluctuations. He comments that, "In Latin America, if you know what you are doing, you can make more money managing your balance sheet than by selling products."[6] The emphasis on managing the balance sheet in countries with high rates of inflation has led Kativo managers to develop a distinctive competence in finance.

In spite of the competitive challenge of operating under unstable political and economic conditions, Kativo managers emphasized in the annual report[7] the importance of going beyond the bottom line:

> Kativo is an organization with a profound philosophy and ethical conduct, worthy of the most advanced firms. It carries out business with the utmost respect for ethical and legal principles and its orientation is not solely directed to the customer, who has the highest priority, but also to the shareholders, and communities where it operates.

In the early 1980s the managers of Kativo, which was primarily a paint company, decided to enter the adhesive market in Latin America. Their strategy was to combine their marketing experience with H. B. Fuller's products. Kativo found the adhesive market potentially profitable in Latin America because it lacked strong competitors. Kativo's initial concern was to win market share. Resistol was the brand name for all adhesive products including the water-based school glue.

Kativo and the Street Children

In 1983, Honduran newspapers carried articles about police arrests of Resistoleros—street children drugging themselves by sniffing glue. In response to these newspaper articles, Kativo's Honduras advertising agency, Calderon Publicidad, informed the newspapers that Resistol was not the only substance abused by street children and that the image of the manufacturer was being damaged by using a prestigious trademark as a synonym for drug abusers. Moreover, glue sniffing was not caused by something inherent in the product but was a social problem. For example, on one occasion the company complained to the editor, requesting that he "make the necessary effort to recommend to the editorial staff that they abstain from using the brand name Resistol as a synonym for the drug, and the adjective Resistolero, as a synonym for the drug addict."

The man on the spot was Kativo's vice president, Humberto Larach ("Beto"), a Honduran, who headed Kativo's North Adhesives Division. Managers in nine countries, including all of Central America, Mexico, the Caribbean, and two South American countries, Ecuador and Columbia, reported to him. (See Appendix I.) He had become manager of the adhesive division after demonstrating his entrepreneurial talents managing Kativo's paint business in Honduras.

Beto had proven his courage and his business creativity when he was among 105 taken hostage in the Chamber of Commerce building in downtown San Pedro Sula by guerrillas from the Communist Popular Liberation Front. Despite fire fights between the guerrillas and government troops, threats of execution, and being used as a human shield, Beto had sold his product to two clients (fellow hostages) who had previously been buying products from Kativo's chief competitor. Beto also has a reputation for emphasizing the importance of "making the bottom line," as a part of Kativo corporate culture.

By the summer of 1985, more than corporate image was at stake. As a solution to the glue sniffing problem, social activists working with street children suggested that oil of mutard, allyl isothiocyanate could be added to the product to prevent its abuse. They argued that a person attempting to sniff glue with oil of mustard added would find it too powerful to tolerate. Sniffing it has been described like getting an "overdose of horseradish." An attempt to legislate the addition of oil of mustard received a boost when Honduran Peace Corps volunteer, Timothy Bicknell, convinced a local group called the Committee for the Prevention of Drugs at the National Level of the necessity of adding oil of mustard to Resistol. All members of the committee were prominent members of Honduran society.

Beto, in response to the growing publicity about the Resistoleros, requested staff members of H. B. Fuller's U.S. headquarters to look into the viability of oil of mustard as a solution with special attention to side effects and whether it was required or used in the U.S. H. B. Fuller's corporate industrial hygiene staff found 1983 toxicology reports that oil of mustard was a cancer-causing agent in tests run with rats. A 1986 toxicology report from the Aldrich Chemical Company described the health hazard data of allyl isothiocyanate as follows:

Acute Effects
May be fatal if inhaled, swallowed, or absorbed through skin.
Carcinogen.

Causes burns.

Material is extremely destructive to tissue of the mucous membranes and upper respiratory tract, eyes, and skin.

Prolonged Contact Can Cause:
Nausea, dizziness, and headache.
Severe irritation or burns.
Lung irritation, chest pain, and edema, which may be fatal.
Repeated exposure may cause asthma.

In addition the product had a maximum shelf life of six months.

To the best of our knowledge, the chemical, physical, and toxicological properties have not been thoroughly investigated.

In 1986, Beto contacted Hugh Young, president of Solvent Abuse Foundation for Education (SAFE), and gathered information on programs SAFE had developed in Mexico. Young, who believed that there was no effective deterrent, took the position that the only viable approach to substance abuse was education, not product modification. He argued that reformulating the product was an exercise in futility because "nothing is available in the solvent area that is not abusable." With these reports in hand, Beto attempted to persuade Resistol's critics, relief agencies, and government officials that adding oil of mustard to Resistol was not the solution to the glue sniffing problem.

During the summer of 1986 Beto had his first success in changing the mind of one journalist. Earlier in the year Mary Kawas, an independent writer, wrote an article sympathetic to the position of Timothy Bicknell and the Committee for the Prevention of Drugs in Honduras. In June, Beto met with her and explained how both SAFE and Kativo sought a solution that was not product oriented but that was directed at changing human behavior. She was also informed of the research on the dangers of oil of mustard (about which additional information had been obtained). Kawas then wrote an article:

Education Is the Solution for Drug Addiction

LA CEIBA
BY MARIE J. KAWAS

A lot of people have been interested in combating drug addiction among youths and children, but few have sought solutions, and almost no one looks into the feasibility of the alternatives that are so desperately proposed . . .

Oil of mustard (allyl isothiocyanate) may well have been an irresponsible solution in the United States of America during the sixties and seventies, and the Hondurans want to adopt this as a panacea without realizing that their information sources are out of date.

Through scientific progress, it has been found that the inclusion of oil of mustard in products which contain solvents, in order to prevent their perversion into use as an addictive drug, only causes greater harm to the consumers and workers involved in their manufacture . . .

Education is a primordial instrument for destroying a social cancer. An effort of this magnitude requires the cooperation of different individuals and organizations . . .

Future generations of Hondurans will

be in danger of turning into human parasites, without a clear awareness of what is harmful to them. But if drugs and ignorance are to blame, it is even more harmful to sin by indifference before those very beings who are growing up in an environment without the basic advantages for a healthy physical and mental existence. Who will be the standard bearer in the philanthropic activities which will provide Honduras with the education necessary to combat drug addiction? Who will be remiss in their duty in the face of the nations's altruism?

At first, Beto did not have much success at the governmental level. In September 1986, Dr. Rosalis Zavala, Head of the Mental Health Division of the Honduran Ministry of Health, wrote an article attacking the improper use of Resistol by youth. Beto was unsuccessful in his attempt to contact Dr. Zavala. He had better luck with Mrs. Norma Castro, Governor of the State of Cortes, who, after a conversation with Beto, became convinced that oil of mustard had serious dangers and that glue sniffing was a social problem.

Beto's efforts continued into the new year. Early in 1987, Kativo began to establish Community Affairs Councils, as a planned expansion of the worldwide company's philosophy of community involvement. These employee committees had already been in place in the U.S. since 1978.

A company document gave the purpose of Community Affairs Councils:

> To educate employees about community issues.
>
> To develop understanding of, and be responsible to, the communities near our facilities.
>
> To contribute to Kativo/H. B. Fuller's corporate presence in the neighborhoods and communities we are a part of.
>
> To encourage and support employee involvement in the community.
>
> To spark a true interest in the concerns of the communities in which we live and work.

The document goes on to state, "We want to be more than just bricks, mortar, machines and people. We want to be a company with recognized values, demonstrating involvement, and commitment to the betterment of the communities we are a part of." Later that year, the Honduran community affairs committees went on to make contributions to several organizations working with street children.

In March 1987, Beto visited Jose Oqueli, Vice-Minister of Public Health, to explain the philosophy behind H. B. Fuller's Community Affairs program. He also informed him of the health hazards with oil of mustard; they discussed the cultural, family, and economic roots of the problem of glue sniffing among street children.

In June 1987, Parents Resource Institute for Drug Education (PRIDE) set up an office in San Pedro Sula. PRIDE's philosophy was that through adequate *parental* education on the drug problem, it would be possible to deal with the problems of inhalant use. PRIDE was a North American organization that had taken international Nancy Reagan's "just say no" approach to inhalant abuse. Like SAFE, PRIDE took the position that oil of mustard was not the solution to glue sniffing.

Through PRIDE, Beto was introduced to Wilfredo Alvarado, the new Head of the Mental Health Division in the Ministry of Health. Dr. Alvarado, an advisor to the Congressional Committee on Health, was in charge of preparing draft legislation and evaluating legislation received by Congress. Together with Dr. Alvarado, the Kativo staff worked to prepare draft legislation addressing the problem of inhalant-addicted children. At the same time, five congressmen drafted a proposed law that required the use of oil of mustard in locally produced or imported solvent-based adhesives.

In June 1988, Dr. Alvarado asked the Congressional Committee on Health to reject the legislation proposed by the five congressmen. Alvarado was given 60 days to present a complete draft of legislation. In August 1988, however, he retired from his position and Kativo lost its primary communication channel with the Committee. This was critical because Beto was relying on Alvarado to help insure that the legislation reflected the technical information that he had collected.

The company did not have an active lobbying or government monitoring function in Tegucigalpa, the capital, which tends to be isolated from the rest of the country. (In fact, the company's philosophy has generally been not to lobby on behalf of its own narrow self-interest.) Beto, located in San Pedro Sula, had no staff support to help him monitor political developments. Monitoring, unfortunately was an addition to his regular, daily responsibilities. His ability to keep track of political developments was made more difficult by the fact that he traveled about 45 percent of the time outside of Honduras. It took over two months for Beto to learn of Alvarado's departure from government. When the legislation was passed in March, he was completely absorbed in reviewing strategic plans for the nine country divisions which report to him.

On March 30, 1989, the Honduran Congress approved the legislation drafted by the five congressmen. (See Appendix II for the text of the legislation.)

After the law's passage, Beto spoke to the press about the problems with the legislation. He argued:

> This type of cement is utilized in industry, in crafts, in the home, schools, and other places where it has become indispensable; thus by altering the product, not only will the drug addiction problem not be solved, but rather, the country's development would be slowed.
>
> In order to put an end to the inhalation of Resistol by dozens of people, various products which are daily necessities would have to be eliminated from the marketplace. This is impossible, since it would mean a serious setback to industry at several levels . . .
>
> There are studies that show that the problem is not the glue itself, but rather the individual. The mere removal of this substance would immediately be substituted by some other, to play the same hallucinogenic trip for the person who was sniffing it.

H. B. Fuller: The Corporate Response

In late April 1986, Elmer Andersen, H. B. Fuller Chairman of the Board, received the following letter:

Elmer L. Andersen
H. B. Fuller Co.   4/21/86

Dear Mr. Andersen:

I heard part of your talk on public radio recently, and was favorably impressed with your philosophy that business should not be primarily for profit. This was consistent with my previous impression of H. B. Fuller Co. since I am a public health nurse and have been aware of your benevolence to the nursing profession.

However, on a recent trip to Honduras, I spent some time at a new home for chemically dependent "street boys" who are addicted to glue sniffing. It was estimated that there are 600 of these children still on the streets in San Pedro Sula alone. The glue is sold for repairing *tennis shoes* and I am told it is made by H. B. Fuller in *Costa Rica*. These children also suffer toxic effects of liver and brain damage from the glue . . .

Hearing you on the radio, I immediately wondered how this condemnation of H. B. Fuller Company could be consistent with the company as I knew it before and with your business philosophy.

Are you aware of this problem in Honduras, and, if so, how are you dealing with it?

That a stockholder should write the 76-year-old Chairman of the Board directly is significant. Elmer Andersen is a legendary figure in Minnesota. He is responsible for the financial success of H. B. Fuller from 1941 to 1971, and his values reflected in his actions as CEO are embodied in H. B. Fuller's mission statement. (For a brief corporate history of H. B. Fuller, see Appendix III).

The H. B. Fuller corporate mission is to be a leading and profitable worldwide formulator, manufacturer, and marketer of quality specialty chemicals, emphasizing service to customers and managed in accordance with a strategic plan.

H. B. Fuller Company is committed to its responsibilities, in order of priority, to its customers, employees, and shareholders. H. B. Fuller will conduct business legally and ethically, support the activities of its employees in their communities, and be a responsible corporate citizen.

Elmer Andersen, CEO, served a brief term as governor and was extraordinarily active in civic affairs. In 1990 he was elected Minnesotan of the year, and thousands of citizens attended his eightieth birthday, which was celebrated on the steps of the State Capitol in St. Paul.

It was also Elmer Andersen, who as President and CEO, made the decision that foreign acquisitions should be managed by locals. Concerning the 1967 acquisition of Kativo Chemical Industries Ltd., Elmer Andersen said:

We had two objectives in mind. One was directly business related and one was altruistic. Just as we had expanded in America, our international business strategy was to pursue markets where our competitors were not active. We were convinced that we had something to offer Latin America that the region did not have locally. In our own small way, we also wanted to be of help to that part of the world. We believed that by producing adhesives in Latin America and by employing only local people, we would create new jobs and help elevate the standard of living. We were convinced that the way to aid world peace was to help Latin America become more prosperous.[8]

Three years later a stockholder dramatically raised the Resistol issue for a second time directly by a stockholder. On June 7, 1989, Vice President for Corporate Relations, Dick Johnson, received a call from a stockholder whose daughter was in the Peace Corps in Honduras. She asked, "How can a company like H. B. Fuller claim to have a social conscience and continue to sell Resistol which is 'literally burning out the brains' of children in Latin America?"

Johnson was galvanized into action. This complaint was of special concern because he was about to meet with a national group of socially responsible investors who were considering including H. B. Fuller's stock in their portfolio. Fortunately Karen Muller, Director of Community Affairs, had been keeping a file on the glue sniffing problem. Within 24 hours of receiving the call, Dick had written a memo to CEO Tony Andersen.

In that memo he set forth the basic values to be considered as H. B. Fuller wrestled with the problem. Among them were the following:

1. H. B. Fuller's explicitly stated public concern about substance abuse.
2. H. B. Fuller's "Concern for Youth" focus in its community affairs projects.
3. H. B. Fuller's reputation as a socially responsible company.
4. H. B. Fuller's history of ethical conduct.
5. H. B. Fuller's commitment to the intrinsic value of each individual.

Whatever "solution" was ultimately adopted would have to be consistent with these values. In addition, Dick suggested a number of options including the company's withdrawal from the market or perhaps altering the formula to make Resistol a water-based product, eliminating sniffing as an issue.

Tony responded by suggesting that Dick create a task force to find a solution and a plan to implement it. Dick decided to accept Beto's invitation to travel to Honduras to view the situation first hand. He understood that the problem crossed functional and divisional responsibilities. Given H. B. Fuller's high visibility as a socially responsible corporation, the glue sniffing problem had the potential for becoming a public relations nightmare. The brand name of one of H. B. Fuller's products had become synonymous with a serious social problem. Additionally, Dick understood that there was an issue larger than product misuse involved, and it had social and community ramifications. The issue was substance abuse by children, whether the substance is an H. B. Fuller product or not. As a part of the solution, a community relations response was required. Therefore, he invited Karen to join him on his trip to Honduras.

Karen recalled a memo she had written about a year earlier directed to Beto. In it she had suggested a community relations approach rather than Beto's government relations approach. In that memo Karen wrote:

> This community relations process involves developing a community-wide coalition from all those with a vested interest in solving the community issue—those providing services in dealing with the street children and drug users, other businesses, and the government. It does require leadership over the long-term both with a clear set of objectives and a commitment on the part of each group represented to share in the solution . . .

In support of the community relations approach, Karen argued that

1. It takes the focus and pressure off H. B. Fuller as one individual company.
2. It can educate the broader community and focus on the *best* solution, not just the easiest ones.

3. It holds everyone responsible, the government, educators, H. B. Fuller's customers, legitimate consumers of our product, social service workers and agencies.
4. It provides H. B. Fuller with an expanded good image as a company that cares and will stay with the problem—that we are willing to go the second mile.
5. It can depoliticize the issue.
6. It offers the opportunity to counterbalance the negative impact of the use of our product named Resistol by reidentifying the problem.

Karen and Dick left on a four-day trip to Honduras September 18. Upon arriving, they were joined by Beto, Oscar Sahuri, General Manager for Kativo's adhesives business in Honduras, and Jorge Walter Bolanos, Vice President Director of Finance, Kativo. Karen had also asked Mark Connelly, a health consultant from an international agency working with street children, to join the group. They began the process of looking at all aspects of the situation. Visits to two different small shoe manufacturing shops and a shoe supply distributor helped to clarify the issues around pricing, sales, distribution, and the packaging of the product.

A visit to a well-run shelter for street children provided them with some insight into the dynamics of substance abuse among this vulnerable population in the streets of Tegucigalpa and San Pedro Sula. At a meeting with the officials at the Ministry of Health, they reviewed the issue of implementing the oil-of-mustard law, and the Kativo managers offered to assist the committee as it reviewed the details of the law. In both Tegucigalpa and San Pedro Sula, the National Commission for Technical Assistance to Children in Irregular Situations (CONATNSI), a county-wide association of private and public agencies working with street children, organized meetings of its members at which the Kativo managers offered an explanation of the company's philosophy and the hazards involved in the use of oil of mustard.

As they returned from their trip to Honduras, Karen and Dick had the opportunity to reflect on what they had learned. They agreed that removing Resistol from the market would not resolve the problem. However, the problem was extremely complex. The use of inhalants by street children was a symptom of Honduras's underlying economic problems—problems with social, cultural, and political aspects as well as economic dimensions.

Honduran street children come from many different circumstances. Some are true orphans while others are abandoned. Some are runaways, while others are working the streets to help support their parents. Children working at street jobs or begging usually earn more than the minimum wage. Nevertheless, they are often punished if they bring home too little. This creates a vicious circle; they would rather be on the street than take punishment at home—a situation that increases the likelihood they will fall victim to drug addiction. The street children's problems are exacerbated by the general lack of opportunities and a lack of enforcement of school attendance laws. In addition, the police sometimes abuse street children.

Karen and Dick realized that Resistol appeared to be the drug of choice for young street children, and were able to obtain it in a number of different ways. There was no clear pattern and, hence, the solution could not be found in simply changing some features of the distribution system. Children might obtain the glue from legitimate customers, small shoe repair stalls, by theft, from "illegal" dealers, or from third parties who purchased it from legitimate stores and then sold it to children. For some sellers the sale of Resistol to children could be profitable. The glue was available in small packages, which made it more affordable, but the economic circumstances of the typical legitimate customer made packaging in small packages economically sensible.

The government had long been unstable. As a result there was a tendency for people working with the government to hope that new policy initiatives would fade away within a few months. Moreover, there was a large continuing turnover of government, so that any knowledge of H. B. Fuller and its corporate philosophy soon disappeared. Government officials usually had to settle for a quick fix, for they were seldom around long enough to manage any other kind of policy. (See Appendix VII for a brief background on Honduran politics.) Although it was on the books for six months by the time of their trip, the oil-of-mustard law had not yet been implemented, and national elections were to be held in three months. During meetings with government officials, it appeared to Karen and Dick that no further actions would be taken as current officials waited for the election outcome.

Kativo company officers, Jorge Walter Bolanos and Humberto Larach, discussed continuing the government relations strategy hoping that the law might be repealed or modified. They were also concerned with the damage done to H. B. Fuller's image. Karen and Dick thought the focus should be on community relations. From their perspective, efforts directed toward changing the law seemed important but would do nothing to help with the long-term solution to the problems of the street children who abused glue.

Much of the concern for street children was found in private agencies. The chief coordinating association was CONATNSI, created as a result of a seminar sponsored by UNICEF in 1987. CONATNSI was under the direction of a general assembly and a board of directors elected by the General Assembly. It began its work in 1988; its objectives included (a) improving the quality of services, (b) promoting interchange of experiences, (c) coordinating human and material resources, (d) offering technical support, and (e) promoting research. Karen and the others believed that CONATNSI had a shortage of both financial and human resources, but it appeared to be well-organized and was a potential intermediary for the company.

As a result of their trip, they knew that a community relations strategy would be complex and risky. H. B. Fuller was committed to a community relations approach, but what would a community relations solution look like in Honduras? The mission statement did not provide a complete answer. It indicated that the company had responsibilities to its Honduran customers and employees, but exactly what kind? Were there other responsibilities beyond that directly involving its product? What effect can a single company have in solving an intractable social problem? How should the differing emphases in perspective of Kativo and its parent, H. B. Fuller, be handled? What does corporate citizenship require in situations like this?

Notes

1. The Subsidiaries of the North Adhesives Division of Kativo Chemical Industries, S.A. go by the name "H. B. Fuller (Country of Operation)," e.g., H. B. Fuller S.A. Honduras. To prevent confusion with the parent company, we will refer to H. B. Fuller S.A. Honduras by the name of its parent, "Kativo."

2. Edward Sheehan, *Agony in the Garden: A Stranger in Central America* (Boston: Houghton Mifflin) 1989, p. 46.

3. See *Honduras: A Country Study,* 2nd ed., James D. Rudoph, ed. (Washington, D.C.: Department of the Army), 1984, for further data and information.

4. The following discussion is based on *Honduras: A Country Study,* 2nd ed., James D. Rudolph, ed., (Washington, D.C.: Department of the Army), 1984.

5. Unless otherwise indicated, all references and quotations regarding H. B. Fuller and its subsidiary Kativo Chemical Industries S.A. are from company documents.

6. Eric Schine, "Preparing for Banana Republic U.S.," *Corporate Finance* (December, 1987).

7. *Annual Report,* 1989, p. 8.

8. H. B. Fuller Company, *A Fuller Life: The Story of H. B. Fuller Company: 1887–1987* (St. Paul, H. B. Fuller Company), 1986, pp. 101–102.

9. Alison Acker, *The Making of a Banana Republic* (Boston: South End Press), 1988, p. 124.

10. Ibid.

11. Ibid., p. 128.

12. Ibid., p. 129.

13. *The New York Times,* October 15, 1989.

Questions for discussion

1. Even when the company intends to do the right thing, is it responsible when its actions produce unintended, harmful consequences?

2. Did H. B. Fuller adequately respond to the abuse of its product?

APPENDIX I
Organization Chart of Kativo Chemical Industries S.A.

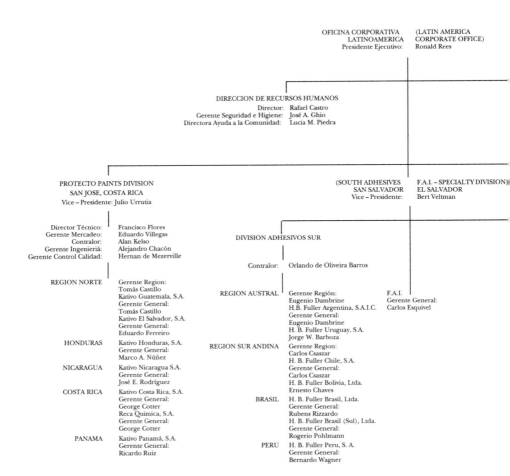

OFICINA CORPORATIVA   (LATIN AMERICA
LATINOAMERICA   CORPORATE OFFICE)
Presidente Ejecutivo: Ronald Rees

DIRECCION DE RECURSOS HUMANOS
Director: Rafael Castro
Gerente Seguridad e Higiene: José A. Ghio
Directora Ayuda a la Comunidad: Lucia M. Piedra

PROTECTO PAINTS DIVISION
SAN JOSE, COSTA RICA
Vice – Presidente: Julio Urrutia

(SOUTH ADHESIVES   F.A.I. – SPECIALTY DIVISION)
SAN SALVADOR   EL SALVADOR
Vice – Presidente: Bert Veltman

Director Técnico:	Francisco Flores
Gerente Mercadeo:	Eduardo Villegas
Contralor:	Alan Kelso
Gerente Ingeniería:	Alejandro Chacón
Gerente Control Calidad:	Hernan de Mezerville

DIVISION ADHESIVOS SUR

Contralor: Orlando de Oliveira Barros

REGION NORTE	Gerente Region: Tomás Castillo Kativo Guatemala, S.A. Gerente General: Tomás Castillo Kativo El Salvador, S.A. Gerente General: Eduardo Ferreiro
HONDURAS	Kativo Honduras, S.A. Gerente General: Marco A. Núñez
NICARAGUA	Kativo Nicaragua S.A. Gerente General: José E. Rodríguez
COSTA RICA	Kativo Costa Rica, S.A. Gerente General: George Cotter Reca Quimica, S.A. Gerente General: George Cotter
PANAMA	Kativo Panamá, S.A. Gerente General: Ricardo Ruiz

REGION AUSTRAL	Gerente Región: Eugenio Dambrine H.B. Fuller Argentina, S.A.I.C. Gerente General: Eugenio Dambrine H. B. Fuller Uruguay, S.A. Jorge W. Barboza
REGION SUR ANDINA	Gerente Region: Carlos Csaszar H. B. Fuller Chile, S.A. Gerente General: Carlos Csaszar H. B. Fuller Bolivia, Ltda. Ernesto Chaves
BRASIL	H. B. Fuller Brasil, Ltda. Gerente General: Rubens Rizzardo H. B. Fuller Brasil (Sul), Ltda. Gerente General: Rogerio Pohlmann
PERU	H. B. Fuller Peru, S. A. Gerente General: Bernardo Wagner

F.A.I.
Gerente General:
Carlos Esquivel

DIRECCION DE FINANZAS
Vice-President: Jorge Walter Bolaños
Gerente Contabilidad: Omar Bolaños
Gerente Auditoria: Carlos Fdo. Rodríguez
Gerente Cómputo Gerardo Ortuño
Gerente Planeamiento: Xenia Mora

(NORTH ADHESIVES DIVISION)
SAN PEDRO SULA, HONDURAS
Vice – President: Humberto Larach

GRUPO ESPECIALIDADES

Director Técnico: Sebastian Gilbert
Gerente Mercadeo: Ricardo Sanchez
Contralor: Rodolfo Zapata

Gerente Grupo:	Francisco López	
Contralor:	Silena Alvarado	
Gerente Recursos Humanos:	Lucia M. Piedra	

REGION CARIBE	Gerente Región:
	Ricardo Román
	H. B. Fuller Dominicana, S.A.
	Gerente General:
	Nelson Villanueva
	H. B. Fuller Puerto Rico, S.A.*

COSTA RICA — Sintéticos, S. A.
Gerente General:
Francisco Lopez
Alfombras Canon, S.A.
Gerente General:
Jorge Porras
Acrílicos de Centroamerica, S.A.
Gerente General:
Luis Langlois
Deco Tintas, S.A.
Gerente General:
Andres Dehais
Operaciones Centroamérica
Gerente General:
Edgar Usaga
El Salvador: Walter Villalobos
Honduras: Orlando Cáceres
Guatemala
Panamá

	Gerente General:
	Ricardo Roman
MEXICO	H. B. Fuller México, S.A. (D.F.)
	Gerente General:
	Carlos Diéguez
	H. B. Fuller México, S.A. (Ensenda)
	Gerente General:
	Jóse Mendoza
EL SALVADOR	H. B. Fuller El Salvador, S.A.
	Gerente General:
	Miguel Angel Flores
HONDURAS	H. B. Fuller Honduras, S.A.
	Gerente General:
	Oscar Sahuri
NICARAGUA	Mercadeo Industrial, S.A.
	Gerente General:
	Milton Gómez
COSTA RICA	H. B. Fuller Costa Rica, S.A.
	Gerente General:
	Carlos Fischel
ECUADOR	H. B. Fuller Ecuador, S.A.
	Gerente General:
	Nadim Kuri
COLOMBIA	H. B. Fuller Colombia, S.A.
	Gerente General:
	Miguel Cadena

*Non consolidated

APPENDIX II

La Gaceta—Republic of Honduras—Tegucigalpa, D.C., April 17, 1989

WHEREAS, the inhalation of certain products utilized in shoe making, carpentry, offices, or in domestic or school activities, on the part of children, youths, and adults, has become a serious danger for our society, and,

WHEREAS, the drug addiction resulting from these behaviors, instead of diminishing, tends to increase, involving children and youths, who in other circumstances would be in conditions to become a part of the national productive process, and to reach full development as useful individuals both for their families and society as a whole; and,

WHEREAS, it is the duty of the Government of Honduras, as representative of the State, to watch over the safety, security and happiness of our children and youths, through the promulgation of preventive dispositions which can avoid further deleterious afflictions for the health and personal integrity of the populace;

THEREFORE,

DOES DECREE:

ARTICLE 1: The prohibition of the introduction into the country of contact adhesive products whose formulation does not include Allyl Isocyanate (oil of mustard).

ARTICLE 2: The Secretariat of Public Health shall oversee that the products introduced prior to this disposition are sole pursuant to the prescriptions of the present Decree.

ARTICLE 3: National producers of articles known generically as rapid setting contact cements, adhesives, or glues, and whose composition includes volatile organic solvents, and which due to their penetrating odor are susceptible to being inhaled, must incorporate a proportion of oil of mustard in their composition, so that the content thereof becomes repulsive for human aspiration.

ARTICLE 4: This Decree will become effective upon publication in the Journal of Official Proceedings *La Gaceta*.

APPENDIX III
Brief History of the H. B. Fuller Company

Harvey Fuller founded the H. B. Fuller company in 1887, St. Paul, Minnesota, as a manufacturer of glue, mucilage, inks, blueing, and blacking. He was an inventor of a flour-based wet paste that paperhangers found especially effective. Harvey's oldest son Albert joined his father in 1888, and the company grew rapidly, making its first acquisition, the Minnesota Paste Company, in 1892.

Harvey continued to invent new products, including an adjustable leg scaffolding and a dry wall cleaner that could be mixed with cold water. By 1905 H. B. Fuller went international with customers in England, Germany, and Australia. Harvey Fuller imprinted on H. B. Fuller a business philosophy that was customer based, growth oriented, and international in scope.

Harvey's third son, Harvey, Jr. joined the company in 1909 and succeeded his father as president of the company upon Harvey, Sr.'s death in 1921. Although the company's fortunes had declined in the early 1920s, Harvey, Jr. reversed them by entering the industrial adhesives market. The hiring of chemist Ray Burgess was especially fortuitous. Although he had no formal degree in chemistry, he developed dozens of new products and the company prospered.

Another hiring decision was even more momentous. Elmer L. Andersen joined H. B. Fuller October 8, 1934.

Andersen became sales manager the year the company celebrated its fiftieth anniversary. Despite the addition of new products and new acquisitions during the 1930s, by 1938 the depression began to take its toll on sales. In 1939 Harvey, Jr. suffered a stroke from which he never fully recovered. In 1941, H. B. Fuller received an acquisition offer from Paisley Products. But Elmer Andersen, using his savings, a loan against his house, and financial help from his wife's family, purchased the company.

The defense needs for adhesives turned H. B. Fuller's financial fortunes around. Under Andersen's leadership the company grew rapidly as it built facilities throughout the country and became an industry leader. But financial success was not sufficient for Elmer Andersen. He wanted H. B. Fuller to be known as a socially responsible company. H. B. Fuller's mission statement reflected Elmer Andersen's corporate philosophy. In 1959 the company had $10 million in sales, nine affiliated companies, over fifteen plants from coast to coast, and sales in all parts of the world.

While serving as president of H. B. Fuller, Elmer Andersen also served in the Minnesota Senate from 1949 to 1959. In 1960, he was elected governor of Minnesota and Al Vigard became president of H. B. Fuller. The company continued to prosper. In 1962, the seventy-fifth anniversary, sales totaled $14.2 million. Vigard also reported a 57 percent increase in contribution to the employee profit sharing plan.

After losing the election for a second term as governor by 0.007 percent in 1962, Elmer Andersen returned to H. B. Fuller as Chairman of the Board. Vigard remained as company president. At this time H. B. Fuller initiated a series of international joint ventures and acquisitions, including Kativo Chemical Industries, Ltd., in 1967.

In 1971 Elmer Andersen stepped down as president and his son Tony became president of H. B. Fuller at the age of 35. Elmer became Chairman of the Board. Both hold the same positions today. Tony Andersen's business goals are in the tradition of his father's. His priorities were acquisition and growth, particularly in the international arena. In pursuit of the goals, he traveled incessantly throughout the world. He also intended to double the company's sales every five years. 1971 brought joint ventures with Japan and a listing in *Fortune*'s top 1,000 corporations. In 1982, H. B. Fuller acquired Asar-Rokall Chemie, a division of Schering AG, West Germany, enabling it to triple its European sales from $30 to $90 million. In 1984 it was listed in the *Fortune* 500, and the next year it signed a joint venture agreement with Guangdong province, China.

During the 1970s and 1980s H. B. Fuller developed its philosophy of corporate responsibility. Employee benefits were broadened. A unique feature was the bonus vacation time given on the tenth anniversary of employment plus a substantial check so that employees could travel and see the world. H. B. Fuller joined the 5 percent club in 1976 (a group of Minnesota corporations that contribute 5 percent of their pretax profits to the community). In 1983, it opened the energy-efficient environmentally "correct" Weldon Lake research center. H. B. Fuller had continually won awards for its responsibility to the environment.

The year H. B. Fuller made the *Fortune* 500 it also made *Fortune*'s "Best 100 Companies to Work for in America." As Elmer Andersen said at the celebration gathering, "We always wanted to grow and be large, but we also wanted to be good."

APPENDIX IV
KATIVO CHEMICAL INDUSTRIES, S.A.
(an affiliate of H. B. Fuller Company)
CONSOLIDATED BALANCE SHEETS
(expressed in U.S. dollars—Note 1*)

	September 30,	
Assets	*1989*	*1988*
Current Assets:		
Cash	2,263,126	$2,427,855
Marketable securities, at cost	3,099,630	3,577,347
Notes and accounts receivable	16,424,038	14,329,467
Inventories	22,290,441	22,378,498
Prepaid expenses	1,330,847	1,281,621
Total current assets	45,408,082	43,994,788
Property, plant, and equipment, at cost less		
accumulated depreciation	22,148,085	17,480,467
Investments	1,083,567	1,754,407
Negotiable certificates of deposit	1,837,310	2,038,859
Other assets	835,380	705,013
Excess of cost over net book value of purchased		
subsidiaries, net of accumulated amortization	108,670	247,920
	$71,421,094	$66,221,454
LIABILITIES AND STOCKHOLDERS' EQUITY		
Current liabilities:		
Current portion of long-term debt	$1,204,819	$1,128,959
Short-term loans and notes payable	7,627,806	5,748,116
Accounts payable—		
Trade	3,520,988	3,309,133
Affiliated companies	11,120,326	10,864,851
Other accounts payable and accrued expenses	4,860,752	4,523,092
Total current liabilities	28,334,691	25,574,151
Long-term debt	2,178,040	2,234,873
Deferred income taxes and other deferred credits	431,327	289,181
Minority interest	1,005	101,051
Stockholders' equity:		
Capital stock	8,676,435	4,319,924
Additional paid-in capital	7,023,790	6,841,586
Retained earnings	30,381,801	32,307,880
Less—Treasury stock	(5,605,955)	(5,447,192)
	40,476,031	38,022,198
	$71,421,094	$66,221,454

(continued)

APPENDIX IV *(Continued)*

| | September 30, | |
Assets	1989	1988
Net sales	$87,131,658	$82,961,220
Cost of sales	55,357,894	52,010,162
Gross profit	31,773,764	30,951,058
Selling, general, and administrative expenses	19,555,969	18,786,646
Operating earnings	12,217,795	12,164,412
Interest expense	3,662,517	2,771,894
Other (income) expense, net	2,525,540	2,584,933
Earnings before income taxes	6,029,738	6,807,585
Provision for income taxes	1,948,958	2,537,702
Net earnings	$ 4,080,780	$ 4,269,883
Net earnings per share	$0.29	$0.31

*Various notes are omitted.
From Kativo Chemical Industries S.A. 1989 Annual Report.

APPENDIX V
Honduras: Statistical Profile

Area (km²)	112,088
Population: Total 1988 (4.2% urban)	4,829,000
Annual growth rate (1980–88)	3.5
Birth rate (1980–85)	43.9
Mortality per 1000 inhabitants (1980–85)	10.1
Infant mortality per 1000 live births (1983)	78.6
Life expectancy at birth (1980–85)	59.9
Literacy rate (1982)	59.7
Labor force by sector (1987)	(Percentages)
Agriculture	52.5
Mining	0.3
Manufacturing	13.7
Construction	4.4
Others	29.2

	1984	1985	1986	1987	1988*
Real production (GDP at market prices)		(Growth rates)			
Total GDP	2.8	3.2	3.1	4.2	3.8
Agricultural sector	1.3	2.9	2.4	6.7	2.5
Mining sector	11.5	2.3	−2.2	−13.8	6.7
Construction sector	−1.3	−1.8	−8.3	−17.0	1.8
Central government**		(Percentage of GDP)			
Current revenues	15.1	15.6	15.5	16.4	16.2
Current expenditures	16.7	17.8	17.8	18.8	18.5
Current savings	−1.6	−2.2	−2.3	−2.4	−2.3
Capital expenditures	3.0	2.9	2.7	2.6	2.7
Deficit or surplus	−9.5	−7.4	−6.1	−6.0	−6.1
Domestic financing	2.8	2.9	3.1	3.3	3.4
Money, prices, and salaries		(Growth rates)			
Domestic credit	10.9	8.8	8.0	15.8	6.1
Public sector	11.5	0.8	7.6	17.9	14.8
Private sector	10.7	11.5	8.2	15.1	3.4
Money supply (M1)	4.1	1.4	8.6	17.9	11.6
Consumer prices (annual average)	4.7	3.3	4.4	2.5	4.5
Real wages (minimum wages)	−4.7	−3.3	−4.4	−2.5	−4.5
Exchange rate					
Official rate (national currency unit per dollar, annual average)	2.0	2.0	2.0	2.0	2.0
Real effective exchange rate (Index 1980 = 100)	8.20	80.6	82.7	85.4	n.a.
Term of trade (index 1980 = 100)	96.0	82.0	101.0	90.0	100.0

(continued)

APPENDIX V *(Continued)*

	1984	1985	1986	1987	1988*
Balance of payments		(Millions of dollars)			
Current account balance	−316.4	−204.2	−105.0	−183.1	−229.3
Merchandise balance	−147.8	−89.6	17.2	−31.3	−23.6
Merchandise exports (FOB)	737.0	789.6	891.3	862.6	893.0
Merchandise imports (FOB)	884.8	879.2	874.0	893.9	916.6
Net services	−248.6	−260.1	−280.6	−298.2	−340.7
Transfers	80.0	145.5	158.4	146.4	135.0
Capital account (net)	335.5	242.5	125.1	200.8	133.4
Change in reserves (− = increase)	−10.7	17.6	−29.8	−77.8	−20.6
Total external debt		(Millions of dollars)			
Disbursed debt	2296.9	2731.5	2981.3	3296.9	3331.3
Debt service actually paid (long-term)	171.9	186.2	221.6	259.0	244.1
			(Percentages)		
Interest payments due/export of goods and NFS	15.9	16.1	15.3	16.5	19.

*Preliminary estimate.
**"Capital expenditures" does not include capital transfer.
n.a. = Not available.
Taken from *Economic and Social Progress in Latin America 1989 Report,* Washington, D.C.: Inter American Development Bank, 1989.

APPENDIX VI
HB Fuller 1984–1989 in Review and Selected Financial Data
(Dollars in thousands, except per share amounts)

| | Annual Growth Rate | | | | | | | | | |
	1-yr 1988–1989	5-yr 1984–1989	10-yr 1979–1989	1989	1988	1987	1986	1985	1984	1983
Income Statement Data:										
Net sales	10.0%	11.0%	11.6%	$753,374	685,034	597,061	528,483	457,937	447,984	414,210
Operating earnings	(.9)	7.4	8.3	$46,009	46,430	47,748	39,483	30,733	32,179	32,452
Earnings from continuing operations	(25.7)	3.8	7.7	$15,671	21,081	25,812	18,822	13,355	13,033	13,624
Earnings before extraordinary items	(25.7)	4.4	7.0	$15,671	21,081	25,812	18,922	13,335	12,624	13,832
Net earnings	(25.7)	5.7	7.6	$15,671	21,081	25,812	18,922	14,909	11,895	13,832
Depreciation	14.5	16.0	15.3	$16,571	14,469	13,197	10,566	9,318	7,898	6,546
Interest expense	56.2	8.3	12.4	$13,237	8,477	5,479	6,208	7,627	8,894	
Income taxes	(3.0)	7.0	6.0	$13,936	14,361	16,320	14,107	9,525	9,944	10,108
Balance Sheet Data:										
Total assets	4.8%	14.0%	12.6%	$455,172	434,293	329,636	291,180	253.571	236,489	225,154
Working capital	(8.1)	7.0	11.3	$95,645	104,071	86,598	74,232	69,477	68,072	59,848
Current ratio				1.8	1.9	1.9	1.9	2.0	2.1	2.0
Net property, plant, and equipment	15.5	16.4	16.0	$186,631	161,605	126,905	108,989	97,173	87,357	80,427
Long-term debt, excluding current installments	2.5	14.5	15.8	$100,974	98,473	33,015	37,211	44,207	51,381	51,755
Stockholders' equity	4.3	13.3	12.4	$186,515	178,871	161,355	135,479	113,417	99,908	92,212

(continued)

APPENDIX VI (*Continued*)

Annual Growth Rate			Income Statement Data:	1989	1988	1987	1986	1985	1984	1983
1-yr 1988–1989	5-yr 1984–1989	10-yr 1979–1989								
			Stockholder Data:							
			Earnings from continuing operations:							
(25.5)%	3.2%	7.0%	Per common share.........	1.64	2.20	2.69	2.00	1.44	1.40	1.47
			Percent of net sales	2.1	3.1	4.3	3.6	2.9	2.9	3.3
			Earnings before extra-ordinary items:							
(25.5)	3.8	6.3	Per common share.........	1.64	2.20	2.69	2.00	1.44	1.36	1.49
			Percent of net sales	2.1	3.1	4.3	3.6	2.9	2.8	3.3
			Net earnings:							
(25.5)	5.1	6.9	Per common share.........	1.64	2.20	2.69	2.00	1.61	1.28	1.49
			Percent of net sales	2.1	3.1	4.3	3.6	3.3	2.7	3.3
			Dividends paid:							
9.5	14.3	12.6	Per common share.........	.575	.525	.405	.35	.315	.295	.275
			Stockholders' equity:							
5.6	12.9	11.9	Per common share.........	19.90	18.84	17.02	14.43	12.28	10.84	10.00
			Return on average stock-holders' equity...............	8.6	12.4	17.4	15.2	14.0	12.4	15.9
			Common stock prices:							
(11.6)	10.9	18.2	High...............	34.25	38.75	48.50	31.00	16.88	20.44	19.88
(13.5)	12.0	15.6	Low...............	20.75	24.00	24.25	15.38	12.25	11.75	11.44
			Average common share out-							
(.2)	1.7	.6	standing (in thousands)	9,572	9,591	9,586	9,464	9,253	9,254	9,272
(3.8)	4.7	4.7	Number of employees.........	5,400	5,200	4,600	4,500	4,400	4,300	4,100

Taken from H. B. Fuller 1989 Annual Report.

APPENDIX VII
Political Profile of Honduras

The Honduran government has been unable and, in some cases, perhaps unwilling to address the poverty issue. A democratically elected government headed by Roberto Suazo Cordova took power in 1982. After his election a liberal newspaper, *El Tiempo,* wrote that Cordova's election was "a vote against corruption and the presence of the military in power."[9] Two years later another liberal newspaper, *La Tribuna,* accused the government of corruption and undermining of liberal party democracy.[10] After taking office, Cordova implemented an austerity program at the suggestion of the International Monetary Fund (IMF) and the U.S. government. By 1983, Cordova wrote President Reagan requesting aid:

> The austerity measures are contributing toward increasing unemployment. We greatly fear that if this situation continues it will become a politically destabilizing factor and weaken our people's belief in the capacity of the democratic system to resolve the problems that we are trying to remedy through these economic policies.[11]

This request resulted in $2.3 million in U.S. aid to Honduras. The aid, for both the military and economic development, exacerbated dependency and corruption within the Honduran government. Alison Acker wrote that by 1987:

> There were hunger marches to the capital, and strikes for a reasonable wage. Clinics and schools closed for lack of supplies or money to pay staff. Glue-sniffing was rampant among Tegucigalpa's street kids, who could not shine shoes because that was now the job of grownups who could find no other work.[12]

Jose Axcona Hoyo, a Liberal Party member, elected in November 1985, proved no more able than Cordova to bring Honduras out of its economic decline. In 1988 credit remained very tight because of the government's monetary policy; growth in the economy was made possible only by U.S. aid. By 1989, to avoid raising taxes and implementing a currency devaluation during an election year, Axcono refused to sign an agreement for more foreign aid with the IMF. As a result, with Honduras $248 million in arrears on its foreign debt payments and negotiations with the World Bank and the U.S., over $300 million in aid from the IMF, the World Bank, and the U.S. were suspended. Also in 1989, senior officers in the Honduran armed forces accused General Humberto Regalado Hernandez of misappropriating millions of dollars in U.S. military aid. The officers claimed that Regalado treated the military equipment as personal gifts and sold it to units under his command.[13]

In November 1989, Rafal Leonardo Callejas of the conservative National Party won the general elections. The aims of the Callejas government included the renegotiation of the foreign debt, the reduction of the fiscal deficit, and privatization of State owned enterprises. On March 3, 1990, the Honduran government passed new legislation that included devaluing the currency from L2 = $1 to L4.5 = $1, a reduction in tariffs, and income tax reforms.

• *Case Study* •
The Project at Moza Island*

JOHN SEEGER • BALACHANDRAN MANYADATH

THE PROJECT AT MOZA ISLAND (A)

Sameer had just finished a marathon four-hour meeting with Gulf Sargam's General Manager, Joe Fernandes. The meeting had proved, as expected, inconclusive. In his own matter-of-fact and dry manner, Joe had pointed out the magnitude of the loss on the project. A loss this size would wipe out the limited capital of the firm. It would also adversely affect future relations with Bank of Arabia. Worst of all, it would threaten the very existence of the firm. There was no choice but to negotiate for the release of the impounded funds.

Sameer Mustafa did not blame Joe for thinking the way he did. Nor did he blame his partner, Nawab, the Director and Chief Executive (D&CE) of Sargam International. (Figure 1 shows the relationships of the firms.) Nawab had called three times during the last 24 hours, urging Sameer to consider the issue carefully in view of the serious long-term effects on the joint venture. Sameer Mustafa shared all the apprehensions. Yet he knew that his role demanded that he look at the issue more broadly. And he strongly believed that inherent values were as important to a company as the necessity to conduct business profitably and increase the wealth of the owners.

Company Background

Sameer Mustafa was a Palestinian national with a Jordanian passport and a business degree from the University of Texas. He had extensive connections with the government officials and businessmen in the East Arabian Sultanate, and his Gulf Trading Company had formed joint ventures with several leading multinational firms.

In 1948 Sohsee Brothers, Switzerland, and Sorabhjee Group, India, had joined together to form Sargam International Ltd., one of the ten largest multinational corporations in India. The company specialized in building large turnkey construction projects and had successfully completed many contracts in India, Africa, Southeast Asia, and the Middle East. It employed 12,000 people, had 115 offices (108 of them in India), and in 1984 had sales revenues of $700 million (US). Sohsse Brothers and Sorabhjee Group still owned 40 percent of the shares of the company, the balance being held by the Indian public.

The Joint Venture

The salient features of the joint-ventures agreement between Gulf Trading Company and Sargam International were simple:

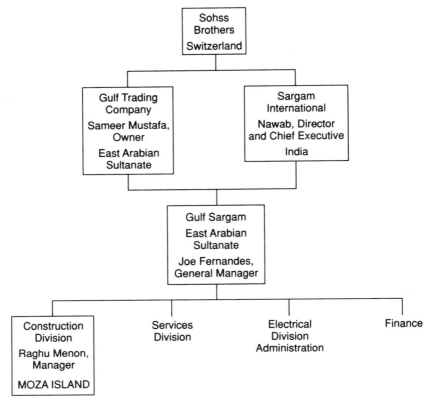

FIGURE 1. Organization of Gulf System

51 percent of Gulf Sargam's capital would be contributed by Gulf Trading Company and 49 percent by Sargam International. Total initial capital was Riyal (R) 1,200,000.

Gulf Trading Company would use its good offices to secure contracts from the government and private firms in East Arabia. It would also arrange for bank facilities for the execution of large projects. Guarantees against such facilities would be provided by Sameer Mustafa in his capacity as the Owner of Gulf Trading Company (Exhibit 1 defines the nature of the guarantees).

Sargam International would operate the joint venture and it would send one of its managers from India for this purpose. All other technical, administrative and support staff would also be provided by Sargam International.

Gulf Trading Company and Sargam International would share profits in the ratio of 55 percent for Gulf, to 45 percent for Sargam International. Losses, if any, would be equally shared.

Organization

Joe Fernandes was the first General Manager of Gulf Sargam. A native of Goa, India (an area once claimed by Portugal), he was an engineer by profession. Joe had joined Sargam International in 1974 and had quickly climbed into middle management ranks. His outstanding performance on several com-

EXHIBIT 1
Financial Results of Operations, Gulf Sargam (in Riyals* 000)

	1980	1981	1982	1983	1984	1985	1986
Sales (Projects)	20	500	1000	1400	1900	12000†	6000
Sales (Services)	500	600	1800	2000	1800	2000	2500
Sales (Total)	520	1100	2800	3400	3700	14000	8500
Cost of Sales‡	320	503	1643	1830	2070	11470	6300
Gross Margin	200	597	1157	1570	1630	2570	2300
O&A	100	366	800	1050	1100	2000	2200
Net Profit	100	231	357	520	530	570	100

*Exchange rate 3.7 Riyals per U.S. dollar.
†Includes Rys 11,000,000 revenue from the Moza Island Project—booked in 1985 with the concurrence of the auditors for Gulf Trading Co. and Gulf Sargam (a "Big Eight" CPA firm).
‡Includes cost of goods sold for both projects and services.

Personal Financial Guarantees Given by Sameer Mustafa (in Riyals)

1. Bank overdraft facilities
   (open line of credit)   3,000,000
2. Letter of Credit
   (guarantees payment for goods received)   2,000,000
3. Tender Guarantees
   (bid bond, forfeited if job not completed)   3,000,000

plex construction projects made him the unanimous choice to head the new Middle Eastern joint venture.

At Gulf Sargam, Joe's technical and management staff—all from Sargam International—consisted of five field engineers, one financial analyst, and an administrative officer. All other hiring was done locally. Joe had extensive authority and powers for day-to-day operations of the firm, but he had to get the consent of Sameer Mustafa for "non-routine" decisions.

Four divisions reported to Joe Fernandes in 1986. The largest was Construction, which installed mechanical equipment for heating, ventilating, and air conditioning (HVAC) as required by contract specifications. Sargam International held the exclusive area licenses for several world-wide brands of this heavy equipment. A separate Service division provided on-going maintenance of HVAC equipment and serviced elevators and fire alarm systems. An Electrical division constructed and maintained electrical switchgear, transformers, transmission lines, and equipment. A small Finance and Administration division completed the organization. Although total employment fluctuated with contracts, Gulf Sargam typically employed 300 to 400 people.

The Economic Environment

The economies of the Middle East countries witnessed unprecedented growth during the oil boom period of the 1970s. But beginning in 1980 most of these countries experienced a glut of oil as demand for petroleum leveled off or declined. Their people realized the good times were far behind them. East Arabia was no exception. With the sharp drop in oil prices and the quota imposed by the Organization of Petroleum Exporting Countries (OPEC), the government's revenues fell sharply, and its development construction activity dropped to 15 percent of the level sustained in the 1970s. For the few new construction projects that were brought to market for bids, competition was intense. A study undertaken by the Sultanate government during this period indicated that competition and the scarcity of business forced firms to accept contracts with margins as low as five to seven percent. Joe Fernandes reported to Sargam International:

> We have no choice in this matter. With a staff of over 250 people, we need projects to keep our people busy, to cover our overhead expenses, and to at least make a nominal profit for our partners. If we refuse to participate in such projects because of low margins, we would be without work and the cash reserves that we currently possess may carry us through only four months. You may say that this is not a healthy situation but we know that better times are ahead and we have to survive to make substantial profits in the future.

Between 1980 and 1983 Sargam won and completed several projects. Most of them were at very low margins, but through effective control and the dedication of its engineers, it was able to make nominal profits for the two partners. In the summer of 1984, however, the picture changed dramatically.

The Development Project at Moza Island

In June 1983, the government decided to modernize the living facilities on Moza, an island 150 miles to the southeast of Abu Sidar, where the country's major liquified petroleum gas (LPG) plants were located. Moza was critically important to the Sultanate's income, but the harsh living conditions there and the primitive state of employee living quarters made it nearly impossible to attract good workers. Modernization was essential.

Moza was a contractor's nightmare. The island could only be accessed by air, flying time from Abu Sidar was one hour. In summer, temperatures averaged around 130°F and relative humidity rarely dropped below 95 percent. The air was severely polluted through minor but constant gas leaks and reeked of hydrogen sulfide (the smell of rotten eggs). Government regulations therefore specified that the maximum "ON" period on the island for any worker should not exceed 12 weeks. Sandstorms were common during the nine summer months, and the combination of temperature, humidity, and gas made the island one of the most difficult places in the world for heavy construction.

The East Arabian Sultanate invited bids from international construction firms in early 1983, and in September the contract for the Moza Island Project was awarded, at a price of R100,000,000, to Al Hasker Contracting Company, a Lebanese organization based in Athens. Hasker, primarily a civil engineering contractor, in turn, awarded various subcontracts to local firms in good standing. In April 1984, Gulf Sargam was awarded the mechanical subcontract at a price of R11,000,000—almost ten times the company's original capital. Joe Fernandes recalled:

> Both Sameer Mustafa and Nawab were unhappy over the low margin—only R1,000,000 estimated profit on the project. Nawab in particular felt that the mar-

gin was dangerously low for a project spanning 18 months at a remote location. He saw that a large portion of the contract value involved equipment from European sources, and that exchange rate variations would constitute a potent risk. But I convinced them that it was easier for the Company to execute one large project and earn R1,000,000 than to derive the same benefit from several smaller projects, each of a different type.

To supervise the construction job, the government employed a prominent consulting firm with offices throughout the Middle East, called Yusuf al Yusuf. This firm in turn appointed Habib Sharif as Engineer-in-Charge and in May 1984, Sharif moved to Moza with his six field engineers. (Yusuf al Yusuf was affiliated with a London consulting firm; several of the supervising engineers were British.)

The contract documents stated that the Engineer-in-Charge was the final authority on every aspect of the project including, but not limited to, approvals of equipment, approval of finished work, approval of variation claims, issue of change orders, interpretation of delays, and grants of extension period. Because the client was the government of the East Arabian Sultanate, disagreements between contractors and the Engineer-in-Charge could be resolved only by a complex civil arbitration system administered by the government in Abu Sidar.

Joe Fernandes selected Raghu Menon to serve as Moza Island Project Manager for Gulf Sargam. The two men had been associated on several previous projects, and Joe knew Raghu as a dedicated, competent, and friendly individual, who got along well with supervising authorities. A good relationship with the Engineer-in-Charge was a necessity on such large projects.

Execution of the Moza Island Contract

From the beginning, Raghu noticed that Habib Sharif often went out of his way to strictly enforce the contract specifications on Gulf Sargam, but not on Al Hasker Construction Company. All construction contracts, by their nature, contain clauses with ambiguous meanings, open to various interpretations; the Moza Island contract was no exception. In normal practice, a contractor would win a favorable interpretation in some of these cases, and would lose in others.

At Moza Island, however, Habib consistently interpreted these clauses to the advantage of the East Arabian Sultanate government, insisting on absolute compliance with the smallest details. Construction drawings, for example, were routinely delayed and then returned for correction of flaws so minute they would not be noticed in normal practice (an example might be a misspelled word like *refrigeration*). In defense, Raghu filed claims for reimbursement of the additional costs Gulf Sargam was forced to pay.

Raghu's weekly report to his head office during this first three months of the Moza Island project regularly reported Habib's attitude of extreme tolerance with Al Hasker Contracting Company and extreme intolerance with Gulf Sargam. His report on the episode of the X-ray welder provided an example:

> On August 4, 1984, our X-ray welder failed the welding test, even though photographs taken on a sample of 60 welds indicated 100 percent finishes. I was furious but helpless. The contract specifies that the British "Code of Welding Practice" sets our standards, and the Code defines the characteristics of both a perfect weld

and a perfect workman. An acceptable workman must have basic communication skills in order to handle emergency situations. Habib argued that our worker lacked communication skills, and shut down the job.

Our man had superb technical skills and was fluent in two languages—Hindi and Malayalam (the native tongue of Kerala province in India)—and he could converse in English too. But not well enough to suit Habib in August. We had to fly in a substitute welder. A month later we put the original through the test again and he passed.

There was no comment about the welder from Habib Sharif, but in Raghu's eyes, a familiar picture was unfolding. Most construction consultants in the region expected to gain personally from their work, but none would ask an outright bribe. The consultant normally initiated the move with subtle "feelers" and awaited responses from the contractor. If a favorable response did not materialize, stronger signals were sent—each signal causing more disruption to the contractor's work than the earlier one. Raghu had faced this situation in several earlier projects and had, through a combination of diplomacy and skill, survived each situation. Sameer Mustafa had strong feelings on the subject:

> The fact that gratuities are often paid in the Middle East does not make it right to pay them. The practice exists because people—very often foreign corporations— pay when they are asked. There is no law saying you must pay. Taking part in a corrupt system is immoral and it perpetuates the corruption. Giving in now would set a precedent for all my other operations.
>
> Habib Shamir is playing a game with us. As always, we must make it clear we don't play by those rules. If we hold fast, the man will see we mean it. He will come around.

The game was a nightmare for Raghu. By June 1985, Gulf Sargam had incurred costs on an additional 9,000 man-hours due to delays in approval of drawings and rejection of site work by Yusuf al Yusuf. Gulf Sargam had filed variation claims totalling R1,000,000, but not a single one had been approved.

By early 1986, the game was still in progress. The delays imposed on Gulf Sargam had slowed the entire Moza Island project, but Habib had not wavered. Joe recalled Raghu's eightieth progress report from the site, as the project neared conclusion:

> We are 6 months behind schedule and the situation is worsening every day. Habib rarely approves our work the first time. Al Hasker Contracting Company's approvals are granted from the office without Habib even visiting the job site. Last evening the space frame (a structure covering an indoor swimming pool, made of lightweight aluminum tubing) erected by Hasker between grids E–H and 21–26 came crashing down. Fortunately, no one was hurt. Habib attributed this mishap to metal fatigue not to Hasker's workmanship. Last night I met Habib at the club and decided to take him on directly as we must resolve this matter before the end of the project. Habib mentioned to me that Al Hasker Contracting Company had taken "good care" of him and he was accordingly reciprocating their gesture. He expressed surprise that Gulf Sargam had not followed the same policy for the last 12 months, a policy that was common in the Middle East and essential for the smooth execution of a project. But, he said, it was still not too late. He had authority to approve variation claims up to a total of R3,000,000 and Gulf Sargam could still make a profit. The cost of this consideration would be R300,000—10 percent of the claims approved for payment.

Habib Sharif argued that, as Engineer-in-Charge on the job, he had every right to enforce the spirit of the contract agreement on Gulf Sargam. He was only, logically, executing his responsibilities in the fullest sense. The firm had bid on the project on the basis of the specifications. They were given an opportunity to review every single part of the contract prior to acceptance and award of the bid. Gulf Sargam's price to his client was based on full knowledge of the job's terms and conditions and should have allowed for all nuances; after all, the practice of providing gratuities to consultants was hardly new. If the company now wanted "softer" terms, to increase its profits, it was only reasonable to expect that they part with a small portion of the added reward. The government had budgeted a 20 percent increase in contract value, to allow for change orders and variation claims from contractors, so the funds were available for disbursement, provided Habib, too, shared in the benefits.

Raghu Menon reported on his response to this argument:

> I repeated our company's policy on such financial arrangements, but said I would relay Habib's information to higher authorities. Then I asked how we could be sure he really had the power to deliver. This morning, Habib approved one of my claims—the most dubious one of them all—for R77,000. He has the power.
>
> . . . I am tired and would like to return to India. You cannot match knowledge and expertise with corruption and greed. I suggest that Sameer and you should think over this matter carefully.

Concluding the Moza Island Project

On the last day of Ramadam, June 1986, Sameer Mustafa read Joe's internal memo several times. The final scenario was frightening. The Moza Island contract had been completed six months behind schedule, and the firm was exposed to the possibility that Habib could impose the contract's penalty clause. At ten percent of the contract's total value, that would add another R1,100,000 to Gulf Sargam's losses. Even without the penalty, the net loss was R2,138,000 as against an estimated profit of R1,000,000. Variation claims on the client totalled R2,860,000, and only a single one had been approved. Raghu had suffered from exhaustion and had returned to India a month earlier. His last progress report had been appended to Joe's memo, with a copy marked for Nawab:

> You have to decide on the variation claims before Habib finalizes the contract on June 30. I feel that we are in a hopeless position and we must accede to his request in order to recover our losses. Bear in mind that after this date we can pursue our claims only in the Abu Sidar arbitration committee, and I hope you will appreciate that we would be against the Government. Secondly Habib has, at this stage, every right to impose the penalty clause.

Joe fully endorsed Raghu's views on the matter. He added that as an employee of Sargam International he was obliged to take all possible steps to avoid losses to his parent company and, since all other avenues were exhausted, he believed that Sameer should endorse the payment to Habib. Sameer's partner, the D&CE of Sargam International, also had a point of view. Nawab's telephone calls had pointed out the Indian government's interest in the performance of joint ventures; financial results were monitored regularly, and a loss of this size would be difficult to explain. While Sameer was a single owner, answering to no one, Nawab had important shareholders who would insist on knowing the details of Gulf Sargam's performance.

Sameer paused and shook his head. The decision was made. He picked up the telephone to summon Joe back to his office.

THE PROJECT AT MOZA ISLAND (B)

Sameer Mustafa held firm. The principle was clear, he said. If he succumbed to the pressure of a blackmailer at Moza Island, which was a relatively small part of his holdings in Gulf Trading Company, then the precedent would be set for all his divisions and for all his managers. He might say it was "just this once," but every employee who ever faced a similar situation in the future would know he had given in once, and so might do it again.

Gulf Sargam closed its 1987 books with a loss of R2,233,000 on the Moza Island project. Habib Shamir invoked the penalty clause, but Gulf Sargam fought it successfully through the Abu Sidar arbitration procedure. Gulf Sargam also filed claims against the client for R2,300,000, for excess costs on work carried out under duress, beyond the contract's terms. The East Arabian arbitrator allowed R220,000 as reasonable, after a long and costly legal battle. The rest of the claims were dismissed as unsupported.

Gulf Sargam never fully recovered but continued in business through 1990, earning enough to pay the interest on funds it borrowed to replenish its working capital after the loss. Relations between Sameer Mustafa and his partner Nawab were strained, however, and in mid-1988 Sameer sold Gulf Trading Company to a prominent East Arabian citizen and emigrated to Jordan. Raghu resigned to start a small consulting firm with some close associates. In July 1989, Joe Fernandes tendered his resignation from Gulf Sargam, feeling that his future with the firm was limited. Nawab, however, refused to accept the resignation.

Questions for discussion

1. How true is the old cliché, "when in Rome do as the Romans"?
2. What are the moral and ethical responsibilities of an MNC operating in a foreign country?

• *Case Study* •

Merck & Co., Inc.

THE BUSINESS ENTERPRISE TRUST

A*

In 1978, Dr. P. Roy Vagelos, then head of the Merck research labs, received a provocative memorandum from a senior researcher in parasitology, Dr. William C. Campbell. Dr. Campbell had made an intriguing observation while working with ivermectin, a new antiparastic compound under investigation for use in animals.

Campbell thought that ivermectin might be the answer to a disease called river blindness that plagued millions in the Third World. But to find out if Campbell's hypothesis had merit, Merck would have to spend millions of dollars to develop the right formulation for human use and to conduct the field trials in the most remote parts of the world. Even if these efforts produced an effective and safe drug, virtually all of those afflicted with river blindness could not afford to buy it. Vagelos, originally a university researcher but by then a Merck executive, had to decide whether to invest in research for a drug that, even if successful, might never pay for itself.

River Blindness

River blindness, formally known as *onchocerciasis*, was a disease labeled by the World Health Organization (WHO) as a public health and socioeconomic problem of considerable magnitude in over 35 developing countries throughout the Third World. Some 85 million people in thousands of tiny settlements throughout Africa and parts of the Middle East and Latin America were thought to be at risk. The cause: a parasitic worm carried by a tiny black fly which bred along fast-moving rivers. When the flies bit humans—a single person could be bitten thousands of times a day—the larvae of a parasitic worm, *Onchocerca volvulus*, entered the body.

These worms grew to more than two feet in length, causing grotesque but relatively innocuous nodules in the skin. The real harm began when the adult worms reproduced, releasing millions of microscopic offspring, known as microfilariae, which swarmed through body tissue. A terrible itching resulted, so bad that some victims committed suicide. After several years, the microfilariae caused lesions and depigmentation of the skin. Eventually they invaded the eyes, often causing blindness.

The World Health Organization estimated in 1978 that some 340,000 people were blind because of onchocerciasis, and that a million more suffered from varying degrees of visual impairment. At that time, 18 million or more people were infected with the parasite, though half did not yet have serious symptoms. In some villages close to fly-breeding sites, nearly all residents were infected and a majority of those over age 45 were blind. In such places, it was said, children believed that severe itching, skin infections and blindness were simply part of growing up.

In desperate efforts to escape the flies, entire villages abandoned fertile areas near rivers, and moved to poorer land. As a result, food shortages were frequent. Community life disintegrated as new burdens arose for already impoverished families.

The disease was first identified in 1893 by scientists and in 1926 was found to be related to the black flies. But by the 1970s, there was still no cure that could safely be used for community-wide treatment. Two drugs, diethylcarbamazine (DEC) & Suramin, were useful in killing the parasite, but both had severe side effects in infected individuals, needed close monitoring, and had even caused deaths. In 1974, the Onchocerciasis Control Program was created to be administered by the World Health Organization, in the hope that the flies could be killed through spraying of larvacides at breeding sites, but success was slow and uncertain. The flies in many areas developed resistance to the treatment, and were also known to disappear and then reinfest areas.

Merck & Co., Inc.

Merck & Co., Inc. was, in 1978, one of the largest producers of prescription drugs in the world. Headquartered in Rahway, New Jersey, Merck traced its origins to Germany in 1668 when Friedrich Jacob Merck purchased an apothecary in the city of Darmstadt. Over three hundred years later, Merck, having become an American firm, employed over 28,000 people and had operations all over the world.

In the late 1970s, Merck was coming off a 10 year drought in terms of new products. For nearly a decade, the company had relied on two prescription drugs for a significant percentage of its approximately $2 billion in annual sales: Indocin, a treatment for rheumatoid arthritis, and Aldomet, a treatment for high blood pressure. Henry W. Gadsden, Merck's chief executive from 1965 to 1976, along with his successor, John J. Horan, were concerned that the 17 year patent protection on Merck's two big moneymakers would soon expire, and began investing an enormous amount in research.

Merck management spent a great deal of money on research because it knew that its success ten and twenty years in the future critically depended upon present investments. The company deliberately fashioned a corporate culture to nurture the most creative, fruitful research. Merck scientists were among the best-paid in the industry, and were given great latitude to pursue intriguing leads. Moreover, they were inspired to think of their work as a quest to alleviate human disease and suffering world-wide. Within certain proprietary constraints, researchers were encouraged to publish in academic journals and to share ideas with their scientific peers. Nearly a billion dollars was spent between 1975 and 1978, and the investment paid off. In that period, under the direction of head of research, Dr. P. Roy Vagelos, Merck introduced Clinoril, a painkiller for arthritis; a general antibiotic called Mefoxin; a drug for glaucoma named Timoptic; and Ivomec (ivermectin, MSD), an antiparasitic for cattle.

In 1978, Merck had sales of $1.98 billion and net income of $307 million. Sales had risen steadily between 1969 and 1978 from $691 million to almost $2 billion. Income during the same period rose from $106 million to over $300 million.

At that time, Merck employed 28,700 people, up from 22,200 ten years earlier. Human and animal health products constituted 84% of the company's sales, with environmental health products and services representing an additional 14% of sales. Merck's foreign sales had grown more rapidly during the 1970's than had domestic sales, and in 1978 represented 47% of total sales. Much of the company's research operations were organized separately as the Merck Sharp & Dohme Research Laboratories, headed by Vagelos. Other Merck operations included the Merck Sharp & Dohme Division, the Merck Sharp & Dohme International Division, Kelco Division, Merck Chemical Manufacturing Division, Merck Animal Health Division, Calgon Corporation, Baltimore Aircoil Company, and Hubbard Farms.

The company had 24 plants in the United States, including one in Puerto Rico, and 44 in other countries. Six research laboratories were located in the United States and four abroad.

While Merck executives sometimes squirmed when they quoted the "unbusinesslike" language of George W. Merck, son of the company's founder and its former chairman, there could be no doubt that Merck employees found the words inspirational. "We try never to forget that medicine is for the people," Merck said. "It is not for the profits. The profits follow, and if we have remembered that, they have never failed to appear. The better we have remembered it, the larger they have been." These words formed the basis of Merck's overall corporate philosophy.

The Drug Investment Decision

Merck invested hundreds of millions of dollars each year in research. Allocating those funds amongst various projects, however, was a rather involved and inexact process. At a company as large as Merck, there was never a single method by which projects were approved or money distributed.

Studies showed that, on the average, it took 12 years and $200 million to bring a new drug to market. Thousands of scientists were continually working on new ideas and following new leads. Drug development was always a matter of trial and error; with each new iteration, scientists would close some doors and open others. When a Merck researcher came across an apparent breakthrough—either in an unexpected direction, or as a derivative of the original lead—he or she would conduct preliminary research. If the idea proved promising, it was brought to the attention of the department heads.

Every year, Merck's research division held a large review meeting at which all research programs were examined. Projects were coordinated and consolidated, established programs were reviewed and new possibilities were considered. Final approval on research was not made, however, until the head of research met later with a committee of scientific advisors. Each potential program was extensively reviewed, analyzed on the basis of the likelihood of success, the existing market, competition, potential safety problems, manufacturing feasibility and patent status before the decision was made whether to allocate funds for continued experimentation.

The Problem of Rare Diseases and Poor Customers

Many potential drugs offered little chance of financial return. Some diseases were so rare that treatments developed could never be priced high enough to recoup the investment in research, while other diseases afflicted only the poor in rural and remote areas of the Third World. These victims had limited ability to pay even a small amount for drugs or treatment.

In the United States, Congress sought to encourage drug companies to conduct research on rare diseases. In 1978 legislation had been proposed which would grant drug companies tax benefits and seven-year exclusive marketing rights if they would manufacture drugs for diseases afflicting fewer than 200,000 Americans. It was expected that this "orphan drug" program would eventually be passed into law.

There was, however, no U.S. or international program that would create incentives for companies to develop drugs for diseases like river blindness which afflicted millions of the poor in the Third World. The only hope was that some Third World government, foundation, or international aid organization might step in and partially fund the distribution of a drug that had already been developed.

The Discovery of Ivermectin

The process of investigating promising drug compounds was always long, laborious and fraught with failure. For every pharmaceutical compound that became a "product candidate," thousands of others failed to meet the most rudimentary pre-clinical tests for safety and efficacy. With so much room for failure, it became especially important for drug companies to have sophisticated research managers who could identify the most productive research strategies.

Merck had long been a pioneer in developing major new antibiotic compounds, beginning with penicillin and streptomycin in the 1940s. In the 1970s, Merck Sharp & Dohme Research Laboratories were continuing this tradition. To help investigate for new microbial agents of potential therapeutic value, Merck researchers obtained 54 soil samples from the Kitasato Institute of Japan in 1974. These samples seemed novel and the researchers hoped they might disclose some naturally occurring antibiotics.

As Merck researchers methodically put the soil through hundreds of tests, Merck scientists were pleasantly surprised to detect strong antiparasitic activity in Sample No. OS3153, a scoop of soil dug up at a golf course near Ito, Japan. The Merck labs quickly brought together an interdisciplinary team to try to isolate a pure active ingredient from the microbial culture. The compound eventually isolated—avermectin—proved to have an astonishing potency and effectiveness against a wide range of parasites in cattle, swine, horses and other animals. Within a year, the Merck team also began to suspect that a group of related compounds discovered in the same soil sample could be effective against many other intestinal worms, mites, ticks and insects.

After toxicological tests suggested that ivermectin would be safer than related compounds, Merck decided to develop the substance for the animal health market. In 1978 the first ivermectin-based animal drug, Ivomec, was nearing approval by the U.S. Department of Agriculture and foreign regulatory bodies. Many variations would likely follow: drugs for sheep and pigs, horses, dogs, and others. Ivomec had the potential to become a major advance in animal health treatment.

As clinical testing of ivermectin progressed in the late 1970s, Dr. William Campbell's ongoing research brought him face-to-face with an intriguing hypothesis. Ivermectin, when tested in horses, was effective against the microfilariae of an exotic, fairly unimportant gastrointestinal parasite, Onchocerca cervicalis. This particular worm, while harmless in horses, had characteristics similar to the insidious human parasite that causes river blindness, Onchocerca volvulus.

Dr. Campbell wondered: Could ivermectin be formulated to work against the human parasite? Could a safe, effective drug suitable for community-wide treatment of river blindness be developed? Both Campbell and Vagelos knew that it was very much a gamble that it would succeed. Furthermore, both knew that even if success were attained, the economic viability of such a project would be nil. On the other hand, because such a significant amount of money had already been invested in the development of the animal drug, the cost of developing a human formulation would be much less than that for developing a new compound. It was also widely believed at this point that ivermectin, though still in its final development stages, was likely to be very successful.

A decision to proceed would not be without risks. If a new derivative proved to have any adverse health effects when used on humans, its reputation as a veterinary drug could be tainted and sales negatively affected, no matter how irrelevant the experience with humans. In early tests, ivermectin had had some negative side effects on some specific species of mammals. Dr. Brian Duke of the Armed Forces Institute of Pathology in Washington, D.C. said the cross-species effectiveness of antiparasitic drugs are unpredictable, and there is "always a worry that some race or subsection of the human population" might be adversely affected.

Isolated instances of harm to humans or improper use in Third World settings might also raise some unsettling questions: Could drug residues turn up in meat eaten by humans? Would any human version of ivermectin distributed to the Third World be diverted into the black market, undercutting sales of the veterinary drug? Could the drug harm certain animals in unknown ways?

Despite these risks, Vagelos wondered what the impact might be of turning down Campbell's proposal. Merck had built a research team dedicated to alleviating human suffering. What would a refusal to pursue a possible treatment for river blindness to do morale?

Ultimately, it was Dr. Vagelos who had to make the decision whether or not to fund research toward a treatment for river blindness.

B*

In 1978, Dr. P. Roy Vagelos, then head of Merck's research labs, approved initial funding for research into a potential treatment for river blindness.

Vagelos believed there were several reasons Merck ought to go forward

---

*This case was adapted by Stephanie Weiss from a monograph "Merck & Co., Inc.," by David Bollier, under the supervision of Kirk O. Hanson, President of The Business Enterprise Trust and Senior Lecturer at the Stanford Graduate School of Business.

with the research, first being the potential impact of a negative decision on the Merck culture. Failure to investigate Dr. Campbell's tantalizing hypothesis could demoralize Merck scientists, especially since the inquiry focused on a widespread, intractable disease that produced great suffering.

Vagelos also believed that the prevalence of the disease in the Third World would motivate someone—Third World governments, private foundations, or even the U.S. Government—to buy a successful drug and donate it to the victims.

The fact that a successful drug for onchocerciasis would not generate much revenue for Merck was a secondary concern to Dr. Vagelos and his associates. "Until you can demonstrate that the drug is capable of doing something," Dr. Vagelos noted, "you don't even bring the marketing people into it. Because, until you can characterize a drug, they can't put numbers on it." Dr. Vagelos admitted, however, that "we knew that it was going to be a borderline economically viable project at the start."

Finally, Dr. Vagelos believed the company should proceed because the project would further Merck's knowledge of parasitology, already an established field in Merck. Even if the research failed to produce a treatment for river blindness, it might produce findings of future use to the company.

For Dr. Vagelos and Dr. William C. Campbell, the scientist who had proposed the research, investing in the development of the drug for this dread Third World disease was an irresistible possibility. "Emotionally, you become very involved in what you can accomplish, as a research group and as a company," Dr. Vagelos explained. "And so we could hardly wait to start these experiments." It made sense for Merck, Dr. Vagelos believed, to learn as much as possible about its fledgling class of compounds, avermectins, as possible.

Clinical Trials Approved

By 1980, ivermectin had traversed quite a distance on its journey to becoming a river blindness therapy: from the original parasitological research (led by Dr. Campbell) to the microbiology and chemical identification programs (led by Drs. Tom Miller, Richard W. Burg and Georg Albers-Schonberg) to the chemical synthesis of ivermectin (Drs. John C. Chabala and Michael H. Fisher) to development of the animal drug formulations. Eighteen months had elapsed since the compound's potential human application was first suspected.

Then, in January 1980, the baton was passed to Dr. Mohammed A. Aziz, senior director of clinical research at Merck. A quiet man of steely determination, Dr. Aziz was widely credited for championing the drug, which would come to be known as Mectizan, within Merck and shepherding it past numerous scientific and corporate obstacles. His obsession with developing Mectizan, cited by all who knew him, was due in large part to his personal background. As a tropical disease expert, native of the region now called Bangladesh and former World Health Organization (WHO) scientist with experience in Sierra Leone, Dr. Aziz knew firsthand what river blindness meant for Third World people. Dr. Aziz got his chance to proceed in January 1980, when Merck research management agreed to move forward with human clinical trials.

It was a momentous decision for Merck. The company was now committed to a lengthy, expensive set of tests for a drug that was not likely to generate much, if any, revenue. "We had never undertaken the development of a drug that was going to be broadly used, such as 18 million patients, with the idea that we were not going to make money," Dr. Vagelos later explained. In general, drugs that earn $20 million or less a year are at risk of being discontinued, he said, and certainly no one expected Mectizan to generate a fraction of that sum.

"On the other hand," Dr. Vagelos continued, "the company is so large and the laboratories so prolific, that one can never guess what is going to come out." A clinical investigation of ivermectin, however problematic, could yield useful knowledge.

At the outset of research, Dr. Bruce M. Greene, a prominent university scientist associated with the development of Mectizan recalled there was "a lot of turmoil in the company [in the early 1980s] about whether we should expose this fabulous commercial product to the risk of human usage." Dr. Vagelos, who had become chief executive in 1985, quieted the debate, and as it turned out, Merck's concerns regarding negative side effects of ivermectin on humans were unwarranted.

The clinical trials would pose a special challenge. Victims of river blindness rarely lived within hailing distance of modern medical facilities. Yet clinical trials needed to be held in such settings to ensure proper medical oversight of test subjects and collection of rigorous data.

Cooperation with WHO

Realizing that it would need help in this phase of the drug's development, Merck turned to the World Health Organization (WHO), the Geneva-based consortium of 166 member nations. Talks began in July 1982 to determine the most appropriate approach to the problem—from medical, political and commercial points of view.

There was a certain incongruity in Merck working closely with WHO. On some policy issues, the U.S. drug industry and WHO had had bitter disagreements. In the 1970s and 1980s, for example, multinational drug companies generally resisted WHO-backed standards for international drug marketing. They also denounced a WHO "essential drugs list" initiative designed to help Third World nations spend their limited resources on the most basic, widely needed drugs.

Notwithstanding such policy clashes, WHO had often collaborated with private drug companies to develop drugs for Third World nations, which typically did not have the marketplace clout, despite their large populations, to stimulate such research. According to a 1988 WHO report, less than 4% of the global drug industry's research expenditures focused on diseases endemic to developing countries, even though 25% of the world's population lived in the Third World. In developing ivermectin, Merck and WHO complemented each other's needs quite well. Merck had a compound that might treat river blindness, and WHO had access to a global network of government health officials and scientists who could help run clinical trials.

Despite these common interests, the initial collaboration between WHO and Merck was at times strained. WHO was already deeply invested in a $26 million a year program to eliminate black flies through aerial larvacide spraying. WHO officials were initially concerned that this program might be abandoned if ivermectin looked promising. Merck officials reassured WHO that they would continue to support spraying as well as the development of the new drug.

WHO scientists also questioned the medical promise of ivermectin. "Initially, when Merck came to us and said it had this fancy new drug," recalled Dr. Duke, who then headed the WHO filariasis disease program, "my reaction was, 'We've got several drugs and they all incite violent reactions.'" There was skepticism that any drug could overcome the side-effects induced by these drugs, which required close medical supervision. Furthermore, WHO scientists believed that any new drug for river blindness must attack the adult parasite, not the microfilariae offspring, because only then could new generations of microfilariae be conclusively stopped.

Notwithstanding periodic clashes of scientific judgment and institutional cultures, a working collaboration evolved over time. Working with Professor Michel LaRiviere of the University of Paris, Dr. Aziz eventually decided to conduct the first human tests of ivermectin at the University of Dakar, Senegal, in February 1981. Merck supplied the drug, grants-in-aid for the studies, and the resources to apply for regulatory approval; WHO provided scientists and research facilities.

Dr. Aziz and his associates moved ahead with great caution, administering extremely small doses. One scientist recalled how Professor LaRiviere personally stayed up all night with test subjects to monitor for adverse reactions. By the end of 1981, the early results were promising: no adverse reactions, and a single, extremely small dose of ivermectin dramatically reduced microfilariae counts. A second study in Paris was conducted to confirm the Dakar results.

But the skeptics remained. In November 1982, Andre Rougemont, a highly respected scientist at the University of Geneva and former WHO official, wrote a stinging letter to *Lancet*, the prestigious British medical journal. Rougemont charged that ivermectin "brings no really new or interesting feature to the treatment of onchocerciasis," and accused Dr. Aziz and his colleagues of being "over-optimistic."

Prodded by such a public attack, Dr. Aziz redoubled his efforts to prove that ivermectin was indeed superior to the existing drug of choice, DEC. With the help of Drs. Bruce Greene, Hugh Taylor and other university scientists, Aziz plunged ahead with Phase II tests in Senegal, Mali, Ghana and Liberia in 1983–1984. The complex tests further confirmed the promise of ivermectin, and led to a subsequent set of trials in 1985. With mounting excitement, Dr. Aziz and his associates planned the final, Phase III tests the following year with 1,200 patients in Ghana and Liberia. These tests succeeded in establishing the optimum dosage level and in further confirming the drug's safety.

Application for Approval of Drug

By early 1987, nearly seven years after Merck executives had authorized the first clinical trials and nearly ten yeas after Dr. Campbell first proposed the research, the company had the clinical data needed to seek final regulatory approval for Mectizan. The materials were submitted to the French Directorate of Pharmacy and Drugs, whose judgments are widely accepted by Francophone African nations where onchocerciasis is a major public health program. Final approval came in October 1987.

It was a buoyant time at Merck, especially for Dr. Campbell, Dr. Aziz and Dr. Vagelos. It was also a critical turning point. Less than two months after the last regulatory hurdle had been cleared, Dr. Aziz died at age 58 of cancer. And Merck, which had spent nearly a decade developing a remarkable treatment for river blindness, could not simply bask in the glory of its triumph. Its achievement would be of little consequence unless it could surmount another daunting challenge—delivering the new wonder drug to the people who needed it.

Selling the Drug

As early as 1982, after Dr. Aziz's first clinical trials proved successful, Merck knew that some unorthodox plan to distribute Mectizan would be needed. Early research confirmed what many had suspected: no conventional market for the drug was likely to materialize. The victims were too poor; they lived in utterly isolated locations; and they had no access to pharmacies or routine medical care.

From this point on, according to Dr. Vagelos, Merck moved forward in developing Mectizan with a blind faith that some third party, at some point in the future, would step forward with funding. The anticipated funders included foundations, international health or development organizations, Third World governments, and the U.S. Government.

When regulatory approval for Mectizan seemed certain in 1986, Dr. Vagelos, then Chairman and CEO, set out on a series of trips to Washington, D.C., searching for parties to buy and distribute Mectizan. His first stop was Deputy Secretary of State John Whitehead. Later he visited Donald Regan, then President Reagan's White House Chief of Staff. "Each of these people understood the potential importance of the drug, and they thought it must be distributed," recalled Dr. Vagelos. "And each of them referred the project to the U.S. Agency for International Development"— a foreign assistance agency that makes grants and loans for various Third World development projects.

Whitehead introduced Dr. Vagelos to M. Peter McPherson, the head of U.S. AID at the time. As Dr. Vagelos recalled, Whitehead said, "'Now, Peter, we've got to do this program.' And McPherson looked up at him and said, 'Mr. Secretary, we don't have any money.'" Follow-up conversations yielded the same answer.

Dr. Vagelos was highly skeptical—and disappointed. The proposed distribution program would require an initial commitment of only $2 million a year, eventually growing to a sum of $20 million a year. It would be hard to imagine a more cost-effective way for the U.S. to curry goodwill with Third World nations.

Dr. Vagelos was disappointed by the U.S. Government's failure to come up with funding because he was spending so much time on the matter. He felt that it was beginning to detract from his normal responsibilities as Merck Chairman and CEO. "I was doing more for this than I'd done for any other drug," he said. "I mean, this [advocacy for a specific drug] is normally covered by our regulatory affairs and marketing people."

A series of visits to other potential funders—African health ministries, foundations, and others—were also to no avail. Merck even called upon noted international figures to advise them, but none of these efforts succeeded.

Should Merck Simply Give the Drug Away?

At this point, an impertinent, offhand suggestion made several years earlier resurfaced at Merck headquarters. In 1983 or 1984, Dr. Brian Duke had made a provocative suggestion—with no authorization from WHO—that Merck simply donate Mectizan outright. To his chagrin, Dr. Duke saw his casual remark to a reporter turn up in print in *South*, a Third World business magazine. The suggestion was not appreciated by Merck management who were still hoping to find third-party funding.

"That's not the way you do things in a commercial organization," Dr. Vagelos said in 1991. "You don't start out by thinking you're going to give something away. . . . We hadn't gone through our process of determining what it would take [to distribute the drug]." When the search for third-party funding failed, however, Dr. Duke's suggestion began to sound much more plausible. Dr. Aziz had long favored such a solution. As Dr. Campbell recalled, "Aziz was constantly pushing the idea that Mectizan should be given away with pride."

The idea of a drug company donating an unlimited supply of a breakthrough drug to millions of people was unprecedented. It was a proposed commitment that would prompt any company to think long and hard. As senior executives debated the issue internally and consulted with peers in the drug industry, they wondered: Would this set a "bad precedent"—an expectation that future drugs for Third World diseases should also be donated, which could itself discourage companies from conducting research on such diseases? Would Merck face intolerable legal liability if some Mectizan recipients suffered adverse reactions? Would the sheer cost of administering such a program and manufacturing the drug be prohibitive?

Questions for discussion

1. Can a corporation follow George W. Merck's philosophy and remain profitable?

2. What is Merck's, or any pharmaceutical company's, moral responsibility regarding orphan drugs such as Mectizan?

3. Should Merck have funded the research for a human version of Mectizan, given the risks and likelihood that it would not be profitable, and might even produce an operating loss for Merck?

4. Should Merck manufacture Mectizan and simply give it away, especially considering that its users are in other countries?

• *Case Study* •
Three Scenarios*

THOMAS W. DUNFEE

No Wage Out?

You are the owner and chief executive of a small, currently unprofitable manufacturing company in your country. There is substantial unemployment in the area and the average wage for unskilled labor has fallen 20% during the past year. You could easily replace your current workers with equally qualified people at the lower wage. A new competitor has just entered the area and has hired workers at the current lower rate. What would you do during this period of unprofitability?

1. Ask your workers to accept a 20% wage cut and replace those who objected.
2. Maintain the current wage rate.
3. Split the difference and ask your workers to accept a 10% cut.
4. Replace any workers who leave of their own accord with new workers at the market rates, thereby establishing a dual rate.

Folders Keepers?

You are negotiating an important contract with a foreign firm with a reputation for driving a hard bargain. After a full day of negotiating, the other firm's representatives leave the room and leave behind a folder which appears to contain key information about their negotiating options. What would you do?

1. Do nothing and leave the folder where it is.
2. Look over the material in the folder and then leave it in the room in the exact location that you found it.
3. Take the folder and call the other managers and tell them that you found it.
4. Take the folder, study it during the night and then return it prior to the beginning of the next day's meeting.

Dial "M" for Monitor

You supervise a group of salespeople in a foreign country who take telephone orders for delivery of products. You want to make sure that they describe the product accurately and that they are professional in their dealings with clients. You are also concerned about some employees making personal calls on company time. What would you do?

1. Limit your actions to steps fully disclosed to employees so that their privacy is protected.
2. If the problems are bad enough, institute a system of secret monitoring of calls.

• EIGHT •
Success Stories
It Can Be Done!

Many business ethics scholars have argued that in choosing to do good, businesses can also wind up doing well. That is, doing the right thing pays off in profits and success. Of course, there is an important caveat involved in this argument. To be truly ethical and possibly successful, businesses must do the right thing for the right reasons. They have to do good intentionally. Doing the right thing because it's fashionable or simply in your own best interest doesn't ethically count—even if the desired results are achieved. As Stephen R. Covey has argued, ethics is an "inside-out" proposition. Ethics is the external expression of our internal values and beliefs. Beneficent behavior, moral conduct based on pretense or accommodation can only rarely be sustained. This claim for "doing good and doing well" is not always an immediately self-fulfilling prophesy in the short-run. However, in the long-run, it is a strategy that can and does work—at least for some organizations, like the ones discussed in this section.

Doing the right thing in business is neither magic nor esoteric. It's simply doing business with *more* than the "bottom line" in view. It's doing business with due concern for the rights and expectations of all the stakeholders involved. It means doing business as if people mattered, and not just profits. It means offering your customers a decent product at a fair price; respecting the rights and dignity of your employees; honoring your contracts and commitments to your vendors and suppliers; recognizing your civil and social responsibilities to your community; and producing a reasonable profit for the financial risk-taking of your stockholders or owners. It's a canon that's easy to state, hard to do, and all too often, only accomplished by a few organizations.

Perhaps the major reason for the inclusion of this new section in the Fourth Edition of this text is our students. For the last few years, both our undergraduates and graduate students have been complaining to us about the negative tone of the kinds of cases we have been using in the classroom. They have been collectively telling us that they're tired of reading about the failures and foibles of ethically bankrupt business and corporations. They told us they wanted to read about a few success stories too. They said they wanted to examine how and why "good companies" do what they do. The "bad companies,"

310

they said, clearly showed them "what went wrong." Now they wanted a few models and examples of "what went right." On reflection, their logic seemed impeccable to us—and so we have added this section.

The first essay "Nice Guys Finish First?" reports that the rules are beginning to change. Instead of the old game of "let the buyer beware" and "make as much as you can as fast as you can," the new strategy is "a decent product at a fair price," and "make a friend, not just a deal." What a concept! Few "good guy" corporations have been more written about than Ben & Jerry's Homemade, Inc., manufacturers of premium ice cream and yogurt. "Ice Cream and Integrity" is a snapshot of how Ben & Jerry's started, how it operates, and why it continues to be held up as a classic example of modern corporate social responsibility. "Roger Meade: Running on People Power" is a case study of how the culture and success of a corporation can be formed and driven by effective leadership. Roger Meade, CEO of Scitor Corporation, "walks the walk" and "talks the talk." He lives what he believes. He trusts people, empowers them, expects them to succeed—and, they do. "People," says Meade, "are the keys to productivity. Scitor is about people, our employees and customers. If we can satisfy all of our people's needs, we'll be a success." "Kresa's Cleanup" is another study in effective leadership. Kent Kresa, CEO of Northrup Corp., believes that ethics must be built-in to the corporate structure, and not just tacked-on as an afterthought. In Kresa's words: "Ethics is not a policing function. It's about creating the kind of climate in which people are encouraged to make the right decisions in the first place." The final essay in this section is not an entirely successful "success story." "The Smoke at General Electric" is the story of GE's often-times failed attempts to do the right thing. If there is a lesson to be learned from the GE experience, perhaps it is that policy statements, ethical codes of conduct, and *just* "talking the talk" are never enough in and of themselves.

• *Essay* •

Nice Guys Finish First?*

PAUL GRAY

Tom Gill, 38, owns an Oldsmobile dealership in Columbus, Ohio, that in the past year has moved $30 million worth of Achievas and '95 Auroras and whatnots out of its showroom and off the lot. Plenty of people bought new and used cars from this man, and he talks openly about how he got them to do so: "I never let a customer walk in my life. I had just one goal in life: to be the No. 1 volume dealer. What could I do to close that customer on the showroom floor now? Our approach was to deliver them now, sell them now, control the deal now. We didn't have that much trust in the customer. The belief was that he would sell us out down the street for $50."

Wait a minute. Tom Gill is still trying to sell Oldsmobiles in Columbus. Why is he describing his methods in the past tense?

Listening to Don Flow, 39, who owns nine import, Saturn and GM dealerships, mainly in the Southeast, raises the same question. "The old game," he says, "was let the buyers beware, crush 'em if you can, make as much as you could off everybody. Better to make a kill now than a friend for life. We basically also made our customers turn into s.o.b.s. If a really nice person walked in, they were a lay-down in front of us. The industry had a lot of fun with those techniques."

Old game? *Had* fun? That's what car dealers like Gill and Flow are saying these days, and the valedictory chorus is swelling. Of the 178,000 people who peddle new automobiles in the U.S., most form the brash bottom line between the products of Detroit's Big Three and potential customers. A growing number among these vendors of domestic wares are claiming to have found a kinder, more humane way to do their job. This new breed speaks, often in near evangelical terms, of basic values and touchy-feely sympathies that have traditionally been anathema in the cutthroat race to roll new cars the hell off the inventories as fast as possible. Says Gill: "We've found it's O.K. to be fair to the customer." Flow, whose dealership last year handled $250 million in sales, insists, "Our focus is on creating friends rather than making deals."

Hearing such sentiments, veteran U.S. car buyers might justifiably pat the pockets where they hope their wallets still are and maybe run a pre-emptive check on their dentures, just to make sure. Are automobile dealers really deciding to treat customers like decent, autonomous human beings, or is this just another ruse—call it the integrity scam—to lure suckers back into the showrooms?

Whatever the motives, a lot of people in the industry hope that being nicer to the purchasing public will prove it is possible to do well by doing good. There is plenty of room for improvement. U.S. automakers have begun to compete more successfully against foreign imports; American cars last year accounted for 79% of domestic sales, as opposed to 69% in 1987, the year of the industry's worst performance against imports. A prime reason for this recovery is better products. Since J. D. Power & Associates, the auto industry's leading research firm, began tracking consumer satisfaction eight years ago, customers' ratings of the quality of U.S. cars have gone up 34%. On the other hand, satisfaction with how those cars were sold and serviced rose only 22%. This discrepancy worries Big Three officials, who want customers to be so happy that they will keep coming back. Sour sales experiences work against that goal.

"One of the 10 least pleasurable things you can do is go out and buy a car," says Ford vice president Tom Wagner, who heads the automaker's customer-satisfaction operations. Chrysler sales vice president Tom Pappert agrees: "We have got to get away from intimidation. Even for people who don't mind shopping and bargain hunting, it's the distrust factor that causes the heartburn."

Each of the Big Three has begun taking steps to try to improve its dealers' sales-floor behavior. This spring Ford sent out a list of directions on how to treat the buying public, including such steps as "customers courteously acknowledged within two minutes of arrival," "test drive offered to all customers," and "advisory relationship established by knowledgeable sales consultant who listens to customers, identifies needs and ensures needs are met." Chrysler offers financial incentives; to earn the highest $300 factory payment on each unit, a

Chrysler dealer must rate in the 95th percentile or better on Chrysler's internal customer-satisfaction index. General Motors has initiated a ground-breaking project in California for the training—or retraining—of its sales force; the company also gathers some of its most important dealers for round-table discussions and pep talks, usually led by one of their own who, like Don Flow, has seen the light.

For if honesty is to break out across U.S. showrooms, it will have to do so as a grassroots movement. There is only so much muscle the Big Three can apply to change its dealers' ways. To own one of the 23,000 dealerships in the U.S. is to be a member of a clannish, well-to-do and often fiercely independent society. Dealerships are regularly traded or sold among friends or inlaws; 40% of them at present were inherited from a family member. Oldsmobile general manager John Rock, who is the son of a Chevrolet dealer and whose wife is the daughter of a Buick dealer, notes half jokingly, "Most of our dealers seem to come from the same sperm bank."

Some see signs of change within this tight circle. Mark Rikess, 45, once ran his family Chevrolet dealerships in Minnesota and now heads a Los Angeles consulting firm that advises other dealers on ways to improve their selling practices. He has noticed that his clients tend to fall into the same pattern: second- or third-generation owners, college educated, between 35 and 45. "They want to change," Rikess says, "not because they are going to see a financial advantage today. They just don't want to run the business the way that Daddy ran it."

If this trend continues, somebody will have to tell the salespeople, the ones who deal with customers face-to-face. To help this process along, Oldsmobile has opened a $25 million "Vision Center" in a nondescript industrial park outside Detroit. Inside, the facility resembles a movie sound stage, with flowing spaces and a spiffy, glass-walled showroom of the future. Large framed printed slogans (OLDMOBILE'S FUTURE IS IN THE HANDS OF OUR CUSTOMERS) hang on the walls.

By the end of the year, more than half of the 15,000-member Olds sales force will have spent a mandatory and intensive week of 12-hour daily classes here, rooming and boarding together and drilling on such subjects as "building T.R.U.S.T. with warp speed." One of their instructors, or "facilitators" in Vision Center terminology, is Ken Winkelman, 30, who has been borrowed by Oldsmobile from a Saturn dealership in Orlando, Florida. Winkelman admits that most of his recruits are not, at the outset, happy campers: "The general feeling among people who arrive is that they don't want to be here." Accordingly, he divides his captive audience into "prisoners, vacationers and learners." Under Winkelman's enthusiastic guidance, most of them soon turn into happy collaborators.

During a recent class, he asked his pupils to list some of the bad old tricks of their trade. They eagerly volunteered, coming up with:

Lowballing. Setting a price ridiculously below dealer costs, knowing that a customer will not find anything cheaper elsewhere, and then "uploading" the package with piffles when the buyer returns.

Double Dipping. Billing again for services such as shipping and lot charges that are already included in the sticker price.

Grounding. Making it almost impossible for buyers to leave the lot, employing ruses such as fictitious waits for sales managers to arrive to dicker or the temporary "loss" of vital car keys.

Flipping/Turning Over. Rotating customers from one sales representative to another in order to confuse them and break down their resistance.

As this litany grows, so does the excitement among class members. The atmosphere begins to resemble a 12-step program; they are recovering car salespeople, and these are the habits they are trying to kick. Winkelman skillfully steers them toward repentance and "the new, soft, soft, soft sell. It's not about being wimpy. It's about building your future. It's about professionalism and earning the customer's right to ask for the sale." He then quotes a maxim: "You can shear a sheep many times in its life, but you can only skin it once." Apparently converted, a thirtyish salesman from Chicago blurts out, "That's how we were taught. If you teach us to be nice, we can be nice."

Not everyone in the business shares in the warm glow emanating from such sessions. Ed Mullane, 82, a Ford dealer for 40 years, argues that the Big Three created the conditions they now deplore by saturating their markets with dealerships: "There are too many of us. By crowding us in like Dairy Queens, you cannibalize the price, cannibalize the service, cannibalize the reputation of the dealer. That's why we're rated with pirates and bank robbers and lawyers, and all we end up doing is swapping dissatisfied customers." And not all the converts remain converted. Los Angeles consultant Rikess admits that as many as one-third of his dealer-clients drop out of his programs.

Even Tom Gill of Columbus has had moments of doubt. During the first three months of his new, nice-guy dispensation this spring, his Oldsmobile dealership's sales dropped nearly 50%, largely, he believes, because his competitors were shiftily using the old, illusory tactics—lowballing him—to undercut his prices. "It got real frustrating," he says. "For me to tell a customer I'm not coming down in price was like steering a ship in reverse. It was hard." Then, unexpectedly, Gill had the best May and June in the five-year history of his operation. Customers came back in droves, bringing Toyotas and Hondas with them as trade-ins, import models he had never seen on his lot before.

Was this upward blip an accident or a reward for good behavior? Gill does not know for sure, and neither, at this point, do the many observers who are pondering what has become the auto industry's most intriguing question: will the era of skinned customers give way to the age of the golden fleeced?

Questions for discussion

1. Do you think the "Saturn Syndrome" represents a real change in the way that the American automobile industry does business, or is it just another trick?

2. Were the "traditional" methods of car selling immoral?

3. Is good ethics really good business?

• *Case Study* •
Ice Cream & Integrity*

MARY SCOTT • HOWARD ROTHMAN

It is seven-thirty on an unseasonable warm November morning in Vermont, and Ben Cohen wants orange juice. The kitchen in a quaint country inn where he has scheduled a breakfast meeting is not yet open for business, so Cohen decides to fend for himself. He searches through a few cabinets until he finds a glass, then roots through a walk-in refrigerator for the juice. "I need liquids," he says with a husky laugh. "Now."

Cohen, wearing scruffy sneakers and a T-shirt plastered with the image of a smiling sun, looks like the kind of guy who always pours his own beverages—and helps his breakfast companions do the same. He does not look like the co-founder and chief executive officer (CEO) of a $135 million food company that employs 600 people and draws more visitors than any other tourist attraction in the Green Mountain State. He also doesn't look like half the team that oversees ninety retail franchises and company-owned stores in three countries as well as a fledgling manufacturing and retailing operation in the Soviet Union.

Cohen still looks—with the exception of a little gray in his beard—and acts much as he did when he and partner Jerry Greenfield first opened an ice cream shop in an abandoned Vermont gas station in 1978. Then both twenty-eight, they vowed to stay in business for one year. Their now phenomenally popular and successful company, Ben & Jerry's Homemade Inc., may have grown by leaps and bounds since that time, but Jerry and Ben themselves have remained true to their roots.

Cohen and Greenfield have created one of the most impressive examples of corporate responsibility that the business world has ever seen. At the same time their company was achieving an almost mythical status in the minds of ice cream lovers everywhere, the boyhood friends managed to keep treating their employees like family, purchase as many ingredients as possible from suppliers that adhere to their principles and philosophies, and support worthy causes and organizations in both their home state and around the world. They even created a nonprofit foundation to give away a full 7.5 percent of their company's pretax profits each year.

As becomes apparent to everyone they meet, Ben and Jerry also remained surprisingly free of pretensions. They're still "regular" guys who haven't strayed one iota from their sixties roots as they set about the task of building a very nineties company. Their hair may be a little sparser than it used to be, but it's never been trimmed to fit the standard corporate mold, and neither have they.

Their company has been faced with challenges and problems, though. Like any growing business, theirs has certainly had its ups and downs. But as an example of caring capitalism—as the duo refers to their overall corporate

*From *Companies with a Conscience* by Mary Scott and Howard Rothman. Copyright © 1992 by Mary Scott and Howard Rothman. Published by arrangement with Carol Publishing Group. A Birch Lane Press Book.

philosophy—Ben & Jerry's is hard to beat. The company produces an excellent product, helps its suppliers, aids its community, and supports it workers. It is precisely what it purports to be.

The same can be said about Jerry and Ben. The only thing different about the two old friends today, in fact, is their ability to now help more of the causes that they and their colleagues deem worthy of support. Unlike most of their peers in corporate America, their willingness and enthusiasm for such philanthropy never faded.

"In the past, people who consciously decided to go into business usually did so because they saw it as a way to make a lot of money. People who were motivated by social and humanitarian values tended not to go into business because they saw business as valueless," Cohen says, settling into his breakfast meeting with a glass of fresh orange juice. "But some of these people with strong social and humanitarian values—like Jerry and me—got into business by accident and were not sorted through that grid. So, through some quirk of fate, instead of ending up in a nonprofit social service agency, we happen to be trapped in a for-profit business."

Cohen laughs heartily once again and reiterates two quotes that his company has lived by since its first anniversary—which they commemorated by giving away free ice cream cones. One was from Jerry: "If it's not fun, why do it?" The other was from Ben: "Business has a responsibility to give back to the community." And even when it was hard to do so, Cohen now recalls, the two have diligently adhered to both of these tenets.

"I think it's always difficult to do anything right," he muses aloud. "It's like that song by Jethro Tull, 'Nothing is easy.' If what you are trying to do is produce the highest-quality ice cream, that's difficult. If you're trying to make a lot of money, that's difficult. And if you're trying to run your business in a way that benefits the community, that's difficult, too. But I don't think any of those things are difficult to the point of not being possible," he adds. "I think it's really just a matter of priorities."

At Home in Vermont

The town of Waterbury is just a blip on Vermont's Interstate 89, nestled in a scenic valley about halfway between the state's capital and its largest city. Despite its prime location, Waterbury has been essentially unremarkable for most of its lengthy history. It is home to a few shops and restaurants, a couple of country inns, the Vermont state police, and some spectacular views. But it wasn't until the arrival of Ben and Jerry—and the decision to locate their main ice cream plant as well as their corporate offices in this community of about eight thousand—that Waterbury really showed up on the map.

The 43,000-square-foot plant began operating in 1985, and faithful ice cream lovers from around the world have been flocking to it ever since. Surprised company officials admitted 41,000 visitors during the first six months after they opened their doors to tourists, but they got over their shock by 1991, when an even larger number walked through the plant every month during peak season. Some 220,000 took the tour that year, making Ben & Jerry's Homemade the number-one tourist attraction in this very tourist oriented state.

But visits were not the only thing that skyrocketed between the mid- and late 1980s. An employee named Mary, who had driven a Ben & Jerry's ice cream truck in 1982 and was later hired to organize the new tour program, recalls that there were only forty-two employees at the company when she came on board in 1986. The year before, sales were just $9 million. But the company then embarked on a rapid nationwide expansion, thanks to funds raised through a special stock offering open only to Vermont residents and a second traditional option for investors across the country. The employee ranks and the corporate revenues were soon to increase tenfold.

All of the activity that brought about such growth, however, was accomplished without the company's altering any of its counterculture business practices: Tons of ice cream and lots of money were still given away, traditional advertising was never employed, and a unique management style remained in force. Longtime employees, such as Mary—as well as newcomers like a woman named Sarah, who started in the gift shop in late 1990—attribute this to the purposeful vision of Cohen and Greenfield, who never deviated from the unorthodox path that they chose long before.

"For a while we were growing at about a hundred percent a year," recalls Cohen, who freely admits to being troubled by a pace that would delight most other business leaders. "Our outside sales were expanding faster than our internal organization and our infrastructure. We knew we were growing too fast. So we made a very conscious decision to slow our outward growth and devote a large amount of energy and resources to improving the quality of our organization—the way we work together as a team and the way we develop each of our employees."

The company, he continues, dramatically changed the way it did business—something that Ben & Jerry's remained able to do because of the way it was structured. Movement into new markets was slowed; expansion of franchised "scoop shops" was curtailed. These actions put the company back on track, Cohen notes, and growth then continued as an organized juggernaut that shows no sign of abating as the nineties wear on.

But none of this is really surprising when one considers the history of the company and the background of its founders, two boyhood friends from Merrick, New York. They first bonded together as outsiders (and lovers of food) in the seventh grade, when they couldn't run track as well as the others in their junior high school class. Neither could find their niche as young adults, either—Greenfield tried his hand as a lab technician while hoping to get into medical school; Cohen studied pottery, drove a taxi, and taught crafts—and their drift to Vermont was as aimless as their career paths.

But then serendipity: The two discovered a correspondence course in ice cream making that was offered by Penn State and only cost five dollars. They took it, Greenfield and Cohen often say, because they could afford it and because they liked ice cream. And after achieving a perfect score on the open-book final exam, the duo took a $12,000 investment ($4,000 of which was borrowed) and in 1978 opened their first scoop shop in the college town of Burlington.

Financial success didn't come overnight—it actually took about five years before the young company turned a profit—but notoriety was theirs right from the start. It came in part from their strongly flavored homemade concoctions with unusual names. For example, Dastardly Mash and New York Super Fudge Chunk. But it also came in part from the two owners, who endeared themselves to locals by working hard and plastering their images on the pint containers of their product that they soon began selling throughout the winter in order to keep the business going.

The Seeds of Giving

In the summer of 1991, Ben & Jerry's sponsored free "One World, One Heart" festivals in Chicago, San Francisco, and Stowe, Vermont. Each included performances by such popular musicians as Dr. John, David Bromberg, John Prine, and Carlos Santana. Each included family-oriented activities like Dye Your Own Tie Dye T-shirts and Ben & Jerry's New Vaudeville Light Circus Bus. Each included presentations by a group called 20/20 Vision, which aims to cut military spending and meet environmental and human needs, as well as free ice cream cones for attendees who wrote postcards or made videos on-site for their congressional representatives.

Each also included the dumping of a billion seeds of grass on festival grounds to point out the excesses of the U.S. military budget by illustrating how much a billion of something is.

By all accounts, the festivals were a huge success. As many as 100,000 people attended in each location. Hundreds of shirts were tie dyed, and performances on the circus bus were viewed by hundreds more. Thousands of postcards and video messages were sent to Washington, and tons of grass seeds were scooped into recycled paper bags by festival goers who could not help but think about the relationship they had to the billions of dollars spent annually on America's war-making machinery.

"One of the nice things about becoming bigger is that you can throw bigger parties," Jerry and Ben said in the flier announcing each event. "This festival is a time to play and celebrate together—it's also an opportunity to take the first step in a sustained effort at working together for a more just world."

But this message and the medium that carried it were only the latest manifestations of a concern for their environment that Greenfield and Cohen have been espousing since their company's beginnings.

"When we first started, our only goal was to have our homemade ice cream parlor on the corner; we didn't plan on being anything larger than that," Cohen remembers. "And while we had strong feelings about wanting to be a business that benefited the community, we didn't know what that meant at the time. So on our first anniversary, we gave out free cones to everybody to celebrate our first year in business and our amazement that we hadn't gone bankrupt yet."

As the company evolved, so did Ben and Jerry's commitment to their constituents. They continued their annual cone giveaways and instituted free summer movies and a yearly fall festival. But, Cohen notes, "these things just came about organically. The movie series came about because we were located at a gas station that had a big white wall next to it and we figured it was a great place to put up chairs where the cars used to go. And after our first summer, we really wanted to thank our customers for patronizing us and allowing us to survive, so we started our Fall Down festivals, which were family days of fun and games held in the park across the street from our shop."

In addition, the company began donating a lot of ice cream to a variety of local community organizations. But it wasn't really difficult yet to juggle business and social concerns, because the company wasn't even making a profit.

Ben & Jerry's eventually reached the point where its balance sheets were written in black ink; however, in 1981 it opened its first franchise, and by 1983 it was distributing ice cream outside of Vermont. Fred "Chico" Lager, a local nightclub owner, was brought in as president. And the company was giving away more and more ice cream and money. Everything, in fact, looked terrific—for a while.

"Originally, Jerry and I were ice cream men working in this ice cream shop," Cohen says. "But then the business started to become more of a business, and we had a bunch of employees and were spending our time talking on the phone and writing letters and memos and hiring and firing. We turned to each other and realized we were no longer ice cream men; we were businessmen. Our immediate reaction was to sell the business, because we didn't want to be businessmen. But then I ran into this old restaurateur down in Brattleboro, and he convinced me to keep the business. He said that if there was something I didn't like, I should just change it. That really hadn't occurred to me before."

They decided to raise capital for expansion in a novel way: by offering residents of their adopted state a chance to buy a piece of their company. In 1984, they sponsored the first-ever Vermont in-state public stock offering with a low minimum buy of $126 to allow everyone in who wanted a chance to participate. The sale was advertised in the front section of local newspapers, and it eventually raised $750,000—enough to finance construction of their Waterbury plant. A traditional nationwide public offering in 1985 permitted the expansion to continue, and their evolving commitment to social issues also continued as their financial resources grew.

A Foundation for Success

"We knew the main thing business does is make money, and if we were going to give back to the community, we had to give away a whole bunch of money," Cohen says. "So that's what we started to do."

To keep this commitment viable—and to appease the legions of new stockholders who sometimes wanted Ben & Jerry's run more like the public company that it had become—the partners created the nonprofit Ben & Jerry's Foundation in 1985. Initially established through a donation of company stock, the foundation was designed to "support projects which are models for social change; projects infused with a spirit of generosity and hopefulness; projects which enhance people's quality of life; and projects which exhibit creative problem solving."

Some of the causes Ben and Jerry support are the Devastators, an all-children's Afro-Latin percussion bank that works to combat drug abuse, AIDS, and homelessness; the Heifer Project, which provides agricultural animals to impoverished communities; Boston's Women's Institute for Housing and Economic Development; and the Worker Owned Network of Athens, Georgia.

Each year since, the company has kept the foundation alive by donating to it 7.5 percent of Ben & Jerry's pretax profits. Grant proposals are solicited that relate to children and families, disadvantaged groups, and the environment.

That, however, is only the beginning of the company's philanthropic efforts. A special Employee Community Fund—financed by half of all revenue taken in from the one dollar charged to each adult who takes the plant tour—

is granted to nonprofit community and statewide groups in Vermont. Funding decisions are made by voluntary employee committees, and recipients range from the Association of Vermont Recyclers to a group of woodworkers who produce toys for underprivileged local youngsters.

Factory seconds are also either given away to community organizations in the state, donated to food banks, or sold by special arrangement in Vermont stores—with a portion of that income also donated to community organizations, such as libraries, recreation centers, and local fire and rescue squads. In 1990, these payments totaled nearly $210,000. According to estimates from an employee named Eloise, who handles the community relations program, the company gave away about eight thousand gallons of free ice cream in 1991 to approximately one thousand Vermont organizations that simply requested it.

"Every day I come to work I feel I'm making the world a better place," says plant manager Don "Mac" MacLaughlin. His sentiments, in one form or another, are commonly echoed at every level in the company.

Despite such solidly based good feelings and the charitable activity on which they are based, Jerry, Ben, and others in the company felt they weren't doing enough. So in 1988 they wrote a Statement of Mission that dedicated the firm "to the creation and demonstration of a new corporate concept of linked prosperity." It consisted of three interrelated parts: a product mission ("to make, distribute and sell the finest-quality all-natural ice cream. . . ."), a social mission ("to operate the company in a way that actively recognizes the central role that business plays in the structure of society by initiating innovative ways to improve the quality of life. . . ."), and an economic mission ("to operate the company on a sound financial basis. . . .").

But this, it seems, was still not enough for Ben & Jerry's. For even with this new mission and a foundation giving away maybe $300,000 a year, the partners noticed that they were flooded with requests for assistance that they simply could not fill.

"All of them were worthy causes," Cohen recalls, "and we realized we were never going to solve all the problems that we were looking to solve. Our contributions were just a drop in the bucket. We started thinking about why there were all these social needs that went unmet, and it didn't take long to realize that it was because 40 percent of the national budget was going to the military. So we came to the conclusion that if we were really going to help the community and meet these social needs, we had to use our power as a business to direct money out of the military and into human and environmental needs."

Fortuitously, at just about that time, the company was coming out with a chocolate-covered ice cream bar on a stick. It decided to call the product a Peace Pop and use the packaging to talk to customers about a new organization that Ben & Jerry's was helping to found called One Percent for Peace. The group would actively promote the idea of redirecting 1 percent of the U.S. military budget to peaceful and humanitarian activities, and the Peace Pop would represent the first attempt by Ben & Jerry's to use its packaging to advance a social cause.

The company has continued with this theme ever since, too, attaching various messages onto its pints—such as those about the disappearance of America's family farms and the destruction of the world's rain forests. And this led quite naturally into another innovative area that Ben & Jerry's has successfully pioneered: that of purchasing its raw materials in a way that aids both the environment and the individual causes it chooses to support.

Blueberries, Peaches, Nuts, and Brownies

Few people outside of Maine know that the state's Passamaquoddy Indians, a group that has long been excluded from economic prosperity, works hard at the business of harvesting and processing wild blueberries on their reservation. Ben & Jerry's found out, however, and in the summer of 1990 the company contracted to buy $330,000 worth of fresh berries for use in its Wild Maine Blueberry ice cream from them.

At the same time, Ben & Jerry's was buying Brazil and cashew nuts from the Amazon rain forest for its Rainforest Crunch ice cream, brownies prepared by homeless employees of Greyston Bakery for Chocolate Fudge Brownie ice cream, peaches grown by African-American farmers in Georgia for Fresh Georgia Peach ice cream, and dairy ingredients from the five-hundred-member St. Albans Cooperative in Vermont for every one of its products. Developing such relationships with suppliers that address unmet social needs has become just another aspect of Ben & Jerry's ongoing mission and another way to meet its unique "two-part bottom line."

"This act—just consciously sourcing our ingredients, even though it might cost us more than somewhere else—ends up bringing about a more positive benefit than probably all of the money that we give away through our foundation," Cohen believes.

"We now do this on every level," he continues, "because we made it an integral part of our bottom line. We tried to figure out why business tends to be valueless and uncaring and in the worst situations actually harmful to the community and exploitative to its workers and its environment. And we found that this is because the success of business is measured solely by the traditional bottom line—that is, by how much money is left at the end of the year."

So Jerry and Ben decided to change the way their company measured success. They developed an alternative "two-part bottom line" that assesses the year by how much money is left over as well as by how much the company has helped the community. It didn't work right away; managers felt that the two goals were mutually exclusive. But the founders convinced them to simply add a new variable to their purchasing decisions and taught them to pick vendors according to three factors (social benefit, price, and quality) rather than the usual two (price and quality).

And once they began, the task became easier. Along with food products, Ben & Jerry's applied this philosophy to the millions of dollars of office and building supplies it regularly purchased. It switched to an insurance company and a credit-card issuer that place their premiums and profits in low-income housing and other similar investments. And it initiated proactive programs, like one in Newark, New Jersey, where Ben & Jerry's ice cream carts are operated by a foundation that runs a food bank and works with homeless people.

"Just by choosing these vendors, we're benefiting those other causes," Cohen explains. "Our goal is to integrate a concern for the community in all of our day-to-day business decisions. So far, we've been successful in maybe ten to twenty-five percent, so we've got a ways to go. But the trend is there; each year we find more and more ways to integrate this concern into our activities."

This move, not surprisingly, it also manifested in the company's resource-management efforts. Its environmental programs manager leads companywide efforts to raise awareness of recycling options and find markets for recyclable materials. Its art department works with suppliers that use recycled paper and soybean-based inks. Solid waste, such as cardboard and plastic pails, are reused whenever possible. And the company has even developed an incredible Solar Aquatics Greenhouse at its main plant that successfully purifies the waste from dairy production by means of a natural ecosystem of flowers, fish, and compost.

Ben & Jerry's also concentrates on the direct development of a variety of social and family activities, such as its free summer festivals. Other sponsorships of this nature include the Giraffe Project, which identifies and supports people who "stick their necks out" by doing exceptional things for their communities; the annual Halloween parade in New York's Greenwich Village, which distributes proceeds to various causes; free performances of the *Nutcracker Suite* for needy youngsters in several cities; and traveling voter-registration drives.

These projects not only extend Ben & Jerry's considerable social reach still farther; they also serve as the primary marketing tool for a company that never places traditional advertising in traditional media. "Rather than spending $35,000 on a full-page glossy ad, we'd rather do something that our public will enjoy," says Holly Alves, the marketing director. This concept must work, too: Consumers across the country clamor for the product, and more than fifteen thousand unsolicited job applications are received at the firm's headquarters each year.

Working for a Living

In the main plant, Peter, the company's flavor designer, toils in a room labeled "alchemy lab"; his business card officially proclaims him "primal ice cream therapist." The cabinets in his working space are tagged "sour things," "sinful things," "magical elixir," "secret stuff," "cold metallic things," and "I don't know."

Full-color life-sized cutouts of James Dean, John Wayne, and other movie stars, each wearing the pastel hair covering that is required headgear in all food-preparation areas, adorn numerous offices throughout the organization. White trash cans, emblazoned with the black markings of dairy cows, are everywhere. Wild and crazy artwork personalizes practically every work area. And if all that weren't enough, an officially designated group called the Joy Gang regularly sponsors a variety of companywide events, including a miniature car derby and an Elvis look-alike contest.

Alves remembers how this penchant for institutionalized fun once left her with some explaining to do. Shortly after she joined the company in 1990, her mother came up to Vermont from her home on Philadelphia's Main Line to see Alves in her new surroundings. Ironically, it was on the same day that sixties activist/prankster Wavy Gravy was visiting the plant to announce a new flavor named in his honor. The guest of honor was dressed, as usual, in a tie-dyed clown outfit; employees were acting even loonier than usual, and many were walking around with paper bags on their heads. "My mother was wondering what I had gotten myself into," Alves recalls.

Alves, too, wondered at first whether she made the right decision to leave a six-figure salary and a penthouse on San Francisco's Russian Hill for a lower-paying position and a smaller house in the hills of Vermont. "I was nervous that the company wouldn't be what it was supposed to be," she says. "But I was pleasantly surprised to find that it was."

Not everyone fits into the wacky atmosphere and liberal philosophy promoted by Ben and Jerry, of course, and those who don't tend to exit quickly. Overall, however, the turnover rate is only 8 percent, and most of those who stay are passionately committed to the founders' ideas and ideals.

Not surprisingly, the company also treats its primarily young work force quite well. Usual benefits, like health, dental, and life insurance, are supplemented by progressive programs, such as maternity and paternity leaves, stock-purchase options, educational assistance, profit sharing based on longevity, free membership at health clubs, wellness programs (cholesterol, blood pressure, smoking cessation, and substance-abuse counseling), and on-site educational seminars (writing skills, management, and financial advice). Even more unique is the domestic-partner coverage, which extends applicable benefits to nonmarried and homosexual partners of employees. And then there is the right to take home up to three free pints of ice cream every day.

Still, according to an employee named Carol in the benefits administration department, "the philosophy and social mission helps keep people more than the benefits."

One area that has occasionally proven a problem in recent years, however, is the company's salary structure. Ben & Jerry's works on a so-called compressed salary ratio, which means that the highest-paid employee can not make more than seven times the lowest full-time wage. The range was recently increased from its previous five-to-one ratio, but this policy—a visible extension of the "linked prosperity" philosophy—has caused several high-level job candidates to turn down employment offers.

Still, Ben & Jerry's appears to be a truly great place to work. People are committed to the company and to each other. And for those who come on board, the salary program that caps even Jerry and Ben's annual at less than $120,000 each is no deterrent.

"Money's not always the issue," notes plant manager Mac MacLaughlin, a former pro football player with fourteen years of management experience who bypassed several higher-paying offers when he chose to accept the job at Ben & Jerry's. "Sometimes in life you have to give something back."

Planning for the Future

At first glance, Ben & Jerry's looks a lot like other midsized companies. A communications coordinator keeps the burgeoning employee base informed about comings and goings. A manager of investor relations deals with Wall Street's growing interest. A human resources director manages personnel operations and employee development, while a quality assurance director plans and implements a companywide program in quality control. But the similarities stop there. Look deeper and Ben & Jerry's structure is all its own.

The quality assurance director, for example, developed a Ben & Jerry's version of the currently popular Total Quality Management program that implores workers to "keep that euphoric feeling" by doing the "ten steps of the

Improvement Boogie." The human resources director is a self-proclaimed jack-of-all-trades who arrived as a consultant in 1984, moves into jobs where he is needed, and wouldn't stick around if the company wasn't committed to its social mission. And the manager of investor relations, who grew up in Vermont and has a primary background in agriculture, rarely travels to New York, because "we don't want to hype the stock."

And then there is the communications coordinator. Part of her increasingly difficult job is to publish a monthly newsletter that informs the expanding work force about items of interest while also striving to be as irreverent and as entertaining as everything else the company does. The publication reports on important activities (e.g., the free summer festivals) and interesting phenomenon (the tattoos of employees). And sometimes it is dedicated to a seminal corporate event, such as the December 1990 retirement of popular company president "Chico" Lager. (This tribute included sarcastic reminiscences, old photos, and a series of artist's renderings detailing Lager's dramatic hair loss during his tenure.)

Keeping this type of wild and crazy attitude alive in a company growing as fast as this one is no easy task, but Ben and Jerry are both working hard to ensure that it is retained. Unless they are traveling, they come into the office every day. Cohen has moved into the media forefront as the official spokesperson and marketing guru. Greenfield has solidified his position as an employee cheerleader and is apt to be found on the plant floor in the middle of the night, working with the late shift as it packages ice cream on the assembly line.

Changes, though, are part of the game. New president Chuck Lacy has brought continuity to the organization (he was promoted from within) and solidified its professional direction, even if he doesn't have the emotional persona and acknowledged wit of his predecessor. The nationwide movement toward healthier, low-fat food prompted the introduction of several frozen yogurt flavors. And while the firm has barely adjusted to the opening of a second plant in Springfield, Vermont, and the relocation of its support offices to a building a few miles away from the main Waterbury plant, more construction is afoot: a $3 million distribution center was recently built in Rockingham and a $12 million manufacturing facility is planned for the town of St. Albans.

Financial gains continue at an almost staggering pace, too, despite the company's conscious effort to slow its growth. Sales increased 23 percent in 1989, 32 percent in 1990, and 30 percent in 1991, while Ben & Jerry's share of the national premium ice cream market grew from 23 percent to more than 31 percent during that time. And now that the company has moved its products into most major supermarket chains throughout the United States, future expansion will stem from the introduction of new products and their increased presence in independent grocery outlets across the country.

Moreover, the social side of Ben & Jerry's remains inseparable from the business side. Controversial stands are as common as ever: In 1990 alone the company officially opposed licensing of the Seabrook nuclear power plant in New Hampshire and military action in the Persian Gulf while supporting workplace rights for AIDS sufferers and a boycott of Salvadoran coffee. And the company's success, despite this penchant for unconventionality, continues to illustrate that even public corporations can make a profit while helping their communities.

Ben Cohen speaks of all this proudly, if not with more than a bit of awe, as he wraps up his early breakfast meeting on that uncommonly warm November morning in Vermont. It is time to point his well-worn sneakers toward company headquarters, where a meeting is scheduled for Ben & Jerry's board of directors. (Cohen is chairperson; Greenfield is assistant secretary.)

"When we started out, our only goal was to remain in business for a year at the old ice cream shop in that Burlington gas station," he notes, slipping on his jacket and heading toward the door. "We never had any idea that it would evolve into this."

Questions for discussion

1. Do you think that Ben & Jerry's will really be able to sustain their program of corporate social responsibility in the light of market pressures from their competitors?
2. Would you prefer to work for a company like Ben & Jerry's?
3. Should Ben & Jerry's customers subsidize Ben & Jerry's moral vision?
4. What's your favorite flavor?

• *Case Study* •

Roger Meade: Running on People Power*

MICHAEL A. VERESPEJ

Your first tendency is to dismiss the people-first policies of Scitor Corp. as simply a case of too much California sunshine. There are no limits—or tracking—of sick days, no lost wages when an employee is sick, and three weeks of vacation for new hires.

In addition to a company-paid, benefit-rich health-care plan, each employee has a $1,400 medical fund for dental costs, vision care, or unreimbursed medical expenses.

And you'd be hard-pressed to find a more comprehensive set of work/family policies. At no cost to its employees, Scitor provides both an emergency-care center for mildly ill children of employees and in-home emergency care for children. New mothers get 12 weeks of paid maternity leave, and the option of full- or part-time work when they return. Scitor provides flextime, job-sharing, and benefits for employees who work more than 17.5 hours a week.

Not enough? How about tickets—once a year—to a San Francisco 49ers home football game and company picnics, chili cook-offs, ski trips, fishing trips, wine trips, and road rallies.

And we've saved the best for last. The fiscal-year Kickoff Meeting in October—held at resorts such as the Rancho Bernardo Inn in San Diego, The Point

*Reprinted with permission from *IndustryWeek*, Oct. 18, 1993. Copyright Penton Publishing, Inc., Cleveland, Ohio.

at Tapatio Cliffs in Phoenix, and the Princess Resort in Palm Springs, Calif.—is usually the premier social weekend for Scitor's 200 employees. Scitor pays the travel, food, and lodging expenses for each employee *and his or her guest* for the three-day event, where the company celebrates the accomplishments of the past year and shares ideas for the upcoming year.

But, in reality, the lavish attention to employee needs is simply the people-first attitude of Scitor (which in Latin means "to seek to know") CEO Roger E. Meade, who in 1979 co-founded the Sunnyvale, Calif., firm that provides products and services in program management, systems engineering, and customized computer information systems.

"Scitor is our people," says Mr. Meade. "Our success depends on them. Knowledge resides in their minds and their feet. Too many companies fail to grasp that feet can walk out the door as easily as they walked in."

That's why he doesn't see his people-oriented programs as overhead.

"They are investments that add value to the corporation, not costs or overhead—because people are your resources, not your products or equipment," says Mr. Meade. "Taking care of people's needs is the key to productivity."

Every work-family policy at Scitor, he says, "is based upon analysis, not emotion. Our benefits exist because they support our attract-and-retain objectives. It isn't being generous. And it certainly isn't being liberal. It's simple economics." For example, Scitor estimates that by investing $2,400 to provide sick-care service for employees' children, it saves the firm $17,000 in lost customer billings.

"Everything we do is driven toward increasing our competitiveness and productivity," says Mr. Meade. "To increase productivity you start by first understanding the human heart. Only by understanding the heart will you know how to stir the passion that fuels productivity."

Clearly, it works for Scitor. It's had 13 years of continuous profitable growth even though Mr. Meade never—and, in fact, refuses to—set any growth or profit targets. "Profits and growth are the byproduct of doing the job right and focusing on customer satisfaction," he explains. "Satisfy the customers and make them successful, and *we'll* be successful."

To empower employees to do that, Mr. Meade has a straightforward core policy—against which he tells employees to make all decisions.

It reads: "Utilize your best judgment at all times. Ask yourself: Is it fair and reasonable? Is it honest? Does it make good business sense in the context of our established objectives? If you can answer yes to all of these, then proceed. Remember, you are accountable against this policy for all your actions."

And he tells employees point-blank: "If you find that management's direction is out of touch with the reality of the situation at hand, it is your responsibility to act based upon your best judgment. Never, and I mean never, use the excuse of following orders as the rationale for following a poor course of action. This is compounding stupidity, and it is inexcusable."

"That's the bottom line," says Mr. Meade. "We try to do everything within that context. Except for government-mandated policies, we try to run Scitor without any other policies."

In that vein, he doesn't monitor employees' activities. He's never asked for or required a status report. He lets individuals and work teams set their own goals and doesn't ask how they'll achieve them.

"I don't ask them, 'What are you doing this week, this month?'" says Mr. Meade. "I give people the whole job and let them accomplish it. We just need to know what you're going to do. The how is up to you." And he'll intervene only if something appears to be "way off course."

Information technology links the entire organization. Thus, the entire budget and goals-achievement process, a bottom-up endeavor, is paperless. A team's goals—there may be five of them—are in the computer where anyone can check progress, thanks to color-coding. Red means a goal is in trouble, yellow indicates some concern, green signifies on course, and blue means a goal has been accomplished.

Scitor's focus on individual responsibility is underscored by several other elements of its corporate culture.

There are no secretaries. All employees take their own messages, open their own mail, write their own letters, and make their own travel arrangements. Scitor teaches all employees how to use a computer and expects everyone to be computer-literate. If an engineer has a speech or a presentation to make, he or she has to create it on his or her own—including any graphic or overhead material.

Much of the corporate culture at Scitor stems from the frustrations Mr. Meade encountered when working for larger organizations that wouldn't step aside and let the workers—not managers—make the key decisions.

"I always used to feel frustrated with how organizations operate," says Mr. Meade. "People at the lowest level always knew what had to be done, and I always asked myself, why did bright people do stupid things? Then I realized that the management structure imposed organizational stupidity.

"Management should always remember that we are ignorant of what is really happening because we simply aren't involved in the day-to-day work. So when decisions aren't delegated as low as possible, individually bright people can collectively achieve a high degree of organizational stupidity. The plays should be called by the people on the field."

Corporations "should get rid of their policy manuals and let fairness dictate all their decisions," says Mr. Meade. "If a policy manual is general, it's useless. The only ones who read them are goldbricks. If you are going to have one, publish the Ten Commandments.

"Management has to stop stifling people and productivity. Just be quiet and listen, and you'll learn more than if you ask a lot of questions. Every stupid thing I do is because I didn't talk to the people involved in a project."

Thus, Mr. Meade will let employees discuss strategy with him, but he won't review or make decisions for employees.

For example, when his real-estate manager wants to lease office space, Mr. Meade won't read the contract put in front of him. "I've told them, 'Any lease you put in front of me, I'll sign,'" says Mr. Meade. "Don't say to me, 'Did you consider it?' because I won't read it. As soon as you start doing that, employees [subconsciously] relax, because they know Roger's going to read it. I am not going to review and overrule things. When too many people get involved, no one knows who has authority or control, so everything gets locked up, performance stops, and there is no customer service."

The you-make-the-call philosophy isn't just used internally. Scitor insists workers use it in their dealings with customers.

"The customer is the person you work for," says Mr. Meade. "We don't want an employee to make a decision based on what he or she thinks is some internal Scitor strategy. If it's a project and you're in charge, it's you and the customer, and the corporation stays out of the decision-making."

And if something goes wrong?

"You have to learn to keep your mouth shut, and let workers try, succeed, fail, or deliver," says Mr. Meade. "If you grab people every time they try to work, they will never learn from what went wrong. Besides, what you perceive to be a mistake may not be. It may turn out to be wonderful. So you have to gulp hard and learn to distance yourself to keep from telling people no."

In addition, Mr. Meade won't let anyone "put any energy into autopsies. When you try to fix blame, it just causes people not to take risks."

To keep himself attuned to employee and corporate needs, Mr. Meade has an open-door policy. And, to reinforce that, each spring he asks employees to tell him, in writing, what's good, bad, and ugly about the company. He then responds to each of those comments in writing, in a package that's delivered to all employees. "It institutionalizes two-way feedback and keeps you on the path," says Mr. Meade.

All of which ties back to his philosophy that achieving corporate needs requires meeting employees' needs.

"Companies are always asking employees to help them adjust to the ups and downs of business," says Mr. Meade. "So how can you ask people to unselfishly support the needs of the company, if the company won't support the needs of its people? It is simply not fair to expect your people to give to the corporation if you do not reciprocate and help them absorb the shocks in their life."

That's why Scitor has unlimited sick time and strong work-family policies. "If you're sick, you're sick," says Mr. Meade. "We go over sick time in the U.S. as if it can be managed statistically. That's foolish."

The proof is in the numbers. Scitor employees average just five sick days a year. And in an area of California where turnover rates for computer-software engineers is 16.5%, Scitor's is 2.1%. What's more, it retains 90% of all employees who have just become mothers.

"Financial people too often deal with numbers, not what drives numbers," says Mr. Meade. "Besides, if you just go by the numbers," he adds in a mocking tone, "you can increase productivity 12.8% if you just cut out all sickness and vacation time. Numbers are good, but a terrible trap to fall into."

On the rare occasion when a worker abuses the privilege of working in an environment with no set policies, Scitor lets the team leader deal with the situation.

"We had a work-team leader come to human resources and ask us to put together a sick-day policy because he felt an individual was abusing the 'policy,'" says Mr. Meade. Instead, the team leader was told to talk to the individual himself. The end result: The worker admitted he had been abusing the system and stopped. "When you have an environment of trust, there is tremendous peer pressure to adapt your behavior to get back in line," says Mr. Meade. Besides, he says, "we don't think it makes sense to develop a policy to deal with a single individual. You can't let the 1% of employees who are problems drive all the rules and procedures at a corporation. You need to deal with them individually if you want to be fair to all. Otherwise, you end up with stacks of regulations that stifle risk and strangle the other 99%."

Mr. Meade also intends to keep Scitor private. "When you go public, you have an excess attention on quarterly profits," he says. "That clashes with our philosophy of having no growth or profit objectives, and it distracts from customer service as well. By remaining private we can focus on things that we think are important, as opposed to what the financial community thinks are important."

But, still the ultimate bottom line for Mr. Meade is his people orientation. "I believe in the worth of the individual," says Mr. Meade. "If you don't have an environment that allows individual initiative, you are not going to be successful. Individual initiative is the fuel on which our company and our nation run."

Questions for discussion

1. Are Scitor's policies people-driven or profit-driven? Does it matter what the motives are?
2. Do you think Scitor is doing better or worse than they'd do without such people-oriented policies?
3. Would you have the patience and courage to be a manager at Scitor? Would you enjoy being an employee there?

• *Essay* •

Kresa's Cleanup*

DAN CORDTZ

When Kent Kresa was appointed CEO of Northrop Corp. in 1990, the company's public reputation for ethics was, even for the scandal-plagued defense industry, distressingly low.

On the very same day Thomas V. Jones, Kresa's predecessor, announced his retirement, an international arbitration panel concluded that Northrop had paid a Korean businessman $6.25 million during the 1980s to help procure an order from the Korean government for the company's F-20 fighter planes.

Officers and directors were embroiled in a shareholders' lawsuit (later settled by the company's insurer for $18 million) accusing them of misconduct and unlawful business practices.

Worst of all, Northrop was about to plead guilty to 34 felony counts for selling the government defective weapons parts, pay a $17 million fine and be barred for two years from bidding for new Pentagon contracts.

No wonder Kresa has devoted a lot of time, attention and corporate resources to the issue of ethics. While he was still serving as president under

Jones, Kresa established an internal office of ethics and business conduct, headed by a corporate vice president, Shirley V. Peterson, recruited from the U.S. Labor Department. That office now runs an array of programs that constantly remind managers and workers of their agreed-upon code of conduct and check how well they are living up to those standards.

Today, the company's public image is clearly better, and Northrop is back in the good graces of the U.S. military. Managers and employees say the damage inflicted by those earlier embarrassments is gone, and they have concrete evidence that employees from top to bottom are observing higher standards of conduct.

For a number of reasons, the Northrop experience is a good example of a corporate ethics initiative.

To begin with, it was launched after events clearly revealed that not all was well. The story is laid out in a remarkably candid videotape called "When Things Went Wrong," produced by Peterson's office, to explain to employees and managers how and why the costly defense parts scandal, which involved the company's Norwood division, came about.

In brief, Norwood manufactured parts for missiles and aircraft at a small plant in Pomona, Calif., far from division headquarters in Massachusetts and largely ignored by the parent corporation. Although some of the specifications were extreme, the plant seemed able to turn out its products at a cost that amazed and delighted division bosses. But as a Northrop executive ruefully acknowledged in the videotape, if something looks too good to be true, it probably is. It turned out that the manufacturing process was not actually yielding parts that measured up to the specifications, and inadequate testing equipment—abetted by some deliberate thumb-on-the-scale behavior by individual managers—failed to detect the shortcomings. When it all came to light, a number of missiles had to be recalled and replacement parts installed at great expense. Not only did heads roll at Norwood (two managers went to prison), the entire Pomona operation was closed down, with many innocent employees losing their jobs.

All of this is laid out unsparingly in the videotape, together with a searching attempt to understand the pressures that prompted Pomona managers to cut corners. Several of Northrop's top executives, including Kresa, concede their own share of the responsibility. There is no attempt to paint the episode as an aberration that could never happen again, or merely the work of one or two unscrupulous people.

"It showed that the system was not working the way we expected it to," Kresa says. Adds Peterson: "Norwood was a symptom, not the problem. Small units doing their own thing get less supervision. But the real danger is that when people are pushed from above to produce results, they may have different perceptions of what's acceptable quality. And having rules won't necessarily change behavior."

What's required, she believes (and Kresa agrees), is a careful process of identifying and spelling out a shared set of values, mutually agreeing to observe them, working continuously to keep everyone aware of their implications for business behavior, and providing means to monitor and reinforce the results.

The ultimate purpose is expressed in a top executive's comment in the videotape: "We're not really in the business of teaching people to be ethical. We're teaching ethical people how to make the tough decisions."

And in Kresa's words: "Ethics is not a policing function. It's about creating the kind of climate in which people are encouraged to make the right decisions in the first place."

The Northrop program also exemplifies the missionary style of exhortation and reinforcement employed by many firms to make certain their value systems are absorbed by every member of the organization.

It began with a series of meetings, at all levels of the company, to identify Northrop's "core ethical principles." These, Peterson says, are "honesty, integrity, fairness, caring/respect, accountability, promise-keeping, loyalty, law-abiding and pursuit of excellence." Those qualities are the base of what Northrop labels "the ethics pyramid." Growing out of that base are Northrop values: customer satisfaction, people, suppliers, quality, integrity and leadership. And above them are a code of business conduct and a variety of procedures and processes intended to guarantee—at the apex of the pyramid—"acceptable behavior."

(Like most firms with highly organized ethics programs, Northrop employs a lot of sloganizing and gimmicks to help fix ideas and concepts in workers' minds. For example, baseball caps and other items are emblazoned with the acronym QCLIPS, which stands for quality, customers, leadership, integrity, people and suppliers.)

The reason all this endless reiteration is needed, according to Peterson, is that the ethics program is really about shaping the culture of the corporation. Kresa agrees, and points out that setting high standards and making sure that they are understood and adhered to will be the key to Northrop's success in the future. For one thing, he says, "it eliminates a lot of extra costs if you have agreed ethical standards, because you don't spend so much time having to see that things are done right. Of course, you have to have some checks and balances to find mistakes, but there won't be as many. It's just good business."

Kresa also notes that in today's workplace efficiency means pushing decisions down to lower levels, and workers need to know exactly what's expected in order to make those decisions. "There are a lot of gray areas," he says. "We [in management] have the responsibility to let people do the right thing."

To carry out this cultural reformation, Peterson and her staff have devised a vast array of tools: videotapes on such topics as "Values in Action: Honest Talking & Honest Listening" that are used to prompt discussion groups; interactive computer training programs to teach the law and the ethical rules of contract negotiations and other everyday business situations; case studies on subjects like kickbacks and gratuities; an ongoing "leadership inventory" in which Northrop employees grade their bosses (all the way up to Kresa) on how well they measure up to the company's values; and even a program that lets people send "ValueGrams" to co-workers "to let them know their efforts are noticed and valued." It may sound a bit corny, but Peterson says they were well received. During Value Week in August 1993, employees sent out 23,000 of these little billets doux.

The leadership inventory is an important component in the company's attempts to measure the effectiveness and progress of the ethics program. Managers have been through the process twice and received feedback both times. Over that time, Kresa says, the average manager scored 12.5% improvement on the 80 items that make up the inventory, from showing respect for customers to accepting constructive criticism.

In light of the Pomona experience, Northrop is understandably sensitive to the issue of protecting whistle-blowers from retaliation. So it has also gone to considerable lengths to develop what it calls the "open line"—a telephone number that workers can call anonymously for advice on ethical and other issues. Peterson says the company rejected the more popular term "hotline" because it implies that its purpose is simply reporting wrongdoing. (In many firms, employees are more likely to call it the "rat line" or "snitch line.")

The most important reason for the open line, she says, is so people will have a place to turn for help in making decisions. It can back them up in refusing a superior's unethical or questionable orders. But the line actually seems mainly useful as a source of information. Of almost 2,000 calls last year, almost three-quarters were about workplace issues that did not involve business conduct. When allegations of ethical violations were received, they were examined by an ethics committee and the decision later reviewed by a board consisting of Kresa, Northrop's general counsel and four other top executives. Last year over 300 such reviews were completed and a mere 77 were found to merit disciplinary action.

The bottom line, of course, is: Does all this work? Kresa is firmly convinced that it does. "I believe it has changed the way we think culturally," he declares. "Are we done? No. Can we do better? Of course. But I'm a believer in continual improvement."

Questions for discussion

1. Does ethics have to be built into the corporate culture in order to be effective?
2. Does ethics have to come from the top down to be effective?
3. Does Kresa's cleanup seem to be profit driven, rather than ethics driven?

• *Essay* •
The Smoke at General Electric*

NANETTE BYRNES

There are few companies in the U.S. as successful as General Electric, the maker of everything from Thomas Edison's illuminating light bulb to the engines on the President's jet. GE is the fifth-largest industrial company in the U.S. Revenues in 1993 from its 12 business groups exceeded $60 billion, up 6% over 1992, of which the company will have paid the tax collector $2 billion. It employs 222,000 people. And by the measurement investors hold most dear, GE has been a phenomenal winner: Its stockprice has soared 80% over the last three years.

Unfortunately for GE, there are also few companies in the U.S. with as checkered an ethical record. In addition to 72 Superfund environmental cleanup sites in which it is named a "potentially responsible party" (total cost to GE to date: $500 million), GE has paid fines or settlement fees in 16 cases of abuse, fraud and waste in government contracting since 1990. This year alone, GE is facing a highly publicized trading scandal at its Kidder, Peabody subsidiary and a Justice Department investigation for alleged contract violation at its aircraft engine unit, and will go to trial in October to face accusations of price fixing and antitrust violations in the industrial diamond market.

If the old adage is true, and there is fire where there's smoke, General Electric must be in the midst of an ethical bonfire.

The irony is that GE has one of the most extensive ethics programs in corporate America. Extensive, but apparently ineffective, which helps keep outside lawyers like James Helmer busy. Helmer, who calls himself a "garbage man for General Electric," specializes in wrongful dismissal and qui tam, or whistleblower, suits, and has by his own count handled more than 10 cases against GE.

"Its written policy is as good as anyone's in the U.S.," Helmer says of the company's ethics rules. "The problem that I keep running into is they talk the talk but don't walk the walk."

Clearly there's been plenty to speak up about at GE's government contracting units. According to the Project on Government Oversight, the Department of Defense and the U.S. General Accounting Office, GE paid $163 million in fines and settlements for fraud, waste and abuse in government contracting between 1990 and February 1994. That figure stems from 16 examples of crimes ranging from money laundering to procurement fraud.

The tale of Chester Walsh alone accounted for $69 million of those fines. Walsh spent four years gathering evidence that members of the company's aircraft engine business were helping to divert U.S. funds in cahoots with an Israeli general named Rami Dotan. Dotan is now serving a 13-year jail sentence in Israel stemming from these accusations. In mid-July former GE employee Herbert Steindler pled guilty to four felony counts stemming from the case.

During the case, GE complained bitterly that Walsh had not reported those evil doings through the company's internal ethics system. That system supplements the traditional method of reporting misdeeds to your supervisor, with 14 toll-free help lines employees can call. Many divisions also have their own ombudsman in charge of that particular business's ethical code.

GE contended that because the whistle-blower law provides for the blower to collect 15% to 25% of what the government recovers, it was more personally profitable for Walsh to report through the courts than to the company.

Lisa Hovelson, executive director of Taxpayers Against Fraud, a nonprofit organization that supports whistle-blowers and received a chunk of Walsh's $13.4 million take, says there were much more serious issues at stake. "In the Chet Walsh case, he had some very grave concerns about what would happen [when he reported what he'd found]," says Hovelson.

In testimony before Congress just after the case was concluded, CEO Jack Welch admitted GE's ethical failure, "We must rely on the integrity of our people as our first defense, in addition to what many agree are the most rigorous standards and policies of any company in America for monitoring our dealings with the government," said Welch. "Unfortunately, I regret that that system wasn't good enough in this case."

Dealings with the government are far from the only area in which GE has fallen off the ethical wagon.

At Kidder, Peabody, the Wall Street brokerage firm GE unsuccessfully tried to sell two years ago, a scandal broke this past spring powerful enough to bring down the business's top management.

Michael Carpenter lost his spot as Kidder's CEO, despite his personal friendship with Welch. His replacement, Dennis Dammerman, GE's CFO, is rumored to be the inside choice for Welch's own job when the time comes— Welch is only 58.

The scandal that caused the shifts at Kidder became public on April 17, when Joseph Jett, the firm's head government bond trader, was fired and accused of single-handedly fabricating $350 million in false trading profits. Since his dismissal, Jett has claimed that Kidder, which lost $29 million in the second quarter of this year and has required $200 million in cash infusions from GE since April, is using him as a scapegoat. Even if they aren't, it's pretty hard to understand why trades that generated such large profits were not being more carefully overseen or reviewed. Especially since Edward Cerullo, Jett's direct supervisor, was an expert in sophisticated trades, a "rocket scientist" who ran financial futures arbitrage and mortgage-backed securities for the firm before taking over the entire fixed-income group. Cerullo clearly should have been able to flag transgressions.

Unfortunately for GE, the theories as to why Jett—or his bosses, if they did know what was happening—would have pursued these phantom profits sound a lot like the explanations for other GE scandals: Success at GE is apparently measured by profitability.

John Gravitt,the first of GE's aircraft engine whistle-blowers, paints this picture: "If you Mickey Mouse the numbers around, then it shows that your department or section is making money. Whatever the plus side is on the dollar sign, you get a bonus out of that."

Jett earned $9 million last year, partly on the strength of those phony trades. That was $2 million more than Welch himself made.

Also unfortunate for GE is the fact that this is not Kidder's first transgression. It's the second fraudulent bond trading scandal GE has suffered through since it bought the 129-year-old trading house in 1986. In 1991, Cerullo was disciplined by the National Association of Securities Dealers for lapses in supervision of one of his bond traders.

To give the devil his due, GE does clearly take action once a breach of ethics comes to light. Consider what happened at GE's NBC division in late 1992. NBC's new magazine *Dateline* infamously helped along its journalistic "investigation" of badly placed GM fuel tanks by staging a phony accident. It could not get the tank to blow up on its own, so it helped the investigation along with the aid of some strategically placed explosives. The people responsible were fired. An office of the ombudsman was also created to reinforce NBC's code of ethics and review anything appearing on NBC news programs. *Dateline* is still on the air.

As TV news changes and news magazines like *Dateline* increase in number and viewership, those ethics guidelines face new challenges.

"A lot of new people are coming into the business, people who haven't come up in the hard news tradition," comments NBC News ombudsman and senior producer David McCormick. "[Prime-time news shows] are competing with entertainment. I don't think we're putting out entertainment programs; we're putting out news programs that compete with entertainment. We're dealing with real issues and reality."

The reality is that *Dateline*'s on-air admission of guilt in early 1993 seems to have had little impact on NBC's profit performance for the year. GE's broadcasting division enjoyed a 29% jump in operating profits despite an 8% drop in revenues.

While all of these ethical snafus are unpleasant, the worst may be yet to come. In early June the U.S. Department of Justice joined a whistle-blower suit charging that GE made false statements to the government about its jet engines. The accusation is that the company misrepresented its engines' ability to meet contractual requirements that they be able to withstand certain levels of electromagnetic interference. (Such interference is a kind of machine babble that when strong enough can cause engines to malfunction—that's why passengers must turn off their CD Walkmans when an airplane takes off.)

The Justice Department is investigating the charges but says that joining Ian Johnson, the GE engineer who blew the whistle, does not imply that it concurs with the factual allegations about the engines. But it is picking up the legal tab from now on.

Helmer, the whistle-blower's lawyer, says that doing what his client Ian Johnson thought should be done to comply with the contracts would have originally cost $15,000 an engine. To fix them now, Helmer estimates the cost could be more than $100,000 a unit.

"It's enormous," says Helmer, "These other [whistler-blower] problems were major problems for the company, but they are small compared to the fraud that's involved in the Johnson case."

Helmer continues: "The problem here is the contractor did not live up to the specifications of the contract. [GE] knew they were not doing it and they made efforts to cover up that they were not fulfilling the contractual specifications. We have hundreds of hours of tape recordings of GE officials discussing this subject, made by [Johnson] as well as the FBI."

The FBI has a policy of not discussing any of its ongoing investigations.

GE vehemently supports the performance of its engines, pointing out that there have been no recorded problems with them, and says the engines, found in commercial and military planes as well as the President's Air Force One jet, is safe.

Another serious issue GE faces is a price-fixing suit scheduled for trial in October. In this case, which stemmed from allegations leveled by Edward Russell, former GE Superabrasives vice president, the company is accused of violating antitrust laws by conspiring with diamond giant De Beers to fix the price of industrial diamonds. A separate wrongful discharge suit brought by Russell has been settled. But the Justice Department plans to continue its case against GE and De Beers, which together control more than 80% of the world's industrial diamond production. GE says the case is circumstantial and without merit.

In spite of these high-profile ethical issues, GE-trained executives are being given chief executive positions all over corporate America.

According to Lee Pomeroy, a headhunter at Egon Zehnder, one of the largest search firms in the world, GE offers employees rare exposure to a variety of businesses and business lines on a global basis. "There aren't that many training grounds left," says Pomeroy, who calls a GE background a "Harvard-like credential." He continues, "We don't have the fear of GE as we do with IBM, that their people will fail in their first job out [of the company]."

Pomeroy says ethics issues are not raised when discussing the qualifications of candidates from GE for positions in other companies. Jack Welch himself is thought of as one of the best managers in the world. He's so adored that a whole book of his pearls of wisdom has been published under the title *Get Better or Get Beaten! 31 Leadership Secrets from GE's Jack Welch.*

Welch's tough "No. 1, No. 2" (in market share) strategy resulted in GE's sale of 400 businesses and product lines, the purchase of another 600 and the elimination of 170,000 jobs in the 1980s. It also made GE into the lean and tough competitor that has recently rewarded shareholders so well.

In the book, Welch endorses "unleashing the energy and intelligence and raw, ornery self-confidence of the American worker," which has helped generate strong earnings at the company.

But one is left wondering if his philosophy of minimum management wasn't taken a bit too far in the case of Joseph Jett, for example. Or in those 16 defense-contracting violations. Or, perhaps, with diamond prices.

And in the end, toll-free numbers and ombudsmen don't mean much if they are not effective.

As Ed Petry, a professor at Bentley College who helps run the college's Center for Business Ethics, puts it: "GE has one of the best corporate codes of ethics and an outstanding ombudsman program, and yet time after time we see problems there. Having an ethics program is no guarantee of propriety."

Questions for discussion

1. Would GE have been as financially successful without having been unethical?

2. Should company management and employees feel obligated to behave unethically in order to serve stockholders' interests?

3. Is GE's ethics program successful? Why/Why not?